C000241119

RIVER OF LIFE, RIVER OF DEATH

Praise for *River of Life, River of Death*

'An extraordinary and fascinating combination of history, geography, environment, politics, religion, and much more. This is a river of unsurpassed significance on the world stage, whose flow and life is traced from the Himalayas to the Sunderbans and the Bay of Bengal.'

Nicholas Stern, IG Patel Professor of Economics and Government at LSE

'To try and fathom the wonders and follies of India through a river is grand ambition…and Victor Mallet pulls it off!'

Gurcharan Das, author of *India Unbound and The Difficulty of Being Good*.

'In prose that is as sanguine and fluid as his subject, Victor Mallet's *River of Life, River of Death* charts the course of the Ganges, the spiritual and material lifeline of northern India, through the vicissitudes of time, space, and the hubris of men. Rich in detail and sparkling with the insight of a trained observer, Mallet's chronicle is an engaging and enlightening read.'

Shashi Tharoor, Indian MP and author of *Inglorious Empire*

'Masterfully combining fascinating history with acute observation of India today, *River of Life, River of Death* is brilliantly effective in its central argument—that the threats facing the Ganges—from pollution, overpopulation, climate change, and often bad policies—are also the severest problems threatening India's progress. Mallet is at times brutally realistic about the prospects for rapid improvement, but passionately concerned that success must eventually be achieved. The result is a splendid and important book.'

Adair Turner, Economist and Chair of the Energy Transitions Commission

'Victor Mallet demonstrates vividly why India needs to get to grips with the huge challenge of antibiotic resistance…I hope Mr Modi's policy advisers read his powerful narrative.'

Jim O'Neill, economist, inventor of the BRICS acronym and chair of the Review on Antimicrobial Resistance

'Victor is one of those rare foreign journalists who not only likes and understands India but, in addition, has the capacity to see its faults as well as impartially assess the efforts it's making to correct them. This means his coverage of India is always informed and thought-provoking. Even when sympathetic he's never biased.'

Karan Thapar, Indian television anchor

Also by Victor Mallet

The Trouble with Tigers: The Rise and Fall of South-East Asia

VICTOR MALLET

RIVER OF LIFE, RIVER OF DEATH

The Ganges and India's Future

OXFORD
UNIVERSITY PRESS

OXFORD

UNIVERSITY PRESS

Great Clarendon Street, Oxford, OX2 6DP,
United Kingdom

Oxford University Press is a department of the University of Oxford.
It furthers the University's objective of excellence in research, scholarship,
and education by publishing worldwide. Oxford is a registered trade mark of
Oxford University Press in the UK and in certain other countries

©Victor Mallet 2017

The moral rights of the author have been asserted

First Edition published in 2017

Impression: 1

All rights reserved. No part of this publication may be reproduced, stored in
a retrieval system, or transmitted, in any form or by any means, without the
prior permission in writing of Oxford University Press, or as expressly permitted
by law, by licence or under terms agreed with the appropriate reprographics
rights organization. Enquiries concerning reproduction outside the scope of the
above should be sent to the Rights Department, Oxford University Press, at the
address above

You must not circulate this work in any other form
and you must impose this same condition on any acquirer

Published in the United States of America by Oxford University Press
198 Madison Avenue, New York, NY 10016, United States of America

British Library Cataloguing in Publication Data
Data available

Library of Congress Control Number: 2017939064

ISBN 978-0-19-878617-7

Printed in Great Britain by
Clays Ltd, St Ives plc

Links to third party websites are provided by Oxford in good faith and
for information only. Oxford disclaims any responsibility for the materials
contained in any third party website referenced in this work.

For Philip and Mary,
who taught me to love rivers,
from the Rother to the Nile

Acknowledgements

This book would not have been possible without the help of my friend and colleague Jyotsna Singh. I am profoundly grateful for her patience and good humour, her knowledge of India (from ancient history to the latest Bollywood films), her journalistic and linguistic skills, and her ability to organise journeys and meetings across the subcontinent in sometimes difficult circumstances.

I also thank: my colleagues and editors at the *Financial Times* for tolerating my obsession with the Ganges and the environment, and for polishing and publishing the articles I have written on these topics over the years; our wonderful New Delhi landladies Meher Wilshaw and Rasil Basu for the use of the haven of their house and garden; my ever-dynamic agent Kelly Falconer; the editors and staff at Oxford University Press, including Matt Cotton, Luciana O'Flaherty, Kizzy Taylor-Richelieu, Martha Cunneen, and Solene van der Wielen; the staff of the British Library; and above all my family for putting up with a writer's moods—my wife Michèle Weldon, our daughters Natasha and Geneviève, and my mother Mary Mallet (whose home in Kent I occupied for weeks of writing).

Like any foreign correspondent I rely heavily on the local media - in this case mostly Indian and Bangladeshi - for ideas and news, and this has been as true for the Ganges as for any other story. I was also inspired by earlier books about the Ganges and India, and those about the world's other great rivers; they are listed in the bibliography. Any errors or omissions, including in the list of people below, are my own.

Only a very few interviewees asked to remain anonymous. Most of those who helped me with this book are named in the text or the notes, for India remains a vigorous democracy where it is normal for people of all sorts to speak their minds. Nevertheless, apart from those named above, I want to thank in particular for their help and inspiration: Mohamed Alam, Stephen Alter, Anuj Bahri and all the staff at Bahri Sons bookshop in New Delhi's Khan Market, Owen Bennett-Jones,

Dharmiyan Singh Bisht, J. J. Biswas, 'Gulu' Ram Chander, Clay Chandler, Ramesh Chandra, Devesh Chaturvedi, Bimla Chauhan, Brahma Chellaney, Lakshmi Chowdhury, Raghunandan Singh Chundawat and Joanna Van Gruisen, Clive Cookson, William and Olivia Dalrymple, Gurcharan Das, Tapan Das, Love Raj Singh Dharmshaktu, Faith Doherty, Arunabha Ghosh, Tapan Kumar Ghosh, John Gomes, David Graham, Ramachandra Guha, Surojit Gupta, Gardiner Harris, S. Jain, Rakesh Jaiswal, Andrew Jenkins, Raj Pal Singh Kahlon, Shyam Khadka, Sunil Khilnani, Prashant Kishor, Pradip Krishen, Bharat Lal, Ramanan Laxminarayan, Tshering Lepcha, James Mallinson, Sam Miller, Piers Moore Ede, Nripendra Misra, Rajat Nag, M. V. Nath, Ainun Nishat, Baijayant 'Jay' Panda, Amod Panwar, Prashant Rajankar, Janakiraman Ramachandran, Jairam Ramesh, Mohit Ray, Adam Roberts and Anne Hammerstad, Simon Roberts, Justin and Bee Rowlatt, Kalyan Rudra, Onno Ruhl, Sadhvi Bhagawati Saraswati, Swami Chidanand Saraswati, Bharat Lal Seth, Ziauddin Shaikh, Shashi Shekhar, Arun Shourie, Imran Siddiqui, Ram Pratap Singh, Sanjeev Singla, Jayant Sinha, R. K. Sinha, Ayesha Sitara, T. R. Sreekrishnan, Arvind Subramanian, Swami Sundaranand, R. Sushila, Vinod Tare, Himanshu Thakkar, Karan Thapar, Romila Thapar, B. D. Tripathi, Kameshwar Upadhyay, Munir Virani, Adil Zainulbhai, and Joseph Zeitlyn.

Contents

List of Plates

Note on Spelling

In this book the names Ganges and Ganga are used interchangeably for the river. In most Indian languages the river and the goddess are both Ganga, and Indians usually use Ganga even when speaking in English, but abroad and among native English-speakers the commonly used name for the river is Ganges. Similarly, I have used the most familiar international spellings for Indian place names, even if there is a recently introduced official alternative. Calcutta is spelt thus, not as Kolkata, but Mumbai is now sufficiently well-known abroad for the name to be used instead of the old Bombay.

The topic of Indian place names is often politicized.[1] Usually the nationalist demand is that foreigners use a close approximation of the local pronunciation in their own language, which would be like the British insisting that the French and Italians stop calling the capital city Londres and Londra and call it London. Bombay over the years has been spelt variously by the British, French, and Portuguese as Mombaim, Bombaim, Manbai, Mayambu, Mombaya, Bombain, Bombaym, Monbaym, Bambaye, Bombaiim, Bombeye, and Boon Bay.

1. For a fuller discussion of the politicization of place names, see Victor Mallet, 'Pride, patriotism and the baffling politics of Indian place names', *Financial Times*, 24 March 2015, https://www.ft.com/content/5ac9ceb6-cf23-11e4-9949-00144feab7de (accessed 16 April 2017).

Preface

I love rivers

        —Eric Newby, in *Slowly Down the Ganges* (1966)[1]

Human civilization was born on a river bank

        —WWF[2]

This book began by accident. Within two days of arriving with my family to live in Delhi during the monsoon of 2012, I noticed a baffling but enticing symbol in the map book kept in the door of the car: next to the Yamuna River here in the heart of north India was a little image of a sailing boat in a red circle—the universal sign for a yacht marina or a sailing club. I love boats, but I found it hard to believe that it was possible to enjoy an outing under sail so far from the sea on a notoriously polluted river—a river, furthermore that passes through modern Delhi almost unnoticed by the mass of its population.

In a way, I was right. No one I met knew anything about boats in Delhi, although my interest was further piqued by an old photograph reprinted in the *Hindustan Times* showing weekend dinghy sailing on the Yamuna in the 1970s. Months later, when I finally reached the spot marked on the map—the street leading to it in the midst of the industrial zone of Okhla in south Delhi is still called Sailing Club Road—I was surprised to find an immaculately kept building and garden called the Defence Services Sailing Club. Across the lawn, sailing dinghies were stacked neatly on racks facing the river. Yet it was a melancholy

---

1. Newby, 22.
2. People and Freshwater, http://wwf.panda.org/about_our_earth/about_freshwater/people_freshwater/ (accessed 21 September 2016).

sight. It was obvious that the boats were rarely, if ever, actually used. The caretaker confirmed it.

The reason was there in front of the club: the stinking, foamy black filth that was once a river. The Yamuna, one of the great tributaries of the Ganges, is portrayed in India's legends and paintings and remembered in its histories as a natural paradise of lilies, turtles, and fish. On its banks, the cheerful god Krishna would play his flute amid a troupe of adoring *gopis*, the female cowherds who attend him. The blue god would be wise to avoid the place today. Almost all the Yamuna's water is diverted above Delhi for irrigation or for the capital itself. In the dry season, much of what flows downstream past Mathura and on to Agra and the Taj Mahal, the famous seventeenth-century mausoleum built by the Mughal emperor Shah Jahan in memory of his beloved wife Mumtaz, is raw sewage and industrial waste from greater Delhi's 25 million inhabitants. Okhla, at the downstream end of Delhi, is particularly vile. As the remains of the river churns across the weir, it forms giant heaps of foam. At dawn the surreal heaps of white spume reflect the orange of the morning sun and are blown hither and thither like lightweight icebergs across the oily black surface. At its worst, the water at Okhla is so polluted by human waste that it contains nearly half a million times the maximum level of faecal coliform bacteria established as the Indian standard for bathing water.

If this stuff goes into the Ganges, I thought, then what of the Ganges itself? Even I, an Englishman recently arrived in India, knew that the Ganges was a holy river, a river celebrated in history and literature. And more than the Yamuna, the Ganges—or Ganga as she is called in most Indian languages—is prominent even today in India's religious, social, economic, and political life. She is a mother-goddess whose uniquely purifying water brings salvation and is kept in pots and jars for use in worship by hundreds of millions of Hindus. It is on the banks of the Ganges that Hindus want to be cremated and in its waters that they devoutly hope their remains will be scattered. Even the secular Jawaharlal Nehru, first prime minister of India after independence from Britain in 1947, asked for some of his ashes to be thrown in the Ganges, which he called 'a symbol of India's age-long culture and civilisation, ever-changing, ever flowing, and yet ever the same Ganga'. Narendra Modi, the Indian prime minister who won a sweeping election victory at the head of the Hindu nationalist Bharatiya Janata Party (BJP) in 2014, deliberately chose the ancient city of Varanasi (Benares) on the Ganges as his parliamentary seat. He praised the river as his mother—*Ma Ganga*—and immediately promised to organize a clean-up of its polluted waters, renaming the relevant ministry as the Ministry of Water Resources, River Development & Ganga Rejuvenation.

The Ganges is important even beyond the shores of India. As I write this, I have just returned from Sri Lanka, where I happened to visit a Buddhist temple in Colombo, crowded with images of Hindu gods such as Ganesh and Vishnu as well as of the Buddha. The name of the temple, it turned out, was Gangaramaya, a tribute, according to the senior monk I questioned, to the great river some 3,000 kilometres to the north. 'There was a lake here that's been filled in', he said. 'Ganga water.'

The Ganges has a numinous presence even in far-away England. During my research, I stumbled across the curious story of how Ganges water was ceremonially poured into a village water well in the presence of Prince Philip, the Duke of Edinburgh, in 1964. He was there to pro-mote UK–India relations and celebrate the centenary of the well in Stoke Row, near Reading, which had been dug and maintained in the nine-teenth century on the orders of a generous Indian maharajah. This Indian aid project for Britain came about because Edward Anderson Reade, a British functionary in the United Provinces (a vast area that includes today's Uttar Pradesh, India's most populous state), is said to have men-tioned a drought then afflicting the Chiltern Hills while having dinner at the palace of the Maharajah of Benares. On hearing of a boy being beaten by his mother for drinking the last drop of water in their home, the maharajah decided to pay for the construction of the deep well, still known today as the Maharajah's Well. It no doubt helped that the maha-rajah knew of Reade's financing of a well in India three decades earlier.

As I criss-crossed India and South Asia in pursuit of stories for the *Financial Times* about everything from elections and industrial automa-tion to climate change and religious conflicts, it dawned on me that writing about the Ganges from source to mouth would be a good way of telling at least part of the almost impossibly complicated but excit-ing story of contemporary India. Having seen the industrial effluents of Kanpur, the sewage of Varanasi, and the garbage of Patna and Calcutta, I wanted to understand why a river that is so important a part of Indian culture and history and the religious identity of Hindus could be so carelessly abused. I wanted to know what was happening to India's greatest river and what needed to be done to save it.

Some friends suggested I should write a book about Modi himself. I have met him and interviewed him and he plays a part in this book about the river, but he is a politician who has risen and will fall like those

who have gone before. Others misheard me when I said Ganges and
thought I was writing about the Gandhis, the political family of Nehru's
descendants now represented by Sonia Gandhi and her son Rahul, who
together lead the Congress Party defeated by Modi and the BJP in 2014.
Again, however, I found the meandering Ganges to be a more enduring
thread around which to weave an interpretation of today's India than the
Nehru-Gandhi dynasty. As Winston Churchill once said of the River
Thames and Britain, the Ganges is 'the golden thread' of Indian history.[3]
On its banks are great cities, some living, others ruined and abandoned,
that have been there for thousands of years and date back to the era
when India was the world's largest economy, greater than China or the
Roman Empire and three times the size of Western Europe.[4]

So how can the Ganges be worshipped by so many Indians and be
simultaneously abused by the same people? Why do Indians and their
governments tolerate for even a week the over-exploitation of their
holy river—sometimes to the point of total dehydration—by irrigation dams, and its poisoning by human waste and industrial toxins? Is
it true that Hindus insist their Ganga is so pure that she cannot be
sullied by such pollution? Can the river be saved?

In this book I explain that Indians are killing the Ganges with pollution and that the polluted Ganges, in turn, is killing Indians. But the story
is not without hope. In writing it, I came to understand much of what is
right with India as well as what is wrong, and to believe that Indians can
save the Ganges just as Europeans and Americans have already saved the
Thames, the Rhine, and the Chicago River. I also realized (as do growing
numbers of worried Indians) that it is absurd for devout Hindus to try to
separate in their minds the actual physical filth of the river from its eternal
spiritual purity, to pretend that the physical world does not and cannot
impinge on the spiritual one. As a wise holy man once said of the Yamuna,
it is the river itself, not some distant symbolic representation of it, that is

---

3. Quoted in Hardyment, 5. She also quoted the Liberal MP John Burns telling a visiting
   American who sneered at the puny size of the Thames in 1929: 'The St Lawrence is
   water, the Mississippi is muddy water, but the Thames is liquid history.'
4. Angus Maddison said India accounted for 33 per cent of world gross domestic product in
   the first century AD; China had 26 per cent and the Roman Empire 21 per cent. (Quoted
   in Sanyal, 120 and available via the University of Groningen and the Maddison project
   at http://www.ggdc.net/maddison/Historical_Statistics/horizontal-file_03-2007.xls and
   http://www.ggdc.net/maddison/maddison-project/home.htm (accessed 20 September
   2016).

'the real goddess'.[5] It is precisely *because* the Ganges is so important in its physical form of life-giving water and fertile silt for so many of the world's people that it came to be worshipped in the first place as a spirit of nature and finally as a fully fledged goddess of the Hindu pantheon.

I am not a Hindu, and can perhaps therefore never revere the Ganga with as much fervour as hundreds of millions of Indians. But I love this river as I love all great rivers—perhaps more, because of my attempt to understand it—and I care about its future. Foreigners, especially those with environmental agendas, are easily accused of hypocritical meddling in the affairs of developing countries: 'You destroyed your natural environment in the pursuit of economic growth, and now you want to stop us exploiting ours', the argument goes. 'The Thames was vile and yet you claim to be shocked by our polluted rivers.' I have been on the receiving end of such criticism in China and South-east Asia, but surprisingly few Indians have bristled resentfully about how the Western media portrays their holy river and its problems. I think that is because almost everyone knows the problems are real.

The direction of this book is (loosely) downstream. It starts at the source of the Ganges in the Himalayan foothills and ends at the river's mouth in the Bay of Bengal. Some friends insisted that this would be a pessimistic way of approaching the topic. Their argument was that the river rises in the icy purity of the mountains and becomes steadily dirtier and more polluted the further you head downstream and the more cities you pass. But I do not see it that way. Much as I enjoy the clean air and water of the upper Ganges, I relish the notion of reaching the navigable river, of leaving behind the chaotic delights of the great cities on its banks and ultimately of attaining the open sea with all its possibilities. Nor is it even true that the Ganges becomes steadily dirtier the further it flows; the varied nature and volume of the water added by its tributaries—notably the Brahmaputra originating in Tibet—and the settlement and dispersal of pollutants along the way make it a lot more complicated than that.

Chapter by chapter, then, we follow the Ganges on its downhill journey, encountering on the way the tragedies, triumphs, and mysteries of India ancient and modern and the characters who have performed in them—pilgrims, politicians, industrialists, scientists, farmers, artists, and adventurers—to end in the mangrove swamps of the Ganges delta in the Bay of Bengal.

5. Haberman, 139.

Map of the Ganges

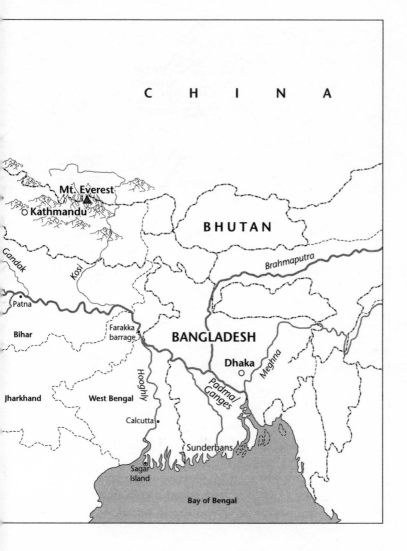

I

Introduction

Killing the Mother Goddess

If Ganga dies, India dies. If Ganga thrives, India thrives. The lives of 500 million people is not a small thing.

—Indian holy man Swami Chidanand Saraswati[1]

The Ganga, especially, is the river of India, beloved of her people, round which are intertwined her racial memories, her hopes and fears, her songs of triumph, her victories and her defeats. She has been a symbol of India's age-long culture and civilization, ever-changing, ever-flowing, and yet ever the same Ganga. She reminds me of the snow-covered peaks and the deep valleys of the Himalayas, which I have loved so much, and of the rich and vast plains below, where my life and work have been cast. Smiling and dancing in the morning sunlight, and dark and gloomy and full of mystery as the evening shadows fall, a narrow, slow and graceful stream in winter, and a vast roaring thing during the monsoon, broad-bosomed almost as the sea, and with something of the sea's power to destroy, the Ganga has been to me a symbol and a memory of the past of India, running into the present and flowing on to the great ocean of the future.

—Jawaharlal Nehru, first prime minister of India, in his will, 1954[2]

When I said that Ma Ganga [Mother Ganges] has called me, these words spontaneously emerged from within. Perhaps these were not even words, they were the manifestation of a spiritual stream flowing within me.

—Narendra Modi, when about to become Indian prime minister, 2014[3]

Nearly 13,000 feet up in the hills where the Himalayas begin, Amod Panwar, an Indian hotel-owner and devout Hindu, reverently places offerings of almonds, sultanas, and a coconut into the water cascading from an icy cavern known as Gaumukh, the Cow's Mouth. This is the source of the River Ganges. The water rushing from underneath the foot of a glacier—the ice cave really does look like a gaping mouth—seizes Panwar's offerings and tumbles them down the valley towards the north Indian plain.

Moments ago, the snowy peaks of Shivling and the three Bhagirathi mountains were brightly lit by the setting sun, but dusk is falling. A block of ice the size of a house is calved from the glacier and plunges into the stream with a roar, sending me scurrying for safety across the grey stones of the riverbank. Panwar, my guide for the high-altitude trek from the roadhead at Gangotri, is undeterred. He continues his devotions, strips off his clothes, and immerses himself in water flecked with shards of ice. Only when we have filled plastic bottles with the holy liquid to take home in our backpacks do we walk downhill to an isolated ashram. There we will take sweet tea and shelter from the cold October night.

Gaumukh is one of the most sacred places in India, and the association with the cow, an animal holy to Hindus, gives it added sanctity. In fact the entire river is holy, flowing more than 2,500 kilometres across north India from the mountainous haunts of the snow leopard to the mangrove swamps of the Bay of Bengal and their man-eating tigers. This glacier is where it all starts: the water emerging from the ice is unfettered by dams and unsullied by the filth that flows into the Ganges downstream.

Examined cartographically, the Ganges appears to be simply a large river that flows from west to east and dominates north India. Yet its religious and social importance reaches far beyond the Gangetic plain, no doubt because the rich silt its waters bring down from the Himalayas has fed and enriched a tenth of humanity almost since the dawn of history. For millennia, the Gangetic plain has been one of the wealthiest and most densely populated zones on earth, which is why the Mughals from Central Asia and the British traders of the East India Company found India such an attractive country to invade, occupy, and pillage. And the Ganges is worshipped as a life-giver not merely by the farmers and fishermen who live on its shifting banks of sand and mud. The river, in the words of the Sanskrit scholar Diana Eck, is the 'archetype of sacred waters',[4] spiritually present in all kinds of waterways, ponds, and wells across South Asia and beyond.

The goddess Ganga's renown was spread in part by the diaspora of Hindu indentured labourers, the peasant farmers from the Gangetic plain who were ferried down the river and shipped from Calcutta to

Mauritius and the West Indies to work on sugar plantations. (In the former British colony of Guyana on the northern coast of South America, where my family lived for a few years in the 1970s, about half the population is of Indian origin.) Less than a year after becoming India's prime minister, Modi was praying at a Hindu holy site in Mauritius, a lake in a volcanic crater called Ganga Talao (also known in French simply as Grand Bassin) into which he ceremonially poured *Ganga jal*— Ganges water. And in South Asia, it is not only Hindus who are in thrall to the Ganges and the supposedly magical properties of its waters. The Muslim Mughal Emperor Akbar preferred the river's 'water of immortality' for drinking and cooking. Buddhism was founded and taught by the Buddha Gautama Siddhartha on the banks of the Ganges.

Thousands of years ago, the focus of early South Asian civilization moved eastwards from the area of the Indus valley (mostly in present-day Pakistan) to the Ganges. So although it is the Indus, not the Ganges, that is most mentioned in the earliest Sanskrit texts, it is the Ganges that has held sway in the world's imagination for the past three millennia. The river is mentioned by the classical Roman poets Ovid and Virgil. Greek, Arab, Chinese, and European pilgrims and explorers wrote of its wonders and of the great cities on its banks: Patna, the now unremarkable capital city of the Indian state of Bihar, was once the magnificent Pataliputra, founded in the sixth century BC and in its day possibly the largest city in the world, described by one historian as 'an Indian Rome'.[5]

The Ganges is far from being the world's longest river, an honour usually accorded to the Nile or the Amazon, but it is one of the most important for humanity by virtue of the massive volumes of water and fertile silt it carries during the monsoon season and the 700 million or so people who depend on it. 'If the Ganga lives, India lives. If the Ganga dies, India dies', says Vandana Shiva, an Indian scientist and environmental campaigner.[6] The whole Ganges basin covers more than a million square kilometres, and in places the sediment is over a kilometre deep, forming a vast store of fertility for rice, wheat, and other crops as well as one of the world's biggest reservoirs of groundwater. North India is already extraordinarily densely populated—as is the neighbouring nation of Bangladesh, which occupies most of the Ganges delta on the Bay of Bengal—and the number of inhabitants continues to rise. India's population in 2016 was about 1.3 billion, more than a sixth of the planet's total, and the country will soon overtake China to become the most populous nation on earth, with the United Nations estimating that the number of Indians will peak above 1.7 billion some time after 2050. The Ganges is vital for nearly half the population of India and for almost all of Bangladesh's 160 million. Nepal is watered by some of its most important tributaries.

By Indian calculations the river is 2,525 kilometres from source to mouth. River measurements are complicated because of arguments over the 'true' source of a river and the way one accounts for different tributaries, but some Indian researchers say it is only the twentieth longest in Asia and forty-first in the world.[7] It is less than half as long as any of the top seven, and easily outranked on that basis by waterways that are little known outside their home countries: the Ob-Irtysh of Central Asia, the Purús of Brazil and Peru, the Lena of Russia, and Canada's Mackenzie-Slave-Peace-Finlay. Even the Ganges's own great tributary the Brahmaputra—which rises in China on the Tibetan plateau as the Yarlung Tsangpo before plunging through the mountainous Indian state of Arunachal Pradesh into the plains of Assam—is 500 kilometres longer than the Ganges itself by the time it joins the river near its delta in Bangladesh.

The sources of the Ganges are on the middle slopes of the Himalayas in the Indian state of Uttarakhand. Hindu mythology now places the source firmly at Gaumukh, the ice cave where the Bhagirathi River emerges in a rush from underneath a receding glacier near the temple town of Gangotri. Geographers might choose as the real source the nearby Alaknanda, which swoops down to the east from the same massif, because of its greater length, but the two soon meet to form the Ganges. The turbid river tumbles down through the steep gorges of the foothills, past Rishikesh—where the Beatles studied transcendental meditation in the 1960s and these days tourists in their dozens shoot the white-water rapids in inflatable boats—towards the meat-free, alcohol-free Hindu holy city of Haridwar on the plains.

By the time the river begins its long, meandering journey from Haridwar across north India to the sea, it is already being tapped for hydro-electricity and irrigation on a large scale. In the spring dry season before the coming of the monsoon in June, the original river is all but exhausted by the time it reaches the industrial town of Kanpur, known to the British as Cawnpore, in Uttar Pradesh.

It is only in Allahabad, where it is replenished by the Yamuna, that the Ganges regains its vigour—and the Yamuna, sullied by the filth of

Delhi and its satellite towns, is able to perform this service only because it has been replenished in its turn by the purer waters of the Chambal. From here, the Ganges passes the big cities of the plains—Varanasi in Uttar Pradesh and Patna in Bihar—and absorbs billions of litres of human sewage and industrial waste from towns and villages on the main stream and on polluted tributaries such as the Ram Ganga. The main stream passes the north-eastern tip of Jharkhand state and crosses West Bengal before entering Bangladesh, where it is named the Padma; there it is joined by the mighty Brahmaputra and reaches the Bay of Bengal in a chaotic and ever-shifting delta of so-called distributaries. Part of the Ganges, helped by the diversionary power of the Farraka dam, turns sharply southward inside West Bengal and continues on what is thought to have been its main route until a few centuries ago, down the Hooghly River and through Calcutta (Kolkata), where Job Charnock of the East India Company in 1690 established the trading post that was to become the capital of British India.

Geologically and hydrographically, of course, it is all one delta. The international border between India and what was then East Pakistan has existed only since the violent partition of British India to create a separate homeland for Muslims at independence in 1947, while the Bengali-speakers of Pakistan broke away from the rest of the country to establish the independent nation of Bangladesh ('Land of the Bengalis') in 1971. South of the now-vast cities of Calcutta and Dhaka, over thousands of years, the silt of the sea-bound arms of the Ganges fanned out into the Bay of Bengal to create a tidal mangrove forest— the world's largest—in a confusion of islands, swamps, and waterways. Protected to some extent on both sides of the border as a national park, the area is called the Sunderbans, or 'the beautiful forest'. This is where the Ganges finally meets the sea, where it ceases to provide direct sustenance for the hundreds of millions of people along its length or the wild animals—freshwater dolphins, crocodiles, birds, tigers, deer—that frequent its waters and its banks.

For anyone familiar with the steadily flowing rivers of Europe, or deceived by the conventional big-river appearance of the Ganges in pictures of Varanasi over the centuries, it is important to explain that for most of its distance the Ganges is a very unreliable river and a very mobile one, with its main bed liable to move laterally by hundreds of metres, or even by kilometres, in a single season. Over decades and centuries, it has wandered much further. The same is true of most of its tributaries, including the Yamuna and the Brahmaputra. One reason is that the rains of the south-west monsoon, concentrated in three or four months of each year, provide most of the fresh water. In the dry season, India's rivers typically shrink to a fraction of their high-season flow. Towards the end of the monsoon, they swell to become dangerous torrents of sometimes awe-inspiring extent, thrashing wildly across the countryside, making and unmaking islands, demolishing villages, and flooding expanses of low-lying farmland.

The second reason for the lateral mobility of the Ganges is the gradualness of its descent to the sea once it has come crashing out the steep Himalayan foothills at Haridwar; driven by gravity, the river water has ample opportunities for diversions and by-passes as it hunts for lower ground on the almost flat north Indian plains. Haridwar is only about 1,000 feet above sea level, but at this point the Ganges still has more than 2,000 kilometres to go before it reaches the Sunderbans. At Kanpur, the altitude is just over 400 feet. Patna, still more than 1,000 kilometres by river from the sea, is below 200 feet. Calcutta and Dhaka are only a few feet above sea level.

These features may seem peculiar to someone who, if asked to think of a river, imagines the reliable if seasonal flow of the Thames in London, say, the Nile in Cairo, or the Potomac in Washington DC. But they do not detract from the importance of the Ganges to humanity and the ecosystems of South Asia. Like almost all the rivers that have become familiar names even outside the countries where they flow, the Ganges was and is essential to the development of agriculture, the establishment of industry, and the growth of cities.

Rivers are more than mere providers of water and food. River-borne trade has long contributed to the development and prosperity of nations. Many great cities are river ports into which it is still possible (and was once essential) to sail, among them Calcutta, London, New York, and Guangzhou (Canton). Even the little Rother near my home in southern England, I recently learned, was plied in Roman times by vessels exporting English iron ore across the Channel, and it carried coal far inland until after World War Two. In fact, the sheer navigational awkwardness of the vagrant Ganges and its tributaries means, in spite of their importance to Hindus, that they do not always get the attention they deserve from modern India. That is especially true of the Yamuna in the Indian capital, a river described by one author as 'Delhi's shameful, rancid secret'.[8] There is no shame or ignorance, however, about the Ganges itself in Haridwar, Varanasi, or Calcutta, where the river's reputation as salvatory goddess, provider of food, and even sometimes as a trade route is undimmed. The British established their capital at the mouth of the Ganges, despite the dangerous shoals of the delta and storms in the Bay of Bengal, because it gave them access to the wealth of India and because it lay at the junction of trade routes linking the Indian subcontinent to the west (the Arab world and Europe); to the north (China, Tibet, and central Asia); and the east (the maritime states of South-east Asia).

The Ganges is known as a wondrous river of legend and history whose epithets in Sanskrit texts include 'eternally pure', 'a light amid the darkness of ignorance', and 'daughter of the Lord of Himalaya'. One hymn calls it the 'sublime wine of immortality'. Yet the river whose waters and fertile silt have supported the densest populations of humans on earth for millennia is now under threat. Where its waters are not diverted for irrigation and hydro-electricity, they are befouled by sewage and poisoned by pesticides, industrial waste, carcinogenic heavy metals, and bacterial genes that make lethal infections resistant to modern antibiotics. When I first wrote this sentence in the middle of the dry season, I was looking at a front-page story in *The Hindu* newspaper headlined 'Is the mighty Ganga drying up?'[9] The conclusions of official measurements, academic papers, and the evidence of one's own eyes are alarming for anyone who cares about human health or the environment.

After decades of false starts, scandals, and wasted money under previous governments, Indian prime minister Narendra Modi launched a campaign in 2014 to clean the Ganges and save it for future generations. More than two years on, many of those who thought he would achieve something are bitterly disappointed by the lack of progress. It will in any case be a huge and costly task. But it is not impossible, as river clean-ups in Europe and America have shown.

The story starts high in the hills at the Cow's Mouth, where Panwar made his offerings to the river goddess. It is here that the river emerges from its ice-cave in the Himalayan foothills.

2

Mouth of the Cow
The Himalayan Source

We were surrounded by gigantic peaks, entirely cased in snow, and almost beyond the regions of animal and vegetable life . . . A most wonderful scene.
—Captain J. A. Hodgson, first European to describe the source of the Ganges, 1817[1]

After 20 or 25 years the Ganga will be finished because the glaciers are melting. Look how warm it is here!
—Swami Sundaranand, yogi and mountaineer, 2013[2]

Up here, you can hear the mountains move. As you negotiate precipitous trails and clamber across deep gullies where the paths have been washed away, you are frequently startled by the sound of rockfalls and minor landslides. Earthquakes are not infrequent: the Indian tectonic plate, having separated itself from Gondwana and crossed the ocean over millions of years, is crunching remorselessly into the Eurasian landmass. To reach Gaumukh does not require the skills or equipment of a mountaineer, but the journey through this starkly beautiful terrain helps explain why Hindus have long been in awe of the mountains that give birth to their holy river. It is also one reason why Panwar, my guide, and some of the hundreds of thousands of pilgrims who come to the highlands each summer want to perform their *puja*—their act of worship—at the very source of the Ganges.

Captain J. A. Hodgson, the British surveyor and soldier of the Native Infantry who became the first European to see and describe Gaumukh in 1817, was right to call it 'a most wonderful scene'. But he also knew from experience that the Himalayas are as fragile as they are magnificent. As he passed the Lohari Nag falls—now the site of a hydro-electricity project abandoned a decade ago because of environmental objections—he wrote that the scene was 'fully of sublimity and wildness, and the roar of the water is astounding'. So steep were the mountains on either side that it was impossible to see the Pole Star to help ascertain his position ('hid by the mountains as usual'). And when his expedition camped in Gangotri, they were lucky to escape the effects of a series of earthquakes that flung huge rocks from the mountaintops into the river bed 'with a hideous noise not be described, and never to be forgotten'.

As they approached Gaumukh, they heard 'the thundering peals of falling avalanches' in wild, cold scenery such that 'a Pagan might aptly imagine the place a fit abode for demons'. The two Brahmins they met in Gangotri told them that they had no information about the river upstream and had never heard of any rock or place like a cow's mouth.[3] Finally, on 31 May, they reached the foot of the glacier:

A most wonderful scene.—The *B'hágirat'hí* or *Ganges* issues from under a very low arch at the foot of the grand snow bed—The river is here bounded to the right and left by high snow and rocks; but in front over the *Debouche*, the mass of snow is perfectly perpendicular, and from the bed of the stream to the summit, we estimate the thickness at little less than 300 feet of solid frozen snow, probably the accumulation of ages;—it is in layers of some feet thick, each seemingly the remains of a fall of a separate year . . . I cannot think of any place to which they might more aptly give the name of a Cow's Mouth than to this extraordinary *Debouche*.—The height of the arch of snow is only sufficient to let the stream flow under it. Blocks of snow were falling about us, so there was little time to do more here than to measure the size of the stream . . . Believing this to be, (as I have every reason to suppose it is), the first appearance of the famous and true *Ganges* in day light, saluted her with a Bugle march and proceeded . . .[4]

We had no bugle to salute the Ganges, so I merely admired the glacier— a fractured cliff face of opaque blue, mixed with dirt and chunks of rock—and peered cautiously into the cave at its base from which gushed the beginnings of the river. I noticed strange-shaped holes in the ice walls in front of us, and rocks lying on ledges above the stream or balanced in isolation atop mounds of ice. Then—with the glacier dripping, cracking, and flaking behind us—we retreated down the valley in the gathering darkness of the Himalayan night.

The legends of the Ganges—the goddess *Ma Ganga* or Mother Ganges—encompass heaven and earth, gods, kings, and sages and explain how she came rushing from the Cow's Mouth. They are tales compellingly strange to non-Hindus and come in many versions and varieties. In the Vedic myth as recounted by the Sanskrit scholar Diana Eck, Indra, the king of the gods, frees the nectar-like waters of heaven to nourish the earth by defeating the great serpent Vritra, who has coiled around the vault of heaven and imprisoned the waters of immortality. The god Vishnu, dwarf-turned-giant, takes possession of the threefold universe by striding through the earth, the sky, and the heavens, and pierces heaven's upper limit with his toe to release the waters:

Through this opening, the Ganga flowed into the heavens, landing first in Indra's heaven, where the river was caught by the steady Pole Star, Dhruva. From there she ran down the sky to the moon as the Milky Way, and from the moon to the realm of Brahma, situated just above Mount Meru... The river split into four parts and ran out upon the four lotus-petal continents. One branch, the Alakananda, flowed into Bharata [India] as the Ganga.[5]

In a Buddhist version of the origin of the Ganges—cited by Xuanzang, a Chinese scholar who visited India in the seventh century AD and may have reached as far upstream as Uttarkashi—the river, like the Indus, the Oxus, and the Yellow River, comes from the Anavatapta Lake south of the Fragrant Mountain and north of the Great Snow Mountains (the Himalayas). 'Its banks are adorned with gold, silver, lapis lazuli, and crystal. It is full of golden sand, and its water is as pure and clean as a mirror. A Bodhisattva of the eighth stage, having transformed himself into a Naga king by the power of his resolute will, makes his abode at the bottom of the lake and supplies water for the Jambu continent [Earth].' The Ganges, in this version, issues from a cow's mouth—the mouth of the Silver Ox at the east side of the lake.[6]

The source of the Ganges remained a mystery to explorers for centuries, and the myth persisted among both Indians and foreigners that its waters issued from Mt Kailash or Lake Manasarovar in Tibet and then forced their way southward through the mountains to India in an underground passage. The source, in fact, turned to be much lower and more accessible than the high-altitude Tibetan origins of some of Asia's other great rivers. James Baillie Fraser, a Scottish traveller and landscape artist, was the first European to reach Gangotri, which he achieved in 1815, two years ahead of Hodgson. 'We were now in the centre of the stupendous Himala, the loftiest and perhaps most rugged range of mountains in the world', wrote Fraser. 'We were at the acknowledged source of that noble river, equally an object of veneration and a source of fertility, plenty, and opulence to Hindostan; and we had now reached the holiest shrine of Hindoo worship which these holy hills contain.' His journal contains an elegant map of the area and chapter headings that give an insight into the mind of the colonial traveller experiencing the Himalayas for the first time: 'In total and eternal snow—The people suffer—Magnificent view by moonlight—The coolies troublesome—the people complain of fatigues and of the bis, or poisoned wind—I felt my breast and breathing oppressed, and my strength decline—Cold excessive...' He had the grace to acknowledge that, although he might have been the first European to see Gangotri, he had little to boast about since he had faced no great danger and the path was open to determined pilgrims. Fraser also learned that the real source of the river was only a few miles upstream—not more than 5 miles, according to a local *pandit* [priest]—but there was no path and he decided the way would be impassable: 'and beyond this place it is in all probability chiefly supplied by the melting of the great bosom of snow which terminates the valley, and which lies between the peaks'. When he asked about the story that the Ganges came from a rock shaped like the mouth of a cow, the *pandit* laughed and said the pilgrims asked the same question. He assured Fraser that the river was simply fed by melting snow.[7]

Perhaps the strangest and most evocative myth of all—recounted in outline to me by my guide Panwar and familiar to most of the world's 1 billion Hindus—concerns Lord Shiva's part in curbing the raging violence of the river by catching her in the locks of his hair and releasing the water in streams to nourish the earth. A king called Sagar has performed a royal rite in which a horse is released to wander the earth for a year, effectively claiming sovereignty for him over the lands it passes through. When the horse disappears, Sagar sends his sons—all 60,000 of them—to find it. They finally locate the stolen horse at the ashram of Kapil Muni, a famous ascetic, and storm in while he is meditating. Enraged, Kapil Muni burns all the sons to ashes with his fiery gaze. Sagar sends his grandson Anshuman to pray and plead with Kapil Muni, who responds that the 60,000 can only be brought back to life by the waters of the Ganges, which has yet to fall to earth. It is Anshuman's descendant Bhagirath who lives as an ascetic in the

Himalayas and so eventually wins the release of the river from the heavens and persuades Shiva to break its otherwise destructive fall to earth. Shiva catches and slows Ganga's raging torrents in his long hair and divides her with his locks into the three main source streams that flow from the Himalayan foothills today—the Bhagirathi, the Alaknanda, and the Mandakini, all considered holy by Hindus. Shiva and Bhagirath are also remembered—in Shiva's case it is his lingam or male organ that is recalled in the name and shape of Shivling—in the mountains visible from the uppermost stretch of the Ganges; the patriotic Briton Hodgson named the four peaks St George, St Patrick, St Andrew, and St David after the patron saints of the four countries of the British isles, but the names did not stick.

The stream from Gaumukh is thus known at first as the Bhagirathi, after King Bhagirath. It joins the Alaknanda to become the Ganga or Ganges at Devprayag. Many others, of course, have been to Gaumukh before me. Ilija Trojanow, the travel writer, was possessed by visions of the Indian gods when he camped next to the glacier more than a decade ago. He described his altitude-induced headache, the visible effects of climate change, and the relentless roar of the emerging river, and imagined Shiva dancing wildly with Ganga. 'With every whirl he crowned himself with froth and threw another sound at the world, until the roar dissolved into uncountable sounds and tones . . . The front of the glacier glowed turquoise, a faded amethyst. The ice was covered with debris; it humped under the weight of constant change.'[8] Eck reached the roadhead at Gangotri one year in early May in the course of her research, but did not make it to the glacier. Few pilgrims had arrived and those returning from Gaumukh said they had seen a frozen ascetic who had died at the spot during the winter.

I, too, nearly failed to reach the glacier on my first attempt in October 2013, but not because of the cold. Access through the hills had been blocked for most of the summer pilgrimage season after raging floods had swept down the Alaknanda and the Bhagirathi in June. Torrential rains triggered thousands of landslides that tore away the snaking roads precariously carved into steep hillsides; it took me nearly two days by car simply to travel the 250 kilometres from Dehradun airport to the end of the road at Gangotri—the pilgrimage town from where you walk and clamber the 20 kilometres or so to Gaumukh and which is reputed to have been the site of the river's source before the glacier retreated.

The situation was much worse over the hills in the Alaknanda valley. Between 15 and 17 June, flash floods surged past the temple at Kedarnath, sweeping away hundreds of pilgrims where people had built hotels and shops along the old courses of the Alaknanda river and its tributary, the Mandakini. The death toll in a disaster barely recalled by the outside world was 5,748, according to the government. Tens of thousands of stranded pilgrims were evacuated by the army and its helicopters. Many disappeared, and some locals insist that the official toll is only a fifth of the true number of fatalities. But there was no argument about the extensive damage to roads, bridges, and buildings, even as tourists and hardy pilgrims started to trickle back to the holy sites on the upper Ganges before the onset of winter. The disaster became known as the 'Himalayan tsunami'.

Photographs and videos of the river surging around the statue of Shiva meditating in Rishikesh vividly portray the violence of the upper Ganges in spate. The statue was constructed on the bank of the river, but the swelling floodwaters, blackened by mud and rock ripped from the mountainsides, can be seen submerging the beatific Shiva up to his shoulders before they sweep him away. The evidence was everywhere as we crossed paths with the sheep being brought down from the mountains for the winter and drove slowly up the Bhagirathi gorge, first past terraced rice fields, then apple orchards and pine forests. Hillsides were scarred by rockfalls. Hundreds of uprooted trees lay on the riverbed where they had been flung aside by the torrent. The bridge linking the two sides of Uttarkashi, the district capital, was gone, knocked down by the flood. A bulldozer that had been swept away lay abandoned in the gorge beside the now peaceful river.

Uttarkashi is no stranger to disaster. Panwar and other locals told me of the great flood of 1978, the 1991 earthquake, and the collapse of the Varunavat hill in a landslide onto the town in 2003. For Panwar, though, the 2013 catastrophe was particularly hard. He is a farmer's son who started working in a hotel one summer at the age of 11 and learned some English. He went on to rent and manage small hotels and, when I met him at the age of 30, felt he had started to achieve something: the previous year he had built his own sixteen-room hotel 50 metres from the Ganges. Like other hotels in the area it was packed with summer season pilgrims on their way to Gangotri on 15 June when the flooding began and the river swelled and shifted its course. He showed me the building as we crawled up the road to Gangotri from Uttarkashi: it was abandoned and perched precariously on the new river bank, while the college next door had been knocked down by the force of the water. At least his guests had not suffered the fate of those in a nearby ashram, swept away entirely with the loss of twenty lives. But he was not sure whether he could salvage his hotel. In a cynical play of words on the environmental concerns about the Ganges, he said: 'People used to say "Save the Ganges". This year they are saying "Save us from the Ganges".'

Everyone from holy men to hoteliers was affected up here by the road closures and the loss of trade from the tens of thousands of pilgrims on their way to Gangotri. 'Before the flood', said Chandan Singh Rawat, who runs a ramshackle tea house perched above the mountain torrent of the upper Ganges, 'business was great. We didn't even have time to talk to people.' Now he had time on his hands and little source of income. 'We live from day to day.' Further up the road, I came across a group of people packing boxes of apples for an aid programme that would give women work making jam and chutney. 'Now there are no tourists, no pilgrims', Gopal Thapliyal, programme manager for a local aid organization, told me.

Panwar, however, had set me thinking about the causes of the flood disaster, which began with heavy June rain in the mountains at the beginning of the monsoon. 'I had a friend up there and he said that it normally rains and then turns to snow. This time it was three days of just rain, and heavy rain. That could be linked to global warming.' It could indeed. This is not scientifically controversial: the upper reaches of the Ganges in the Himalayan foothills—and all the great rivers of Asia that rise in the high Himalayas of Tibet—are already affected by climate change. A geological study published in May 2015 by researchers from Europe and Nepal said glacier volumes around Mt Everest shrank 15–20 per cent between 1961 and 2007 and could be reduced by 70–99 per cent before 2100 in a 'sustained mass loss from glaciers in the Everest region through the 21st century'.[9] The floods could be a sign of exactly the kind of problems that climate scientists have been predicting, including more intense and variable monsoon rains and a sharp rise in average temperatures in the north of the Indian subcontinent. Cyclone Phailin, which struck India's east coast four months after the Himalayan floods, was one of the most severe recorded in the Indian Ocean. Anup Malik, a senior official of the Indian Forestry Service visiting Gangotri to assess the damage, had much the same explanation for the flash flooding as Panwar. 'Usually in the upper reaches of the Himalayas, it doesn't rain that heavily', he told me. 'This year it did. One reason to which it's being attributed is climate change. Even last year there was a lot of rain in Uttarkashi.' The floods, he said, had destabilized the river bed, washed away swathes of hill forest and uprooted trees, silted up wetlands downstream and disturbed the wild-life. 'This is nature's fury.'

I had become aware of south Asia's extreme vulnerability to climate change as soon as I moved to India in 2012 and attended a mountain literature festival in the hill station of Mussourie. At the time, global warming was already starting to benefit oil exploration and shipping in the previously ice-bound Arctic seas, but in the Indian Himalayas climate change was being blamed for human, environmental, and eco-nomic catastrophes. What we heard in Mussourie from the climbers, guides, and naturalists who scale the peaks and work in the mountains should have dispelled any lingering scepticism about the realities of global warming. 'Throughout our field trips, we've seen that strange things have started to happen', said Rajarshi Chakraborty, a biologist working for WWF, the conservation group. After enthusing about the discovery of more than 350 species of plants and animals in the eastern Himalayas in the two decades up to 2008, Chakraborty expressed dis-may about the retreat of glaciers and surprise that rhododendrons had begun flowering in February instead of April. He was not alone. Love Raj Singh Dharmshaktu, an Indian mountaineer who by then had scaled Mt Everest four times, said apple harvests at his home in the highlands of Uttarakhand had been diminished by the decrease in cold weather and snowfall in winter and by extreme weather at other times of the year. 'The temperature has definitely increased. I've seen the glaciers recede very fast', he said. 'The flow of streams and waterfalls has really gone down. A long time ago, people used to fish, but now they [the rivers] are all dried up.'[10] Trojanow had a neat description of the phenomenon in his book on the Ganges. It was, he wrote, 'as if mankind had left the freezer open' and allowed the ice to melt.[11]

Indians—because they are so numerous and because climate change is predicted to be particularly drastic in the heavily populated regions of north India where the Ganges runs along the southern side of the Himalayas—are likely to be among the worst affected victims of global climate change. According to one recent report by senior UK and Indian government scientists, temperatures in India will rise sharply within decades, just as the country overtakes China to become the world's most populous nation, while the monsoon downpours become stronger and less predictable. The scientists' conclusions show that average temperatures in north India are projected to rise by 2.9–5°C by about 2080—an extraordinary change in one lifetime—if greenhouse gases continue to be emitted globally in large quantities. Their predictions in 2012 that floods would probably be more severe, that rainfall would be more variable, and that cyclones were likely to be more intense were confirmed almost immediately by the disaster on the upper reaches of the Ganges.

And in May 2015, at the peak of the pre-monsoon hot season in India, some 2,000 people were reported to have died of heat-stroke, dehydration, and other heat-related ailments as daytime temperatures approached 50°C. Urban 'heat islands' where buildings and roads absorb and retain heat only make matters worse. That prompted Verisk Maplecroft, a risk consultancy, to calculate that 'heat stress' days would increase and labour productivity decline in the coming thirty years, while the number of 'very hot' days each year in Delhi would more than quadruple from fourteen to fifty-seven. Arjuna Srinidhi, programme manager for climate change at India's Centre for Science and Environment, noted that human-induced global warming had already turned 2014 into the hottest year on record and triggered other extreme weather events. 'This year, we saw the wettest March in about 50 years, and we have already seen the second major flood in Kashmir in a period of six months. These are all extreme weather events.'[12] In early 2016, northern and western India were hit by a severe drought, but the arrival of the monsoon on schedule in the middle of the year brought severe flooding and swelled the Ganges to record levels. Globally, 2016 was on track to be the hottest year on record.[13]

Climate change, according to Strobe Talbott, president of the Brookings Institution think-tank and a former official in the Clinton administration, is a critical security issue. 'This is not a problem that exists in the future conditional tense. It exists in the present tense.' Rajat Nag, then managing director-general of the Asian Development Bank (ADB), said environmental problems—including climate change—should not be ignored while developed and developing countries argue about who is to blame and who should act first:

Over the past four decades, Asia has lost 40 per cent of its coral reefs, China has lost 70 per cent of its mangroves in the past 50 years, and south-east Asia has lost 13 per cent of its forest areas in the past 20 years . . . We think that we are actually seeing the effects of climate change in the number of cyclones, floods and earthquakes. Asia has been vulnerable to many natural disasters. What we are saying is that a large part of this is surely to do with climate change, though not all.[14]

There have certainly been tragic events directly related to weather and climate in the Himalayas in recent years—including the sudden, heavy snowfall in the Annapurna region of western Nepal in the early autumn of 2014 that surprised trekkers and guides and left thirty-eight of them dead. Earthquakes are an even greater danger. The 7.8-magnitude Himalayan quake of 25 April 2015 killed more than 8,000 people in Nepal and north India, a reminder that the world's highest mountains are still being formed by the massive geological force of the Indian tectonic plate's continuing northward march and its multi-million year collision with Eurasia.

The steepness and fragility of the hills and mountains is one of the first things I noticed about the terrain as I drove and then walked along the upper Ganges to its source. This is a landscape still in the making. The rock is friable, and roads built on near-vertical slopes are inevitably unstable. Frequent rockfalls when you are walking or camping prompt you to glance up and try to identify the source of the noise: perhaps a group of *tahr*, the Himalayan mountain goat, or merely the result of the relentless erosion engineered by wind and rain. As a British governor-general remarked in the early nineteenth century on a visit to Haridwar: 'In all other countries which now occur to my recollection, minor hills rise in succession before you come to a principal range. Here the mountains start abruptly from the plain, and with such steep acclivity, that they are to be ascended at particular passes.'[15]

Harsh conditions here have long attracted Hindu holy men and hermits, who are eager to practise the religion's long tradition of asceticism and self-denying austerities. Some, like the unspeaking *sadhu* or holy man I met at the ashram in Bhujbas near the glacier, spend half the year meditating on mountain tops and have taken a vow of silence. There are said to be about 150 such *sadhus* living in Gangotri, and they too have noticed the changing climate and the pressures on the environment from India's growing population. The oldest must surely be Swami Sundaranand, who was born in 1926 and came to Gangotri in 1948 from Andhra Pradesh. He was 87 when I met him. Yogi, holy man, photographer, climber, and colleague of mountaineers—he was friends with Everest conquerors Sir Edmund Hillary and Tenzing

Norgay and knew Heinrich Harrer, the Austrian tutor of the Dalai Lama and author of *Seven Years in Tibet*—the white-bearded Swami told me the Gaumukh glacier had retreated 3 kilometres since 1982 and the winters had grown milder. 'In October, all the mountains used to be covered in snow. Not now', he told me, sitting cross-legged in his ashram, protected by a sheepskin jacket. 'Before we used to have four feet of snow, and now it's one and a half feet in Gangotri.' The old man condemned the pilgrims for throwing rubbish in the river, the *pandits* for caring only about money, and the locals for building hotels without sewage treatment. 'Nature one day will finish us and Kedarnath is an example', he concluded. 'After 20 or 25 years the Ganga will be finished because the glaciers are melting. Look how warm it is here! Before we would be sitting near the fire...All the night and day I'm thinking about the Ganga and the Himalayas. Oh Ganga, save us, the bad people!'

The huts and meditation centres of the *sadhus* are perched above the narrow gorge where the roaring Ganges carves curvaceous, Henry Moore-style sculptures in the rock. 'Both in color and texture the rocks look like whipped meringue', one American traveller wrote, 'even though they are as hard as bone.'[16] Next door to Sundaranand, the Swami calling himself Brahmacharya Anil Surukh was equally scathing about the locals and their commercial enterprises; but he was also sceptical about the credentials of some of his fellow-*sadhus*. 'As a *sadhu*, I must say that the *sadhus* are not playing their role. The *sadhus* down on the plain, in Delhi and so on, they are not doing their duties', he said, after explaining how he was born in Hyderabad, moved from place to place as the child of an army officer, and then arrived in Gangotri a decade ago. 'They are living a normal life in society. Their duty is doing real *sadhana* [religious discipline] of the heart, not of the mind. This is not my view. It's a fact. Everybody's lifestyle is changing— *sadhus* have a Western life, the luxurious life. They are not fully turning their attention towards the gods.'

I asked if the gods were angry. He smiled. 'No, it's not like that. God is a disciplined power.' But the divine powers are warning us, through floods and disease, about the error of our ways, said the *sadhu*, who was wearing an orange woolly hat, a pink anorak, and a duvet over his feet in the autumn evening chill. He believed the places with good and plentiful *sadhus*—such as Gangotri, obviously—were protected from disaster in the flash flooding that devastated Kedarnath. 'Four thousand five hundred people were here, but nobody got killed, because here there are many *sadhus*, doing *sadhana* in caves, in ashrams.' I asked what people should do to save the Ganges. 'Leave her alone', he replied promptly. 'Don't do anything. It will be very hard. They are earning many *crores* [tens of millions of rupees] from Ganga ... Leave the banks of the Ganga— the government says 200 metres [back from the river, a limit for building]. I say 500 metres. There's no need for money. Only willpower is needed. There's money here too for [saving] Ganga. But they don't want to save it. Ganga is not a matter of money. You have to think.'

Erosion, deforestation, and melting glaciers, together with multiple Chinese dams on Himalayan rivers in Tibet, make for apocalyptic predictions about the fate of India and the Ganges. By one reckoning, if you include the Brahmaputra which joins the Ganges near its terminus in the east, meltwater from the Himalayas contributes 70 per cent of the flow of the Ganges; as the world warms and glaciers melt, the flow will at first increase and then dwindle as the glaciers shrink and disappear.[17]

Even if catastrophe has yet to strike, some of those who appreciate the oddities and beauties of the mountainous Garhwal region where the Ganges rises are already a little melancholy about the ravages of modernity. This is a place where *rishis* or sages would sit motionless in the so-called 'green posture' for nine days after smearing their bodies with a mixture of mud, cowdung, and millet seeds; the millet seeds would sprout and the *rishis* would turn green and blend in with the landscape. These are the hills where the piping song of the blue whistling thrush recalls the story of how the Lord Krishna lost his flute. He fell asleep next to a mountain stream and a small boy stole the instrument, so he turned the thief into a bird. But playing the flute had taught the boy-turned-bird bits and pieces of Krishna's magical repertoire, and so 'he continued, in his disrespectful way, to play the music of the gods, only stopping now and then (as the whistling thrush does) when he couldn't remember the tune'.[18]

But these are also the hills climbed by hundreds of thousands of careless pilgrims, by herb collectors who strip the slopes bare of rare plants, and by poachers in search of leopard, musk deer, and black bear. Stephen Alter, an American writer who has lived in the area since he was a child, calls the hot springs that tout for tourists and pilgrims at Gangnani above Uttarkashi 'possibly the most disheartening place in the Himalayas ... little more than a steaming, fetid drain', and it is hard to disagree. In Gangotri, on one of a series of treks to the sources of the Ganges, he found vendors selling 'musk deer glands' that were actually goat scrotums stuffed with sawdust and scented with cheap perfume. It is a far cry from the 'landscape of overwhelming beauty, a sanctuary where nature captivates the imagination' described in the Vedas and Puranas, the 'unspoiled world where one could easily believe the gods retreated in meditation'.[19]

There was garbage littering the river bank just upstream of the temple when I went to Gangotri, but the shops were closed after the flood disaster in the summer and there was not a sawdust-stuffed goat scrotum in sight. My last stop in the town was at the temple to Ganga, said by the chief *pujari* or priest, Pandit Bhageswar Semwal, to have been built in the eighteenth century by a Nepali king and subsequently enlarged by another *raja* from Jaipur. Pilgrims present offerings to Ganga's image, 'a small golden image of the goddess on a silver throne embossed with a relief image of her *makara*, the Gangetic "crocodile" that is her vehicle, bearing in her hands auspicious emblems of her generosity—a water pot and a lotus'.[20]

Other images in the temple include those involved in the legend of her descent to earth—Shiva and Bhagirathi—as well as Saraswati and Yamuna, her mythical and actual tributaries, and the goddesses Durga and Annapurna. Semwal tells me that normally about 350,000 pilgrims visit each year before the image is taken downstream to Mukhwa for the winter, although that year less than half that number made it before the roads were blocked by landslides. Rajanikant Semwal, the treasurer (they are from the same Brahmin family), tells me something I have often heard before but can now almost believe so near are we to the source—that Ganga water has almost magical properties of purity. 'The water of Ganga can never be destroyed or spoiled', he says. 'If you open the bottle after ten years, the water will be the same.' Rajanikant has sung traditional Garhwali songs for the movies, and recorded one specially for the flood victims at Kedarnath. He is in no doubt that the gods are angry with people for abusing the environment and debasing Hinduism for financial gain. 'God took vengeance on people—people did things wrong', he says. 'God said, "If you don't control yourselves, we will start controlling you." Many people are coming here and it's become commercialized. We crossed the natural limits, so God sent a message to us: "If you don't understand it, I will punish you and maintain it myself."'[21]

At dusk I watch the *pujari* emerge from the temple for the dramatic 'lamp offering', accompanied by the sound of the temple bells and some garish illuminations in blue and magenta, to worship the river on its way to the rest of India and the sea. The ceremony ends with the singing of a sixteenth-century hymn to Ganga by the poet Jagannatha.

> O *Mother Ganga, may your water,*
> *abundant blessing of the world,*
> *treasure of Lord Shiva, playful Lord of all the world,*
> *essence of the scriptures and*
> *embodied goodness of the gods,*
> May *your water, sublime wine of immortality,*
> Soothe *our troubled souls.*[22]

I have learned much about the fragility of the Himalayan environment. I have seen some extraordinary birds and animals, including the massive lammergeier or bearded vulture, flocks of *bharal* or blue sheep, and snakes. I have even seen the footprints of a snow leopard on the path. I have begun to understand the interdependent relationships between Hinduism, India, and the Ganges.

Panwar, my guide, offers a silent prayer and touches the bridge he is crossing each time he encounters the Ganges or one of its streams. I have even learned something about politics. It turns out that Panwar is a member of the Rashtriya Swayamsevak Sangh or RSS, the right-wing Hindu cultural organization that fathered the Hindu nationalist Bharatiya Janata Party (BJP) of Narendra Modi. His wife, he tells me, is a BJP representative in the area. Uttarakhand used to be part of India's most populous state, Uttar Pradesh next door, and he correctly predicts—nearly a year before the election—that the BJP will win a majority of seats in the state and thus see Modi installed as prime minister of the world's largest democracy.

The two of us have had some fruitful arguments during the long hours of trekking up and down the valley. He defends Hindu nationalism and suggests that Pakistan's status as an Islamic state born out of the British *Raj* means that India, by the same token, should be a Hindu nation. I contend that secular, multi-religious states are more successful than their intolerant cousins, and offer the same nation state that he has pointed to—Pakistan—as an example of abject failure: first it was a state for all Muslims, and non-Muslims faced persecution; then Sunni Muslim militants began to persecute and murder non-Sunnis, such as the Shia and the Ahmadis; and now Sunni extremists are killing other

Sunnis for failing to adhere to an imported, Saudi-inspired version of Islam. Furthermore, I say, all this religious factionalism is absurd when the earth is such an insignificant speck in the universe. The only time I feel I have the upper hand in our debate is when we pause to look at the crystal-clear night sky as we descend rather late in the evening from the glacier. Panwar points to the band of thin cloud across the stars. Those aren't clouds, I laugh. That's the Milky Way. No, he says, I'm a guide, and those are clouds. No, I retort, I'm a sailor, and they're stars. I hand him my birdwatching binoculars so that he can see for himself the countless stars of our galaxy. For once he has no reply.

It is time for me to leave and head back down the slow road to the teeming plains of north India; past Mukhwa and Harsil (the remote spot where Frederick Wilson or 'Raja Wilson', a deserter from the British forces in the nineteenth century, established himself as a trader in timber, fur, and musk and married a local girl); through Uttarkashi again; past the massive Tehri dam on the Ganges; along the river at Rishikesh; and so to Dehradun, and the great pilgrimage cities of the Gangetic plain.

3

Holy Waters

What need of expensive sacrifices,
or of difficult penances?
Worship Ganga, asking for happiness
and good fortune,
and she will bring you heaven
and salvation.

—From the Padma Purana[1]

When they had bathed they felt cleansed: not just bodily but in spirit.
—The Ramayana, describing a day by the holy river[2]

North India can be cold in mid February. In Delhi at night the city's ubiquitous 'security guards'—usually just old men who open and close the gates of the rich—huddle around noxious fires of plastic waste or fallen tree branches. Even the wealthy shroud themselves in blankets and lean over electric radiators in homes ill-designed for winter. The Ganges at Allahabad in February is cold too, cold enough (and murky enough) to remind potential swimmers of James Joyce's 'snotgreen, scrotumtightening' sea off Dublin. It is, however, hard to resist the peer pressure from 100 million people who are participating in an activity that is said to attain this degree of auspiciousness only once every 144 years. So in I jumped, immersing myself in the chilly, muddy waters of the Ganges to become a bit player in one of the most astonishing spectacles on earth. The Kumbh Mela, reputed on occasion to be the largest concentrated gathering of humans anywhere, is a month-long celebration of holy waters that occurs in four different Indian river towns in a twelve-year cycle, attracting Hindu pilgrims and holy men from across the country and the world.

River confluences are considered especially sacred. Allahabad—site of the 2013 Kumbh Mela—is where the Yamuna and the invisible Saraswati (probably once a real river west of here that disappeared in ancient times) meet the Ganges. On the first day, monks in silver chariots and naked holy men smeared with ashes and wielding tridents lead crowds of ecstatic men and women who surge into the water in their millions to cleanse their sins. The scene brings to mind a vast medieval fair, a chaotic mixture of commerce and religion where you will be talking one moment to a visiting Mumbai businessman and the next to a marijuana-stoned yogi. 'It is like a spiritual expo', says Sri Sri Ravishankar, a contemporary Indian guru.[3]

The bathing festival in some form dates back many centuries and is rooted in Hindu mythology: the accepted story today is that as gods and demons fought over a jug of nectar, drops of it spilled onto the four river sites—at Allahabad, Haridwar, Nasik, and Ujjain—that now take turns to host a festival of varying degrees of auspiciousness and importance. 'Every year the Mela is vast. On the 12th year, as in 2013, the size is almost unimaginable. This is the Kumbh Mela', says a report by a social science group from British and Indian universities.[4] (They concluded that although the *mela* was a noisy ordeal for pilgrims, they were so happy to be taking part that 'participation at the Mela actually increases people's mental and physical wellbeing'.) According to a Hindi-English guide to the Kumbh[5] handed out at the event, the gods and demons fought for twelve days—equivalent to twelve years for humans. 'There is a complete rotation of the planets after every 144 years', it concludes firmly. 'This causes the extra significance of Maha [Great] Kumbh, at the planetary return after twelve successive Kumbh Melas. There are twelve zodiacal signs and a day has two sets of twelve planetary hours. Kumbh also has a period of twelve years, a Maha Kumbh comes every 144 years or 12x12 years.'

Like so many things in India, particularly those that pertain to Hinduism and its 330 million gods, the history of the Kumbh is not quite that simple. Megasthenes, a Greek ambassador who came to India in about 302 BC, may have been the first foreigner to refer to the festival when he mentions an annual 'great assembly' of philosophers in north India.[6] Xuanzang, the Chinese Buddhist monk who travelled to India in the seventh century AD, left us with a written record of an event at Prayag (now Allahabad)—but he suggested a five-year cycle and recorded ceremonies of alms-giving presided over by the Buddhist king Harsha, who emptied his treasury and gave away even the jewels he wore, although his wealth was quickly replenished by the lords and kings of the various countries under his sway. 'At the confluence of the two rivers to the east of the Grand Place of Alms-Giving, several hundred people drown themselves every day', wrote Xuanzang. 'It is the custom of the people to believe that in order to be reborn in the heavens, they should starve and sink into the river at this spot.' Xuanzang, although his Buddhism led him to disapprove of river-worship and sun-worship, also observed the strange ascetic practices of Indian holy men at Prayag; they would plant a pole in the middle of the river, climb it at dusk and cling to it with only one hand and one foot, turning their eyes on the sun as it set.[7]

More than a thousand years later, Niccolao Manucci, an Italian traveller and writer who served at the Mughal court, also referred to a five-yearly event.[8] What seems to have happened, according to Sanskrit scholar Jim Mallinson,[9] is that the *pandits* or priests, confronted with British colonial suspicion of large gatherings of Indians (they feared both cholera outbreaks and political agitation) decided to invent a tradition or harden the existing ones to give the Kumbh Mela an unassailable legitimacy. That, says Mallinson, is why there is no early written record of the story about the drops of *amrit*, the nectar, falling on the four holy places for the Kumbh. It is also why the encampments and status of the various orders of *sadhus* at the Kumbh Melas—the holy men at one time fought battles against each other—are thought to be largely unchanged since they were systematized under the British.

Invention of tradition, of course, is itself a great Indian tradition. In yoga, Mallinson says the apparently timeless sun salutation is probably only about 100 years old and was heavily influenced by Swedish body building, gymnastics, and the military drills of the British army. In a self-deprecating radio broadcast a couple of years ago, a BBC correspondent and friend explained how he had witnessed and reported on an ancient Hindu ceremony on the Ganges—all white-robed priests, booming conch-shells and incense—while in the city of Varanasi for the 2014 general election. Shortly afterwards, a young Indian journalist who had heard the report told him: 'You know the whole thing was invented by the manager of a luxury hotel in Varanasi about 20 years ago. He was trying to drum up the number of tourists coming to town.' The chastened BBC correspondent said: 'I see', but was noble enough to broadcast another story about the experience.[10]

There is, however, nothing artificial about the matter-of-fact reverence felt by Indians for the holy waters of the Ganges. A couple of days
before I arrive in Allahabad for the Kumbh Mela, a freak rainstorm has
flooded the encampment on the sandbanks and sent holy men and
pilgrims fleeing for the relative safety of the mainland, but now they
are marching back into the temporary city at the river confluence. At
dawn, a cool wind blows off the river. A pied kingfisher hovers over
the water as it starts the day's fishing. Pilgrims make their way over the
damp ground to the riverbank, which is reinforced by sandbags to
prevent erosion by the movements of millions of bathers. The organizers have also planted wooden barriers in the water to stop pilgrims,
most of them non-swimmers, from going too deep or being swept
away in the current. I meet an elderly man called H. N. Tripathi clad
only in blue underpants who is cheerfully immersing himself. 'We do
believe that anyone who takes dip in this water, he becomes pure also,
because it is always pure', he explains, 'though it looks like it is impure.
It looks like dirty water.' It does indeed, and I notice when I dunk
myself at the confluence later that day that underwater visibility is no
more than a few inches. For once, there is nothing sinister about this.
Although some holy men have been reported in the local press to be
so appalled by pollution that they drink only bottled water,[11] the
Ganges is a silty river. For the smooth running of the Kumbh Mela,
furthermore, the government has released additional water from the
Tehri dam upstream and shut down the tanneries of Kanpur that usually add a daily load of toxic waste to the water.[12]

For obvious reasons, humans have long worshipped river spirits and
built their settlements on riverbanks and confluences. The rivers provide us with drinking water, fertilize and irrigate our fields, and give
us access to the hinterland upstream and the sea below. Rivers and river
confluences have been sacred in other cultures too, from ancient Egypt
to ancient Britain. 'The gods were meant to dance at the confluence
of waters. The mingling of the tributary and the main river was deemed
to be sacred', wrote the historian Peter Ackroyd about the Thames in
England. 'So the meeting of the rivers is an occasion for spiritual ritual.'[13] In the ceremonial naming of children, Christians recall the bap-
tism of Jesus in the holy waters of the River Jordan. Yet among Hindus
this reverence for rivers, especially the Ganges, persists into modern
times in a profound way that rarely fails to astonish outsiders. Even a
conservative estimate of the number of pilgrims during the two

months of the 2013 Kumbh Mela suggests that the number of those who bathed was greater than the entire population of Britain.

A river cult that started on the Indus to the west seems to have moved east over the millennia to the Saraswati and eventually the Ganges, as people settled and cultivated the once jungle-thick Gangetic plain and established there the historical civilizations and kingdoms we classify today as Hindu, Buddhist, and eventually Muslim and Christian. 'Water is potent: it trickles through human dreams, permeates lives, dictates agriculture, religion and warfare', wrote Alice Albinia in *Empires of the Indus*, her adventurous historical travelogue about that river. 'Ever since *Homo sapiens* first migrated out of Africa, the Indus has drawn thirsty conquerors to its banks.' She charts the eastward movement of the river cult from the territory that is now Pakistan. She found the Mohanas, an Indus boat people, still living on the Indus near the Pakistani town of Sukkur and using wooden boats propelled by sails, rudders, and poles identical in outline to the boats etched on the 5,000-year-old seals of the Mohenjo-daro city civilization. The Mohanas, she says, are a direct connection to a prehistoric river cult. Albinia also recalls that the ancient *Rig Veda*, a collection of Sanskrit hymns dating back to about 1500 BC, is mainly about the Punjab (divided today between Pakistan and India). It mentions the Ganges just twice and the Yamuna only occasionally, while the now lost Saraswati appears only 'in later layers of the text'. More centuries must pass before the classical Sanskrit texts have promoted the Ganges to the position of the 'ultimate sin-cleansing goddess, the holiest of holies'. Lamenting the loss of status for the Indus, Albinia writes: 'In the centuries after the RigVeda was first sung, a whole culture went east into the easy world of the monsoon-fed Ganges.'[14]

Even before the arrival of Islam and long before the establishment of Pakistan as a Muslim homeland, the move east and south of Sanskrit had led to a reorientation of the *aryavarta* or 'Hindu sacred landscape'. Punjabis were vilified as barbarians who drank alcohol, ate beef with garlic, and whose women danced naked, while the loyalties of river-worshippers shifted east from the Indus to the mythical Saraswati (a river which also conveniently moved eastward in the imagination to join the Ganges at Prayag/Allahabad) and yet further eastwards to the Ganges itself. Saraswati, goddess of wisdom, still has a cult following among Hindus, especially in Bengal; there you can see countless Saraswati idols floating down the Hooghly River (a branch of the Ganges) towards the sea after being immersed in the river by worshippers along its banks during her annual festival. The scholar Steven Darian says it is hard to resist the conclusion that 'the image and sanctity of Ganga have evolved from that of the Sarasvati—as a mythological projection of the ancient Aryan river'.[15]

The Indus, however, has been largely forgotten by Hindus, and its lower reaches are in any case cut off from the vast majority of Indians by the Pakistan–India confrontation—few Hindus or members of other non-Muslim minorities remain in the Islamic Republic of Pakistan seventy years after partition—and the difficulties of obtaining visas. And yet as recently as the nineteenth century, according to Albinia, Hindu priests at the Sadhubela temple in Sukkur on the Indus tried to launch the Kumbh Mela there, claiming Sukkur as the original location of a ceremony that was eradicated by Buddhists two millennia earlier and whose revival was later suppressed by Muslims. And in 1997, L. K. Advani, who went on to become home minister for the Hindu nationalist Bharatiya Janata Party government, tried to relaunch the cult of the Indus when he visited a section of the river running through Indian-controlled territory in Ladakh, a traditionally Buddhist region of Tibet incorporated into the Indian state of Jammu and Kashmir. Advani, himself a Hindu from Sindh in what is now Pakistan, helped found the 'Sindhu Darshan', an annual celebration of the Indus and Indian heritage in which pilgrims bring water from other rivers—notably the Ganges—to add to the Indus as it flows from its source in Tibet towards the Muslim land of Pakistan. Atal Bihari Vajpayee, BJP prime minister at the time, inaugurated the festival in 2000 and described the Indus as a unifying symbol of 5,000 years of Indian civilization.[16] International rivers remain politically sensitive. In September 2016, after a militant attack in Indian-controlled Kashmir that killed eighteen soldiers, Modi considered punishing Pakistan by abrogating the half-century-old Indus Waters Treaty under which the two countries share the river's flow.[17]

The word 'Hindu', it should be mentioned here, has been widely adopted as a religious label rather than a geographical one only since colonial days; previously, 'Hindu' and 'Hindustan' were simply the words used by Muslim invaders to describe the people and territories east of the Indus. Indus is a version of *Sindhu*, the Sanskrit word for a large river, and it is this river that gave its name to Hindustan and to Hindus, and so to India and Indians. (Following the partition of British India in 1947, the Indus flows mostly in what is today Pakistan. Mohammed Ali Jinnah, the father of Pakistani independence, was said to be furious that independent India had kept the Indus-derived name and failed to opt for the Sanskrit alternative *Bharat*.)[18]

Among rivers, in any case, it is the Ganges that now lies at the heart of Hinduism and Indian spiritual consciousness. She is a goddess and a mother to everyone from Narendra Modi, the BJP prime minister, to the humblest Hindu living in the far south of India or running a motel in the United States. 'There are few things on which Hindu India, diverse as it is, speaks with one voice as clearly as it does on *Ganga Mata* [Mother Ganges]', says the Harvard scholar Diana Eck. 'The river carries an immense cultural and religious significance for Hindus, no matter what part of the subcontinent they call home, no matter what their sectarian leaning might be.' She goes on:

Hindus bathe everywhere along the Ganga and especially at important *tirthas* [spiritual crossing points], taking the waters cupped in their hands and pour-ing them back into the river as offerings to the *pitrs* and the *devas*, the departed ancestors and the gods. They present offerings of flowers and oil lamps in the river, as they would in the sanctum of a temple. On great occasions, they ford the river in boats, trailing garlands of flowers or ropes of saris hundreds of feet long to adorn the goddess river, chanting '*Ganga Mata ki Jai!*' 'Victory to Mother Ganga!'. Finally, pilgrims will come from all over India bringing the ashes of their beloved dead to commit ritually to the Ganga's waters. When they return to their homes, perhaps hundreds of miles away, they carry vessels of Ganga water to, one day, moisten the lips of the dying. The Ganga is holy all along its course, from its source to the sea.[19]

The Ganges today still plays a central role in Hindu rituals of birth, marriage, and death and has done since the third century AD. Farmers in Bihar still put Ganges water in a pot in their fields to ensure a good harvest, and among those who live along the river 'a newly married woman unfolds her sari to Ganga and prays for children and the long life of her husband'. Ganga, furthermore always confers benediction. 'She shares none of the chthonian affinities associated with Kali or Durga or the sepulchral goddesses of Greece. Even in the underworld, the river has pointed the way to paradise.'[20]

The legend of how the river came into being is a typically elaborate and colourful epic tale, with many variants but whose core elements are known by most Indians and will be related with relish to strangers from abroad when they visit the river—especially if they go to the river's source or to Sagar island at the mouth on the Bay of Bengal. As I was told at the source of the river, a mighty king called Sagar (the

name means 'ocean') lost his 60,000 sons when they were burnt to
ashes by the angry gaze of a sage whose meditations they had interrupted while searching for their father's missing horse. Sagar had
decided it was time for him to become a *chakravartin* or world ruler
and he had released a mare to wander where it pleased for a year, in a
ceremony known as an *asvamedha*, a horse sacrifice in which the territory traversed by the horse becomes the king's territory. The gods, not
unlike the whimsical and fractious gods of Greek mythology in their
relations with humans, had set up the confrontation between Sagar's
sons and the sage because they were worried that Sagar's empire was
reaching the ocean shore and might attain their dominions in heaven.
So they hid the horse at the ashram of the *rishi* Kapil Muni, whose
temple now stands where the Ganges meets the sea at Sagar Island
south of Calcutta. It is, according to some practical Bengalis, an etio-
logical myth—a story, that is, to explain something that actually happened. Captain J. J. Biswas of the Kolkata Port Trust, the government
organization that runs the commercial harbours at the mouth of the
Ganges, told me that the 60,000 sons represented the inhabitants of
Bhagirath's own kingdom, who were tormented by drought and disease and indeed rescued by the waters of the river. 'In reality, no one
can have 60,000 children, so these were subjects', said Capt. Biswas.
'His subjects were suffering from jaundice because no fresh water was
available. So Bhagirath's son built a canal and prayed for it to flow. You
can say he was an engineer.'[21]

There are countless versions of the myths and stories about Ganga,
as there are about the millions of other members of the pantheon. One
broadcaster travelling down the river for a radio documentary was told
by a priest in Haridwar that Ganga came to earth from the sweat of
Vishnu's toe when he became over-excited watching a young woman
dance.[22] Stephen Alter, a writer who lives in the Himalayan foothills
and has explored the headwaters of the Ganges, relates a version in
which Narada, the somewhat comic messenger of the gods, comes
across a group of men and women in the hills. They are beautiful, but
each is missing some body part—a foot, an eye, an arm. They explain
that they are *Ragas* and *Raginis*, the divine spirits of music, who have
been mutilated by hearing his less than divine singing. Narada, morti-
fied, asks what he can do to repair the damage, and they tell him that
only the perfection of Shiva's music will make them whole again.
Shiva agrees to Narada's plea for him to perform, but only if he can do

so in front of an equally perfect audience: Brahma and Vishnu. The concert begins and the *Ragas* and *Raginis* are healed. 'Vishnu became so absorbed in the music that he began to melt. The stream of liquid that flowed from his toe became the Ganga and this explains the purity of her waters.'[23] In one sub-plot of the Bhagirath legend, after he has succeeded in releasing Ganga from the heavens and persuading Shiva to break her fall, the river is stopped by another angry sage, the *rishi* Jahnu, who swallows the whole river because it flowed past his hermitage, overturned his pots and pans, and disturbed his meditations.[24]

Ganga also features in the Sanskrit epics, the *Mahabharata* and the *Ramayana*, especially the first, a massive tale describing the war between the Pandava and Kaurava princes that ushers in the *Kali Yuga*, the age of darkness in which we live today. At the start of the story, Shantanu, the as yet unmarried fourteenth king of the Kuru line, has been unsuccessfully hunting leopards and stags on horseback all day when he comes to the banks of the river.

'Ganga!' breathed Shantanu when he saw her: she who had fallen from the sky in pristine times. She was as wide as a sea and he could hardly make out her far bank. He dismounted and led his horse to the susurrant water's edge, where the river lapped at banks of green moss.

He knelt beside his beast and, bending down to the crystal flow, drank deeply, splashing his arms and face with the sweet water. Suddenly, the king became aware that he was not alone.

He turned and saw her: a vision swathed in the last rays of the saffron sun, her skin like soft gold. She appeared perfect of face and body. Her eyes were luminous, her black hair fell to her waist in a cascade, as she stood staring at him and made his blood quicken as no other woman ever had. And she was no stranger: she had visited his dreams since he was a boy.[25]

The woman is, of course, the embodiment of the river. He kneels before her 'to slake the thirst of his young manhood' and she agrees to be his wife, but only on one mysterious condition: he must never ask who she is nor question her actions, however terrible they may be. He accepts and they return to his home in Hastinapura—still a town today near the main stream of the Ganges—and she soon falls pregnant. Shantanu discovers that each time she has a baby son she casts him into the river, but the tormented king holds his peace until the eighth child is born and is taken by her to the riverbank. He howls at her to stop, whereupon she reminds him of his oath not to interfere, reveals herself as the goddess—'the river of heaven and earth' who washes away the sins of humanity—and vanishes with the surviving child, promising only that the child will be restored to Hastinapura at the age of 16 and one day become a Kuru king. This is Devavrata, who after being schooled in scripture, politics, and archery is indeed returned by Ganga to the happy Shantanu, who makes him crown prince.

But there is no happy ending. In a colourful legend that illuminates all the delicious complexities of love, marriage, caste, and class, Shantanu encounters another beautiful woman by another river, this time the Yamuna, one of the big tributaries of the Ganges. The woman is Satyavati, daughter of the fisher-king. She had smelled of fish herself until she was ravished by a holy man she was ferrying across the river, and now her dark body emits an 'irresistible heavenly scent'. Shantanu, beside himself, finds the girl's father, an uncouth but wily negotiator with betel-stained teeth. The fisherman tells the royal suitor he can marry the daughter only if he guarantees that her son will become king. An agonized, unfulfilled Shantanu departs, but his son Devavrata eventually uncovers the source of the king's unhappiness. He finds the fisherman and makes a vow to all the gods not only to relinquish his claim to the throne but also to remain celibate so that no children are born to inherit his formidable qualities as warrior and ruler. Devavrata henceforth becomes known as Bhishma, variously translated as 'the fierce one' or 'he of the terrible oath'. As great-uncle to both the Pandavas and the Kauravas, he is revered by the two rival families in the Mahabharata and remains a popular figure in Indian films. He even gave his name to the Indian version of the Russian-made T-90 battle tank.

Like the *Mahabharata*, the *Ramayana* takes the reader back to a time of ecological innocence, when all the follies of mankind could not sully the pure and abundant waters of the Ganges. Early in the tale, the god Ram, with his companion Lakshman and the sage Viswamitra, needs to cross the great river:

It was midday when they arrived on the banks of the Ganga. She lay before them like an inland sea; shading their eyes, they could barely discern her far shore. Swans and lotuses floated upon her in equal profusion, and so deep was her attraction they decided to spend the rest of the day beside her murmuring currents.

They bathed in her water and sat beside her, some dozing, others staring out across the enchanted flow; and they saw luminous daydreams, as they had not even during their *dhyana* [meditations] in the mountains. Surely, she was awesome, she was magical, and her nearness made the body feel so light it seemed the soul could soar out and be free. In the late afternoon, the desire took the princes and the rishis alike and they waded once more into the calm, warm water. When they had bathed they felt cleansed: not just bodily but in spirit.[26]

Ganga, Eck notes, is the only deity claimed as consort by all three of the great gods—Brahma, Vishnu, and Shiva—while the *amrit* or nectar of immortality contained in her waters endows her with unique properties for the salvation of humans. Even the despicable Vahika, who had killed a cow, kicked his own mother, and was addicted to gambling, is rescued on his way to hell by a chance encounter with the Ganges. Vahika was killed by a tiger in the forest, and while his soul was being judged and then transported to the underworld, vultures were tearing apart his corpse. One of them, fighting in mid-flight with another vulture over a bone from his foot, dropped it into the Ganges, whereupon a chariot arrives to take his now blessed soul to paradise.[27] 'The Ganges', Eck writes, 'is the liquid essence of the scriptures, the gods, and the wisdom of the Hindu tradition. She is the liquid essence, in sum, of Shakti—the energy and power of the Supreme, flowing in the life of the world.'[28]

Three years after immersing myself at the Maha Kumbh Mela in Allahabad, I decided to witness another famous ceremony of the many regularly celebrated on the Ganges and other Indian rivers by Hindu devotees. This time, in January 2016, the destination was Sagar island at the mouth of the Ganges and the annual festival known as *Ganga Sagar*, when hundreds of thousands of pilgrims bathe in the auspicious confluence of the Ganges and the sea, visit the temple of Kapil Muni (the sage whose angry gaze turned the 60,000 sons of King Sagar to ashes), and seek blessings from the scores of naked, ash-smeared *sadhus* who sit in alcoves along the road leading away from the temple.

I am accompanied by Jyotsna Singh, a journalist colleague whose family comes from near Varanasi on the Ganges and who speaks Bengali and Hindi as well as English. As we drive south from Calcutta one hazy evening past rice fields, dusty palm trees, dilapidated shacks, half-finished houses, brightly painted advertisements for cement and mobile telephone services, and children playing football or cricket, we are treated to the latest manifestations of the personality cult of Mamata Banerjee, the feisty, flip-flop wearing chief minister of West Bengal. Her favourite colours are blue and white and everything from the bridges, walls, and houses of Calcutta to the trees along the road to Sagar have been painted thus by her loyal supporters, overwhelming the now infrequent, red-painted hammer-and-sickle symbols of her leftist rivals.[29]

We drive under newly constructed arches across the road bearing 12-foot-high photographs of Banerjee before reaching the crowded terminal for the ferry that will take us to Sagar once the tide comes in. By now I have been thoroughly disabused of my earlier romantic notion that the green colour of the island on my map meant an uninhabited natural and spiritual paradise. In fact it is hard to imagine anything less natural or less spiritual than this bus park with its sodium-orange floodlights or the relentless, 24-hour-a-day shouting over loudspeakers that will greet us at the holy bathing beach on the island itself. Perhaps my feelings about light and sound are peculiar to foreigners. I recall that Ilija Trojanow, another foreigner, wrote drily at the start of his description of his journey in *Along the Ganges*: 'The most important instrument of contemporary spirituality is the loudspeaker; its volume set high as if the world were deaf.'[30]

It is the night before the auspicious new moon. We pass tens of thousands of pilgrims, bundles of food and clothes on their heads, being herded along bamboo corridors to the ferries, and as the murky waters of the incoming tide fill the river we board our little launch. The arrival is as unromantic to Western eyes as the departure. A big welcome arch at the Sagar terminal, beyond the billboards advertising Airtel 3G and Idea Cellular, is lit up like a funfair with a host of flashing LED bulbs in an array of garish colours: they portray spouting fountains of light, purple swastikas, and the word *Om*. After driving down to the sacred site near the Kapil Muni temple, we find beds in a hostel and try to sleep to the astonishingly loud announcements over the ubiquitous PA system about missing people, staff movements, and garbage disposal: 'Please use the toilets and don't make the place untidy.'

Noise and crowds are not new at such festivals. Lieutenant G. F. White, a nineteenth-century British officer and amateur artist, was stunned by the 'swarms' of people and the sounds of the *mela* at Haridwar. 'The noise baffles all description; the shouts and cries of men come mingled with the neighing of horses, the trumpeting of elephants, the grunts of camels, the lowing of cattle, the bellowing of bulls, the screams of birds, and the loud sharp roars of the wild beasts; and, as if these were not enough, there are gongs and drums beating, trumpets blaring, conch-shells blowing, and bells ringing, which never cease for a single instant.'[31]

At first, the Sagar festival seems to me more like a giant and exceptionally noisy exercise in crowd control than a spiritual occasion. Yet it is obvious the next morning that the thousands of pilgrims—most, but not all of them, humble peasants from Bengal, Bihar, and Uttar Pradesh—who are surging down to the beach do not share my misgivings. Like the Kumbh Mela, the event is a chaotic mixture of the sacred and the profane. Group leaders are guiding huddles of their followers, sometimes herding them with ropes held between two people at waist level to stop them straying. For food, stall-holders are selling pastries, cakes of toffee and nuts, chillis, apples, and cucumbers. For ceremonial purposes, they sell water bottles for *Ganga jal* (Ganges water); offerings of coloured threads, rings, coconuts, and flattened rice to be given to beggars; and vermilion powder in special plastic boxes. They sell walking sticks and cheap shirts. They sell products from the sea, exotic for those from far inland, including cuttlefish bones, whelk-shells, and cosmetics in the form of oyster shells ('It's good for skin problems when crushed', says the young woman who has piled them in front of her). There are crudely made souvenir images of the temple, the pictures stuck to a piece of cardboard box with the outside edges fixed with black plastic tape to make a frame. 'All this is superstition', mutters one man in Hindi to his family.

A group of women pilgrims from the dry lands of Rajasthan or Haryana far to the west stand out from the mass because their faces are invisible, completely covered with coloured scarves. Like the Christian pilgrims in the Canterbury Tales, the Hindus here are from all ranks and professions and regions, from bearded *sadhus* and retired professors to subsistence farmers and day labourers. As the sun rises through the mist on the river, dozens of villagers squat on the ground devouring a steaming potato dish from wrappings of newspaper. A man in an orange *dhoti* beats a tambourine. Beggars, cripples, and lepers in increasing numbers line the sandy path through the market and cry for attention as we approach the water, and the devotees heading that way for their *puja* fling handfuls of the flattened rice at the bowls on the ground in front of the beggars. At a junction of the crowded lanes between the stalls two male beggars fight over the best spot. An apparently lunatic woman lies on the ground waving her arms and moaning.

At the shore, a sea of humanity—for once, the metaphor is apt—is joining the actual sea of the Bay of Bengal. Tens of thousands of pilgrims are surging towards the muddy brown waters. This year, we are told by the officials organizing the event, between 1.5 and 2 million people will come to this island to pay homage to the river and the sage. A drongo—a black, insect-eating bird with an elegantly forked tail—is perched on a wire leading to one of the many loudspeaker poles, presumably baffled by the once-in-a-year noise and confusion.

One of the pilgrims we approach to ask his thoughts on the Ganges is negotiating with another man over a skinny calf on a string. 'You catch the tail of the calf and give some money to the Brahmin, to go to paradise after death', explains the pilgrim. 'This is a thing of merit. We have to cross the Doleful River. This cow will help in crossing the river. Otherwise you cannot cross.' The pilgrim is Krishna Nanda Dubey, a 67-year-old retired college principal from Varanasi, who took this ten-day round trip with seven members of his family, taking an express train, a boat, and finally a taxi to attend the Ganga Sagar *mela*. He is wearing black underpants, has a pot-belly, stubble on his face, and henna-red hair and says it is his first time at this festival. Life, Dubey says in English, is divided into a time of work and materialism and a time of retirement and contemplation, and he retired five years ago. 'These are the last days. We are preparing for a noble death and for paradise. We are too much materialistic in our prime, but in our latter days we try to be more pious.' He has already been to the holy town of Haridwar on the upper Ganges, and is going next to Puri in Orissa on the east coast for the festival of the god Jagannath, the 'Lord of the Universe' whose huge and supposedly unstoppable, pedestrian-crushing temple chariots gave the word 'juggernaut' to modern English.

On the beach next to the highbrow Pandey and his relatives is another family from upcountry, from a village in Jharkhand, one of the poorest states in India. Holika Devi Mahto has left her husband at home, where they scrape a living from the hills by growing vegetables and rice, and come to Sagar for the first time with her mother and her two children to intercede with the gods for help. 'We are in deep trouble', she says in Hindi, without explaining the precise nature of the trouble. 'We are facing a lot of misery. That's why we've come here for solutions.' Her 16-year-old daughter Rupa adds: 'It's our faith that has brought us here.'

I am eager to question the man with the calf—I notice now that it has a dishcloth draped over its bony back—and he is still there offering contact with the holy animal to passing pilgrims in exchange for cash or clothes. Kedar Pande, aged 45, is also from Jharkhand and says he bought the animal two days earlier for Rs1,500, the equivalent of about $23, and will sell it back to the original owner when he leaves. When I ask how much people pay for the privilege of holding the tail, he replies philosophically 'Yaba shakti, taba shakti', a Sanskrit saying about devotion and ability that translates roughly as 'From each according to his means.' Some pay just one rupee, others pay twenty. And will he make money out of the enterprise? 'I don't know, but the great Kapil Muni [the sadhu from ancient times to whom the local temple is dedicated] will decide.' It must be worthwhile, I think, because he has been buying and reselling a calf like this at the festival every year for the past fifteen years.

We hear music and find a stage constructed on the beach. In front of it, a man on stilts dances to the sound of drums. Orange-robed Baul musicians—the traditional minstrels of Bengal—sing a haunting melody in Bengali to the sound of an ektara, a one stringed instrument made from a gourd, while the audience gapes at them. It sounds beautiful, I tell my Bengali-speaking colleague, what are they singing? She says it is a message from the organizers: 'Use the toilet and wash your hands afterwards. The goddess will be angry if you despoil her.'

Among the hundreds of thousands of people standing on the beach or ankle-deep in the water, I seem to be the only foreigner, apart from a couple of goras—white people—in the Hare Krishna brigade snaking through the crowds and chanting with the help of a man who holds a microphone and carries a large amplifier and loudspeaker on his shoulder. Some of the visitors are Bengali locals. Among them is Shantana Mukherjee, a 46-year-old primary school teacher from Sonarpur, who is clad in a pink shirt and speaking into a smartphone. 'The auspicious time to bathe is tonight between 11.38 p.m. and 3.38 a.m.—that water is very good for human bodies', she says. At first I think the precise times must be something to do with the tide, but they do not correspond and probably come from an astrological almanac: Ganga Sagar is celebrated every year around 14 January according to a solar calendar, not a lunar one, and coincides with Makar Sankranti, the first day of spring.

We walk through the crowds towards the Kapil Muni temple, passing a portable photographic booth (Rs50 for a glossy print from a digital camera) attached to a cycle rickshaw, its wheels half buried in the wet sand. At the temple, pilgrims are herded rapidly past the entrance, through which they can see an orange-painted image of Bhagirath, with Shiva and his wife Parvati to one side. As they pass, the pilgrims throw money, bangles, rice, and other gifts onto a dais where it is rapidly piled and collected by rather thuggish-looking temple attendants.

Rows of mostly naked *sadhus*—a few have miniature loincloths called *langotis*—are installed in the alcoves outside. With the right hand, the *sadhus* wield long, decorated wands adorned with peacock feathers to bless the devotees by tapping them on the head; with the left, they receive payment in notes and coins. Around the corner, in a less favoured position, we find one of the few female *sadhus*—known as *sadhvis*—at the event. Karuna Giri, dressed in orange and wearing glasses, is 60 years old and has been a *sadhvi* for the past twenty. It is almost impossible to hear her because her bamboo shack, with its depression in the mud floor to hold a small wood fire, is right underneath a deafening loud-speaker making constant public announcements. 'I just felt detached from worldly things', she says, explaining that she left her daughters and the rest of her home life behind in Jalpaiguri on the Teesta river (a tributary of the Brahmaputra and so ultimately of the lower Ganges) in northern Bengal.

Most of the busy male *sadhus* are reluctant to have their business interrupted by an inquisitive foreigner, but on the quieter side of the dusty avenue we find a cheerful Naga *baba* called Naresh Giri, who came from Kanpur on the Ganges in Uttar Pradesh and has spent the last twenty-five of his 63 years as a *sadhu*. (Naga *babas* are by tradition warrior-ascetics.) 'I was a farmer. I never married', he says. 'Looking at the Ganga gives you'—he pauses—'it gets rid of the cycle of birth and death. I got involved in religion and so I became a *sadhu*. Yes, I go to all the *kumbh* festivals. In three months, it's Ujjain.' Like many *sadhus,* he has been to Gaumukh, the glacier from which the Ganges emerges in the high country above Gangotri. 'I'm a Naga *baba*. I've been every-where, on the mountains and in the snow caves.' Since he is from the industrial city of Kanpur, I ask him about the pollution in the Ganges. 'I'm very worried about the condition of the river', he replies. 'If the government doesn't do anything, how can we clean the river? Only the government can do it.'

4

How to Build a Megacity—and Save the Ganges

It's like a mega-refugee camp that came up overnight and gets sustained and managed for two months... an incredible logistical operation.
—Onno Ruhl of the World Bank on the Kumbh Mela's 'pop-up megacity'[1]

What it means is: India can do it. All of the villages, all of the cities can have electricity, they can have running water, they can have roads.
—Bhagawati Saraswati, Hindu devotee[2]

'Only the government can do it', says the *sadhu*. This points to a crucial question about the future of the Ganges. Can governments, with their well-deserved reputation among Indians for corruption and incompetence, really be trusted to organize the salvation of the sacred river? The idea is not quite as outlandish as it sounds. India, after all, is a nuclear-armed state. In 2014, it placed a satellite in orbit around Mars on a budget of $72 million, confirming its place as a cost-effective explorer of outer space and becoming only the fourth nation to succeed in a scientific mission to the red planet. As for crisis management and project implementation on earth, India has been effective in the past and it can be again. *Airlift*, a 2016 Bollywood political thriller based on real events, celebrates the evacuation of 170,000 Indian migrant workers from Kuwait after Iraq invaded in 1990. Most were bussed to Jordan and then flown by state-owned airlines on hundreds of flights from Amman to Mumbai in one of the world's biggest rescue operations. In 2016, the Delhi government banned cars on alternate days from the streets of the capital, in an attempt to curb horrific air pollution. The predicted chaos did not materialize. Most drivers obeyed the new restrictions while continuing to ignore normal traffic rules as they had done in the past. Although the air remained filthy because much of the pollution comes from other sources, the authorities proved that they could enforce radical measures if necessary in the public interest.

Large religious festivals also tend to be well managed. Both the central government in New Delhi and state governments such as those of Uttar Pradesh and West Bengal regularly demonstrate their organizational skills in the running of the Kumbh Mela and the annual Ganga Sagar. Onno Ruhl, then head of the World Bank in India and—like me—one of the few foreigners among the millions who bathed at the river confluence during the 2013 Kumbh Mela, calls it 'an incredible logistical operation'. Harvard University researchers describe it as 'a pop-up megacity'. On the sandbanks of the Ganges at Allahabad, the bureaucrats and workers of Uttar Pradesh—with over 200 million inhabitants, it is India's largest and one of its poorest states and more populous than Brazil—took less than three months to build a tent city for 2 million residents complete with hard roads, toilets, running water, electricity, food shops, garbage collection, and well-manned police stations. Organizers do much the same every three years at the four different locations. In 2016 it was the turn of Ujjain to the south in Madhya Pradesh. Indeed, the Ujjain festival could not have happened at all had the authorities not built a $65 million, 50-kilometre pipeline and pumped water directly into the dried-up Shipra River from the Narmada River. (The Shipra flows into the Chambal and so eventually into the Yamuna and the Ganges.)

At these instant cities, fresh water comes out of the taps. Toilets are disinfected. Trained police carefully shepherd the crowds to the bathing areas. The lights come on at night. In the minds of both Indians and foreigners, this raises important questions. How? Why? Or rather: if the authorities can build infrastructure so efficiently for this short but very large festival, why can they not do the same for permanent villages and towns? Ruhl says Allahabad's Kumbh Mela city on the sandbanks, which is quickly dismantled before the river floods in the monsoon, 'has water, sanitation, power, solid waste management—everything, actually, that many Indian cities lack'. To someone like himself who manages big projects, 'It's like a mega-refugee camp that came up overnight and gets sustained and managed for two months with people filtering [in and out] at a rate of millions a day. I've never seen anything like it in my life.' And yet all this is managed by the Uttar

Pradesh (UP) government. 'If somehow we could translate that capacity to day-to-day business, you could transform UP. It's a really powerful thought.' Uttar Pradesh is often seen as the epitome of all that is wrong with India, especially in sanitation. Yet the Kumbh Mela runs like clockwork.

Devesh Chaturvedi, a senior official who was divisional commissioner of Allahabad at the time, is proud of the 'huge task' that he and around 100,000 workers completed in organizing the 2013 festival. He mentions 14 clinics and hospitals, 960 kilometres of power lines, 25,000 street lights, 52 electricity substations, 200,000 electricity connections, 280 kilometres of roads, 5.5 kilometres of prepared bathing space along the river, 18 pontoon bridges, 690 kilometres of water pipes, 34,000 toilets, 20,000 police officers, 1,000 anti-terrorist agents, and 275 food shops for essential supplies such as flour, rice, milk, and cooking gas. Chaturvedi has two explanations for the contrast between the successful provision of these services and the lacklustre performance of the authorities the rest of the time and in the rest of the state. First, the organizers ensure that all those working on the project are accountable for their actions and the money they spend. Second, those involved are highly motivated. 'They feel it's a real service to all these pilgrims who have come here, the *sadhus* and the seers, so it's a sort of mission which motivates them to work extra, despite difficult working conditions.'

Good organization and efficient infrastructure, in short, are no more impossible in India than anywhere else. 'The lesson is, it can be done', says Bhagawati Saraswati, a Californian-born Hindu devotee camped on the river bank with other members of an ashram based on the upper Ganges. She notes the 'phenomenal' number of man-hours and employees devoted to the Kumbh Mela, but says the event still shows that India can organize itself. 'It's an amazing lesson', she says. 'What it means is: India can do it. All of the villages, all of the cities can have electricity, they can have running water, they can have roads. That attention, that focus, that clarity, that commitment, just has to be there.'

So remarkable was the achievement that it is the subject of *Kumbh Mela: Mapping the Ephemeral Megacity*, a book featuring multidisciplinary research from Harvard University's South Asia Institute. At the book's launch in Mumbai in early 2016, Chaturvedi mentioned most of the same statistics about street lights and toilets that he had given me at the Kumbh three years earlier, but he added some interesting details. The festival not only demanded the temporary closure of most of the polluting tanneries and factories upstream. It also meant arranging the discharge of extra water from the Tehri dam, so there would be enough flowing down the Ganges, and increasing Allahabad's own sewage treatment capacity from 89 million litres a day to 211 million. Those involved in the organization included six central government departments, twenty-eight departments of the Uttar Pradesh state government, and thirteen *akharas*, the guilds of *sadhus* that attend the *melas*.

Stampedes at crowded religious festivals have long been a lethal risk in India and elsewhere. In 1954, at the first big Kumbh Mela of independent India, an elephant charged a crowd of pilgrims near the bathing area. Five hundred people died.[3] Chaturvedi explained that instead of stopping the advance of the crowds—which tends to trigger falls and stampedes rather than prevent them—the authorities funnel them along circuitous routes to delay their arrival at dangerously crowded places, sometimes leading them around for five or six kilometres when in fact they are only 500 metres from the *sangam*, the confluence. 'We cannot stop a crowd. We have to regulate it.' No less than 200,000 lost pilgrims were reunited with their families and friends, Chaturvedi boasted, and 24-hours-a-day scanning with closed-circuit television cameras helped to ensure that there was neither crime nor crowd trouble. Most interesting of all was his assertion that all this cost just $1 per person per day.

The Harvard professors, students, and alumni who attended the *mela*—fifty of them went to the Kumbh and stayed in Allahabad for ten days—had typically varied experiences as they pursued their particular interests, but most were impressed by the way the event was handled. Vikram Gandhi, a venture capitalist and investment banker, called the organization 'quite phenomenal'. He remembered a meeting between a Harvard delegation and Indian officials in which a student brusquely took out a map and demanded to know what the 'business model' was. He received blank looks. And yet, said Gandhi, there was in practice a business model that worked and a whole process for allocating budgets.[4]

For almost the first time, information technology enabled the smooth running of the Kumbh—and helped researchers to study it. The 2013 *mela* was said to be only the second Kumbh to have a website and the first major one at which mobile telephones were ubiquitous. Telephony data from the area showed that at least 72 million people attended the event—below the highest official estimates of 120 million and above the low police calculation of 40–60 million. By comparison, in 1906 there were 2–4 million and in 1989 about 15 million. 'More than any-thing, the Kumbh Mela is a crucible of predictable chaos', said Satchit Balsari, a doctor and a specialist in emergency medicine and disaster management, as he explained how doctors had used computer tablets to monitor diseases and treatments at each of the fourteen clinics. 'We saw hundreds of billions of germs from millions of people from all across India and there were lots of opportunities for these germs to interact.' Fortunately, they did not—at least not in a way so bad that anybody noticed.

The Kumbh was not always so healthy, and the 1817 event was seen as the origin of the first cholera pandemic. Hindu pilgrims and British troops apparently carried the disease back with them to Calcutta and Bombay, helping it on its way to the Haj pilgrimage to Mecca and to China and the Mediterranean. It took the harsh winter of 1824 to end the outbreak. Balsari said he and his colleagues saw no flies during their time at the Kumbh, and he showed a photo of Kumbh *chapatis*— a flat bread that is one of the staple foods of India—burned with a message in Hindi: 'Before you eat your *chapati* make sure you wash your hands with Lifebuoy soap.'

The smaller but still enormous Ganga Sagar event of January 2016, with a million or more visitors, was equally well organized, again by an administration—in this case the West Bengal government—plagued by corruption, incompetence, and unpredictability; when a fly-over under construction in Kolkata collapsed and killed twenty-four people three months later, Narendra Modi, the prime minister, said at a state elec-tion rally that it was 'God's message' to save Bengal from the governing Trinamool Congress Party. For Ganga Sagar, though, Banerjee's gov-ernment repaved the roads, ensured a smooth flow of traffic and over-saw a 'green' festival in which worshippers were forbidden to throw rubbish into the river and were obliged to use toilets, a luxury many of them had never enjoyed in their home villages.

Rahul Mehrotra, an architect and Harvard professor of urban plan-ning, was fascinated by the 'modular' way the Kumbh Mela temporary megacity was built so quickly and efficiently for millions of people with only five basic sorts of materials: 8-foot bamboo poles; rope and coir; screws and nails; corrugated metal sheets; and coverings of cloth and plastic sheeting. But he was also intrigued by the motivation behind the feat, and echoed Chaturvedi in suggesting that everyone involved was focused on a single goal, burying their differences and enjoying a spurt of energy in their mission to make the occasion a success. In an explanation that would appeal to anyone who has attended one of India's extravagant, multi-day nuptial ceremonies, he called it the 'Indian wedding syndrome'. The implication, sadly, is that it cannot be done every day, year in, year out for the routine running of India.

Religious motivation, though, can surely help clean the holy Ganges even if it is not up to the larger task of cleaning India. To gauge whether such a religiously motivated clean-up has any chance of success, we must move downstream from the brand new, instant megacity of the Kumbh Mela at Allahabad to one of the oldest and dirtiest cities in the world: Varanasi.

5

Varanasi

India's Capital for a Day

Ma Ganga is screaming for help. She is saying, 'There must be one of my sons who will come and pull me out of this filth'... There are many tasks that perhaps God has set for me.

—Narendra Modi in Varanasi after his 2014 election victory[1]

Congress with a cow.

—Modi critic Arun Shourie, likening Modi's government to its incompetent predecessor, but with added Hindu religious fervour[2]

Yes, the city of Benares is in effect just a big church, a religious hive, whose every cell is a temple, a shrine or a mosque, and whose every conceivable earthly and heavenly good is procurable under one roof, so to speak—a sort of Army and Navy Stores, theologically stocked.

—Mark Twain in *Following the Equator*[3]

On a hot April day in 2014, a fervent crowd of thousands surged through the streets of Varanasi to catch a glimpse of one man: Narendra Modi, the son of a Gujarati tea-seller who had risen to become the charismatic leader of the Hindu nationalist Bharatiya Janata Party (BJP). For the imminent Indian general election in the world's largest democracy, Modi had effectively abandoned his native Gujarat (where the BJP was already secure) and stood for parliament in Varanasi, also known in English as Benares. He had two reasons. First, Varanasi lies in the middle of Uttar Pradesh (UP), India's largest state, whose population of over 200 million gives it the same population as Brazil. Second, Varanasi with its 5,000-year heritage on the holy Ganges is the cultural heart of India and of Hinduism and, it is said, the world's oldest living city. 'He's brilliant and he will make corruption disappear', said Tanvir Singh, a 32-year-old resident of Varanasi who runs a business selling car accessories. Crowds of young men, drenched in sweat in the early summer heat, chanted 'Modi! Modi!' as their champion garlanded statues of Indian heroes and paraded through the streets atop an open van.

'Varanasi is an extremely important historical, cultural, educational and civilizational centre', said BJP official Navin Kohli. 'In the 2014 elections it's emerged as the political capital ... The BJP felt that by Mr Modi standing from Varanasi—from UP and Varanasi—it would also have an impact on a very large part of the Hindi heartland.' In a blog to mark his nomination, Modi promised to clean up the holy but heavily polluted Ganges, a popular cause in the city which depends on pilgrimages by devout Hindus who come to bathe in the river from its famous *ghats*, the stairways leading to the water. 'The condition of the Ganga [Ganges] in several parts of UP is pitiable', Modi said in his blog. 'We can't let this go on anymore! Need of the hour is to work towards cleaning the Ganga and restoring it to its previous glory.' As he told the crowds in Varanasi: 'When I was coming to this city I thought the BJP was sending me, but after I came here I felt mother Ganges had called me. I feel like a child coming to his mother. I want Kashi [Varanasi] to be the spiritual capital of the world.'[4]

In the short term, Modi's bet paid off handsomely. He won the constituency easily, while the BJP won seventy-one of the eighty parliament seats in Uttar Pradesh and he won control of the country in the most sweeping election victory for a generation. He did not forget the river after his election triumph the following month. 'Ma Ganga has decided some responsibilities for me', he told the crowd at a celebratory meeting. 'She will keep guiding me and I shall fulfil the tasks one by one. From her source to her end, Ma Ganga is screaming for help. She is saying, "There must be one of my sons who will come and pull me out of this filth"... There are many tasks that perhaps God has set for me.'[5] However, by late 2016—more than two years after that suggestion of a divine mission to save the Ganges—it was still not clear whether Modi would be able to fulfil his ambitious promises. Disillusioned residents of Varanasi, referring to Modi's televised launch of a plan to clean tonnes of mud off the city's famous Assi Ghat, criticized the lack of progress on the more important problem of sewage and resorted to a common lament: that such cosmetic projects were like 'putting lipstick on a woman with a dirty sari'. It even seemed possible that Modi would—like other famous politicians before him, including the Congress prime minister Rajiv Gandhi—leave the river in a pitiable state.

Varanasi's combination of spiritual significance and physical squalor has inspired and appalled visitors for centuries, perhaps most famously Mark Twain, who remarked acidly that 'Benares is older than history, older than tradition, older even than legend, and looks twice as old as all of them put together.'[6] The place is best witnessed from a boat on the Ganges at dawn, when the rising sun illuminates the east-facing city's eighty-four (or possibly more) *ghats* and its chaotic jumble of crumbling temples, guesthouses, cremation grounds, and giant, pink-painted pumping stations for water and sewage. I hire a boat each time I go. The experience is irresistible, the scenes always fascinating but never the same. When I was there for Modi's nomination, I scribbled the following observations in my notebook shortly after 5.00 a.m.: old women washing themselves next to discarded flowers and plastic bags in the muddy water—one of the women being of fantastic age, coughing horribly and nearly knocked down by our careless boatman; a man sitting cross-legged and staring at the sun rising through the haze; a riverside yoga lesson transmitted by a sound system so loud that you could hear the teacher breathing before issuing his ear-shattering instructions to the pupils; boats for pilgrims brightly painted with advertisements for the Bank of India, Muthoot Finance, and the Brown Bread Bakery; people slapping their washing on flat stones; the tilted spire of a collapsed and partially submerged Shiva temple; heaps of wood for burning the dead; dogs fighting over human remains on the bank; a man swimming noisily off Raja Ghat, blowing bubbles and having the appearance of hippopotamus; a religious procession coming down to the water, led by a man with a shiny trident; swifts swooping overhead and feeding on flying insects; a grey heron; women in purple saris praying to the sun; a man apparently fishing for crabs with something on the end of a blue string (though subsequent experience tells me he may have been using a magnet to pick up cheap jewellery dropped in the river).

You want to look at the other side, at the rising sun. But you can barely switch your gaze from the city for a moment. All life is here—swimming, praying, washing, chanting, eating, burning the dead. On an earlier visit, I noticed different sorts of people (Japanese tourists, and a family bearing an image of the goddess Saraswati to bathe in the river), other animals dead and alive (cows snuffling through the garbage, and, in the water, the rotten corpse of a monkey, its face in a rictus, caught on a boat's mooring line), alternative advertisements ('Exide Invatubular—the Ultimate Inverter Battery' to provide electricity during Uttar Pradesh's frequent power cuts), and softer sounds (the quiet roar of humanity, the occasional ringing of a temple bell). As Rudyard Kipling, who loved India in all its complexity, put it in his novel Kim: 'The clamour of Benares, oldest of all earth's cities awake before the Gods, day and night, beat round the walls as the sea's roar round a breakwater.'[7]

For Diana Eck, the Sanskrit scholar and biographer of the city who probably knows Varanasi better than any other foreigner, this 'magnificent city, rising from the western bank of the River Ganges... which Hindus call Kashi—the Luminous, the City of Light' is unusual among ancient centres of civilization for having so little political history. It is older, by more than 2,000 years, than the metropolises founded by Muslim or British invaders—Delhi, Madras (Chennai), Bombay (Mumbai), and Calcutta (Kolkata)—and its name survived an attempt by the Islamist Mughal emperor Aurangzeb to call it Muhammadabad. Nevertheless:

It has rarely been an important political center, and the rise and fall of kings through its long history have no role in the tale of the city's sanctity told by its own people. Kashi is said to be the city of Shiva, founded at the dawn of creation. It is not the events of its long history that make it significant to Hindus; rather, it has such a long history, and it has survived and flourished through the changing fortunes of the centuries because it is significant to Hindus.

There is another important difference between Banaras and its contemporaries: its present life reaches back to the sixth century BC in a continuous tradition. If we could imagine the silent Acropolis and the Agora of Athens still alive with the intellectual, cultural, and ritual traditions of classical Greece, we might glimpse the remarkable tenacity of the life of Kashi. Today, Peking [Beijing], Athens and Jerusalem are moved by a different ethos from that which moved them in ancient times, but Kashi is not.[8]

Varanasi, then, is the quintessential Indian city, particularly—though not exclusively—a Hindu city within whose boundaries a Hindu who dies is guaranteed moksha, liberation from the wearisome cycle of birth and rebirth. This is the holy place on whose banks most devout Hindus would wish to be cremated, and where their ashes should be immersed in the Ganges to purify their souls as their physical remains are swept slowly across north India to the sea. Varanasi on the banks of the holy river is the ultimate *tirtha* or crossing point between the human and spiritual worlds. Like the Indus valley to the west, Varanasi's abundant water and its Forest of Bliss (once indeed a forest, like the rest of the Ganges valley) made it in ancient times a centre of worship for the divinities and demons of earth, tree, and river (*devis, rakshasas, yakshas,* and *nagas*)—offerings to them of blood and meat are echoed in today's habit of smearing certain idols with vermilion—before the emergence of the gloriously chaotic mixture that we know as Hinduism today.

For centuries, it has been possible—for devout Hindus at least—to draw a distinction between the spiritual purity of Varanasi and the Ganges and the physical pollution from which both the city and the river suffer in the form of garbage and untreated sewage. To this day, you will be told in Haridwar or Varanasi or Patna or Calcutta that the goddess Ganga remains unsullied by mere human filth; indeed, so strong is her purifying force that she actually cleans polluted water and kills germs. 'Ganga is like a mother', was the view of many Varanasi residents quoted by Kelly Alley in an essay two decades ago on pollution in the city, 'who cleans up the messes her child makes. Many remarked, "The Ganga can never be impure." '[9]

Those views persist, but not as strongly as before. A relentlessly growing population in Varanasi and the rest of north India, combined with increased industrialization and the failure of three decades of official clean-up campaigns to deal with sewage and garbage, have made the Ganges so visibly disgusting and malodorous in places that it discourages some of those who would otherwise take a ritual bath in the river. 'At the age of about 10, I learned swimming,' Manoj Shah, a Varanasi medical engineer, entrepreneur and head of a trust to restore the city, told me when I was researching pollution in the Ganges. Like other residents of Varanasi, he took lessons in the obvious place. 'My father used to take me. I learned to swim in the Ganges. We used to take a boat and go to the opposite bank where the water was cleaner. I would jump out of the boat in the middle and swim.' Had he done the same with his children? I asked. 'No, my children have never swum in the Ganges. My son is 18 years old, my daughter is 20. At the temple they give you *Ganga jal* [Ganges water]. I won't take it. I don't want to put even a few drops of Ganga water in my mouth.' Among educated citizens, those views are typical.

Govind Sharma, a 43-year-old trader, said three generations of his family had lived near Assi Ghat and that is where he went to school, but the Assi river had been transformed into a sewer and the *ghat* until recently covered in a mound of mud. 'I am a very religious person,' he said. 'I offer prayers to the river, but I haven't bathed in the river for the past five years…My son asks me, "You all had so much fun in your time going to the river—what about us?" I have no answer. I feel sad and guilty.' Sharma said he was 'happy that the Prime Minister Mr Modi has started the Clean Ganga campaign', but was frustrated at the lack of progress on sewage treatment. Shah, who runs the Kashi Tirth Sudhar Trust (the Varanasi Tirtha Restoration Trust) called Modi's presence in the city as the victorious parliamentary candidate 'a ray of hope' and felt that he had made residents more aware of the river's troubles and had changed the mindset—but had yet to achieve any concrete results in a city where only a quarter of the sewage was subjected to even basic treatment. 'I have a lot of faith in this government and I have faith in Mr Modi. I have high hopes but it will take time. My children are now older, but I hope that my grandchildren can swim in the Ganges.'[10]

Modi's enemies are often eager to blame his failures on his background as a Hindu religious militant and the BJP's sometimes intolerant brand of Hindu nationalism. Varanasi, after all, is like many other north Indian towns in having a history of confrontation as well as cooperation between Hindus and Muslims. The Kashi Vishvanath temple and the adjoining Gyanvapi mosque recall the religious fault-lines in old Jerusalem, where some of the holiest sites of Judaism, Christianity, and Islam exist awkwardly side by side. The *mandir*, among the holiest of Shiva temples, was destroyed by Muslim conquerors on at least three occasions, most recently by 'that famous bigot' the emperor Aurangzeb in 1669.[11] It is now separated from the mosque that supplanted its early incarnation by a huge metal barrier and the front line between the two holy places is guarded by nervous police. Shortly after a solicitous policeman had urged me to join the queue of pilgrims and touch the holy Shiva *lingam*, the smooth black stone at the heart of the temple, one his colleagues angrily stopped me when I tried to approach the barrier separating the site from the mosque.

Modi, however, went out of his way to court Varanasi's Muslims—they account for nearly a quarter of the city's 1.6 million voters—and to emphasize its multicultural, syncretic traditions when he was on the campaign trail in 2014. He praised not only Hindu but also Muslim cultural figures, including the musician Bismillah Khan, and said Khan was arguably the greatest symbol of *Ganga-Jamuni tehzeeb* (Ganga-Yamuna culture), a riverine phrase often used to describe the intertwined Hindu-Muslim culture of north India where those two rivers flow. Modi also targeted the important Muslim community of sari-weavers in the district of Lallapura. Varanasi's silk wedding saris, lavishly designed and interwoven with gold thread, are much sought after by Indians from across the country and from overseas, and Modi promised to help the weavers acquire modern technology, quality raw materials and better marketing skills so they could compete with Chinese clothing manufacturers. 'The weavers of Varanasi are an integral part of the city's history', he wrote in a blog post on his nomination day. 'It is my resolve to ensure that they stand on their own feet with pride and their future generations have a bright future.'

I went to the alleyways of Lallapura that day to find out what Varanasi's Muslims thought of Modi's overtures and found two problems for Modi, one predictable and the other unexpected. Like many Muslims across India (they make up about 14 per cent of the population), they are suspicious of the Hindu nationalist BJP and particularly of Modi, who had just become chief minister of Gujarat in 2002 when Hindu mobs slaughtered hundreds of Muslims in the aftermath of a suspected firebombing of a train carrying Hindu pilgrims; Modi has strongly denied accusations that he abetted the rioters, but in light of the extent of the riots there can be little doubt that the state government and its police force failed to rein in the murderous crowds. 'Muslims cannot tolerate at any cost a party responsible for the mass assassination of Muslims in Gujarat in 2002', Rais Ahmad of the Congress party told me as he sat with his friends in Lallapura, in a room shuttered to keep out the fierce summer sun. 'Varanasi has been known for centuries for communal harmony, for its saris, for its *Ganga-Jamuni* culture and for education. So now Varanasi people are very concerned that this communal harmony will be disturbed.' Such views are widely shared, although Congress—which reckons it is the natural home of liberals, leftists, secularists, and minorities as well as moderate Hindus—is itself often criticized by educated Muslims for treating the community as a 'vote-bank' that can be bought with special favours handed out like 'lollipops'.[12]

More surprising than these widely shared political views was the discovery that Modi's selling point among young Indian voters—his

successful management of the Gujarat economy for more than a decade and his focus on the need for jobs, investment, and development
across India—completely failed to sway the sari-weavers. 'In his first
rally here Modi said he would update this industry. It's not possible
because this is a very big country', sari-maker Mohammed Hashim
told me dismissively as we sat on the cushioned floor of a small
Lallapura house, from where he runs 200 power-looms in the district.
'He will presumably be the prime minister, and he won't have time for
this constituency. And it's not possible to deal with the problems of the
Varanasi sari industry.' Why not? I asked, pointing out that Varanasi
needed better electricity supply and roads, exactly the sort of benefits
Modi had brought to Gujarat and was now promising the rest of the
country. The industrialized coastal state of Gujarat and its canny businessmen, it turned out, were the problem, not the solution. 'Nowadays
we have suffered due to Gujarat', said Hashim. 'Gujarat is copying our
products—and they are charging 50 per cent less than us. They have
more modern machinery, proper electricity supply, and cheaper yarn.'[13]

Modi's subsequent difficulties with the Ganga clean-up, however,
had more to do with administrative inertia and the recalcitrance of
sections of the Hindu majority than with grumbling Muslim sari-
weavers. Less than a year after the election, Girdhar Malviya, a retired
High Court judge and the very man who had officially proposed
Modi's nomination for the Varanasi seat, was campaigning against the
construction of a sewage treatment plant in the city. The reason was
simply that some of the land where the plant was to have been built
had previously belonged to a *gosala* or cow shelter, and he could not
countenance the idea of holy cows being denied protection merely to
make way for a sewage plant.[14] (Modi too is a passionate believer in
caring for India's wandering cows and has pledged in the past to provide them with extra veterinary care, even eye surgery.)

A few months after the sewage plant row, *sadhus* and other devout
Hindus were marching through the streets of Varanasi to protest against
an Allahabad High Court anti-pollution ruling that banned the immersion of idols in the Ganges. As tensions rose, the police broke up one
demonstration with what is known as a '*lathi* charge', in which policemen with long sticks charge into the crowd and beat people. Ram
Gopal Mohale of the BJP, the Varanasi mayor, agreed it was a 'delicate'
situation. 'Modi-ji and Uma-ji [Uma Bharti, the minister for water and
the Ganges] have made it clear in no uncertain terms that the Ganges

needs to be cleaned. And we will do all it takes to get that done. But it is also true that the immersion of idols is part of our tradition and it isn't easy to convince people to change their habits.' Mohale went on to say that there were ways around the problem. Idol-makers, for example, could be persuaded to use biodegradable paints.[15]

It did not take long for disillusionment to set in, even among those dedicated to saving the Ganges who looked to Modi for deliverance. Successive high priests at the Sankat Mochan temple to Hanuman the monkey god at Tulsi Ghat—another of Varanasi's most important holy sites—have campaigned for more than forty years, so far in vain, to ensure that 'not one drop of sewage' enters the river. The writer Piers Moore Ede describes how he struggled to meet Veer Bhadra Mishra, the temple's *mahant* or senior priest and also a water engineer. He found him demoralized and distracted after years of lobbying politicians—and meeting journalists who had promised to promote the cause of the Ganges. 'They tell me people will be moved by what's happened to this river. I'm afraid I don't really believe that any more. I'm afraid I have lost faith in your trade.' Ede is abruptly dismissed and is then consoled by one of the *mahant*'s assistants, Shiva, who explains the problems: corruption, bureaucracy, and repeated failures starting with the first Ganga Action Plan launched by Prime Minister Rajiv Gandhi of Congress in the mid-1980s. 'So many Ganga meetings, so little Ganga action . . . So many millions wasted. And still she was full of poison. The Ganga Action Plan proved to be a total fiasco.'[16]

The elder Mishra, who was said to have contracted polio, hepatitis, smallpox, and jaundice during his life,[17] died in 2013, before Modi came to power. I went to the temple the following year to meet his son, a professor of electronics engineering who had succeeded his father as *mahant*. There cannot be many high priests around the world of any religion who understand sewage treatment technology, but Mishra's concern for the Ganges means he knows a thing or two about activated sludge plants and faecal coliform bacteria. He met me after a night-time ceremony of chanted prayers, and told me that Varanasi produced 350 million litres a day of sewage and was able to treat only 100 million litres (and that only partially). But he boasted that he had helped Modi to understand the importance of the issue. 'The place where you're sitting'—he pointed at the mat on the floor—'Modi was sitting there on the 20th of December. He was a mute spectator. Whatever I was saying, he was just listening. I said, "Modi-ji, you are

going to address a big crowd. It would be nice if you could consider, if
you could deliberate on this [Ganges] issue. Most people are not aware
of it." ' Mishra told me he would hold Modi to his promises, vowing to
be 'the first person to tell him: "You made this commitment in Sankat
Mochan temple." Our objective is that not even a drop of sewage
should go into the Ganges.'[18]

Modi certainly made his speeches about the Ganges, but his actions
thereafter have left Mishra and others disappointed. The government,
they say, has continued to neglect the basic planning and engineering
needed to treat sewage, and naively tried to use the orderly Japanese
city of Kyoto and its Kamo river as a development model following a
visit to Varanasi with Modi by Shinzo Abe, Japan's prime minister.[19]
For an Indian magazine investigation into Modi's *Swachh Bharat* (Clean
India) campaign—a report that referred to Varanasi as 'God's shithole'—
Mishra said in an interview that the government was wrongly focusing
on shopping malls, ring roads, and metro lines instead of sewage. '[B]y
the time they get done, Banaras will be dead', he said. He complained
that dredging for coal barges and dam-building on the Ganges—which
would 'turn a living river into a series of 16 ponds filled with sewage'—
was being allocated far more government money than the clean-up
operation, and he mocked official proposals to send thousands of
retired soldiers to protect the river from pollution. 'Will they shoot
people who bathe in the river?' On another occasion, Mishra was
asked about a Hindu nationalist's proposal that religious groups, after
suitable training, should run sewage treatment plants in exchange for
access to the Ganga shoreline. At first he was speechless, then said: 'I'm
afraid the solution lies in science, not religion.'[20]

Two years after the election of Modi as their MP, many of Varanasi's
voters seemed inclined to give him the benefit of the doubt, agreeing
that improvements thus far were cosmetic but arguing that he needed
more time to fulfil his campaign promises. Others were disappointed.
Public toilets had been rebuilt, painted saffron and marked 'Inspired by
His Excellency Prime Minister Narendra Modi' in Hindi—but then
not maintained. 'The stench is unbearable', a labourer told a local journalist at one such site. 'The water tank is empty, the pipe has come off,
the taps don't work. They used poor quality material, which didn't last
even a month.'[21] Ashish Yadav, a 25-year-old law student and activist for
Bajrang Dal, a Hindu militant group, explained how he had helped
Modi be elected and watched the prime minister change the country's

mindset. But he was also shocked by the continuing disaster in basic health and education and disappointed by the performance of the BJP in anything other than showcase projects. 'Whenever Modi has to come to Varanasi, the municipal corporation starts repairing a few main roads on a war footing. After Modi-ji goes back to Delhi, they will stop caring about the roads. I suggest Modi-ji comes and takes a different road route every time he comes to Varanasi. That way, we'll get good roads!'[22]

I came to realize that the triumphs and travails of Modi and the BJP in the holy city of Varanasi were mirrored in their performances in less religious parts of India. The country has long been what Lant Pritchett, a Harvard professor, called a 'flailing state', with officials unable or unwilling to implement policies handed down from the top even when those policies are sensible ones. Modi and the BJP never pretended to have much in the way of an economic ideology (the party was the political product of the Rashtriya Swayamsevak Sangh or Organisation of National Volunteers, a right-wing Hindu group, and only took its present form in 1980). Although Modi himself sensibly focused on sanitation and economic development he was undermined by the obstructionism in parliament of the Congress Party (which controlled the upper house when Modi took over), irrepressibly uncooperative bureaucrats, and a shortage of skilled ministers from the untechnocratic upper reaches of the BJP. Uma Bharti, a religious activist and politician by profession, seemed a particularly poor choice for the Water Ministry and was a constant source of frustration for Indians and foreigners trying to implement practical policies for cleaning the Ganges. She appeared more interested in proving the existence 5,000 to 6,000 years ago of the extinct Saraswati River (in Hindu mythology, it still invisibly joins the Ganges along with the Yamuna at the holy *triveni* or triple river junction of Allahabad) than in solving the very real crisis facing the contemporary Ganges.[23]

It was Arun Shourie, the puckish former BJP minister and one-time confidant of Modi, who best summed up the feelings of those disappointed with Modi's administration. They had expected him to usher in radical change but the government had turned out to be like the incompetent and sclerotic Congress one that preceded it, only with added Hindu fervour. 'Congress plus a cow', he said tersely. 'Policies are the same.' When I interviewed Shourie with a colleague from London he added some scathing criticism of Modi's taste for development slogans such as 'Make in India' and 'Digital India' with little substance behind them. 'His concept of development is a few large, shining, and conspicuous projects', he said.

Before he took office, Modi's liberal enemies feared he would become a powerful, authoritarian prime minister in the East Asian mould who would impose—or allow his Hindu religious backers to impose—fundamentalist Hinduism on the country's vast and hetero-geneous population. There was some of that, good and bad. Hindu fundamentalists, energized by Modi's election win, waged campaigns against Muslim men who married Hindu girls, complaining of a con-spiracy to boost the Muslim population. A Muslim man in Uttar Pradesh was lynched by a Hindu crowd for allegedly eating beef at home, and police investigators (along with BJP officials) focused on the nature of the meat consumed ('Was it mutton or beef?') rather than on pursuing the murderers. A BJP state government in Rajasthan deleted crucial references to Jawaharlal Nehru—who led India to independence from Britain and became the first prime minister—from several school textbooks. Nehru, after all, had the temerity to lead the Congress Party at the time when a member of the RSS, spir-itual parent of the BJP, was assassinating Mahatma Gandhi. There was even a bizarre Hindu nationalist campaign on the social media net-work Twitter to erase 300 years of history by abolishing the Mughals (they gave India the Taj Mahal, the capital Delhi, and much else, but are seen by Hindu hardliners as Muslim interlopers), under the hashtag #RemoveMughalsFromBooks.[24]

On the other hand, the government's supporters in business insisted there had been economic progress under Modi, even if few of them agreed with Jayant Sinha, the minister of state for finance and a former McKinsey partner, that the government was 'fundamentally changing the nature of Indian capitalism' to help entrepreneurs. By mid-2016, India (notwithstanding some arguments about the reliability of the statistical data) was growing faster than any other large economy in the world, with gross domestic product rising in real terms by nearly 8 per cent a year. Under Modi, India accelerated road building; invested in an ageing rail network barely expanded since independence from Britain in 1947; launched an ambitious renewable energy and solar power plan; persuaded 200 million previously unbanked Indians to open bank accounts to reduce corruption by allowing electronic transfer of government subsidies and other payments; and increased the shareholding limits for foreign investors in sectors ranging from insurance to arms manufacturing.

In tandem with the Reserve Bank of India, the central bank, the Finance Ministry sought to rejuvenate the state-dominated banking system by pressing reluctant tycoons to repay their debts and forcing banks to recognize on their books the severity of a bad-loan crisis arising from road projects, power stations, and mining ventures that had turned sour. Modi's government also struggled to introduce a nationwide goods and services tax—a GST—that would eliminate a plethora of complicated local taxes and fees, turn India's twenty-nine states into a single market, and boost economic output. This last measure was blocked for more than two years by resistance in the Rajya Sabha, the upper house of parliament, from Congress, a party that had previously tried to introduce GST itself but had been stymied by resistance from a party then in opposition: the BJP.

The GST was eventually passed, although in a form with so many exclusions that its aim of simplifying taxes and generating growth has been severely compromised. In November 2016, Modi also abruptly withdrew some 86 per cent of the value of banknotes in circulation by cancelling the old 500-rupee and 1,000-rupee notes. The purpose was to punish black marketeers and tax-evaders who stored bundles of cash, although small traders and the rural poor, who depend on the cash economy, suffered the most in the early weeks. What Modi did not do was to introduce any transformative, 'big bang' economic reforms at the national level other than GST. Indian and foreign investors, for example, wanted sweeping changes to land acquisition laws that often meant years of delays for building new factories and to restrictive labour regulations that discouraged the hiring of new employees; instead they were granted piecemeal reforms by a few BJP-run states such as Rajasthan and told that others might follow in a burst of fruitful 'competitive federalism'.[25]

Most Indian voters might not care about such reforms—indeed, it was the BJP's fear of popular resistance from workers and peasant farmers, stoked by left-wing Congress politicians, that made liberalization unpalatable—but they do care about jobs. After four years of reporting on India, I reckoned that Modi's failure to create millions of jobs and so fulfil the hopes of the aspirational young Indians who voted for him in 2014 was one of his biggest weaknesses. It was not entirely his fault, of course. India, long resistant to foreign investment and wary of free enterprise, had already comprehensively missed the boat on replacing China as the world's manufacturing hub, and by the time Modi launched his 'Make in India' campaign even companies in India, where wages are relatively low, were replacing factory workers with robots, not hiring hundreds of thousands of new employees to assemble cars or smart-phones. But there are still jobs to be had in construction and some basic services for the unskilled and semi-skilled who make up the bulk of India's workforce, and I was surprised that Modi's government did not move quickly to build sewage and waste treatment plants in cities such as Varanasi on the Ganges: such projects would have a triple benefit, not only creating jobs but also saving the lives of the hundreds of thousands of young children who die each year from waterborne diseases in the Ganges basin and helping to save the holy Ganges itself from pollution.

The blame can be laid at the door of Modi and the central govern-ment, certainly, but the guilty parties also include state governments such as the one in Uttar Pradesh (led by political rivals to Modi from 2012 until a BJP election victory in a state election there in 2017), dys-functional municipalities, and the apathy of the population. Priyankar Upadhyaya, a political scientist at Banaras Hindu University in Varanasi, said Modi 'desperately' wanted economic development and found himself in a 'trap of expectations' set by hopeful voters who will deliver their judgement in the 2019 general election. 'I think he really wants to bring about change', Upadhyaya said. 'But the problem is that the system on which he depends is mired with issues.'[26]

Modi, the Gujarati Hindu activist turned politician, is not the first outsider to struggle with the contradictions and bad sanitation of Varanasi, or what Sunil Khilnani, the historian and politics professor, called the oddity of 'its unworried marriage of religious purity and physical filth'. Khilnani quotes the horrified description of the health risks of Varanasi by the Anglican missionary M.A. Sherring in the 1860s, when India was under British rule:

[W]hen we reflect on the foul wells and tanks in some parts of the city, whose water is of deadly influence, and the vapour from which fills the air with fever-fraught and cholera-breeding miasma; when we consider the loathsome and disgusting state of the popular temples, owing to the rapid decomposition of the offerings, from the intense heat of the sun; when we call to mind the filthy condition of nearly all the by-streets, due to stagnant cesspools, accumu-lated refuse, and dead bodies of animals; and, when, in addition, we remember how utterly regardless of these matters, and incompetent to correct them is the police force scattered over the city, the difficulty becomes overwhelming.[27]

While Sherring is a magnificent example of the appalled Westerner confronting the teeming, filthy streets of an Indian city, it is wrong to think that these are the concerns only of squeamish foreigners. Mahatma Gandhi himself—like Modi, an outsider from Gujarat, albeit one with experience of life in London and South Africa—wrestles with his distaste for Varanasi's noise and dirt and the need to find a *pandit*, or priest 'comparatively cleaner and better than the rest' when he wants to perform his *puja* and bathe in the Ganges. He is 'deeply pained' by the stinking mass of rotten flowers and the broken marble floor he sees when he visits the famous Kashi Vishvanath temple for *darshan*.'The swarming flies and the noise made by the shopkeepers and pilgrims were perfectly insufferable', he wrote in his autobiography, declaring that the authorities should be responsible for creating and maintaining about the temple a 'pure sweet and serene atmosphere, physical as well as moral. Instead of this I found a bazar where cunning shopkeepers were selling sweets and toys of the latest fashion.'[28]

Varanasi, even so, seems always to have been inspirational as well as appalling. It is one of the important Gangetic pilgrimage sites for Buddhists as well as the cynosure of Hindu worshippers. According to some of the Jatakas, the ancient poetic tales about the Buddha, Siddhartha Gautama was an exceptionally rich Varanasi merchant when the city was a significant north Indian trading centre in the Iron Age. In other versions he was a prince in the area. In any case, he abandoned a life of material luxury to meditate on life and death in Gaya, just south of the Gangetic city of Patna. But it was to Varanasi that he came after his enlightenment because it was there that his former companions, the powerful citizens and intellectuals of the day, were clustered. He walked 200 miles from Gaya and crossed the Ganges by ferry, establishing a monastic retreat in a deer park at Sarnath on the outskirts of the city.[29] Although Muslim armies destroyed Sarnath at the turn of the twelfth century, Buddhists still come as pilgrims to the city today from as far as Japan. In Victorian times, the Tibetan *lama* in Kipling's novel Kim notices the smoke rising from the cremation *ghats* and fragments of half-burned corpses 'despite all municipal regulations', bobbing by in the river's current, but is relieved by his reception. 'Benares struck him as a peculiarly filthy city, though it was pleasant to find how his cloth was respected. At least one-third of the population prays eternally to some group or other of the many million deities, and so revere every sort of holy man.'[30]

In the Mughal era, Jagannatha, a seventeenth-century Sanskrit scholar and poet from Andhra Pradesh, served in the court of the Mughal emperor Shah Jahan and wrote what is probably the most famous song in praise of the Ganges, the *Ganga Lahari* ('The Waves of the Ganges'), in Varanasi. This is the same hymn sung at the temple in Gangotri near the river's source. The story goes that Jagannatha, who taught Sanskrit to Shah Jahan's son and was dubbed *Panditraja* or King of the Pandits, was playing chess one day with the emperor. Shah Jahan thought he was about to win, challenged Jagannatha to beat him and promised him whatever he wanted if he did, whereupon a beautiful Muslim princess named Lavangi entered the room and Jagannatha named her as his prize. He duly won the game and was either asked to convert to Islam or be expelled from his Brahmin caste, or possibly both. He travelled to Varanasi and when he went to bathe with his bride at the Panchaganga Ghat even the river shrank from him, receding down the steps until he composed a hymn in fifty-two verses over fifty-two days, praising Ganga, appealing for deliverance, and bringing her up step by step with each verse. On the last day he and his wife were swept away by the purifying river.

> I come a fallen man to you, uplifter of all.
> I come undone by disease to you,
>   the perfect physician.
> I come, my heart dry with thirst, to
>   you, ocean of sweet wine.
> Do with me whatever you will.[31]

The English translation in the trilingual Sanskrit–Hindi–English edition of the hymn popularly available in India is in rather clunky prose, but the little paperback has the merit of including numerous pictures of idols and paintings of the goddess Ganga with her traditional animal vehicle, the crocodile. It also reminds us of the ancient Puranic restrictions on activities in the Ganges, many of which have long been more honoured in the breach than the observance by both humans and gods: defecating; rinsing the mouth; combing the hair; rubbing the body; throwing garbage; discarding the remains of a *puja*; laughing and joking; taking alms and offerings; having erotic enjoyment; praising other holy places; washing clothes; beating the water; and swimming.[32]

An earlier great poet, son of Varanasi and symbol of north India's syncretic traditions, was the fifteenth-century Kabir, whose pithy lines in Hindi are still much quoted today by Indians over social media. Again, the legends surrounding his life are confused. He may have been born into a low-caste Muslim community of weavers or been a Hindu by birth. But he famously mocked the priesthoods and the rituals of both Muslims and Hindus, even to the extent of deliberately leaving holy Varanasi to die in an obscure town, when most north Indians would be heading in the other direction and yearning to expire within the boundaries of the city to find salvation. His contempt for organized religion is reflected in the legend of his death: Hindu and Muslim devotees argued over who should claim the poet's remains, but when the cloth covering his body was lifted, they found nothing underneath but a spray of flowers.[33]

Then in the following century came Tulsi Das, a devotee of the god Ram. Like Kabir, he wrote in the vernacular language of north India, and translated the *Ramayana* from Sanskrit into Hindi. His version of the legend, the *Ramcharitmanas*, 'was attacked at first by orthodox pandits, but it was loved by the people. It remains today the single most popular classic, the Bible of the Hindi-speaking people.'[34] Tulsi's name is given to the *ghat* where he wrote the poem, and he is said to have launched the annual Ram Lila festival in which the stories are played out by actors over several weeks to popular acclaim on the far side of the river.

Varanasi today has lost none of its attractions for writers and artists, nor for Sanskrit scholars and sociologists seeking to unravel the mysteries of India.[35] Arriving in Varanasi for the first time at the age of 25, Moore Ede marvelled at the combination of creeds and colours, the coexistence of astonishing beauty and harrowing ugliness, of madness and wisdom and poetry. 'Until then I had supposed India was essentially unfathomable: it was too fast, too swiftly changing to yield to any categorisation. In Varanasi, however, I found a city whose spirit seemed to denote the whole.'[36] Despite all the pollution and filth, he wrote, 'your spirit soars'. His book touches on the usual interests of visitors— the sari-weavers, the Ganga *aarti* ceremonies offered for the past 5,000 years, the temples and the cremation *ghats*, including the tradition that the corpses of babies and holy men are tied to boulders and dumped unburned in the river because they need no purification by fire—but he also relishes his diversions into lesser-known topics: Varanasi's prostitutes; its sweet-makers; and the *Aghoris*, the extreme *sadhus* in the fast lane to *moksha* or liberation by virtue of their embrace of the 'dark path' rather than the easier but slow path of light. 'Some of us choose to eat the flesh of these corpses, others to eat excrement', one of them confides to him at a cremation ground. There are perhaps only 1,000–1,500 *Aghoris* in the whole of India. 'Sometimes we cook our food on the embers of cremation pyres, or drink water from a cup that is a human skull. There are many other things, some I cannot talk of. This knowledge takes us beyond the Eight Snares of Existence: lust, anger, greed, delusion, envy, shame, disgust and fear, which bind all beings.'[37] After all he sees—corruption, the drug trade, exploitation, dirt—Moore Ede is unashamedly a Varanasi-lover.

[T]he simplicity of life in the old medieval alleys, the poetry of the city's rituals and beliefs, seemed to me to represent the best of India, the best, perhaps, of the human condition. There was a straightforward friendliness to the people there, a jocular sense of humour. Above the basic hunger for survival was a sense of our place in a much larger order alluded to in a thousand subtle phases and offerings. All of this was the language of Banaras, its own private patois. It seemed like a language I'd been waiting to learn my whole life.[38]

6

Varanasi

Broken Promises

Now Modi's sitting there and has painted these buildings, but what else has changed? People here, they shit, they crap, and piss and who can tell them to stop?

Varanasi boatman Deepak Maji[1]

'The Ganges water never used to smell', says Chandramauli Upadhyay, Sanskrit scholar and head of the astrology department of Banaras Hindu University. He is my first stop on a 2016 visit to Varanasi to assess the city's attitude to Modi and his Ganges clean-up plans by talking to everyone from Brahmins to *dalits* (once known as untouchables), from religious scholars to those who burn the corpses on the banks of the river. The prevailing mood is of regret and resignation, still tinged with hope that Modi might be able to make progress in the second half of his term as prime minister.

Upadhyay's office is decorated with images of gods and Hindu saints and a calendar showing the phases of the moon. At the age of 61, he says the two main problems for the river are the lack of water flow because of dams such as the Tehri, far upstream, and the reluctance of Indians to change their behaviour or abide by regulations. 'I used to swim in the Ganges with my father as a child, since the time I was 6 or 7. I used to drink the water and never had any problem—and we used to drink a lot of water from the Ganges. Gradually the water changed.'

He observes that greater wealth, commercialization, and overt religiosity have multiplied the quantity of idols and offerings dumped in the river over the years. 'I believe either we were not as religious as we are today or there was not so much paraphernalia attached to our religious ceremonies as today.' In the more frugal old days Saraswati Puja, Durga Puja, and the festival for Ganesh involved only a few idols, but today 'all these three festivals are producing a lot of toxic waste on such a big scale—it's a major contributor [to pollution]'. Meanwhile, residents routinely flout regulations, whether by building their houses up to five or six floors when only permitted two, or ignoring the requirement to dispose properly of sewage and garbage even when it is possible. 'Modi-ji's idea of having toilets in every household is a good idea, but where is the water going to come from?' Upadhyay asks.

It looks like the government has the good intention of cleaning the Ganges. The TV ads telling people to wash their hands before they eat—it has some effect, it raises awareness . . . [But] it will be ten to fifteen years before things will really change. It's the mindset. If nobody's watching, it's okay to throw garbage. In our childhood, whenever we would go to the Sankat Mochan temple, people used to say it's the Simla of Kashi [Varanasi], it's so nice and cool. The river too. Now it's like a *nullah* [a drain].

I ask him whether people would ever be so upset about abuse of the Ganges that they would take to the streets to demand action. 'That will never happen', he says firmly.

With Upadhyay in his office in Varanasi that morning was K. Chandramouli, a Bangalore-based mechanical engineer, author, and former business executive who has long had an interest in the practical steps needed to save the Ganges. 'Many people talk of Ganga without knowing much of the problems', he said, explaining how he had taken a forty-day trip from Sagar at the mouth to Gangotri near the source by four-wheel-drive vehicle and had produced a booklet on rescuing the river to send to universities and government officials. 'Unless we take on the problems, there's no point taking on the history and the mythology . . . Basically we know things and we don't do things.' Chandramouli, sporting a small moustache and a pink shirt, was philosophical when I asked him what he had discovered on his trip from those who lived along the river. 'The fate of the people is immeasurable. Why are we treating the Ganga like this?'

Like others in the small band of Indians who are trying to clean the river (to the Ganga, he said, had been transferred all the divine attributes of the Saraswati after that river dried up in 3200 BC), he was frustrated by the failed projects of successive Indian governments and pressure groups. When Upadhyay said Modi's cleaning of the *ghats* was not enough to clean the river itself, Chandramouli added: 'It's like a feverish old lady and you give her a manicure and a pedicure.' He described the sewage treatment plants established under the first Ganga Action Plan from the 1980s as fossils. The plants had rusted. 'They are full of rubbish. Pumps are not working.' There were too many organizations working at cross purposes—fourteen or fifteen in Varanasi and five or six in Kanpur. He had been engaged in months of friendly but fruitless to and fro communications with the office of Uma Bharti in which she asked him to become involved; he agreed, and then nothing happened. When I saw him, however, he had been appointed to an Expert Advisory Group formed three weeks previously and was about to attend the group's first meeting in Delhi. 'There are signs, yes, that this time will be different.' The trouble, I suggested, was that it had taken two years for a prime minister and a government vocally committed to save the Ganges merely to establish a committee.

Apart from delay, one of the Modi government's weaknesses has been the ease with which it is distracted from its core tasks by pseudo-scientific or impractical solutions to problems, often proposed by Hindu activists. (The BJP-run Rajasthan government proposed using the urine of holy cows instead of regular disinfectant in government hospitals.)[2] So it was with some dismay that I heard another Ganges-obsessed Varanasi professor later that day try to explain his theories about the river. The eccentric U. K. Choudhary, who taught a master's degree course in river engineering at Banaras Hindu University for thirty-five years before retiring in 2011, concurred with his colleagues in lamenting the ineffectiveness of the Modi government and its predecessors. But his solution has been the establishment of 'The School of Ganga-Geeta-Atomic Theory', supported by various politicians and Hindu holy men but without any discernible scientific basis for its linking of nuclear physics with the Bhagavad Gita, the divine song of the Mahabharata.[3]

For a more down-to-earth assessment of the Ganges in Varanasi, I went with my host in Varanasi to the temple and *ghat* of Nishad Raj Guha, named after a legendary tribal king of the boat people who lived on the river and helped Ram cross the river in his quest to rescue his wife Sita. The temple is a base for the boatmen. We were guided there by Devendra Misra, a smartly dressed local salesman for a pharmaceutical company, who took us along the shore, littered with garbage, past a jumble of temples built by various *rajas* and a large pumping station labelled 'Intake Water Works'; it creates a small whirl-pool where it sucks water for the town out of the river—about 400 metres downstream from the vile Assi drain that pours untreated waste straight into the Ganges.

As we walked past old wooden rowing boats being repaired on the shore and a small Shiva lingam shrine, Misra said Modi was doing what he could—there were even rubbish bins now, he pointed out—and blamed ordinary people for the river's problems. 'People are not used to being hygienic in public spaces. They don't have the nationalistic spirit', he said. 'Modi-ji is doing whatever he can. And it's not just the local people who have been abusing the river. It's the people who come from the villages. They bring stuff with them and leave every-thing on the *ghat*.' But as we reached the Nishad Raj Ghat, he echoed other Varanasi residents in complaining about the lack of water in the river and lamenting the loss of the once 'absolutely translucent' water to bathe in. 'Nowadays I don't even feel like putting water in my mouth. I'm hesitant to do it now.' ('But he has to, he's a Brahmin', whispers my colleague. 'He comes to the *ghat* every morning.')

The temple has recently been repainted in bright red and turquoise (I am reminded that ancient Greek temples and statues, admired now for their honey-coloured stone, were also gaudily coloured in their time) and we examine an image of Nishad Raj himself, adorned with a fine moustache. The first boatman I approach, the 70-year-old Mithai Lal, is initially reluctant to talk but finally agrees to discuss the Ganges and his livelihood. The family owns two wooden boats, one with an engine and one for rowing. My questions about whether anyone remembers sailing vessels on the river draw no response from the boat-men, although Misra says there were some that used to carry 60–70 tonnes of wood for cremations. Lal's hair is grey, he is unshaven and wears a dirty white T-shirt stretched over a substantial pot-belly, and a blue check *dhoti*. 'Our great grandfathers lived here', he says solemnly. 'A lot of changes have happened. The river is very small now, it's gone down. It's in very bad condition and there's no water. All these dams are being built and they are taking away the water for the dams.'

Making a living for his extended family of twenty is hard, partly because potential visitors and pilgrims are deterred by pollution and partly because the government has banned fishing in this stretch of the river ('Yes, people do it at night, illegally', he admits). 'There's so much pollution, the Ganga is so dirty that people have stopped coming, they don't want to come here. We keep drinking it, because we have to.' He too gives Modi the benefit of the doubt, choosing to blame Akhilesh Yadav, then the chief minister of Uttar Pradesh, whose family leads the Samajwadi Party (Socialist Party) and opposes Modi and the BJP. (The BJP under Modi subsequently won the Uttar Pradesh state election in March 2017, ousting Yadav and appointing Yogi Adityanath, a radical Hindu priest, as chief minister.) 'Modi-ji is the head of the family and he's giving money to sort things out and it's Akhilesh's job to make things happen, but he's not doing anything.' Even for the time of year, a few weeks before the arrival of the monsoon, the river is exceptionally low, and Lal points to the sandbanks on the far bank and a stretch of greenery a further 200 metres away. 'There used to be water right up to the green part. Our whole family bathes in the river. We have taps here but when the water supply stops we drink the river water. Mother Ganga is always pure. She will never give us any problem.'

While we are discussing the river with Lal, I notice another man with glasses on the terrace of the temple repairing a fishing net, the enormous size of the mesh suggesting he expects to catch some very large cat-fish. Ram Lakhan Prasad is 67 and as disenchanted as Lal with the state of the Ganges. 'All the tributaries of the Ganges are being dammed, that's why there's no water. I grew up, I was able to get education, all because of her'—he gestures towards the river—'but now it's all gone. Even this river will become a *nullah*. There's still at least six weeks to go [before the monsoon] and the water levels have gone down so much that we don't know what's ahead of us. It's basically all the effluents, the chemicals from the factories. These people say, "Don't bathe your cattle", but we always did that and there was no problem.' I agree with this last complaint—it is absurd to think that washing cows or buffaloes causes serious river pollution—and I ask him whether the real problem is not the growing number of human beings and the flow of their sewage into the river. 'There's pressure on the river, I agree', he replies. 'But can you see how much she is being abused? They are making dams everywhere. Let them unshackle the river.' He points despairingly at the heaps of garbage dumped on the far river bank.

We decide to investigate the Assi *nullah* upstream where we can see a large, concrete waste treatment and pumping plant on the shore. The plant, we are told, was built a decade ago but it is silent and abandoned and clearly has not been functioning for years. Pigs and piglets rootle in the rubbish under a platform holding the large diesel generators designed to power the plant during Varanasi's frequent power cuts. Inside the plant, through gates secured with rusting padlocks, we can see some expensive-looking but now dusty control panels, as well as a heap of sacks and pieces of loose machinery. The Assi *nullah*, one of the biggest and dirtiest drains in Varanasi, flows on unimpeded. I watch a polystyrene box come rushing down the stream before it snags on a bank of old plastic bags and other garbage in the stream bed. We find the caretaker, Dhaman Jay Singh, in a small house nearby, who assures us that renovation work is proceeding—although there is no sign of it. The generators and pumps, he says, were tested four years ago but the test was abandoned when a village upstream was submerged by the pumped water.

Before dawn the next day, we set off to see a cremation *ghat*, where the task of the workers is to burn the corpses of those who die in Varanasi or whose bodies are sent there so that the ashes can be committed to the Ganges. The ever-present cows are still sleeping in the arcades of shops, and the only traders to approach us are selling flowers for offerings or twigs freshly ripped from *neem* trees for cleaning the teeth. Even the orange-robed *sadhus* are asleep on benches by the river. We arrive at the Dashashwamedh Ghat, the *ghat* of ten horse sacrifices, and the Dr Rajendra Prasad Ghat where Rajiv Gandhi launched the first, ill-fated Ganga Action Plan back in 1986. (Prasad was the first president of India.) A large police station stands prominently on the bank, right opposite a place on the far side where rubbish is dumped—presumably illegally—on the sand of the dry river bed. As the sun rises orange through the dust, a family from Orissa are collecting water in plastic containers for their Shiva temple back home. The father emerges from bathing in the river—its surface dotted with pieces of plastic and the occasional floating lamp for a religious offering—and struggles into his underpants.

Deepak Maji, a 60-year-old boatman whose family has worked on the river for generations, is not impressed by Modi's clean-up efforts or by the new toilets near the river. When I ask him if the river has changed, he replies in a hoarse voice: 'No, it's the same. There's been no change except the pollution. Now Modi's sitting there and has painted these buildings, but what else has changed? People here, they shit, they crap and piss and who can tell them to stop? If you tell them, they start fighting. Who can tell anyone what to do?' As he speaks, a child squats next to her mother and leaves a stain of watery yellow diarrhoea on the river bank. We decide to hire a younger boatman, the 35-year-old Madan Maji, for the short trip to the cremation *ghat* where we are headed. As he pulls away from the *ghat* on the oars, I see a couple of boatmen with their craft still tied up near the shore, right underneath the police station, pulling up a fishing net, albeit on the river side hidden from the police and with no fish caught. When I ask him whether fishing is allowed on the river here, he gives a response that I relished for its delicate exposition of flexible Indian attitudes to the law. 'It's *less* allowed between Assi Ghat and Raj Ghat Bridge', he says. He does not need to tell me that we are indeed between those two points.

As we head downstream to Manikarnika Ghat (probably the best known of the cremation sites), he points to a big house overlooking the river, decorated with two painted statues of tigers at the corners of its balustrade. It is the house of Dom Raja, the current king of the Dom community of undertakers. He is theoretically untouchable, but reputed to be immensely rich because wealthy Hindus pay the Doms, guardians of the sacred flame, to carry out the Hindu funeral rites that are their preserve. Later, on our way back, we climb a steep outside staircase from the river front and bang hopelessly on a locked door, and finally gain access from the landward side, passing a chained bull and a cow, only to find that Dom Raja is sleeping and cannot be woken. His family, breakfasting on the balcony, tell us he finishes work at 5.00 a.m. Those who work for him say he does not do much because he is rich and does not need to. But a journalist who met the Dom Raja in 2015 described this palace as a 'large hovel', and found the Dom Raja, by the name of Sanjit, to be a short swarthy man, 'decrepit and pitiful', who claimed to drink several bottles of whisky a day to help him forget the unbearable stench of rotting corpses. His chest and hands were scarred by burns, although the Dom Raja said that was the result of a gas bottle explosion at a wedding six years previously and nothing to do with the cremations.[4]

At the Manikarnika cremation *ghat*, a few human remains are still smoking amid the ashes of their wooden pyres in the morning light. Nearby there are piles of wood waiting for the next customers and blue-painted scales for weighing the logs. A couple of dogs are fighting on the *ghat* and two men are watching television in a makeshift shelter next to the river. They tell us they dispose of 80 to 150 corpses every day. Indians seem to deal with death in a matter-of-fact way in any case, and for devout Hindus death in holy Varanasi is often not merely accepted but welcomed. 'The weather is all right, not too hot, not too cold, so not many people are dying', says Surendra Prasad, who designs saris by day but volunteers for four hours in the early morning to work at the ghat and its three hospices for the dying. Varanasi, after all, is supposed to be the 'city of 10,000 widows', though the true number of usually destitute women who take refuge here is now closer to 40,000.[5] 'This is my *karma* job. I collect *karma* for the next life. We take care of them, we give them food, medicine, and massage, and when they die we burn them.'

It takes between 200 and 360 kilograms of wood to burn a person, depending on their size, and the body usually takes two and a half hours to burn. I ask where the wood comes from. From a big forest in Madhya Pradesh to the south, he says. In Uttar Pradesh, the wood is finished everywhere. Clad in a white vest and *dhoti*, amid the dogs, cows, and goats wandering around the *ghat*, Prasad explains the various parts of the ritual. Relatives open the mouth of the dead person and pour in Ganga water three times; the oldest son or the husband goes to the barber and is shaved and dons white clothes; the relatives buy the wood—minimum 200 kg, Prasad emphasizes—and then pay the fee to the *ghat* for the eternal flame, which is transferred to them for lighting the pyre in the form of burning grass. The body is taken to the pyre and burned. When only the large bones such as the pelvis and the skull are left, the relatives bring water from the Ganges five times to put out the fire. (He does not say this, but the skull either explodes in the fire or is smashed with a stick by the eldest son or one of the cremation workers to release the soul on its way to heaven.) Such fivefold rituals reflect the five elements of the body, says Prasad: earth, water, fire, air, and 'ether' (or space). 'When the ashes are cold, the body has peace.' After the fifth time of bringing the Ganges water, the relatives throw the earthenware pots over their shoulders and the pots are supposed to break. It means, 'You go to heaven, I'm going home.' Then the ashes are deposited in the river and the workers dive down to retrieve nose-rings and other jewellery.

The *ghat* is a calm, businesslike place. I see a painting of the goddess Kali with her necklace of skulls, and inspect the eternal flame in a rectangular stone basin overlooking the Ganges. A man with glasses sits nearby on a mat with a handwritten ledger for the fees. At one of the level places on the *ghat* where the bodies are burned the pyre is still smoking and roasting hot, although the skull has already shattered and the corpse has been reduced to bone and ashes. It is all very casual and there are a few bits of rubbish strewn around: plastic bags, an old water bottle, cow dung, pieces of glittery cloth, and empty cardboard packets for incense sticks. The Ganges, flowing quietly past the *ghat*, is central to the role of Manikarnika as one of the most revered cremation sites in Hinduism. As I leave, I discover one more way in which the river has been woven into the fabric of life and death for Hindus. Manikarnika means 'earring', for there are several legends about how Parvati, goddess of love and fertility and wife of Shiva, lost her earring here—or possibly hid it to tease her husband. By good fortune, I have arrived at the *ghat* on the day of a festival in Parvati's honour and her image is on display, decked with flowers, at the centre of the *ghat*'s whitewashed tank or water pond. The water in the tank, Prasad assures me, comes direct from Gaumukh, the 'mouth of the cow' that is the glacial Himalayan source of the Ganges. When the water from the tank is emptied into the Ganges, he says, it is possible to see the face of a cow at the bottom.

My last meeting on this visit to Varanasi is with another Brahmin concerned about the fate of the Ganges. He is a Sanskrit scholar called Kameshwar Upadhyay whose religious credentials should make him a natural ally of Modi and the BJP—he was astrologer, he says, to Atal Bihari Vajpayee, the first BJP prime minister—but he is as disappointed with BJP governments as he is with those of the secular Congress. He retired from Banaras Hindu University in 2003 to revive Sanskrit studies and Vedic traditions by setting up a 'scholars' parliament' and has written a book on how to live as a true Hindu. Between 2005 and 2007, says Upadhyay, he launched a movement to clean the Ganges so effective that various non-government organizations and the Vishva Hindu Parishad and parts of the Rashtriya Swayamsevak Sangh (right-wing Hindu groups) attacked his efforts. Why? I ask. 'Because we were hitting on the real, genuine causes [of the river's problems].' And what are those? 'I went around telling people that as a son cannot stop his Mum from meeting the Dad after her periods, nobody has a right to make dams on the river, or restrict her, to prevent her flowing…As a woman is purified by her periods, so the river is purified by its flow.' As we discuss the sex of rivers (most are female, although the Brahmaputra—son of Brahma—and the Indus are exceptions) it becomes clear that the main concern of Upadhyay and other Ganges champions in Varanasi is the water that is taken out of the river for irrigation rather than the pollution that is put into it.

Scientifically, this makes some sense because dilution through increased water flow will reduce the damaging effects of pollution even if it does not eliminate the problem entirely, but Upadhyay's concerns are as much religious as practical. He cites tradition and scripture to assert that while chemicals cannot change a river it is not permitted to restrict the water's flow because that really does kill the river. 'Both Rajiv Gandhi's government and Atal Bihari Vajpayee's government built these dams on the river to produce electricity. They interrupted the whole river', he says. 'According to the tradition of India, you can restrict the sea, but not the river.' Both Gandhi and Vajpayee, he continues, committed the 'sin' of breaching a 1916 agreement reached by the British Raj and 119 *rajas* from along the Ganges, brokered by Madan Mohan Malviya, founder of the university, which said that 'the Ganga should be flowing under the open skies eternally and naturally'. (In fact the agreement, still included today in official regulations, is a rather technical document and a compromise over the damming of the Ganges at Haridwar that guarantees some flow—specifically 1,000 cubic feet per second—past the Haridwar *ghats*.)[6]

'I was Vajpayee's astrologer, but I was so upset by these things that I distanced myself from him', he says. I ask whether Modi has changed things. 'No. I've been watching this since 1998. They keep talking about pollution control. But the problem is not pollution. You are not leaving any water in the river, that's the problem ... Milk the cow only as long as it's giving you milk. Don't make it bleed.' For a devout Hindu, that is a very strong statement. When I ask why Modi has failed to make an impact, he turns his ire on Uma Bharti, the cabinet minister in charge of water and the restoration of the Ganges. 'There is a very good reason for that. The ministry responsible and the minister who leads it have no vision, and no *rishi*-thoughts [the thoughts of a holy sage]. She keeps saying that people would not allow bodies to be thrown into the river. But the Ganga was brought onto earth for that purpose only! What is it that the human body contains that is going to pollute the river?' There is, says Upadhyay, a conspiracy to stifle the river. It is not about the vast sums of money that need to be spent but about the flow of the water. 'We cannot put Ganga water in our mouths now, as our tradition has been', he says. 'The next generations, those who are born in the twenty-first century, would not even know the quality of the water. From 2001 I stopped going to the river—I'm very sad to see the state of it ... One signature from Mr Modi would save the Ganges. You will not need 20,000 crore [$3 billion]. Just let the river flow naturally.'

After so much gloom about the fate of the river in Varanasi, it is a relief to leave the city and find the river still flowing peaceably a short way upstream at Chunar Fort. Here the east-flowing Ganges makes a wide turn to the north to run past Varanasi. Vast sandbanks have been exposed by the falling river in the hot, dry season before the monsoon. On the river's edge next to a dilapidated British cemetery, farmers are tending small irrigated fields of millet and *nenua*, a kind of cucumber. From the high walls of the fort, I can see a few fishermen in wooden boats, storks and plovers feeding in the shallows, and—where the water runs turbulently past a sandbank—two Gangetic dolphins hunting for fish. That always cheers me up, although I am on my way to investigate the nature and extent of the pollution that is poisoning India's holy river.

7

Toxic River

The entire waste water is deadly. It's a toxic cocktail of chemicals ... it's killing the river
—Rakesh Jaiswal, environmental campaigner on the Ganges in Kanpur[1]

Can you stop breathing?
—Reply from A. K. Sinha of the Merchants' Chamber of Uttar Pradesh when asked: 'Can you tell your members to stop polluting the river?'[2]

The first glimpse of an Indian river these days is rarely a pretty sight. The river is likely to be turbid. It may be black and evil-smelling, combining raw sewage with untreated industrial effluents and the occasional floating corpse, human or animal. Its banks are almost certain to be strewn with rubbish, the remains of religious offerings, and the detritus of an emerging consumer society that has yet to work out how to manage its waste. Few rivers, however, are like this near their sources. So the obvious way to understand what we are doing to our rivers is to compare locations upstream and downstream of the pollution: before and after. That is what I did with the Ramganga (the Ganges of the god Ram), one of the tributaries of the Ganges that flows in from the north.

The contrast between the idyllic river upstream and the squalid mess below was even more stark than I had imagined. Guided by Indian campaigners of the World Wide Fund for Nature (WWF), I did beautiful before ugly, which counts as a mistake for anyone trying to remain optimistic about the future of the Ganges. After a long day's drive from Delhi across the densely populated Gangetic plain of Uttar Pradesh, we began to wind into the hills behind the Jim Corbett National Park and finally reached the village of Marchula. From there we were on foot.

We traversed the river on a pedestrian suspension bridge, pulled ourselves across a stream with a pulley system attached to a raft of inner
tubes, and checked into a lodge frequented by birdwatchers.

The only sounds on the upper reaches of the Ramganga are birdsong, the gurgling of the river and the occasional bark of a *sambar*, a
type of large deer. The water is so clear that I can see the golden and
silver *mahseer*—the fish of the Himalayan foothills—from the riverbank. Anil Kumar, a guide and ornithologist from the village of
Bakhroti, which we can see high on a hillside in the distance, points to
tiger footprints, the fibrous droppings of wild elephants, and a pool
where he caught a 68-kilogram catfish two years ago. I jump into the
cool water for a swim—the air by day is still warm in November—and
wash off the grime of the long journey.

By Indian standards, this place is remote and sparsely populated, the
haunt of otters and raptors as well as tigers and deer. We watch a Pallas's
fish eagle hunting in the river, then come across a tiny Hindu shrine
to an unknown god or spirit; it is a small square of stones placed one
on top of the other under a tree and marked by the remains of a few
simple offerings—an open packet of cloves, a discarded box of 'Hari
Krishna' incense. Even here in the hills, I see some pieces of rubbish,
plastic bags, and empty cigarette packets. The next morning, as the sun
rises, we pass a gang of laughing thrushes cackling in the bushes and a
find a few stone houses in a clearing above the river.

Basanti Devi, who says she was born here 'about fifty years ago', has
torn down some branches and leaves off a ficus tree to feed her cattle.
She was widowed at the age of 22 and lives from the animals, a few
vegetables she plants, and the income of her sister's son-in-law, a
teacher. I ask about fish from the river and she at first insists that 'we
don't catch fish'—fishing was banned five years ago—before conced-
ing quietly: 'When guests come, *sometimes* people get fish.' For her, the
wild animals are a menace, in spite of the 800-rupee (about $12) gov-
ernment payout if a cow is killed by a tiger. Development is to be
welcomed, particularly the suspension bridge. An earlier bridge was
washed away, leaving the village isolated. 'We used to have a lot of
fields', she says. 'But now there's nothing. It's because of the wildlife.
We can't even grow vegetables because they come and eat and destroy,
the wild elephants and other animals. The new course of the river has
eaten up our farmland too. Previously there were fewer animals and
they've started to encroach on our land, tigers, elephants, *chital* [spotted

deer], you'll find everything here. I saw a tiger right here at my
house'—she points to the path where we are standing—'two months
back. I can't leave my cattle.'

The descent to the plain is a shock. By Indian standards, Moradabad
is not a particularly large city—just 1 million people—but there is no
sewage treatment and there are scores of paper mills, sugar plants, brass
foundries, and plastics factories nearby that spew waste into the
Ramganga and its tributaries. Downstream of the city centre, the sandy
banks and the exposed riverbed present an apocalyptic scene of filth
and garbage, of dead dogs, plastic bags, *nullahs* (drains) spewing pink
dye, and pigs rootling through the muck. All the while, men with trac-
tors and bullock carts are mining sand for construction, while *dhobis*
(washermen) ply their trade in the dirty water and a boy forlornly casts
his net for fish. Farmers wash their buffaloes. In the Lal Bagh district,
men and women squat in the shallows swirling the waste ash from the
foundries in deep bowls to recover tiny remnants of metal. We had
been told that the panning of incinerated electronic waste is done here
at the dead of night—it is illegal because of the known toxicity of
many of the components—but at least one boy is openly panning his
e-waste in the daylight to extract wire and other valuables.

'When I was young this river was very clean and we could even see
the riverbed,' says Mairaj Uddin, a Moradabad dentist who has become
a Ramganga *mitra* (friend), one of a group of anti-pollution volunteers
formed by WWF-India. As he speaks, someone hurls a plastic bag of
rubbish from the walls of the nearby Ganga Mandir, a Hindu temple
to the river goddess, straight into the river. 'Now it's dead. All the sewage from the city comes into the river. But things should change once
the sewer line is laid . . . And I really hope that I'm going to help make
this river go back to its original state. Maybe I'll be too old to bathe in
it. But I want my children to bathe in it.'

A short distance upstream at Agwanpur, where the river enters
Moradabad, the water is still fairly clear and suitable for fish. But by the
time the Ramganga leaves Moradabad, it has been polluted by untreated
waste, including sewage and chemicals, from twenty-three drains. 'The
quality deteriorates and we can't use the water even for bathing', says
Mohammad Alam, a local WWF project officer who works on rivers.
'We do chemical analysis and there are remarkable differences. The
concentration of heavy metals is very high in the city, and the oxygen
levels are so low that fish cannot survive.' The last time he tested the

water at Agwanpur, levels of dissolved oxygen were 6.5 parts per million. In the city it was as low as 2 ppm, and fish need about 4 ppm to live. Even the planned sewage plant would treat only half the city's waste water.

A few months after I visited Moradabad, researchers from the Centre for Science and Environment, the most prominent of India's environmental non-government organizations, went there to look at the e-waste problem and published an alarming report on the phenomenon. They concluded that a decline in the traditional brass industry—itself a source of pollution for the river—had led to a surge in the informal business of extracting metals from the printed circuit boards found in everything from computers and keyboards to mobile telephones and remote-control devices for televisions. 'E-waste recycling has become a home business in the city, with most members in a family involved in processes right from dismantling to metal recovery', the report said.

Dismantling and recycling activities in Moradabad are carried out mostly in basements or rooftops of houses of people engaged in this business. The work involves hammering dismantled gadgets and motherboards to extract copper, silver and gold from the circuits. Workers burn motherboards that contain heavy metals in open piles which release deadly toxic fumes. Circuit boards are cooked over open flames or in shallow pans, exposing workers to lead fumes. Copper is extracted during this process. Gold is extracted from circuit board chips by acid baths, spewing even more toxic gases into the air. These processes are very hazardous to the environment and human health.[3]

Among the pollutants released are various carcinogens and poisons, including mercury—which was found in samples of Ramganga water at levels eight times higher than the Indian standard. The country has no standards for soil contamination. Indeed, one of the worrying aspects of such recycling operations—whether the concern is human health or river pollution—is how little the government or anyone else knows about them. By one estimate, Moradabad city receives nine tonnes of e-waste a day and half of all the discarded circuit boards in India end up in or near the city for this casual and very dangerous reprocessing. Local officials had no idea how many people were involved in the business, with estimates ranging from 20,000 to hundreds of thousands. 'The analysis of soil samples collected from the banks of the Ramganga showed very high levels of heavy metals, such as zinc, copper, arsenic, chromium, lead and nickel', the CSE concluded.

'The water samples also show the presence of heavy metals such as arsenic and mercury above permissible limits. The test results show that the area is highly contaminated.'

It is easy to blame informal workers for the worst of the pollution, but large factories that pour their untreated or half-treated effluent into the rivers, and farmers using pesticides, are far from blameless in a country where the application of environmental laws is notoriously lax and inspectors can be bought off for a few thousand rupees. At Kashipur, north-east of Moradabad, acres of land by the roadside are carpeted in grey waste from a cluster of pulp and paper mills. The waters of the Dhela river here—where it is joined by the Dhandi—run black and stinking towards its eventual junction with the Ramganga. Scores of black-winged stilts—elegant wading birds with long red legs that are noted for their tolerance of pollution—gather in the shallows. All rivers hunt for lower ground, and the black water from here, along with much of the waste of north India, eventually finds its way into the main stream of the holy Ganges.

Heavy metals are found not just in the Ramganga but also in the Yamuna around Delhi and in the Ganges itself. The effects on human health of absorbing excessive amounts of metals such as mercury, arsenic, lead, and cadmium include cancer, kidney failure, and neuro-logical damage. The truth is that neither villagers nor inhabitants of cities such as Delhi, even foreigners particularly wary of unfamiliar health risks, know much about the dangers of heavy metals in water. And they know even less about the poisons they ingest with their food; in large part that is because there is so little available data in India about the dangers of industrial chemicals and the residues of pesticides and fertilizers finding their way into the food chain. (Delhi-ites have recently spent more time worrying about air pollution than water. The dust and smoke is frequently worse than Beijing's and air filters are the latest consumer goods product to see an explosive growth in sales.)[4] Still, at home in central New Delhi, we always make sure the fruits and vegetables we buy or grow in our backyard are disinfected and then washed in purified water. But we do sometimes wonder what is under the nicely cleaned skin of those cucumbers or papayas or tomatoes or potatoes. We still have no idea whether the vegetables we eat are dan-gerous or not, but our suspicions have deepened since the publication of a study of Delhi's Yamuna River, whose wide flood-plain is the source of many of the city's vegetables when the river is not in spate.

The study by Toxics Link, an environmental research and advocacy group, took water and sediment samples upstream and downstream of Delhi both before and after the monsoon. It found the riverbed to be 'highly contaminated' with carcinogenic and poisonous heavy metals, including lead, cadmium, chromium, mercury, and arsenic—all except the naturally occurring arsenic being largely the product of India's rapid industrialization. 'This is alarming', says Toxic Link's Prashant Rajankar. 'We have found a high amount of heavy metals in samples after Wazirabad [where the Yamuna enters Delhi] and if vegetables are grown in that sediment, plants have the ability to absorb heavy metals and minerals from the sediments.' He goes on: 'These are the most dangerous heavy metals... These are locations where vegetables are normally grown on the bank of the Yamuna River. Many people are dependent on these vegetables also, so contaminants can come to our plates and we can get harmed.'[5]

There are no Indian standards for toxins in sediment, and applying the standards for drinking water instead is of limited value because we do not know how much of each toxin ends up in the plants as they grow, nor how much people ingest in the eating of them. Still, with that proviso, it is clearly a worry that at one point the researchers found sediment with 796 parts per million of chromium and 4.7 ppm of mercury, thousands of times above the international toxicity standards for drinking water. Toxics Link recommended further research into the impact on flora and fauna and a drive to stop polluted water entering the river. 'The study found that the river bed is highly contaminated with the heavy metals, so suitable remedial measures are needed to be taken to decontaminate the river bed.' It is highly unlikely that this last recommendation, involving a gigantic clean-up of the extensive river-bed left exposed by the Yamuna in the dry season, will ever happen.

Heavy metals and other pollutants enter the Yamuna and the Ganges from a multiplicity of sources: sewage, factories, farms, and even the painted religious idols immersed in the rivers. Lead, for example, comes from paint, pesticides, batteries, and glass manufacturing and can cause cognitive impairment in children and peripheral neuropathy (damage to the nervous system with results ranging from a tingling sensation in the feet to organ failure) in adults. Zinc is found in the effluent of electroplating industries, in sewage, and in the offerings placed in the river by Hindus; it causes vomiting, diarrhoea, jaundice, and liver and kidney damage. Nickel from stainless steel manufacturing can be neurotoxic, genotoxic (that is, damaging to the genetic material of cells), and carcinogenic. 'Bioaccumulation of the heavy metals may cause damage to the central nervous system, lungs, kidneys, liver, endocrine glands, and bones', was the verdict of some biochemists on toxins in the Yamuna. 'The prevailing condition of the river is of serious concern, and there is an urgent need to take strict measures to ensure cleansing of the river and prevent further contamination.'[6]

Nor are heavy metals the only chemical dangers. One study of organochlorine pesticides examined vegetables such as radishes, cauliflowers, gourds, and brinjals (otherwise known as eggplants or aubergines) grown in the Delhi region and concluded that the hazards and cancer risks from eating them were 'above the acceptable limit and can be considered as a serious concern for Delhi population'.[7] Vegetable farmers interviewed by an Indian newspaper for an article about these alarming findings were dismissive of the idea that the pesticides they used could be the source of the problem, pointing out that the black and polluted water of the Yamuna that they used to irrigate their crops was likely to be even more toxic. 'Can pesticides harm more than the poisonous Yamuna water?' asked one farmer, not unreasonably. 'How can vegetables make you sick? We wash them before they are sold', said another. 'It's the government that has rendered this river poisonous', insisted a third. 'That's the water that comes in our taps and we use on our crops. How can anything be more poisonous than that water?'[8]

The same pollution pattern as in the Ramganga and the Yamuna—cleaner water upstream, chemical and bacterial filth downstream—is repeated around all the great pilgrimage sites and cities along the Ganges and many of its tributaries—and the 'distributaries' near the mouth where the river fans out into the multiple streams of the delta as it reaches the sea. In Varanasi, scientists Anand Singh and Jitendra Pandey at the city's Banaras Hindu University (BHU) have investigated heavy metals in the main stream of the Ganges. They found concentrations increasing steadily as they moved downstream past Varanasi, suggesting that its own waste was the main contributor. After the city, concentrations of both lead and cadmium were typically about three times the World Health Organisation's 'maximum admissible concentrations'. Pandey says most of the city's people use the river water. 'Then it is a health concern directly to human beings', because cadmium and lead can lead to birth defects and accumulate in the body. 'Many toxic manifestations are related with these. They can interfere with the synthesis of haemoglobin [which allows the blood to pick up oxygen] and damage the functioning of the kidneys.' Pandey, who has established that heavy metals are deposited in the river from air pollution as well as through the drains, is doing more research on the levels of heavy metals in the Ganges and their effect on health. 'They are serious for human health, directly through drinking the water and through eating fish and so on', he says.[9]

Scarcely a week goes by without someone complaining of the effects of pollution in one of India's rivers, or a judicial court—often the National Green Tribunal (NGT), a specialized body established in 2010 to deal with environmental cases—ordering that the pollution be stopped. Yet such pleas are usually based on incomplete data about the problem, and anti-pollution orders are rarely enforced. In early 2016, environmentalists complained about the pollution risks of a vast culture festival on the Yamuna floodplain in Delhi organized by the guru Sri Sri Ravi Shankar. Preparations for the event involved the clearing of hundreds of acres of land and the erection of a large stage, and an NGT committee recommended a fine of 1.2 billion rupees—about 18 million dollars—for Ravi Shankar's Art of Living Foundation, with the money to be used for the 'entire ecological restoration' of the area. Supporters of the event, which was attended among others by Narendra Modi, the prime minister, not only insisted that the event was eco-friendly but also pointed out that the river and its banks were already so heavily contaminated with pollution that a few million people attending a three-day event was hardly likely to make a difference. In the end, the day before the three-day festival was due to start, the NGT imposed a fine on the organizers of just 50 million rupees or $750,000 and also imposed small fines on the Delhi Development Authority and the Delhi Pollution Control Committee for lapses in the way they issued the necessary clearances. 'Look at the Yamuna. It is clean, green and calm', said M. Venkaiah Naidu, minister for urban development, and one of several senior government figures to attend. 'Only some minds are polluted. I hope Guru-ji's teachings purify them.' To call the Yamuna in Delhi 'clean' at the height of the dry season is more than absurd, since the contents of the river consist almost entirely of raw sewage at that time of year.[10]

Most, but not all, of the pollution is man-made. It has been known for years that there are alarmingly high rates of certain cancers in the Gangetic plain. Women in Delhi show the highest rates of gall bladder cancer in the world. Indian scientists hesitate to say which heavy metals, if any, are the cause, although a preliminary Indo-Japanese joint study found 'significantly high' levels of chromium, lead, arsenic, and zinc in the cancerous gall bladder tissues of Indian samples when compared with those of Japanese sufferers. What is now better understood is a vast and continuing tragedy of arsenic poisoning in the lower Ganges, in both India and Bangladesh, in what one scientific paper describes as 'the biggest case of mass poisoning in history'.[11]

For once, it is not manufacturing or any other kind of human intervention that first puts the toxic heavy metal in the water. The arsenic is naturally occurring and traces of it have been washed down for centuries with the silt from the Himalayas into the Ganges basin, where it accumulates and descends into the groundwater. A similar process occurs in other countries and continents, but the Ganges is particularly badly affected. What is more, a well-intended (and successful) campaign to save Bangladeshis from the water-borne diseases carried in surface water led to the drilling of millions of boreholes for groundwater, which exposed people to the longer-term dangers of arsenic poisoning. More than 100 million people in Bangladesh and India, and millions of farm animals, are at risk, and the dangers are exacerbated by the extensive use of pumped groundwater for the irrigation of fields. 'This means that arsenic has begun to seep into the crops and into the food chain and could trigger a large scale environmental tragedy, fatally affecting future generations', wrote a group of environmental scientists and cancer researchers in one study published in 2013.

Over twenty-five years, the researchers analysed more than 170,000 water samples from the ubiquitous metal hand pumps that bring up water from tube wells in the Indian subcontinent, and found that half of the samples in badly affected districts contained arsenic above the limit set by the World Health Organisation. Of 100,731 villagers screened, 10,113—about one-tenth—had different sorts of arsenic-related skin lesions. The arsenic also triggered other cancers and problems in childbirth, including spontaneous abortions and stillborn or underweight babies. The authors of the study said 'we can say with certitude that vast tracts of land in many Indian states situated on the Ganga-Brahmaputra plains (Uttar Pradesh, Bihar, Jharkhand, West Bengal, Assam and some of the North Eastern hill states) and Bangladesh in the Padma [Ganges]-Meghna-Brahmaputra plains are

affected by deadly arsenic contamination'. Those at risk, they concluded, 'are facing a slow death and millions more will be affected soon
as groundwater arsenic contamination is deepening and spreading its
tentacles wider'.

The Indian authorities, including the central government and those
of the twenty-nine states, and regulators such as the Central Pollution
Control Board (CPCB) and its state affiliates, are remarkably ineffective
at monitoring pollutants—whether natural or generated by humans—
let alone doing anything to stop them. Even for the main stem of the
Ganges, there is little information about the scale of the crisis involving industrial effluents. The CPCB merely mentions 764 'grossly polluting industries' and says how much wastewater they produce—but
not what is in it.

Still, ask any Indian, expert or not, about the pollution of the Ganges
and they are almost certain to mention the tanneries of Kanpur as a
prime offender. The toxic effluents from the 400 or so tanneries of the
industrial city once known as the Manchester of India have come to
represent everything that is wicked about uncaring industrialists and
incompetent regulators. There is, furthermore, a highly sensitive polit-
ical-religious twist to the story of this pollution: the owners of the
tanneries are Muslim. There should be no surprise about that. Muslims
have long performed tasks involving the disposal of cattle and the working of leather that are highly distasteful to cow-worshipping Hindus.
But it is sometimes convenient for Hindus—especially Hindu industrialists who own other kinds of polluting factories—to be able to
blame members of the Muslim minority for the sullying of their sacred
river. At the same time, the politicians of Uttar Pradesh, rarely known
for their ethical sensibilities or green credentials, have been eager to
court the state's important Muslim voters by going easy on the enforcement of environmental restrictions for Kanpur's tanneries, even at the
expense of the ecological health of the Ganges.

After the 2013 Kumbh Mela, during which the tanneries were
closed to spare the bathers downstream in Allahabad, I drove straight
to Kanpur to investigate. Known to the British as Cawnpore, Kanpur
is a very large industrial centre, and I started passing factories—some
decrepit, some modern—more than 60 kilometres from the centre.
Once there, I met Rakesh Jaiswal, a mild-mannered but determined
environmentalist who runs a non-government organization called Eco
Friends and has been trying to clean up the Ganges for more than two

decades. It was only later, when I started reading more about the river and the journeys adventurers have made along it, that I realized he was one of the few people in Kanpur, or anywhere along the river's length, who care enough about its fate to try to do something about it. In fact, it is extraordinary that among the hundreds of millions of inhabitants of north India, the same characters—a water engineer turned activist in Haridwar, an environmentalist in Kanpur, a Hindu priest in Varanasi, a zoologist in Patna, and a river scientist in Calcutta—feature repeatedly in the modern non-fiction literature of the Ganges. Saving the Ganges is not a majority pursuit, but the enthusiasm of a tiny number of specialists.

There is little that Jaiswal does not know about pollution, tannery effluents, and the inadequacies of waste-water treatment in Kanpur, and he has kept open his lines of communication with the authorities as well as with those tannery owners who are willing to make an effort to cut pollution. A few years back he helped the Blacksmith Institute, a New York-based non-profit group that tackles pollution and recently renamed itself Pure Earth, to protect a Kanpur community of 30,000 from hexavalent chromium (Cr VI) in their groundwater. Known to cause lung cancer, liver failure, and premature dementia, Cr VI had been found at a concentration 124 times the Indian government limit, and the settlement of Noraiakheda had developed 'right on top' of a plume of Cr VI emitted by toxic sludge from an old chemical plant that had supported the tanneries, according to Blacksmith. The group dug new wells and injected a substance into the groundwater that proved successful for 'chemical remediation' of the site, while installing new pumps to supply the community with safe drinking water.[12]

Jaiswal led me to the river bank next to a sewer outfall from the tannery district and told me what was going on. 'The entire waste water is deadly. It's a toxic cocktail of chemicals', he said. 'I have seen governments struggling for the last twenty-five years to deal with tannery pollution and other pollution. In a way it's killing the river.' The tanneries, whose waste includes dyes, salts, acids, and the carcinogenic chromium, often fail to carry out primary treatment of their waste and in any case produce too much for the central plant to handle. 'This chromium containing chemical is really very toxic. It's a heavy metal and it's a known carcinogen . . . It affects the river water quality and the ecology of the river and the flora and fauna of the river, and also people who use the water directly.' I asked about the kinds of problems

suffered by the farmers downstream, where land is irrigated with a
mixture of sewage and treated tannery waste water. 'Various kinds of
rashes, boils, pustules, rotten nails, and even numbness in the limbs', he
replied.

Jaiswal went on to explain the halting efforts to manage the toxic
waste from the tanneries over the years. A 'common effluent treatment
plant' with a theoretical capacity of 36 million litres per day was finally
commissioned in 1994 to manage waste water from all the tanneries
concentrated in the Jajmau area of Kanpur next to the Ganges. Before
sending its waste to the plant, each tannery is supposed to segregate
water containing chromium and recover most of the heavy metal, and
do a basic clean-up of the remaining waste water in a 'primary effluent
treatment plant'. For years, few of the factories segregated the chromium, and although most of them do have primary treatment plants
they do not always want to bear the expense of actually running them,
so they sometimes send their waste straight into the drain or untreated
to the common, secondary treatment plant.

The official limit for chromium waste content going to the secondary plant is 2 milligrams per litre, but Jaiswal said the actual amount
was typically 100–150 mg/l, which the common treatment plant was
unable to manage. Only about a third of the tannery effluent reached
the secondary treatment plant, he added, and in any case the plant
would be unable to cope with all the waste because the number of
tanneries had more than doubled from the 170 that existed when it
was built. 'It's functioning, but there's no adequate treatment,' was
Jaiswal's conclusion. He said organizations such as his could put pressure on the tanneries, especially those that export, by monitoring the
water and publishing the results, but that would be expensive and in
any case there was no need for scientific testing to know that the
Ganges was heavily polluted by tannery and other waste. 'You can see
it with your naked eyes', he said, pointing at the drain. 'You can smell.'

We certainly can. In spite of all the layers of legislation, bureaucracy,
and inspections, the tannery industry—like many others in India—is
in reality very poorly regulated if it can be said to be regulated at all.[13]
On my first visit to Kanpur, Jaiswal took me to the tannery district
through scenes that evoked images of Dickensian Britain. Men with
mule-drawn carts were ferrying hides to and fro. Squatting in the yard
of a small, artisanal tannery, a young man with no protective gear
painted chemicals onto the hides with a brush. Women were washing

clothes on the banks of a large open drain, where three pigs were snuffling in the turbid black water of tannery waste and sewage. One side
of the foetid stream was a garbage dump compacted by decades of use.
Ramshackle huts and houses hung over the creek.

Many of those who live there either work in the tanneries or have
relatives who do, but even they resent the stench coming from the
water. 'It's harmful. The gas comes out', complained Mohammed
Shamim, a 70-year-old man wearing flip-flops, black trousers, and a
dirty white shirt. He has six children. 'It should be stopped. We worry
about it, but who will listen to us? This is poison and it really harms
all of us.' Later that day we met a French photographer who informed
us that he has seen two corpses in the river at the dam upstream built
for Kanpur's drinking water. But the likely pollution from two dead
bodies seems paltry when compared with the toxic waste from the
tanneries.[14]

Not much in the streets seemed to have changed when I went back
to the Jajmau tannery district three years later: the same vile *nullahs*,
the same mules and carts, barrels of chemicals stacked in the streets,
and rubble and offcuts of buffalo-hide heaped against the walls of the
occasional collapsed building, as though the district has been damaged
in a bombing raid. Outside each large tannery is a forlorn signboard
headlined 'Notice of hazardous chemicals and waste' where details of
dangerous products are supposed to be listed by the proprietors. This
time, however, I was armed with an invitation to visit one of the factories whose owners have opted for a policy of social and environmental
responsibility. They have decided to tackle the pollution problem for
the good of the community, their employees, and the Ganges. They also
want to keep their industry alive and exporting to a world increasingly
concerned about sustainability and ethics.

Imran Siddiqui and the Super Tannery operation he runs are unusual
in several respects. He seems like a typically quiet and efficient manager in the Indian private sector, but he serves cappuccino coffee
instead of the sweet, spicy *chai* favoured in most Indian offices. And the
Amin family that founded the company in 1953, he says, have always
been first in line to adopt green technology, building the first tannery
effluent treatment plant in Uttar Pradesh or neighbouring states back
in 1984, and the first chrome recovery system less than ten years later.
At the moment they are demolishing old buildings and investing in
new, more efficient structures and machinery and plan to ensure full

segregation of their waste water within a year. The ultimate aim is to recycle so much water that no effluent needs to leave the plant at all, which would save the company's owners from accusations that they are polluting the Ganges.

We are soon joined by two more tannery owners and treated to a history lesson. Kanpur was a centre for the indigo trade before the blue dye was largely replaced by synthetic versions in the late nineteenth century, according to Naiyer Jamal, a partner in Makhdoom Tanning Industries. At the same time, the city became a big centre for the leather industry under the British because it was an important military supply point for north India. The East India Company's troops needed numerous pieces of leather equipment, including saddles for horses and boots for the soldiers. The first government factory began operations in 1869 and was an important supplier of materiel during the First World War.[15] Cooper Allen & Co., founded in 1880, was reputedly the world's largest leather company, and Kanpur today is still the centre for independent India's leather business, specializing in saddlery and army boots.

The leather industry has grown rapidly since independence, along with India's fast-expanding population. Super Tannery, for example, has three shoe factories and a belt factory and makes safety shoes for the army, the police, and miners. It has three tanneries: the one we are visiting processes 750 hides a day (buffalo hides, not the hides of holy cows, Siddiqui emphasizes) with chemicals, but the company also has a unit that uses vegetable products for the operation—the leather finds a market among consumers concerned about pollution—and a goat skin tannery in Unnao. It is clear that one problem for the Ganges is the sheer scale of the tanning business in modern India. Jamal quotes a British report as saying that there were 2,800 families involved in the leather business in 1840, and only about seven or eight industrial tanneries three years after independence in 1950. That grew to 175 in 1984 and 368 today (the widely used round number of 400, he says, is wrong because several tanneries have closed).[16]

Serious industrial pollution of the Ganges, then, began in the days of the British, but efforts to manage the dangerous effluents have failed since then to keep pace with the growth of the leather industry. Few of the tannery owners will say so publicly, but even those who want to run clean businesses are hampered by the inefficiency of the local authorities and the nightmarish bureaucracy of the ten different government departments with which they are supposed to deal. Corruption is a problem, too, with pumping equipment sometimes lying idle during power cuts because state employees have taken the diesel stored for back-up generators and sold it on the black market, leaving untreated waste pouring into India's rivers.

The common effluent treatment plant in Kanpur—built with Dutch government money and a contribution from the tanneries and jointly funded now by the tanneries and the Uttar Pradesh government—is inefficient at the best of times because it receives more chromium than it can handle from tanneries that fail to carry out primary waste treatment. Even when there is electricity, the pumps are not powerful enough to send more than about a third of the tannery waste for mixing with municipal sewage and processing. Again, the result is that the tannery waste goes straight into the Ganges. A plan for an upgrade of the treatment plant—with the research work financed by the tanneries—has been under discussion for seven years with no sign of a decision. As the owner of one of Kanpur's smaller tanneries told me: 'Even if the waste is treated, it's only when pressure is applied by the CPCB [the Central Pollution Control Board].'

That is not the only complaint of the Muslim tannery owners. They also say the combination of their minority religion and the much publicized dangers of tannery waste make them an easy target for pollution campaigners, government busybodies, and Hindu nationalist politicians. 'In Kanpur there are 28,000 industries', says Siddiqui. 'Dyeing, textiles, electro-plating, pharmaceuticals, paint, automotive, goldsmiths—they release a lot of sodium cyanide—why are the tanneries only blamed?' He points out that other industries elsewhere in Kanpur have turned the Pandu River, a tributary of the Ganges, into a polluted 'big drain'. Jamal says wryly that people reflexively complain about the effects of the tanneries on the river water they use—even when they live upstream of the Kanpur tanneries and cannot possibly be directly affected. In a rather elaborate and roundabout narrative involving a history of animal sacrifices, he explains without actually saying so directly that Muslims are persecuted because they are vulnerable, an easy target. 'People have traditionally sacrificed animals', he concludes obliquely. 'The king of all animals is the lion, but no one sacrifices a lion because they fight. So it is the goat that is sacrificed.'

Politics, however, is a two-way street. While it is true that Hindu politicians might be tempted to focus disproportionately on the pollution generated by Muslim industrialists, all politicians in Uttar Pradesh, including the Yadav family that was in power in 2016, are equally keen to court the state's significant bloc of Muslim voters. About a fifth of Kanpur's inhabitants are Muslim, and more than 100,000 of them are estimated to work in tanneries and leather factories and workshops.

At the central government in New Delhi, Shashi Shekhar, secretary at the Water Ministry, did not deny when I interviewed him that industries other than leather are also big polluters. They include pulp and paper factories, distilleries, and sugar mills. State governments had sometimes obstructed rather than contributed to the clean-up and the State Pollution Control Boards—which are meant to be the main regulators and monitors of pollution on the ground—were 'steeped in corruption'. Tanneries, nevertheless, remained the big pollution problem. 'That's my challenge. The most toxic pollution is this', Shekhar said. 'They have remained outlaws so far.' Shekhar gave one example of how corruption works at the SPCB, explaining that the board gives consent for factories to process a certain number of hides but looks the other way when these limits are exceeded. Most tanning, in short, is illegal but is carried out with the full support of the SPCB.

As for Akhilesh Yadav, who headed the Uttar Pradesh state government, and state ministers of the time such as Azam Khan, an outspoken Muslim politician: 'They pamper Muslims, so we did not get adequate support from the government. What we want is zero liquid discharge from the tanneries.'

The depressing truth is that tannery waste continues to poison the Ganges even though it would be neither impossible nor particularly expensive to curb it. A robustly enforced pollution control programme might even save the tanneries some money by improving their efficiency (in water use, for example) and it would certainly save the industry's reputation in the outside world. Shekhar said the government was willing to build a new common effluent treatment plant costing 8 billion rupees—about $120 million—while each tannery would have to have in-house chromium and solid-waste recovery systems and would buy back treated water from the common treatment plant to finance its maintenance. All this, he said, would increase the average cost of a leather belt by just 90 *paise* (less than one rupee, or about one US cent), a pair of shoes by just 7 rupees, and a horse saddle by 15 rupees. Shoppers, furthermore, would have the satisfaction of seeing the tag that explained how the sustainable product they had bought was saving the Ganges.[17]

Kanpur's residents, whether Hindu or Muslim, are hardly likely to object, since they all depend on the Ganges for the water they use for washing, drinking, and religious ablutions. Siddiqui reminded me that Muslims ritually clean their hands, feet, and face before prayer. 'People have this concept in their minds that we don't care about Ganga', he said. '[But] it's a belief of our religion that the cleaning of your body you have to do in a very perfect way. So for us Ganga is also very important.' About an hour later, I was speaking to some Hindu businessmen on the other side of town and they expressed similar thoughts, agreeing at the same time that cement plants and industries other than leather were also polluting the Ganges. 'Water is needed by Hindus, Muslims, and any other religion', said A. K. Sinha, secretary of the Merchants' Chamber of Uttar Pradesh. 'Water is essential, that's why it's been converted into the spiritual.' So, I ventured, can you tell your members to stop polluting the river? 'Can you stop breathing?' he replied. That dispiriting response suggests it will take many years for India to grasp the nettle of industrial and chemical pollution.

Dealing with sewage is easier than curbing toxic waste or the pesticides and fertilizers that enter the Ganges along most of its length. Or rather it should be. After all, the effects of poor sanitation are more immediately visible than those of industrial toxins and carcinogens: hundreds of thousands of babies and children die each year from diarrhoea, many of them in the Ganges basin. At the start of his election campaign to become prime minister, Narendra Modi confounded some of his Hindu nationalist supporters by cleverly stealing a line from Jairam Ramesh (then minister of rural development in the Congress government) on the need for 'toilets before temples'.[18] In his first speech on Independence Day when prime ministers address the nation from the walls of the seventeenth-century Red Fort in Delhi, Modi played down his background as a Hindu religious activist and emphasized the need for economic modernization and social change. He lamented female foeticide, violence against women in India's traditional societies, and the unsanitary practice of defecating in the open in a country where fewer than half of the inhabitants use toilets, and said the government was targeting sanitation for all in ten years. 'I don't know if people will appreciate my talking about dirt and toilets from the Red Fort but I come from a poor family. I have seen poverty and the attempt to give dignity to the poor starts from there', he said. Shekhar Gupta, editor-in-chief of *India Today*, said presciently at the time that although Modi had focused on modern, quality-of-life concerns such as manufacturing, gender equality, and toilets, 'the challenge for him is to live up to his words, because he is promising a lot'.[19]

So it has proved. Two years after Modi's speech, surprisingly little had been achieved. At a conference on water in New Delhi, I heard a senior water official[20] lay out the government's ambitious plans for cleaning the polluted river by treating every drop of sewage from 118 towns and cleaning the toxic effluent from 764 factories. That was a wonderful presentation, I told him afterwards, but previous governments had launched similar projects in the 1980s and 1990s, and little had been achieved. Had anyone actually laid any concrete for a single sewage plant? The official seemed almost offended by the idea that plans should be acted upon. 'It's going to be quite a huge challenge', he responded. 'They are very old cities and laying sewers is going to take a lot of time.'[21]

Anyone who can read—or use their eyes and nose—knows that India has a big problem with sewage. At every major city along the Ganges or its tributaries, the same pattern is repeated—cleaner water above the towns, filth below. Faecal contamination is 'off the charts, ridiculously high', says one World Bank official.[22] Take Delhi. At its worst—according to the 2011 water quality statistics published by the Central Pollution Control Board (CPCB)—the Yamuna's water at Okhla contains 1.1 billion faecal coliform bacteria per 100 millilitres, nearly half a million times the (Indian) recommended bathing limit of 2,500. The reason is clear. Half of India's 1.3 billion inhabitants lack toilets; if they have them, they may not be connected to drains; if they are, there may be no sewage treatment plant; and if there is, it may not be working. The CPCB says only one-tenth of the sewage produced along the main stream of the Ganges is treated at all.

The lack of action is all the more surprising because construction of sewers and sewage plants would provide jobs to some of the hundreds of millions of unemployed or under-employed people in India's interior—and Modi urgently needs to create jobs to fulfil the aspirations of the young Indians who voted him into power in 2014. Modi's BJP, having swept to victory in the so-called 'cow-belt' states of Uttar Pradesh and Bihar in that general election, suffered a crushing defeat in Bihar's state election only 18 months later, in part because of the perceived failure of his central government to achieve its development goals. I visited Bihar during that election and found widespread disenchantment, not least because of the unchanged and filthy state of the Ganges in the capital Patna. Before heading to an election rally to see Nitish Kumar (a politician who had fallen out with his former allies in the BJP and was re-elected in 2015 as chief minister of Bihar), we went to the riverbank.

It is just after dawn and hundreds of Hindu worshippers are surging through a holiday market to pay their annual homage to the goddess Durga—one of whose incarnations is the dark destroyer Kali—at a riverside temple. Some immerse themselves in the river and perform elaborate *pujas*, or prayer ceremonies, with brass pots filled with the holy water. One man, blowing a conch-horn, has brought an entire banana plant, decorated with green coconuts and representing the wife of the elephant-headed god Ganesha. Through loudspeakers, temple managers urge the crowds at the Kali Ghat to refrain from the traditional practice of throwing offerings into the river. A slogan on the wall of a hut tells them to keep the Ganges clean by using bags of biodegradable paper, jute, or cloth. 'Save the Ganges, Save the Country', says a poster.

Yet the water flowing downstream from Patna seems as filthy as ever, bubbling with raw sewage and dotted with floating plastic. 'All the filth of this town is coming in. There are so many drains which are connected with the Ganges', says Krishnanand Srivastava, a wizened 88-year-old former government official who has just bathed in the Ganges at the nearby Krishna Ghat and is performing a prayer ceremony for his recently deceased wife. 'The Ganges is not as clean as it should be. This government says it will keep it sacred, but it has not been possible as yet.' Shyam Rajak, a minister in the Bihar state government and an opponent of Mr Modi and the BJP, is more scathing. 'The campaign to clean the river was just a publicity stunt', he says. 'There was no vision and the central government has not come up with any plan.'

R. K. Sinha, zoology professor at Patna University and an expert on the threatened Gangetic dolphins that can be seen fishing amid the garbage near the city, seems to agree. 'Nothing much has changed since the Modi government came', he says. For the past two-and-a-half years, according to Sinha, neither his university nor other institutions have even been reimbursed for their contracted work to monitor pollutants in the river and the performance of the few sewage plants still operational. 'Nobody's happy with the work on the Ganga', he says. 'Probably it's going to be a failure of the Modi regime ... In the last thirty years, not even a single drain in Patna has been completely intercepted and diverted away from the Ganga, and they have spent several *crores* [tens of millions] of rupees.' Sewage pumping stations have not been maintained.

In private, Modi has expressed shock at the superficial nature of suggestions for beautifying the Ganges that officials thought would please him, including decorations and new lights in Varanasi. His advisers, furthermore, said in late 2015 that tenders would be issued for some new sewage treatment plants in the coming months, with the focus on demonstration projects in Varanasi, in Uttar Pradesh, as well as the states of Jharkhand and Uttarakhand—although not in Bihar. 'You cannot clean the Ganges just in Bihar', the BJP's Sanjay Mayukh told me in Patna in the midst of the state election campaign. 'There are many cities on its banks. The previous government didn't even think about any of these issues. Not much was done previously and it's not going to happen overnight, [but] the cleaning of the Ganges is on ... At least it's got into the public discourse and that will lead to something.'[23]

There is truth in these excuses. In trying to improve sanitation Modi faces the immense and thankless task of investing in unromantic public sewage works (and convincing the twenty-nine states to do the same) while persuading people to stop defecating outdoors as they have done since the first humans walked the Gangetic plain. Drive across Uttar Pradesh in the early morning and you will see dozens, hundreds, thousands—it depends how far you drive—of men and women squatting in the fields to relieve themselves.

Previous campaigns to build toilets have been abject failures, either because the toilets were not built (the money was stolen) or because they were not used or maintained. On one of my first reporting trips outside Delhi after I arrived in India in 2012 I took a colleague to investigate the so-called 'manual scavengers' who still—in defiance of hygiene and the law—collect faeces from people's houses in some of the many urban areas where there are no flushing toilets or sewage systems. In Budaun, Uttar Pradesh, we met Parmeshwari, a 60-year-old widow, who explained her job to us. A Balmiki—a 'sweeper' categorized as Dalit, the out-of-caste group previously known as untouchables—she is one of hundreds of thousands who clean out primitive toilets by hand and brush, collect the waste in baskets, take it in handcarts, and dump it outside the towns and villages—in spite of a 1993 law that bans the traditional practice. A ban, of course, is not much good if there are no sewers and no alternative way of disposing of waste. So in Budaun's Muslim district of Navada, where residents typically defecate on the cement floor of a fly-infested cubicle separated from the rest of the crowded home by a curtain, she and her fellow Balmikis pass by each day, lift the metal flaps in the street that give access to the stinking privies, scoop up the waste and take it away.

The trip, though, turned out to be memorable not merely because of the manual scavengers (whose continued work is an open secret in India) but because it exposed the institutionalized corruption that undermines sanitation programmes in north India whatever the complexion of the national government. In 2012, the government was a Congress-led alliance, and shortly before we went to Budaun, Jairam Ramesh, the minister whose 'toilets before temples' idea had been borrowed by Modi, had launched yet another hygiene drive. 'India's sanitation challenge, especially in rural India, remains humungous', he said. Ramesh said some 400,000–500,000 children under the age of 5 died each year from diarrhoea in India, 'largely caused by unhygienic practices including improper disposal of human excreta... Cleanliness is more important than godliness in this country.' Ramesh said the sanitation budget had been nearly doubled to $675 million for that financial year. The government also drafted yet another law to abolish the job of manual scavenger, this time with the threat of one-year jail terms for anyone who employed one, while the Supreme Court ordered that all schools should be provided with basic toilet facilities within six months.

It was mostly just rhetoric, and was especially ineffective in Uttar Pradesh. For the ten years up to 2011, the Uttar Pradesh government had dutifully reported steadily rising access to latrines in rural areas with the help of $600 million in public funds under the 'Total Sanitation Campaign'. Households with access to toilets officially increased from 19.23 per cent of the total in 2001 to 82.47 per cent a decade later. With Budaun having been in the past a centre for polio—polio is now officially eradicated in India—this looked like good news. But the reality was very different: the independently performed 2011 national census showed 21.8 per cent of Uttar Pradesh households had toilets—hardly any improvement at all in a decade. Over-reporting of success was rampant across India, but in Uttar Pradesh it was extreme. 'Corruption is institutionalized', one frustrated Indian aid worker in the state told us. (He did not want his name used for fear of retaliation.) 'The moment they pass over the money, they count the job as done. So another ten-year programme has been lost... We found sanitation conditions are quite appalling.' Uttar Pradesh state officials did not return our calls when asked for comment on the missing toilet funds.

There are occasional bright spots in a landscape dominated by corruption and bureaucratic inertia. In the farming village of Urulia, near Budaun, most homes used to have the typical unhygienic 'dry' toilets serviced by manual scavengers. Today—thanks to an active district administration and help from Unicef—they all have lavatories that are flushed with water and connected to underground septic tanks or 'leach pits'. 'Now diarrhoea is reduced, cholera is [under] control, and there are fewer flies', says Zakir Ali, an unemployed householder and member of the village's health and sanitation committee. 'Before we had to depend on someone [to clean] and if they did not turn up for three days there would be a lot of maintenance.' Twenty families of manual scavengers have lost their livelihoods and moved to town to find more conventional sweeping jobs. 'We're very happy', says one of Mr Ali's neighbours. 'Before there were too many flies—and bad smells.'[24]

At a presentation in May 2016 to celebrate two years of the achievements of the Modi government, Prakash Javadekar, India's minister of state for environment, forest, and climate change, announced that new sewage treatment operations had started in Maharashtra and Punjab, and more had been approved under a national river conservation plan.[25] He also boasted about the enforcement of effluent controls on the Ganges and made the remarkable claim that industrial pollution of the river had been cut by a third. His claim will be examined in a later chapter on river clean-ups, but even Javadekar accepted sadly that seventy years after independence, nearly nine-tenths of India's sewage still went untreated. India has barely begun to deal with the backlog of unbuilt and abandoned sewage plants, let alone install new capacity to cope with its fast-growing population.

It turns out, furthermore, that the river water contains not only industrial toxins and harmful bacteria, but something even more ominous: bacterial genes exposing water-users to the risk of infections that resist modern antibiotics. These bacterial infections are popularly known as superbugs.

8

Superbug River

It would be hard to culture [bacteria from] river water in India and not find antibiotic resistance genes.

—Ramanan Laxminarayan of the Public Health Foundation of India[1]

Now, close to 100 percent of the babies referred to us have multidrug resistant infections. It's scary.

—Neelam Kler, a doctor and chairwoman of the department of neonatology at New Delhi's Sir Ganga Ram Hospital[2]

India [is] a perfect system for the spread of antibiotic resistance.

—David Livermore, professor of medical microbiology[3]

It is no secret that visitors to India and other countries in south Asia are frequent victims of stomach bugs—jokingly described as 'Delhi belly'. We also know that the immediate cause of the sometimes violent vomiting and diarrhoea that results is poor hygiene. Half of India's 1.3 billion people have no access to even primitive toilets, they defecate in the open, and infections often find their way into food and water; in fact little of the sewage generated by those who do have toilets is treated in any case; that waste, too, ends up in the Ganges and other waterways. One of my favourite illustrations of the dangers of poor hygiene comes from Atul Gawande, the Indian–American surgeon and writer. He describes in *Being Mortal*—his best-selling book on ageing and death—how he came to Varanasi to commit his father's ashes to the Ganges in keeping with Hindu tradition. Since he is a doctor, and since he knew both the ritual actions he would have to perform and the unhygienic state of the river, he carefully dosed himself with antibiotics, hoping to avoid illness from the three spoonfuls of bacteria-filled river water he was made to drink by the *pandit* presiding over the ceremony. Instead, he caught Giardia, a parasitic infection not susceptible to his precautionary antibiotics.[4]

What few visitors or residents know, however, is that by travelling or living in India they are also liable to pick up a recently discovered bacterial gene that can make various diseases highly resistant to antibiotic drugs. I stumbled upon reports of this gene—of which the first version is known to scientists as bla_{NDM-1} and codes for a defence protein called New Delhi metallo-beta-lactamase (NDM-1)—while I was researching the 'normal' pollutants such as sewage and industrial waste that sully the Ganges and its tributaries. 'It only takes a short visit and exposure to acquire such genes in your gut', I was told by David Graham, a Canadian environmental engineering professor at the UK's Newcastle University, who has studied NDM-1 in India. 'I'm pretty confident I now carry the gene.' Not surprisingly, he was confident that after four years of living and travelling across south Asia I would be a carrier too.[5]

My belated realization about the significance of bla_{NDM-1} for myself, my family, and for anyone in India coincided with a global upsurge of concern about the spread of antimicrobial resistance and so-called 'superbugs'. In 2014, British prime minister David Cameron recruited Jim O'Neill, the former Goldman Sachs chief economist, to chair a review into what seemed to be a growing international medical crisis. The conclusions reached in December of that year by O'Neill—who is better known among investment experts for having invented the Bric acronym for the big emerging economies of Brazil, Russia, India and China—were alarming. A continued rise in microbial resistance to drugs for treating pneumonia, tuberculosis (TB), malaria, HIV, and other diseases would lead by 2050 to at least 10 million people dying every year. That would make it a bigger cause of death than cancer is today. It would also cut global gross domestic product by between 2 and 3.5 per cent, costing the world up to $100 trillion. Although some medical experts think he may have overstated the likely death toll,[6] this is not some theoretical danger that lies in the future. Many of us have friends or relatives who have been hospitalized with infections that are hard to treat because they are resistant to so many classes of antibiotics. The O'Neill report estimated that 700,000 deaths a year worldwide could already be attributed to drug resistance today, compared with

100,000–120,000 from cholera, 60,000 from tetanus, and 1.2 million
in road accidents. The review said:

[B]acteria and other pathogens have always evolved so that they can resist the
new drugs that medicine has used to combat them. Resistance has increasingly
become a problem in recent years because the pace at which we are discovering novel antibiotics has slowed drastically, while antibiotic use is rising. And
it is not just a problem confined to bacteria, but all microbes that have the
potential to mutate and render our drugs ineffective. The great strides forward
made over the past few decades to manage malaria and HIV could be reversed,
with these diseases once again spiralling out of control.[7]

O'Neill's report concluded that India, Nigeria, and Indonesia—all
heavily populated countries—were particularly at risk from rising
resistance to malaria treatments; Russia would suffer from the spread of
TB; and Africa as a whole was exposed to the dangers of drug-resistant
malaria, HIV (which can cause Aids), and TB. At around the same time,
Gardiner Harris, a journalist with the *New York Times* then based in
India, investigated the prevalence of superbugs among Indian babies
and reached conclusions as disturbing about India as O'Neill's were for
the UK and the world and at large. He referred to a study in *The
Lancet*, the British medical journal, showing that more than 58,000
Indian newborns a year were dying from bacterial infections resistant
to most antibiotics. It is true that the number is only a fraction of the
hundreds of thousands of Indian under-5s who die each year from
diarrhoea and other illnesses, but the phenomenon is recent and it is
worsening. 'Five years ago, we almost never saw these kinds of infections', Neelam Kler, a doctor and chairwoman of the department of
neonatology at New Delhi's Sir Ganga Ram Hospital, told Harris.
'Now, close to 100 percent of the babies referred to us have multidrug
resistant infections. It's scary.'[8]

   Vipin Vashishtha, a paediatrician in Bijnor, a town in Uttar Pradesh
on the Ganges, described his horror when babies starting dying in his
hospital in 2009 because bacterial acquisition of bla_{NDM-1} had made
infections resistant to antibiotics. 'What I found out was that there is a
deadly epidemic going on. And very few of us have any clue... The
bacteria in our water, sewage, soil, even the bacteria within us—they
are all immune to nearly all antibiotics.'[9]

   Tales of child deaths in developing countries are distressing enough.
But it would be quite wrong to assume that sick people in wealthy,
industrialized countries are being spared the trauma of antibiotic

resistance or will be only mildly affected in the future. Many will have heard of dreadful superbugs that spread among hospital patients, including MRSA (Methicillin-Resistant *Staphylococcus aureus*), which can cause death from septicaemia or blood poisoning. O'Neill's report warned that modern treatments that rely on prophylactic antibiotics, such as hip replacements or other surgeries, would become far more dangerous if drug resistance continued to spread. Cancer treatments often suppress the immune systems of patients, which makes them open to infection; without effective antibiotics, chemotherapy would become much riskier.

What might a patient's death from a superbug infection in a hospital in New York or London have to do with India, let alone the Ganges— particularly if the victim has never travelled to south Asia? The answer is that the NDM genes that make bacteria highly drug-resistant are being spread across the country in humans and other animals, and through sewers, streams, and rivers, and are ultimately transported onward in people's guts to every part of the world. This is a politically sensitive matter, of course. Some Indian officials and doctors were furious with *The Lancet* for naming the new NDM gene in 2010 after New Delhi, the Indian capital, and the origins of this particular part of the drug-resistance problem are less important now that such genes have spread around the world. But both Indian and international scientists accept that South Asia has been one epicentre of the crisis and agree that India (soon to overtake China as the world's most populous nation) urgently needs to improve hygiene and build toilets and effective sewage treatment plants. It also needs to curb the misuse and overuse of antibiotics that accelerate the evolution of drug-resistant strains of bacteria.

This applies even to the upper reaches of the Ganges and holy towns such as Haridwar, before the river has passed through some of the world's biggest and dirtiest cities on its way to the sea. Haridwar, where meat and alcohol are banned, is famous as a destination for Hindu pilgrims and was memorably described by travel writer Eric Newby, who tried to journey down the length of the river by boat for his 1966 book *Slowly Down the Ganges*. He wrote of the grasping guides trying to extort rupees from the hapless tourists in exchange for dubious religious advice, recalled the violence of the eighteenth century (nearly 2,000 men were said to have been killed in 1760 in a pitched battle between rival sects of *sadhus* or ascetics), and relished the chaotic and

colourful life seen from a sacred *ghat*, the bathing steps that line the
Ganges in the cities that lie on its banks:

Down where we were on the waterfront, limbless beggars moved like crabs
across the stones; on the offshore island which was joined to the land by a pair
of ornamental bridges, non-ritual bathers, intent only on getting clean, soaped
themselves all over before lowering themselves into the stream; men wearing
head-cloths swept downriver on tiny rafts of brushwood supported by hollow
gourds; large, silvery cows excreted sacred excrement, contributing their mite
to the sanctity of the place; while on the river front, the *nais*, the barbers,
regarded by the orthodox as indispensable but unclean, were still engaged in
ritual hair-cutting under the lean-to sheds of corrugated iron, shaving heads,
nostrils and ears, preparing their customers for the bath. The wind was still
cold; it bore the smell of burning dung, mingled with the scent of flowers,
sandalwood and other unidentifiable odours. Everything was bathed in a brilliant, eleven o'clock-light. It was an exciting, pleasant scene.[10]

Surprisingly little has changed in Gangetic towns such as Haridwar,
except that they are much bigger—India's population has tripled since
Newby's trip—and that the river is more polluted than it was when he
swam in it and could see himself being nipped by a 30-pound *mahseer*
fish. And, even up here, just south of the Himalayas, there are NDM
resistance genes in the water.

Of all the academic papers on antibiotic resistance that I examined,
the most arresting on the subject of the Ganges was written by scientists based in India and the UK and carried the less than catchy title:
'Increased waterborne bla_{NDM-1} resistance gene abundances associated
with seasonal human pilgrimages to the upper Ganges River'. It con-
firms that NDM-1 genes are found in the Yamuna River, a Ganges
tributary that runs through Delhi, and in the main stream of the
Ganges River. It also shows that high levels of the gene are associated
with high levels of faecal coliform bacteria and therefore with the flow
of human waste into rivers. More significantly, the samples demonstrate that the (relatively) pristine reaches of the upper Ganges near
Haridwar suffer surges of bacterial pollution and, in turn, bla_{NDM-1} pollution during visits by thousands of urban Indians during the May–
June pilgrimage season. Devout Hindus, in other words, are unwittingly
spreading diseases, and antibiotic resistance to diseases, in the very river
to which they have come to pay homage. For *Ma Ganga* (Mother
Ganges) is worshipped as a goddess and is sacred to Hindus worldwide,
which is why towns and cities that lie on the river, from Rishikesh and

Haridwar to Calcutta by way of Allahabad and Varanasi, have an elevated status in Indian history and culture.[11]

The Ganges is a much-abused river at least in part because Hindus are reluctant to believe its holy waters can be sullied. Even foreign visitors are inclined to assume, wrongly, that the water of the upper Ganges is safe. The Ganges–Yamuna paper blames increased exposure to NDM-1 in the upper Ganges partly on the fact that pilgrims presume water quality to be good and fail to consider the impact of their own mass visits. Its data suggest that the average visiting pilgrim, because he or she is likely to come from Indian cities where NDM genes are more prevalent, harbours well over twenty times as many NDM-1 genes as local residents. 'As such, pilgrimage areas may act as "hot spots" for the broader transmission of bla_{NDM-1} and other ARG [antibiotic resistant genes], especially considering bathing and water consumption occur in Ganges waters and exposed visitors return home after their visit to the region', it concludes.

This struck me as a 'smoking gun', evidence of a serious and internationally important aspect of Indian river pollution that had barely been mentioned in the mainstream media amid all the talk of heavy metals, carcinogens, and pesticides. And it prompted me to call David Graham, one of the co-authors of the paper and the man who then informed me that both he and I were likely to have NDM-1 genes in our guts. Graham told me he had worked for more than fifteen years on the effects of trace contaminants in the environment. After the 9/11 Al-Qaeda terror attacks on New York and Washington, amid 'a great concern' in the United States over possible biological warfare, he was one of those investigating the risks of the poisoning of US water supplies and how to deal with them. He went on to become an expert in genes that code for resistance. Until 2008, he had studied the use and abuse of chemicals and antibiotics in farming.

Studying almost anything in river water is complicated nowadays because humans pour in so many different types of pollutants that it is hard to find out precisely which ingredient is affecting what and how. 'Big rivers are different than little streams. It's very, very difficult to explicitly—with no ambiguity—show cause and effect', says Graham. 'We could have gone [downstream] to Varanasi and come up with a sensational paper that was really very, very scary.' Instead, intrigued by the prevalence of antibiotic resistance in India and Pakistan, and inspired by the suggestions of Ziauddin Shaikh from India, who was then one of his post-doctoral researchers, Graham started studying the Haridwar pilgrimage sites on the Ganges in 2012. Graham and Shaikh have been sampling the river twice a year since then. 'The political implications of this are very substantial', says Graham. 'They've got to stop open defecation. If they are seeing anything like this at other places along the Ganges, they have got to stop it...In some places within India I think things are maybe hopeless. But if we can create beacons of hope along the river, that will create some social momentum.'[12]

Shaikh became an assistant professor at the department of biochemical engineering and biotechnology at the Indian Institute of Technology in Delhi, one of the country's elite academic institutions. I went to see him at the spacious if rather dowdy campus in south Delhi to find him designing sewage treatment technology aimed at reducing the increasingly worrisome bla_{NDM-1} contamination of river water as well as performing the conventional task of eliminating disease-causing bacteria. 'We have to increase the number of treatment plants and improve the operation of existing treatment plants', he said. After three years of Ganges sampling, 'we can see the signature pattern for antibiotic resistance genes and how they are getting stored in the environment...In Rishikesh and Haridwar it's showing an increase in trend.' T. R. Sreekrishnan, the head of the department and another co-author of the study, said: 'The only route it can enter the water is through faecal contamination...If you do not properly treat the waste before it's discharged into the rivers you are not only contaminating the water, you are also assisting the proliferation of antibiotic resistance.'[13]

The global spread of NDM-1 since its discovery less than a decade ago has been startlingly quick. The first-known human carrier of the gene was a 59-year-old diabetic Swedish hospital patient of Indian origin who caught a urinary tract infection on a trip to India in 2009. He had been treated in Ludhiana and Delhi for an abscess on his buttocks and underwent surgery. As described in *The Lancet*, the infection was caused by a strain of the *Klebsiella pneumoniae* bacterium that was resistant to antibiotics because of the presence of a previously unknown bacterial gene that codes for the New Delhi metallo-beta-lactamase protein or NDM-1.

The suggestion that Indian hospitals—a cheap destination for medical tourists from around the world—were the source of the problem prompted a predictably angry reaction at the time from some Indian doctors and government officials. A few even suggested a Western

conspiracy to undermine the Indian economy. 'We feel this is economically motivated', said Dr Raman Sardana, secretary of the Hospital
Infection Society India. Yet hospitals, with their combination of sick
people and multiple drug regimes, are known to be ideal breeding
grounds for the accelerated evolution of pathogens.[14] A hospital in
Delhi conducted a study in 2010 and found twenty-two patients carrying bacteria with NDM-1 genes in three months; others were soon
identified elsewhere in India and in Pakistan. India's poor sanitation
and the abuse of antibiotics (drugs can easily be obtained without a
doctor's prescription and patients frequently fail to complete a course
of medicine, encouraging the survival and proliferation of resistant
strains of disease) only deepen the crisis. The two problems together
'make India a perfect system for the spread of antibiotic resistance', says
David Livermore, professor of medical microbiology at the University
of East Anglia in the UK. 'India and Pakistan are the first countries
where this kind of resistance has got real traction.'

Ramanan Laxminarayan of the Public Health Foundation of India,
an expert on the topic, said India had a 'perfect storm' to produce
highly pathogenic strains of bacteria, in the form of a 'large pharmaceutical industry, high background rates of infectious diseases, and an
affluent population that can afford antibiotics'. Tim Walsh of Cardiff
University, another microbiology professor who co-authored the
report in *The Lancet*, says India's political and medical establishment is
in denial about the scale of the problem, despite some good research
in the country. One reason, he suggests, is that Indian hospitals do not
want to put off patients from abroad: more than 3 million 'medical
tourists' visit the country each year. Walsh says he has not been welcome in India since he led the 2010 study. Instead he is working in
neighbouring Pakistan, where the problem is also serious. 'It is very
easy to do this research there', he says. 'We have just completed the
biggest study of its type in the world, looking at the faecal [bacteria] in
2,000 patients admitted to a public hospital in Karachi.' The results
showed that 25 per cent had picked up NDM-1 infection in the community before admission.[15]

Bacterial infections resistant to most antibiotics because of the
NDM-1 gene are now found in hospitals all over the world. The vic-
tims include those who have travelled to India for cosmetic surgery,
US soldiers who fought in Afghanistan, and returning holidaymakers.
The main 'reservoirs' of bacteria with NDM-1 nevertheless remain in

the Indian subcontinent, the Middle East, and the Balkans. In 2011, Walsh and others published another study in *The Lancet*. They found bacteria containing the NDM-1 gene in nearly a third of the surface water samples they tested in New Delhi, and even in two of the fifty drinking-water samples. The gene, furthermore, was found in eleven species of bacteria where it had not been previously reported, including *Shigella boydii* and *Vibrio cholerae*, which can cause dysentery and cholera respectively. The point, now well established, is that even if bla_{NDM-1} was originally selected and detected in the ideal conditions of a hospital, it is now widespread in the environment, including in Indian rivers such as the Ganges.[16]

NDM-1 has a number of disturbing characteristics. For a start, the bacteria with which it associates are almost indestructible when faced with the array of antibiotics available to doctors today, including those of the carbapenem group that are usually used against other drug-resistant bugs. NDM-1, furthermore, is found in so-called 'gram-negative' bacteria such as the *Klebsiella pneumoniae* where it was first discovered, and these bacteria are now a particular source of concern for doctors. 'Gram-negative bacteria boast thick cell walls and enviable cellular defences; even if an antibiotic can penetrate it is likely to be pumped out quickly', wrote Anjana Ahuja, a science commentator, in an article in which she begged big pharmaceutical companies to invest in developing new antibiotics. She compared the 800 cancer medicines and vaccines being tested or awaiting approval in the United States alone with the 41 antibiotics in the global pipeline, only three of which were deemed to be 'breakthrough antibiotics' for tackling gram-negative pathogens. '[T]hese relative numbers should induce a shiver', she concluded. Lastly, NDM-1 can move not only between bacteria of the same species but between different species in a process known as 'horizontal gene transfer'. The gene, says Graham, 'can be acquired as a whole gene and can be slotted into the right place in a new organism, sort of like instant evolution'. The gene may also lurk unnoticed in the bacteria until the bacteria infect a person, the person falls sick, and a doctor prescribes an antibiotic, creating what scientists call stress. 'Stress can induce or switch on the gene', says Shaikh, 'so then the pathogenic bacteria can be switched on and become antibiotic resistant.'[17]

As if NDM-1 were not worrying enough, I was flicking through the pages of an Indian financial newspaper in September 2014 when I came across a story about a new type of the gene called NDM-4.

Asad Ullah Khan, a professor at the biotechnology department of Aligarh Muslim University, had found NDM-4 in the common *E. coli* bacteria collected from sewage water less than 10 metres from a washroom for a ward at the Aligarh Hospital. This was India's first-known example of NDM-4 in waste water, although the gene had been previously detected in Denmark, Cameroon, France, and the Czech Republic. The NDM-4 gene was intercepted on its way to the Ganges watershed; Aligarh lies between the main stream of the Ganges and its tributary the Yamuna, and is close to Agra and the Taj Mahal, the famous mausoleum built by Mughal emperor Shah Jahan to commemorate his favourite wife. 'NDM-4 is one of the variants of NDM-1', Khan told me, adding that it was resistant to even more drugs than its predecessor and was a danger to hospital patients whose immune systems were already compromised. 'It's more dangerous than NDM-1 . . . We have reported a single example, but the fact is that there are many cases.'[18] Evolution, of course, does not stand still. Scientists have already identified NDM-5, 6, 7, and 8.

India, and the world, appear to be at the threshold of a grave crisis of antibiotic-resistant infections. People of my generation have grown up with the understanding that almost any bacterial infection can be cured with the right drug administered correctly, but the global spread of superbugs threatens to return us to the world of our grandparents, when children and adults often died of common diseases that are regarded in industrialized nations today as no more than a nuisance. For modern Britons, Americans, Japanese, Chileans, and Chinese, child deaths are rare and newsworthy tragedies. Yet the fast-spreading bacteria containing the genes that code them to resist antibiotics can cause numerous and serious infections in the gut, lungs, skin, blood, urinary tract, and elsewhere, and these infections can and do kill some of their victims.

In India, studies have shown very high rates of resistance to drugs, more than 95 per cent in the case of one drug used to treat typhoid. And out of forty-one countries for which up-to-date data were available India had the highest rate of resistance among so-called gram-negative organisms such as *E. coli* and *Klebsiella pneumoniae* to the 'last resort' carbapenem class of antibiotics; those resistance rates, furthermore, have been rising. Doctors are finding that even colistin, an old antibiotic that was brought back to treat infections resistant to modern treatments, has lost its effectiveness for some patients.[19] David Cameron, when he was British prime minister, warned of a return to 'the dark ages of medicine'. As with climate change, there are actions we can take to limit the damage or even reverse the process. But—as with climate change again—success will require governments, corporations, and peoples to invest time, money, and effort and in some cases drastically alter their behaviour.

Microbiologists such as Khan in India and campaigners such as O'Neill[20] in the UK know what needs to be done. The list includes improving hospital hygiene, properly managing the distribution of antibiotics (especially in countries such as India where they are barely controlled), sharing information about antimicrobial resistance (Sweden is trying to help India improve its data systems for this), and fostering investment in new types of antibiotics to treat emerging superbugs. O'Neill, an economist by training who candidly admitted that the world of microbes and medicines was 'like Swahili' to him, said recently that pharmaceutical companies risked a backlash similar to that experience by banks after the 2008 global financial crisis if they failed to invest more in new antibiotics. If they focused only on profitable cancer drugs, they would be blamed for the rising number of deaths from drug-resistant infections, just as banks that concentrated on exotic financial instruments before the crash were accused of neglecting their social responsibilities to the millions who ultimately suffered economically from the crisis. 'If we get closer to 2050 and there are 10 million people around the world dying', he said, 'guess who is going to be blamed?'[21]

O'Neill wants all member states of the United Nations to sign up to an agreement on how to deal with antimicrobial resistance. There is also talk of a $2 billion 'global innovation fund' to stimulate research, to which the pharmaceutical industry as well as governments and international financial institutions should contribute over five years. O'Neill said the money would be 'peanuts' for taxpayers compared with the heavy cost of inaction. His UK-based commission is also trying to adapt the profit incentives that drive private-sector drugs giants such as GlaxoSmithKline (GSK), to make the companies more responsive to the new threat. At present, the companies not only focus too much on profitable cancer drugs at the expense of other medicines, they also have a financial interest in maximizing sales of antibiotics even if that means the drugs are being incorrectly used, and are thus promoting the proliferation of drug-resistant bacteria. So the commission has proposed that governments pay pharmaceutical companies lump sums up front for successful new antibiotics (thus removing the link between sales volumes and profits), though only after the companies have spent billions of dollars—between $16 billion and $37 billion for four new drugs is the estimate—on developing new treatments. That is a lot of money, but then the world's top ten drugs groups alone have been making about $90 billion a year in profit. Some industrialists seem to have taken O'Neill's warnings about the parallels between the hated banks and their own industry to heart. 'The banking industry has found itself out of love with stakeholders in society', Sir Andrew Witty, the GSK chief executive, said recently. 'For us as an industry it's really important we don't end up in a similar situation.'[22]

India obviously has a critical role to play, if only because it is one of the world's most populous countries and one of the most vulnerable to deaths and illnesses caused by drug-resistant strains of bacteria. It also has a large pharmaceutical industry, primarily but not exclusively making cheap 'generic' medicines for world markets, and a small but dynamic biotechnology sector. By far the biggest task facing India, however, is to improve basic sanitation and to build treatment plants to clean the waste that currently flows unchecked into the nation's waterways. Pakistan, India, and Bangladesh between them contain nearly a quarter of the world's population and these three countries and their drains, streams, and rivers are major environmental reservoirs of drug-resistant bacteria and of the genes that give them that resistance; the Ganges delta on the Bay of Bengal spans the India–Bangladesh border and two of its rivers run through Calcutta and Dhaka, which are among the world's biggest cities. 'This problem is about to get a lot worse', says Laxminarayan, who is director of the Center for Disease Dynamics, Economics & Policy in Washington and Delhi and a senior research scholar at Princeton University. 'It would be hard to culture [bacteria from] river water in India and not find antibiotic-resistance genes.'

Few of us residents of India think of this crisis when jumping in the river after white-water rafting in the upper Ganges or while having a drink in Delhi. But the unfortunate truth is that antibiotic resistance is spreading not just via hospitals or because of inappropriate use of drugs in medicine and agriculture, but also via human waste in sewage-polluted south Asian waterways and on through the region's drinking water. An added complication is that various pollutants are known to 'stress' micro-organisms. 'Stress induces cellular gene rearrangement processes, which increase the chance of any cell acquiring and activating

AR [antibiotic resistance] genes, even if no antibiotics are present', Graham and others wrote in an academic paper warning of the contribution of poor water quality to growing drug resistance. 'Pollutant stress increases AR potential in bacteria; therefore, locations with high levels of pollution also have elevated potential for AR transmission.' They went on to warn of the dangers of rapid international transmission through air travel:

One might cynically argue these are local issues in emerging countries; however, international travel and increased human mobility has changed the epidemiology of disease. Individuals can now obtain the genetic potential for multi AR in their guts in one part of the world and then carry that latent AR potential anywhere through travel. Further, global travel is growing as local wealth increases, often to and from countries with poor water quality. Therefore, once a novel resistant determinant emerges, travel habits allow it to spread widely, only becoming evident again when the next antibiotic treatment fails; maybe in a hospital very disconnected from the original cause. As such, the impact of poor water quality is often veiled, but may be as important as how antibiotics are used in many parts of the world. Therefore, we contend improving how we use antibiotics is only one part of the solution, while promoting globally cleaner water quality is also essential.[23]

Neither in India nor Europe nor the United States has much attention been paid to how poor sanitation has allowed the Ganges and other rivers of South Asia to become the agents for the spread of deadly superbugs and of the genes that power their drug resistance. As Graham and his co-authors concluded: 'Unless such a perspective is adopted, we will almost certainly enter a "post-antibiotic age" that many doomsayers are predicting.'

I cannot close this section on the pollution of the Ganges without addressing the age-old question of whether the water of the Ganges is physically—as well as spiritually—purifying: does *Ganga jal*, in short, have the power to kill germs? Many Indians believe it does have this apparently magical property, and probably just as many reflexively scoff at the notion and dismiss the idea as superstitious nonsense. In a way, both groups are right, which is why the ancient legends about the river water and the modern discovery of bacteriophages—viruses that can destroy cholera and other bacteria—combine to make it such an intriguing story.

While few devout Hindu households are without a copper pot for *Ganga jal*, it is also true that there is scarcely a middle-class urban

household without one or more sophisticated water filtration and de-
contamination machines to eliminate harmful bacteria from their tap
water. Water filters and the servicing of the machines is big business in
India. Some machines clean the water by reverse osmosis, others use
ultraviolet radiation to kill bugs and many do both.

But we must start by going back hundreds of years to note that
Indian kings and emperors, including the Muslim rulers who were presumably not swayed by Hindu reverence for the goddess Ganga, set
great store by the quality of the drinking water they obtained from the
Ganges. Both Muslim and European travellers remarked on this phenomenon. Ibn Battuta in the fourteenth century said that Mohammed
bin Tughluq, the Sultan of Delhi, had the water transported for as much
as forty days' voyage to quench the royal thirst. The emperor Akbar
called the product from the Ganges 'the water of immortality'.[24]

Edward Terry, a seventeenth-century chaplain, said Ganges water
found favour with the Mughals because it was unique in a curious
respect: it was lighter, he said, than normal water, although one sus-
pects he did not actually confirm this with any of his own experiments. 'Where this thing remarkable must not passe: that one pinte of
the water of Ganges weigheth lesse by an once then any in the whole
kingdome; and therefore the Mogol, wheresoever hee is, hath it
brought to him that he may drinke it.' Hindus, of course, prized the
water as well. According to Nicholas Withington, a trader and a contemporary of Terry: 'The water of this river Ganges is carried manye
hundred myles from thence by the Banyans [i.e. Hindus], and, as they
affirme, it will never stinke, though kepte never so longe, neyther will
anye wormes or vermine breede therin.'[25] Much later, a British doctor
also remarked that drinking water taken from the Hooghly—the lower
Ganges—lasted much longer aboard ships bound for England than was
the case for English water carried in the other direction.

Ganges water consumed near Indian towns nevertheless made
people sick and probably has done since humans first lived on the river
banks. Jean-Baptiste Tavernier, a French gem merchant in the seventeenth century, had unpleasant first-hand evidence in Allahabad that
the water in the river was not as pure as people thought:

Since we were at the Ganges we each drank a glass of wine in which we
poured some water, which caused us some stomach problems; but our valets,
who drank just the water, were much worse afflicted than we were. The Dutch
who have their house beside the Ganges drink no water from the river unless

it has been boiled. As for the natives of the country, they are habituated to it
from their youth; the king himself and all the court drink only Ganges water.
Every day one sees a great number of camels whose only task is to go to the
Ganges to be loaded with water.

Tavernier is advised by Claude Maille, a surgeon among those tending
the city's governor, not to drink Ganges water—which will give them
diarrhoea—but only well water.[26]

At the end of the nineteenth century, the cleansing qualities of the
Ganges were apparently confirmed by science in a study much mentioned in India to this day by those who insist the river has antibacterial
properties. Ernest Hankin, an English naturalist and expert on cholera
and other bacteria, conducted experiments showing that the water of
the Ganges and the Yamuna killed cholera bacteria in a matter of
hours, which for him explained why cholera epidemics did not spread
downstream despite its being a waterborne disease and why so few
bacteria appeared in water samples even a short distance below large
towns on India's rivers.

He had discovered, he wrote, 'that these waters contain an antiseptic
that exercises a powerful bactericidal action on the cholera microbe'.
He did not identify the agent—the 'Mysterious Factor X' as one
author later put it[27]—but said it would be a good idea to advise pilgrims at Hindu gatherings to avoid using well water and encourage
the consumption of river water instead.[28]

So sensational were Hankin's findings that they came to the attention of the American writer Mark Twain on his trip to India shortly
afterwards. After seeing Indians happily drinking Ganges water at
Varanasi a few steps below a foul sewer and a floating corpse, he writes:

For ages and ages the Hindoos have had absolute faith that the water of the
Ganges was absolutely pure, could not be defiled by any contact whatsoever,
and infallibly made pure and clean whatsoever thing touched it. They still
believe it, and that is why they bathe in it and drink it, caring nothing for its
seeming filthiness and the floating corpses. The Hindoos have been laughed
at, these many generations, but the laughter will need to modify itself a little
from now on. How did they find out the water's secret in those ancient ages?
Had they germ-scientists then? We do not know. We only know that they had
a civilisation long before we emerged from savagery.[29]

Nowadays you can buy a litre of Ganges water from the source at
Gaumukh on Amazon's India website for Rs260 (about £3), plus Rs50 for
delivery inside the country, while Ravi Shankar Prasad, the communica-

tions minister, said he had ordered the Department of Posts to make arrangements for sending 'pure *Gangajal*' from Haridwar or Rishikesh to those who wanted to buy it.[30] In the West, it is more expensive; I found a 200ml bottle on eBay for £6.32 plus £19.14 postage and packing.[31]

Consumers of untreated river water nevertheless frequently fall ill in India. The anthropologist Kelly Alley has come into frequent contact with the river while conducting her research and noted wryly:

I found self-realization through negative paths! A bout with viral hepatitis, contracted while drinking tea made from Ganga water, forced me to look at the distinction between external form and devotion in my own mind and contrast it with the distinction understood by my informants. While my bout with hepatitis brought me closer to the fear of 'water pollution' and pushed me farther from devotion, it did little to press the connection between environmental pollution and public health in the minds of my informants.[32]

Another, British, researcher working in Varanasi told me he had become 'horrifyingly ill' after drinking something made with Ganges water, although the bodies of local residents were inevitably 'quite hardened to this kind of stuff'.[33]

But could it be true nonetheless that Ganges water has special properties that kill, say, cholera bugs either in the river itself or in the bodies of people who drink it? Or should we assume that those who peddle the water and its qualities are charlatans like those who once claimed that the water of the Thames had a similarly magical effect? ('There were perpetual complaints about the salubriousness and safety of the water', wrote Peter Ackroyd of the Thames, 'but the managers of various enterprises repeated the claims—made by certain apothecaries at an earlier date—that somehow the water of the Thames had the gift of self-purification...The water was in fact a killer, as the diseases of the nineteenth century testify.')[34]

The discovery of agents that exist in water called bacteriophages (literally, 'bacteria-eaters') by the Canadian scientist Felix d'Herelle in Paris in 1916–17 seemed like a godsend for proponents of Ganges water, and his work is cited to this day in support of *Ganga jal*'s purportedly bacteria-killing qualities. They were invisible to the microscopes of the day, but these bacteriophages were subsequently identified as viruses and found to exist in huge numbers and in great variety in nature. They appear as tiny, elongated moon-landers with a swollen 'head' containing DNA on top of an extended sheath and protruding 'tail' fibres like the legs of an insect. With mixed success, doctors devised bacteriophage treatments for bacterial diseases—there were, for example, successful experiments using phages on Indian cholera patients in Punjab and Assam in the 1920s and 1930s—and came to realize that they needed to use exactly the right phage for each bacterium, for each type of phage targets a specific bacterial host. Phage therapy fell out of favour with the discovery and dissemination in the 1940s of other antibiotics, whose broad spectrum of action against bacteria made them effective cures for many diseases, although phage therapy was used extensively in the Soviet Union, including in the Afghanistan war in the 1980s.

Today the use of bacteriophages appears to be enjoying the beginnings of a renaissance, not least because they are an alternative to antibiotics increasingly compromised by the spread of antibiotic-resistant bacteria (such as those with NDM-1). 'The antibiotics really don't have a lot going for them', says Janakiraman Ramachandran, one of those who have secured funding from venture capitalists for bacteriophage research and development. 'At some stage there will be more phage-based solutions.'[35] I came to hear of Ramachandran's work because his company, based in Bangalore, is called GangaGen, partly after the river and its place in the history of bacteriophage discoveries and partly after his late mother, whose name was Ganga. Ramachandran, who headed AstraZeneca's Indian pharmaceuticals operation before he founded GangaGen in 2001, told me how he arranged for 5 litres of water to be brought from the bathing area of the Hindu *mela* at Nasik in 2003, from which he and his scientists isolated eight phages against *Staphylococcus* bacteria. GangaGen's main product under development is a treatment[36] consisting of anti-staph phages with their DNA removed (to meet the concerns of regulators and eliminate the risk of bacterial resistance to phage treatments) that kill *Staphylococcus aureus* bacteria, including the hospital 'superbug' MRSA. Other phage companies have gone into the food safety business, developing non-medical phage products for protecting fish and meat from contamination with bacteria such as *Listeria* and *Salmonella*.

Working with phages is difficult. They have proved hard to store and transport. They cannot themselves be patented because they are ubiquitous natural organisms, which discourages investors. They can cause disease as well as cure it; by mixing their genes with those of bacteria they have given rise to the disease diphtheria and food poisoning from E. coli 0.157.[37] Results from phage treatment are frustratingly better *in vitro* than *in vivo*, and one study conducted in the Soviet Union and published in 1971 found bacteriophages to be markedly inferior to antibiotics in treating cholera.[38] 'I don't know anything about the quality of the Ganges water (it does depend on when and where you sample it)', one of the authors told me when I asked him about phages and the Ganges, 'but from a public health perspective, I certainly wouldn't recommend drinking it, anywhere along its route.'[39]

Even if there is some bacteria-killing property in Ganges water, it is clearly not 100 per cent effective, and it may be the result of the river's ability to rapidly re-oxygenate itself, or of magnesium or sulphur or something in the silica-rich silt carried down from the Himalayas rather than the bacteriophages that exist in all rivers and seas. True, there are a lot of bacteriophages in the Ganges, but, as Felix d'Herelle quickly learned (says the science writer Anna Kuchment), 'bacterio-phages are found wherever bacteria thrive: in sewers, in rivers that catch waste runoff from pipes, and in the stool of convalescent patients. Like any predator, bacteriophages are best able to survive and multiply when they are in close proximity to their food supply, where they ful-fill their evolutionary role of keeping bacteria in check.'[40] If there are more bacteriophages in the Ganges, in other words, that is because it has more people living on its banks and more bacteria in its waters. The waters of the river are not a magic cure.

9

Dolphins, Crocodiles, and Tigers

Thus speaks the Beloved of the Gods, the king Piyadassi: When I had been consecrated for twenty-six years I forbade the killing of the following species of animals, namely: parrots, mainas, *red-headed ducks,* cakravaka-geese, swans, nandi-mukhas, *pigeons, bats, ants, tortoises, boneless fish,* vedaveyakas, pupulas *of the Ganges, skate, porcupines, squirrels, deer, lizards, domesticated animals, rhinoceroses, white pigeons, domestic pigeons and all quadrupeds which are of no utility and are not eaten.*

—Fifth pillar edict of Emperor Ashoka, third century BC[1]

The Ganges dolphin is an indicator of health of river Ganga, it is a symbol of Ganga, it is aquatic heritage of India, it is aquatic heritage of the world.

—R. K. Sinha, dolphin researcher in Patna[2]

It is easy to slump into a mood of despair when thinking about superbugs or pollution in India. In Delhi, the air is often thick with smoke and dust and the Yamuna River that runs through it resembles nothing so much as a river-sized open sewer. So it is cheering to leave the capital, sit in a boat on the Ganges, and suddenly see a 2-metre dolphin break the surface. A dolphin! I have seen dolphins of various species at sea, leaping, spinning, and diving around everything from a sailing yacht to a car ferry; they like to show off and to play in a boat's bow-wave or in the turbulence at its stern. I have seen dolphins far up the Amazon River and watched and written about the famous pink dolphins of the Pearl River delta between Hong Kong and Macau. But I never expected to see a dolphin hundreds of miles inland in one of India's busiest cities. Yet there they were, Gangetic dolphins with their peculiarly long, toothed snouts, fishing in the river in the middle of Patna, a city the size of Rome.

I should not have been surprised to see them: a meeting with the river dolphin experts at the University of Patna was one of the reasons for my trip and they were my guides on the river. Yet I had not believed it would be so simple to see an endangered species of mammal that had only recently been declared India's 'National Aquatic Animal' at the urging of R. K. Sinha, the zoology professor known as Mr Dolphin. Gangetic dolphins, unlike several oceanic species, seem to take little interest in human activity and I have not seen one playing around a boat. Yet they do coexist with humans when we let them and have done so for many centuries. Babur, the Mughal emperor, called them 'water-hogs'. Their popular name is *susu*, from the noise they make when surfacing to breathe through their blowholes.

The continued existence of dolphins in Patna, capital of the populous state of Bihar, is encouraging news for the Ganges and those who wish to save it. It also demonstrates one of the most attractive features of modern India: the tolerance, even respect, among its human inhabitants for other species. I do not want to romanticize this or make a crude distinction between East and West. Pradip Krishen, a film-maker and author who has championed native plants and written definitive field guides to the trees of Delhi and central India, says he fears that Indians are not particularly interested in biodiversity or wildlife, despite their habit of distributing food for birds, dogs, and even ants. 'It's all about earning points in heaven', he sighs. 'It's not about loving animals.' [3] Tolerance and respect, it is true, are not the same as love and understanding—in India, as elsewhere, whole populations of wild animals and plants can be inadvertently wiped out by habitat destruction—but cultural and religious traditions do make a difference that is immediately noticeable to anyone who moves to India from another country.

You can see Sarus cranes, the world's tallest birds, mincing along next to factories in the busy fields of Uttar Pradesh. Greater Delhi, with a population of some 25 million, is one of the world's biggest megacities, but the quantity and variety of animals that survive and thrive in the metropolis is almost as striking as the number of people who do the same. Some of the animals are tame, of course: elephants and camels, white horses to carry the grooms at weddings, holy cows, cats, and dogs. Even the smartest shops tend to have a mangy cur dozing on the doorstep. Delhi-ites feed and care for packs of feral dogs and have gone to court in defence of their welfare. I was once told not to worry about rabies if I saw a dog foaming at the mouth in Lodi Gardens in the centre of New Delhi—that would be the one with epilepsy.

Yet wildlife flourishes too, especially but not exclusively in the privileged avenues of the capital—collectively known as 'Lutyens Delhi' after the British architect Edwin Lutyens—and the adjoining parks and gardens. Rats, monkeys, crows, and mynahs have learned how to live on human leavings. In our own yard, the first thing we met was a giant toad relishing the monsoon rains. Walking home at night, it was hard to avoid a series of crunching squelches as you step on giant land snails trying to cross the path. We would be woken by the chattering of squirrels and the cries of hornbills, parakeets, woodpeckers, and the bird of prey my father used to call a 'shite hawk', the scavenging black kites that have learned to swoop silently on unsuspecting baseball spectators at the American school and snatch hamburgers from their hands.

At home we routinely saw and heard the creatures immortalized in Rudyard Kipling's *The Jungle Book* tale 'Rikki-Tikki-Tavi': the eponymous mongoose himself, Darzee the tailorbird, the coppersmith barbet (a bird with a call 'like the beating of a hammer on a copper pot', as Kipling puts it), and Chuchundra the muskrat who is too scared to cross a room and so walks along the walls—but not, thankfully, Nag the cobra and his evil wife Nagaina. Not bad for a megacity, and a far cry from the wildlife-bereft cities of modern China.[4] The Gangetic dolphin may be endangered, but the Baiji, the Chinese river dolphin of the Yangtze, was declared extinct a decade ago in the first global extinction of a 'megafauna' species for half a century.[5]

I am not suggesting that India is an immaculate wildlife paradise. Patna is no pristine wilderness, and one reason for my initial surprise at sighting them was that they were fishing only metres from the shore amid the garbage of what smelled like a sewer outfall. Nearby, twisting in the current, was a partly burned human cadaver caught on some underwater obstruction. Jet-skiers amused themselves by roaring in circles, and dogs gnawed at the ribcage of a dead cow on the river bank. Thankfully, most of my subsequent sightings were in more pleasant surroundings: on open stretches of the Hooghly River north of Calcutta; below Chunar Fort at the great river bend that takes the Ganges north to Varanasi; and in the clean waters of the Chambal—one of the most important tributaries of the Ganges—south of Delhi.

However, my most unexpected encounter of all was in another pol-luted stretch of water, on the outskirts of Dhaka, the Bangladeshi capital. I was on the water on this occasion not to learn about the wildlife of the Ganges but about its boats. Andrew Jenkins, a long-time Dhaka resident and British water expert at Brac, a non-government organization with a big social agenda,[6] had offered to introduce me to some traditional builders of wooden boats and to take me on his own wooden sampan, *Jusna*. We headed west out of Dhaka and over the Turag River (a tributary of the Meghna, which connects downstream to the Padma, the local name for the Ganges). Looking down from Gabtali Bridge, I saw a river packed with freighters and boats large and small, some carving a path through a thick layer of water hyacinth. This floating plant, although its green leaves and lilac-coloured flowers are more attractive than floating garbage, is a notoriously fast-growing invasive species that has become the bane of canal operators and river users the world over since it spread from its home in the Amazon basin to Africa and Asia. Jenkins told me there were various stories about how the pest arrived in what is now Bangladesh. One attributed the plant's obstructive presence to a *memsahib* in the era of British India who wanted to beautify her garden. According to another, the water hyacinth is known as the 'German flower' because the Germans allegedly introduced it here during the First World War to block the waterways and stymie Britain's most important colony.

At first I did not have much luck finding the boatbuilders, and as we set out with a group of friends on our Friday afternoon jaunt (the weekend in mainly Muslim Bangladesh), I noticed gloomily that the water cloven by the bows of our boat was black with filth and smelled oily and slightly putrid. For someone who lived in Delhi, it was no great shock to see children swimming and laughing in the water, or old men lathering themselves with soap outside a timber yard. What was astonishing, in this scene of Dickensian squalor, was the appear-ance of several Gangetic dolphins, their smooth, grey bodies gleaming as they emerged from the black depths. There were dragonflies, too, both blue and orange, and the occasional water hen by the bank. There were even kingfishers, so there must be fish somewhere down there for the birds and dolphins.[7]

Such sightings are simultaneously encouraging and depressing: they lift the spirits because they show that dolphins can survive even in dif-ficult conditions (just as Hong Kong's pink dolphins intelligently

moved away from their regular fishing grounds during the building of
the international airport at Chep Lak Kok, only to return once the
work was finished in 1998); but it is also depressing to see dolphins in
seriously polluted waters, because it shows how grave are the threats to
their survival. And they are vulnerable. A study by Sinha and other
researchers put the total population of *Platanista gangetica gangetica*
across its historical range—from the Himalayan foothills of the upper
Ganges in the west to the Brahmaputra and other rivers of Bangladesh
in the east—at between 2,000 and 2,500. The Indus river dolphin of
Pakistan, once thought to be a separate species but now identified as a
subspecies of the same stock from the time when the two river systems
were connected, has a population half the size of its Gangetic cousin's
and is one of the world's rarest mammals.

The Gangetic dolphin, one of only four surviving river dolphin
species in the world, has primitive cetacean characteristics that make it
peculiarly interesting to zoologists—but it is also particularly hard to
study because it lives in generally murky water and surfaces only
briefly. The long toothy snout, just like the similarly-shaped mouth of
the gharial, the Gangetic crocodile, has evolved to increase the chances
of catching slippery prey. Its eyes are tiny, merely pinhole openings
above the mouth, and their lack of crystalline lenses makes the dolphin
effectively blind (though it may be able to detect light), but that is no
great disadvantage for an animal that hunts by echo-location and lives
in water with zero or poor visibility.[8] They hunt in an unusual manner,
swimming on their sides—usually the right side—near the bottom
and apparently feeling the riverbed with their fin while nodding their
heads in a sweep for prey; the sideways stance positions one eye in a way
that probably allows it to detect the light coming from the surface.[9]

There are many threats to this extraordinary creature that has swum
in the rivers of the Gangetic plain for an estimated 60 million years.
The building of dams and barrages has isolated and extinguished
populations of dolphins in India, Pakistan, Bangladesh, and Nepal
(from which flow some of the Ganges's most important tributaries).
Dolphins disappeared from the main stream of the Ganges above the
barrage at Bijnor twelve years after it was built. The overuse of water
for irrigation has further threatened the dolphin's habitat by dramatically reducing the depth of the river in the dry season, while the riverbed itself in many places has been disturbed by massive sand-mining
operations to provide the raw material for the concrete used in the

construction of modern buildings across India. Fish and the dolphins that prey on them have been affected by pollution from sewage, industrial waste, fertilizers, and pesticides. More studies need to be done on the impact of some of these toxins on animals, including humans and dolphins, but a paper by Sinha and his fellow-researchers said that as far back as 2002, 1.5 million tonnes of chemical fertilizers and 21,000 tonnes of pesticides were finding their way each year into the Ganges–Brahmaputra river system. Polychlorinated biphenyls (PCBs), hexachlorocyclohexane (HCH), chlordane compounds, and hexachlorobenzene (HCB)—collectively known as organochlorines and often banned or restricted in Western countries over fears about their persistence and toxicity—were found to accumulate in the blubber and organs of the dolphins.[10]

Even if they survive this industrial and chemical onslaught, the dolphins frequently become entangled in the gill-nets used by fishermen on the river and die when they cannot surface to breathe. In the past, fishermen used to kill dolphins deliberately so that they could use their oil—like the whale oil of the past—as fuel for lamps, as an aphrodisiac, as a treatment for muscle pains (rubbed into the skin as a liniment), and as bait for catfish (the oil was put in the water as a way of attracting fish towards the fishermen's boats). Sinha helped to ensure the enforcement of a ban on direct killing of dolphins and popularized an alternative to the dolphin oil as fish bait, an equally effective substitute in the form of an oily mulch made from fish scraps.

Sinha now hopes the population of Ganges dolphins has stabilized, albeit in a much smaller range than previously and in a series of segments separated by the dams of the Ganges river system. An animal called the *gangapuputaka*, thought to be the dolphin, was among the animals protected by one of the edicts of the Buddhist emperor Ashoka inscribed on columns across his lands in the third century BC, while the memoirs of Babur, the first Mughal emperor, in the sixteenth century AD, said the 'water-hog' was found in all the rivers of Hindustan, by which he probably meant the northern half of the subcontinent. An account published in 1879 by the Scottish zoologist John Anderson, curator of the Indian Museum in Calcutta, said the dolphin was found in the Ganges–Brahmaputra system across north India and in the Yamuna as far as Delhi, even in May when the river was its lowest before the monsoon. But the ubiquity that the dolphin once enjoyed in north India has long since passed. 'The last record of *susu* in Yamuna at Delhi was in 1967, when a dead dolphin caught in a fishing net was brought to the Delhi Zoo', is the mournful epitaph in the scientific paper by Sinha and his colleagues.

R. K. Sinha is one of only half a dozen Indians living along the river who are outspoken champions of the Ganges. He was born to illiterate parents in a village some 70 kilometres south of Patna, and remembers coming to the Ganges occasionally as a child for family funerals. He noticed the dark shapes in the water and was told that they might be dangerous, although nobody seemed to know whether they were gharials, dolphins, or something else. As a student and teacher in Patna and Munger on the Ganges, he would watch the elusive creatures curiously from the river bank for hours, and was eventually informed by a fisherman that they were not fish but suckled their young (and were therefore mammals). Sinha made the study of the dolphins and their preservation his lifelong passion, despite being ambushed by bandits on at least three occasions while conducting research on the river.[11] Sinha adopted the name 'Mr Dolphin Sinha' and has long argued that the health of the dolphin population reflects the state of the river. 'The Ganges dolphin is an indicator of health of river Ganga, it is a symbol of Ganga, it is aquatic heritage of India, it is aquatic heritage of the world, and it is simply a symbol of what is happening in the overall river system', he said in a film documentary about his work.[12]

Like the royal Bengal tiger that roams the mangrove swamps of the Sunderbans, the Ganges river dolphin is simply a large, photogenic, and well-publicized example of the many mammals, reptiles, amphibians, birds, other animals and plants of the river endangered by the destruction of their habitat and the relentless pressure of India's growing human population.[13] That population in turn is affected by declining supplies of food from the river. Some 265 species of fish are found in the Ganges basin, including the Ganges river shark, as well as rare turtles and endemic freshwater crabs. But catches of various species of carp and of *hilsa*, the bony but delicious fish that is prized in Bengali cooking, have declined sharply in recent decades; one study found *hilsa* catches to have fallen to a twentieth of their previous levels.

Native fish have in some cases been affected by the introduction of exotic species farmed for food, including the Chinese Grass Carp. 'Turtles, gavialis [gharials], crocodiles, birds, otter and freshwater dolphins are exploited heavily throughout the Ganga basin', reported one study of biodiversity in the river. 'Among invertebrates, crabs, bivalves and freshwater prawns are highly exploited for food. Mollusc shells were used on a large scale for making lime as a substitute for cement. Thick shells of the bivalves are commercially exploited from the Gandak river [a Ganges tributary flowing from Nepal] for making buttons for garments.'[14]

The foothills of the Himalayas around the source of the Ganges, the river's vast flood-plain in north India and the delta at its mouth have long been extraordinarily rich in birds, both resident and migratory. One evening on the Hooghly River near Bandel in February I watched a huge, twittering cloud of swallows—perhaps half a million or so—flying up the river, presumably on their annual northward migration at the end of winter. But over four years of criss-crossing the Ganges, admittedly for purposes other than ornithology, I tried and failed to find an Indian skimmer, a tern-like bird that hunts by flying just above the surface of the river with the lower mandible of its red–and–orange bill ploughing at high speed through the water to pick up small fish and other prey; it was not until my final fortnight that I saw one.

Habitat loss and local extinctions are not new phenomena—the Javan rhinoceros was reported extinct in the Sunderbans at the mouth of the Ganges in 1888—and there are still a few places in the vast Ganges catchment area where wildlife is officially protected, typically in mountainous terrain or swamplands unsuitable for farming. Around the river's source, for example, the glacial terrain and forests of conifers and birch are protected by the Gangotri National Park. On a long visit there, you would be unlucky not to see a herd of *bharal*, otherwise known as blue sheep—but very lucky to catch a glimpse of the musk deer and snow leopards that also live in the hills and have been hunted to the brink of extinction.

Moving downstream to the environs of the Hastinapur wildlife sanctuary, between Haridwar and Kanpur, it is almost possible to imagine what the Ganges was like in its stately progress across the north Indian plains before the industrial revolution, the building of dams, and the explosion of the human population. When I went there I encountered a cheerful crowd of pilgrims, waving flags, blowing trumpets, and carrying brass pots of river water as they returned from their prayers to *Ma Ganga*. Ducks and waders were feeding in the shallows, while river turtles and endangered gharials, the bizarre, thin-snouted crocodiles of the Indian subcontinent, basked on the sandbanks.

Further east in the Panna tiger reserve on the Ken river, a tributary of the Yamuna (and therefore ultimately of the Ganges), I had the rare pleasure of watching a pair of red-headed vultures, also known as king vultures, feasting on the rotting skin and carcase of a deer. Vultures—now vanishingly rare in most of India—are an indicator of ecological health, and the scene reminded me of the rich wildlife and open spaces of the African savannah. For all their ugliness, vultures are often the good guys in Indian culture and mythology. In the Ramayana epic, the vulture Jatayu loses his life trying to save Rama's wife Sita from the monster-king Ravana of Lanka, while Jatayu's brother Sampati provides the aerial surveillance that helps Rama and his friends locate and rescue Sita. You would not know it today, but vultures were ubiquitous across India until the 1990s, even in central Delhi and in Mumbai. In a ritual similar to the 'sky burials' of Tibetans to the north, the Zoroastrian Parsis of Mumbai used to expose their dead on so-called 'towers of silence' to be devoured and recycled by vultures.

The sorry story of what happened to India's vultures is a lesson in the unintended consequences of human progress. The number of vultures in India crashed from 40 million to less than 100,000 in a few years, with the three gyps species—the white-backed, long-billed, and slender-billed—particularly affected. 'By 2007, we had lost 99.9 per cent of the population', says Vibhu Prakash, a vulture expert at the Bombay Natural History Society. The culprit was diclofenac, a drug used to treat inflammation in humans and cattle. If a cow dies soon after being given the medicine and is then eaten by vultures, the vultures often die of kidney failure. The consequences have been grim, and not just for the vultures. The birds have evolved into efficient carrion disposal units, with serrated tongues and stomach acids strong enough to kill dangerous pathogens. In their absence, cow carcases lay rotting across India. Rats and feral dogs multiplied and rabies deaths among humans exploded. India banned diclofenac for veterinary use in 2006, and the hope is that vultures bred in captivity can soon be reintroduced to the wild to start rebuilding the population. 'It's quite a daunting task because getting the drugs removed is not easy', says Prakash. 'We are a democratic country, so things don't move that fast.' In the Himalayas, you will still come across the lammergeier, or bearded vulture, dropping animal bones onto slabs of rock to smash them and eat the marrow. There is even a gang of young Egyptian vultures that has been hanging out on the army polo field next to the ridge in New Delhi's diplomatic quarter. But in swaths of India, the vultures are gone.[15]

At the river's mouth, the tidal swamplands of the Sunderbans ('beautiful forest'), the world's largest mangrove area, straddle the delta across the India–Bangladesh border. It is a biologically rich terrain but little appreciated by tourists: the outer islands of the Sunderbans are inaccessible except by water and the thick plant cover makes it difficult to see the swamp's notoriously large and aggressive tigers unless they come to the muddy shore or are seen swimming across the channels in pursuit of prey. Arun Sarkar, my 35-year-old guide on one boat trip into the forest, said tigers killed fifteen to twenty people in the area each year, usually fishermen or those who collect the famously fragrant honey made by bees from the flowers of the mangrove trees. Pointing at a stand of *hental*, a type of scrubby date palm ('The tigers like to hide in this because the colour is very similar to a tiger's'), he told me he had been on around 800 boat trips and seen tigers forty-five times, 'mostly when they are swimming'.[16] Joseph Zeitlyn, a journalist who lived in Bangladesh as a child, came face to face with an adult tiger when he was 9 years old and being towed in a small boat by a launch in the Sunderbans; the swimming tiger was entangled in the tow rope and became enraged, but Zeitlyn was told to lie flat in the boat by the fisherman who was with him and they both escaped unscathed.[17]

Most of those who venture frequently into the Sunderbans have wildlife tales to tell. John Gomes of Vivada, an Indian company that takes tourists on cruises into the forest, showed me pictures on his mobile telephone of a giant Burmese python crushing and then eating a spotted deer on the Bangladesh side of the reserve.[18] Andrew Jenkins, the water expert based in Dhaka, told me of a trip offshore to the Swatch of No Ground, a stretch of deep water off the silty delta in the Bay of Bengal, during which they spotted no less than six species of dolphins. They also saw a Bryde's whale. Jenkins noticed with alarm that the skipper of their boat was trying to shoot it with a kind of cross-bow, until he realized the purpose of the shot was not to kill the whale but to obtain a biopsy of the whale's skin for scientific study of its genetic make-up.[19]

There is more to wildlife than megafauna, and for me it is often the little things that make for an interesting afternoon. In a couple of hours in the Sunderbans, you can watch several different types of fiddler crab—bright blue, bright red, or bright yellow—emerge from their holes in the ooze, observe pied kingfishers performing their characteristic hunting pattern of hover-and-dive in a whir of black and white, and see a rare group of lesser adjutant storks wheeling high above their favourite fresh-water reservoir. (The 'adjutant' name derives from their somewhat military gait.) I watched an Indian pond heron in its fancy breeding plumage—normally a drab, brownish bird, it dons a dark feathery cape and two long white feathers trailing down the back of its neck for the mating season—grappling with a large mud-skipper it had caught. Mudskippers, bulging-eyed fish that can breathe outside the water and walk onto the mud using their fins, are fascinating in themselves, but this one was losing the battle for life. The heron dropped it, caught it again, marched with it to the water's edge, rinsed it thoroughly and swallowed it.

It is tempting to conclude that the existence of such wildlife oases at the extremities of the Ganges is a sign that the battle to improve popular awareness and official oversight of India's natural inheritance is finally being won. In reality, the struggle for the naturalists who care about the river and its wildlife is as daunting as ever. The reserves and parks of India, Bangladesh, and Nepal are under constant threat from poachers, farmers, woodcutters, government officials, and industrialists who want to claim natural resources for other goals, including agriculture and hydro-electricity.

Even the country's protected tigers, many of them numbered and named and confined to tightly managed reserves such as Ranthambore in Rajasthan, have not been entirely safe. In 2005, in what one expert described as 'probably the biggest conservation scandal in modern times', it emerged that not one of the twenty-four tigers supposed to prowl through the nearby Sariska Tiger Reserve was actually alive. Although the reserve has since been restocked, the most visible mammals in Sariska these days are not tigers but monkeys, stray dogs, and people—hundreds of pilgrims who are allowed to visit a Hindu shrine inside the park. Back then the official count for tigers across India was 3,723, though naturalists thought the real number was less than 2,000. Numbers fell to about 1,400 in 2011 and are reckoned to have risen again to 2,226 by 2016, although the increase may have something to with more efficient surveying methods. India has most of the world's 3,890 tigers (they are nearly extinct in China, Laos, Cambodia, Vietnam, and Myanmar). India's tiger habitat, however, is reported to have shrunk by a quarter in the past decade and environmentalists and campaigners remain concerned about the fate of the country's iconic big cat.[20]

It is the same story for less glamorous fauna. The narrow band of forest in the Himalayan foothills where the Ganges rises is threatened by illegal hunting, dam-building, and the inexorable uphill march of luxury condominiums to harbour the wealthy during the hot summer months in Delhi. Downstream near Hastinapur, the rare gharials and turtles are basking on their mid-river sandbanks within earshot of the numerous chugging diesel pumps that extract water from the Ganges to irrigate the fields of vegetables and sugar-cane established on the vast expanse of riverbed exposed in the dry season. Villagers herd their cows or wash their motorcycles in the river nearby, and the Hindu celebrants of the Ganges water ceremonies gaily fling the plastic trash from their picnic onto the sand. Still further south and east at the Panna tiger reserve, where the vultures thrive in the watershed south of the Ganges, there are fears that part of the park will be submerged beneath the reservoir for a planned dam to divert water from the Ken River to the Betwa, even though the Ken itself is short of water. I asked Raghunandan Singh Chundawat, an environmental campaigner who runs a tourist lodge near the reserve, why would any government want to proceed with the project? His response was discouraging: 'Sixteen thousand crores [160 billion rupees, or about $2.4 billion] in civil construction. You can make a lot of money.'[21]

Even the Sunderbans, with its 10,000 square kilometres of mangroves protected as a Unesco world heritage site, is not entirely safe from human exploitation. In much of the forest, locals are allowed to fish and brave the tigers to collect honey and bamboo. I watched women with blue and green nets in rectangular frames wading through the mud to catch 'prawn seed', the tiny juveniles which are sold to prawn farmers. I was puzzled by the brightly coloured nets until I realized they were using fine-meshed mosquito netting, a cheap and highly efficient method of catching almost every living thing in the water. Boat captains say they hardly see Gangetic dolphins in the delta nowadays, although you can spot the baby-faced Irrawaddy dolphin, a marine species that is found in estuaries around the Bay of Bengal and lacks the extended snout of its Gangetic counterpart.

The swelling human populations of India and Bangladesh encroach on the fringes of the forest, and the islands are sinking because dams upstream have deprived them of their annual consignments of silt.

Prawn farms and their large ponds of dirty water destroy the landscape and pollute the waterways. Ships ply the larger channels on their way to and from the ports of Bangladesh and India; a tanker sank on the Bangladeshi side of the Sunderbans in December 2014 after a collision, sending tonnes of black furnace oil snaking up the rivers and onto the shore. Contractors in Bangladesh, meanwhile, are building a 1,320-megawatt coal-fired power station 15 kilometres from the Sunderbans; it will be supplied with 5 million tonnes of coal a year shipped through the park.[22]

There is another riverine wildlife sanctuary in north India, and it is found surprisingly close to Delhi. Intrigued by alluring film footage of gharials, Indian skimmers, spoonbills, bar-headed geese, and an apparently pristine stretch of river in a BBC series about the Ganges,[23] I asked everyone I knew where I could find such an unlikely place on the river. The answer came back: it's not the Ganges, it's the Chambal. I had heard the name mentioned by environmentalists as the saviour of the Yamuna and of the Ganges. Its clean waters join the sewage-laden trickle of the Yamuna and transform it into a respectable river before the Yamuna enters the Ganges at the holy confluence of Prayag or Allahabad. Nearly 1,000 kilometres in length, the Chambal rises in Madhya Pradesh and traverses Rajasthan before joining the Yamuna south-east of Agra in Uttar Pradesh. Yet the Chambal, unlike the Yamuna or the Ganges, is barely mentioned in conversation or in the Indian media, and after four years of living in Delhi I had no inkling that this natural paradise lay only a few hours' drive from the capital. Why? Because the river is accursed.

This irony—that a river with an evil reputation among Hindus supplies its two holiest waterways, the Yamuna and the Ganges, with clean, life-giving water after they have been ravaged by sewage and toxic waste—was explained to me by Ram Pratap Singh, the owner of the Chambal Safari Lodge. There are two stories about the old curse. In the first, Rantideva, a king of ancient times, had so many animals slaughtered for feasting or sacrifices that the blood and juices that flowed became a river, or flowed into a river; the ancient name of the Chambal was Charmanvati or 'Skin River' because animal hides were dried on its banks. The implication is that Hindu holy men were appalled by the death of so many cows and other beasts and so cursed the river.

In the second story, Draupadi, the heroine of the Sanskrit war epic the *Mahabharata*, cursed the Chambal and all who drank from it because it was on its banks that the notorious dice game was played that led to her humiliation. Yudhishtira, one of her husbands, was an obsessive gambler and lost his kingdom and finally his wife in the game against the evil Shakuni. She was called a whore and her enemies tried to strip her in public (although she was saved from total nakedness by divine intervention).

There is a third, more modern reason for the Chambal's notoriety. For hundreds of years the complex topography of the ravines near Agra have been the haunt of bandits, and in the late twentieth century the Chambal became the hideout of Phoolan Devi, the so-called 'Bandit Queen' immortalized in a film of that name. A poor, low-status woman of the boatman caste, she was gang-raped by a group of men from a rival faction and took a brutal revenge with her allies, killing twenty-two (higher-caste) Rajputs. She surrendered in 1983 but was released after eleven years for political reasons as a champion of the lower castes. She was twice elected a member of parliament before being assassinated at the age of 37 by relatives of her victims.[24]

So the Chambal, Singh told me, is probably the only unholy river in India, and that has been a blessing for the wildlife. 'If you follow the length of the Chambal you won't find any temples. The first temple appears at the spot where the Chambal and the Yamuna meet. This leads to a conservation story: no temples, no people, and the habitat is still very pristine.' A narrow 400-kilometre stretch of the river and its banks in three states were declared a wildlife sanctuary in 1979. As well as the rare gharial, endangered turtles, and Gangetic dolphins, more than 330 species of birds are found in and around the river, as well as jungle cats, hyenas, and golden jackals.

Singh's own presence by the Chambal owes something to banditry too. He says his Rajput ancestors of the Tomar clan were pushed out of Delhi a thousand years ago, and the family has lived in this place since 1372. When bandits from the Chambal ravines started raiding Agra in the Mughal era, the Mughals appointed landlord families such as Singh's as local peacekeepers, providing them with horses and soldiers in exchange for policing. The British maintained the *zamindar* system, although a new wave of bandits emerged from the defeat and disbanding of the mutineers who rose up against British rule in 1857. Singh's great-grandfather built the present house, now the lodge, as a plantation mansion and centre for cattle fairs in 1915. His grandfather was reputed to be good friends with Mansingh, one of the leading bandits of his day and described to me by one local as being 'like Robin Hood', a comparison also used for Phoolan Devi. Kidnapping for ransom was the bandits' main business.

The house eventually fell into disrepair, and it was not until the 1990s that Singh and his wife abandoned their town jobs, tried to farm the unproductive land, and finally turned the buildings into a haven for birdwatchers and tourists. He found that bandits were still active and locally popular and the forestry department rangers had a tacit agreement to let them be, never wearing uniforms when they entered bandit territory. In theory, that might have been bad for the Chambal's wildlife, especially since the sanctuary comes under the purview of three Indian states, and is therefore hard to police. Illegal mining of sand from the riverbed is also a persistent threat ('There are big interests in mining, and they don't give up easily', says Singh), and fishermen sneak up from the Yamuna, where they are allowed to operate, to the protected Chambal. Yet the poor quality of grazing in the eroded ravines beside the Chambal has persuaded many local dairy farmers to move out of the river sanctuary and install their villages next to the road. Previously, farmers worked the land right up to the river bank and even on the riverbed in the dry season, leaving the gharials with little of their natural sandbank habitat. The Indian skimmers seem to be extending their range as well. 'The Chambal, over the past twenty years, I've seen it become better', says Singh.[25]

With those rare words of optimism about the Ganges river system ringing in my ears, I head for the Chambal on a fiercely hot day in early June to see for myself. The Chambal, I am assured by Bachu Chitoria, my skinny 36-year-old guide, never dries up and is 'one of the cleanest rivers in India'. Chitoria, from nearby Bharatpur, has been twelve years a naturalist and moved to the Chambal a year ago from Gujarat in north-west India, where he worked with the last survivors of the Asiatic lions that once ranged from Eastern Europe to Central Asia. We meet at 'cow-dust time', when the cattle are being herded home along dusty lanes, and pass a herd of wild *nilgai*—the largest Asian antelope also known as a blue bull—apparently coexisting with farm animals and standing under some trees in search of shade. Here in rural Uttar Pradesh, the main crops are wheat, mustard, millet, and potatoes, and I notice that the land has also been extensively excavated for the earth to make bricks; mustard plant waste is piled high next to a brick kiln, where it is used for fuel.

We drive through Pinahat, a typical market town with a ruined fort where the shops sell snacks, bicycle tyres, and cheap shoes, navigate around a fallen lamp post leaning on a building in the main street and reach a pontoon bridge over the Chambal and a large water pumping station to supply water to an irrigation canal. The river banks are busy: crowds of people are crossing the river, some are watering their cows and buffaloes and I see a small vegetable farm on the sandy bank of the Madhya Pradesh side of the river. Yet within minutes of boarding one of the Forest Department's boats, I have seen my first gharial, a 10-foot female, and some marsh crocodiles, also known as mugger crocodiles. Even a glimpse of an otter. Dozens of birds are feeding around some small islands that have emerged from the river during the season of its lowest natural flow, including great thick-knees, a strange bird with huge eyes that looks permanently surprised, and comb ducks, the males bearing black, semicircular 'combs' above their beaks. I finally see my first Indian skimmer, a high-flying loner left behind by the flocks heading north to cooler rivers on their annual migration. On one of the islands, a warden carefully scrapes the sand away to reveal a crocodile's nest of luminous white eggs. They lay twenty to forty eggs, I am told, and the gharials sixty, but only a tenth survive the depreda-tions of jackals, raptors, and other crocodiles. 'They have a very hard life. If the monsoon is early, they are swept away.'

Shortly afterwards, we are treated to the sight of no less than seven gharials in the river, two of them with their long jaws open and out of the water and pointed diagonally towards the sky. This bizarre-looking beast, *Gavialis gangeticus*, is as emblematic of the Ganges as the dolphin with which it shares the river, and is often identified with the mythical animal vehicle of the goddess Ganga (which is clearly crocodilian though not precisely a gharial). It is also much rarer than the dolphin, having narrowly escaped extinction in the 1970s. The gharial, said to be the oldest surviving crocodile from the era when reptiles dominated the earth, was once abundant in rivers across the subcontinent from Pakistan to Myanmar through India, Nepal, Bhutan, and Bangladesh. By 1976 the adult population was estimated to have collapsed to fewer than 200, from 5,000 to 10,000 in the 1940s.

Gharials, unlike the marsh crocodiles, are harmless to humans, for the adults feed entirely on fish, while the young eat insects, larvae, and frogs. The shape of their jaws is well suited for the capture of their fast-moving prey, according to the researchers of the Worldwide Fund for

Nature: 'Their long, narrow snouts offer very little resistance to water in swiping motions to snap up fish in the water. Their numerous needle-like teeth are ideal for holding on to struggling, slippery fish.' Males have a curious protuberance at the tip of their jaws shaped like a *ghara* or earthenware pot—hence the name—and its presence at their nostrils is apparently used to produce a snorting, hissing noise in displays of male dominance.

But the bulge has proved to be one more cause of their decline. One tribal community in Nepal believed that a crocodile's *ghara* under a pregnant woman's pillow would relieve her of labour pains, that incense sticks made of *ghara* would work as a pesticide when burnt in the fields, and that a gharial's eggs had medicinal value. Another disadvantage for the gharial, according to some scientists, is the unwillingness of the gharial mothers to assist her young into the water after they hatch—perhaps her teeth are too sharp—or to protect them for more than a few days afterwards. (The BBC's researchers, on the contrary, found the typical gharial mother to be exemplary: she hears the cries of her young in their underground nest, guards them for up to six months, and benefits from shared child-care arrangements with other gharials if she needs to go hunting.)[26] Another interesting habit, Ram Pratap Singh has assured me, is that the gharials eat stones so they can sink to the bottom of the river. At first I find this hard to believe, but it turns out to be a practice shared with other crocodilians, and it seems to be to help with the grinding of awkward food in the digestive system as well as for buoyancy adjustment.

Although we are seeing an apparently healthy local population of gharials, they are not secure from sand-mining or poaching. About 100 gharials died a decade ago in a mass killing through kidney damage thought to have been caused by the animals eating poisoned or pollution-affected fish from the Yamuna. The clean waters of the Chambal nevertheless remain a sanctuary for the gharial and are where most of them are found to this day, despite attempts to restock the main stream of the Ganga at Hastinapur with young harvested as eggs and hatched in captivity. Viren Palsingh of the Forest Department on the Chambal explains that he and his colleagues erect nets around the nests of gharials and crocodiles to protect them from jackals and monitor lizards. 'The number of gharials and crocodiles are increasing', he says.[27]

The banks of the Chambal are certainly peaceful here, given how close the river is to the teeming cities of Delhi, Agra, Kanpur, and

Lucknow. You can hear the susurration of the pipal tree—sometimes known as the ghost tree from that haunting rustle of leaves—in the faint evening breeze. Chitoria proves to be a sharp-eyed guide to the wildlife. At night he points out a palm civet creeping through the undergrowth and imitates the call of a spotted owlet with a noise that sounds like a cross between a whistle and someone squashing a plastic bottle half-full of water; it seems an implausible cry for a bird until a real owlet shows up and makes an identical call.

At dawn the following morning we head east through the ramshackle town of Bah to find a more isolated stretch of the Chambal. Even here there are scores of people, some crouched in mud huts with thatched roofs reminiscent of rural Africa, others defecating amid the eroded hillocks and miniature canyons at the water's edge, and yet others herding camels heavily laden with firewood; much of the wood is *babul*, the local name for mesquite, an invasive plant from America that spreads with terrifying speed and which locals are encouraged to cut and uproot, but some of it is from native trees for which they supposedly need permission. Across the river at Ater is a seventeenth-century fort built by Badan Singh of the Bhadoria clan, and on our side we see the brick entrance to the abandoned cave of a holy man who died 70 or 80 years ago.

The birds are abundant, from the ubiquitous wild peacocks (I saw one in the car park once at Delhi's international airport) to the tiny, tail-flicking jungle prinias chirruping and leaping about the trees, and a lone hoopoe, the exotic crested bird of black, white, and orange also found in Africa. The river here is about 50 metres wide and shallow enough to wade most of the way across, reasonably substantial by English standards but tiny compared to its full size during the monsoon. I spot our first turtle, a 4-inch long Indian roof turtle between two huge, beached metal cylinders that are used to make a pontoon bridge. By the end of the day, we have seen at least four turtle species. There are gharials, too, and when we walk with our picnic breakfast to a green peninsula jutting into the river we pass under the occupied nest of an Egyptian vulture, a collection of sticks propped on a ledge in the eroded bank of silt.

I find it hard to believe I am in north India. The only sounds are the rippling of the water in the morning breeze, the lowing of cattle on the far side, and occasional birdsong. A large turtle, its body bigger than a dinner plate, pokes its nose above the water. A marsh crocodile is patrolling just off our island, only the top of its head and the crenellations of its tail showing, and I fancy it is attracted by my hard-boiled eggs. Despite the intense heat and the temptingly clear water, I decide not to swim. On the opposite bank stands a solitary black-necked stork, and on our side we glimpse a coucal, a black-and-chestnut bird with an eerie, hollow call that can be heard in forest and scrubland across Asia. Its Hindi name, Chitoria tells me, is *bhardwaj*, after a famous holy man. 'It's lucky to see a coucal in the morning', he says. 'Your day will be good.' As for the Chambal, he tells another version of the curse from the days of King Ratidev and concludes: 'People were very scared to come close. And construction is forbidden, so the future is bright for the Chambal.'

In truth, even the Chambal River, spared the ravages of man for centuries by its evil reputation, is not secure today. As usual, the basic problem is lack of water. The first dam across the river was built in 1960 on the Rajasthan–Madhya Pradesh border, and since then there have been six major irrigation projects and scores of smaller ones, including the pumping station I saw on the river, to irrigate thousands of hectares of farmland. So much water is extracted that one of India's leading environmental journalists found that along the 435-kilometre stretch of the Chambal suitable for dolphins and gharials only 10–15 per cent of the distance had the minimum depth required in the dry months between May and July. Sand-mining, quarrying, industrial effluent, land clearance for fields, pesticides, fertilizers, and illegal fishing were further threats to wildlife, and the capacity of the three state forest departments concerned to protect the sanctuary was 'woefully inadequate'.[28]

For a vision of how bad the river could be, it is a short trip across the tongue of land that separates the Chambal from the Yamuna before they meet downstream. Bateshwar on the Yamuna is famous for its 101 riverside temples dedicated to Lord Shiva, and in ancient times it was the site of an annual fair famous throughout South Asia. Chitoria tells me that traders came from Peshawar in the north-west to sell camels, from Ladakh in the north to sell donkeys, from Burma in the east to sell elephants, and from everywhere to sell buffaloes. It is a peaceful Monday (Shiva's day) and the sound of tolling temple bells reminds me of an English village on a Sunday morning, although the temperature here is in the high forties in centigrade, sweat is pouring down my back, and there are greater quantities of both worshippers and rubbish than you would find in England's home counties.

I watch in dismay as a man with dark glasses empties a plastic sack into the river at the bottom of a *ghat*. My dismay turns briefly to acceptance when I see that the sack contained plant cuttings and that turtles are crowding round in the water to feed. Dismay returns when I notice that some of the waste is in a tied-up plastic bag, which floats down the river like a white football amid the greenery. I persuade him not to throw the empty sack in as well, but it is clear I am fighting a losing battle. Although the marigold petals scattered by pilgrims on the river's surface and the porridge thrown to the turtles by an orange-robed *sadhu* are obviously biodegradable, the bottom of Bateshwar's ghats is a mulch of plastic bags and *puja* waste. Worshippers are paying homage to Shiva *lingams* in the temples above, a bemused calf is wandering along the steep steps, and stray dogs are lying in the shallow, green, and garbage-thickened water of the Yamuna to seek respite from the midday heat. It is amazing, I reflect, how all this seems completely normal when you live in India.

My optimism about Indian wildlife, I realize, is as vulnerable as a gharial's egg. To be sure, I delight in the biodiversity of the Ganges and the rest of India, and I was pleased to learn that in 2014 alone the Botanical Survey and the Zoological Survey of India recorded 349 new plants and animals, mostly from 'hotspots' such as the Himalayas and the Andaman Islands. Among them is a blue dwarf snakehead fish that can walk ashore—well, wriggle really—breathe air and stay on land for up to four days out of its freshwater home. Another find is a fairyfly that is just 0.16mm long and thought to be the world's smallest flying insect; this species—the *Kikiki huna*, meaning 'tiny bit'—has been found in other countries but never in India.[29]

And yet it is impossible not to understand, with a sense of melancholy, that India's wild animals are increasingly confined to isolated patches of land or ribbons of water in national parks and reserves and that even those sanctuaries are rarely intact. Fewer than 200 great Indian bustards survive today. This creature that stands about a metre high—once considered for the status of national bird but rejected in favour of the peafowl for fear of misspellings and jokes in poor taste—is in imminent danger of extinction because of hunting, habitat loss, and electrocution by overhead cables. There has been immense change to the landscape, the flora, and the fauna since the days of Ashoka more than two millennia ago when he ordered the protection not only of a Ganges denizen that may have been the dolphin but also of parrots,

mynahs, ducks, geese, bats, ants, tortoises, squirrels, deer, lizards, rhinoceroses, and 'all quadrupeds which are neither useful nor edible'.[30]

The Mughal emperor Babur was unimpressed by India's people but
enamoured of its wildlife, including the rhinoceroses that he found as
far west as the forests of Peshawar. Mughal noblemen hunted the lions
once abundant in the country, while the British who replaced the
Mughals concentrated on shooting the tigers. Today, even at the
restocked Sariska reserve, the easiest tiger to see is a dead one—stuffed
and snarling from its showcase in the lobby of the Sariska Palace hotel.
The numerous, century-old photographs displayed on the terrace—of
maharajas and British military officers posing with dead tigers as hunting trophies—shows how common the big cats once were in the area.
These days the closest most Indians will come to a wild cat is when
they watch television pictures of the leopards that periodically fall
down a well or wander by mistake into a village or the grounds of a
school.

The slaughter of South Asia's rich stock of wildlife in the colonial
era was terrifying in its extent and intensity. Before her ship had even
reached India from England, the diarist Fanny Parkes recorded the
shooting of albatrosses and sharks by her fellow passengers and an
attack on a whale, for fun, with a Congreve rocket. After she lands
there are hunting parties, shooting expeditions, and exhibition fights
staged by a north Indian potentate involving elephants and rhinoceroses
and worthy of ancient Rome.

Until the early nineteenth century, the river and its banks teemed
with wildlife of every sort, whereas now the only megafauna are likely
to be found in national parks or zoos or arrive at the river by accident.
In the 2016 monsoon an adult male elephant from Assam was swept
hundreds of kilometres down the Brahmaputra River in a flood, was
repeatedly driven back by stone-throwing villagers when it tried to
scramble ashore in India, and died six weeks later after crossing the
border into the wetlands of Bangladesh.[31] As for the gharials, a ship's
pilot in Bengal who has spent his life guiding vessels up the Hooghly
and into the main stream of the Ganges told me he had last seen one
eight years previously.

The lower slopes of the Himalayas, once remote but now increasingly accessible by road, are vulnerable as well. In the mid-nineteenth
century, Frederick 'Pahari' ('hill man') Wilson, a British military
deserter who became the so-called Raja of Harsil near the source of

the Ganges, was notorious in his day for hunting so many wild animals (those musk deer again) and for cutting so many of the deodar trees that were converted into the railway sleepers of India.

Today only a fraction of that natural wealth survives in the hills. The account by Stephen Alter, an American author born to missionaries in upland India, of his four treks to the sources of the Ganges in 1999 and 2000 is peppered with anecdotes about poachers and plant robbers as well as *sadhus* and pilgrims. He does once see a black bear, but he also encounters a group of men who seem to be poaching musk deer, another man who tries to sell him a leopard skin, and gaggles of Garwhalis and Nepalis digging up roots and flowers to sell as herbal remedies in a trade that has already devastated the highland flora of India and China. In Yamunotri, near the source of the Yamuna, he encounters an elderly *sadhu* who tells him he has lived there since 1967. The *baba* laments the complex of rest-houses and tea stalls that have commercialized the area around the shrines and accuses the forestry department of failing to protect wildlife. 'All kinds of animals used to come here in winter—*bharal*, *tahr*, *ghoral*, leopards and bear, but I haven't seen them for years', he says. 'People are digging up the wild herbs everywhere and burning all the trees for firewood.'[32]

My admiration for the ability of Indians to coexist with wild animals—and for the heroes, Indian and foreign, who have tried and so far succeeded in saving big mammals such as tigers and dolphins for posterity—is inevitably tempered by realism. That is because the pressures on the Ganges and the natural world in general are so intense; they include the repeated extraction of the river's water along its length for irrigation, pollution from sewage and industry, and over-exploitation of everything in the river from fish to turtle eggs and snails. These challenges have an underlying cause that is immensely important for the Ganges, India, and the world and yet is surprisingly little appreciated or discussed: the relentless rise of the human population.

10

People Pressure

Why Population Growth Is Not a Dividend

This is indeed, a most rich and striking land. Here, in the space of little more than 200 miles, along the same river, I have passed six towns, none of them less populous than Chester, two (Patna and Mirzapoor) more so than Birmingham; and one, Benares, more peopled than any city in Europe, except London and Paris! And this besides villages innumerable.

—Reginald Heber, Bishop of Calcutta, describing the Ganges
on his journey of 1824–5[1]

People, people, people, people.

—Paul Ehrlich, author of *The Population Bomb*, describing
a 'hellish' taxi ride in Delhi

Nitish Kumar, the chief minister of the Indian state of Bihar, has a big problem—and that problem is too many people. The state capital Patna on the Ganges—which as the splendid Pataliputra more than 2,000 years ago administered the Mauryan empire and was possibly the world's largest city of the time—became notorious in modern times for crime and poverty. Indians from elsewhere were reluctant to visit and even locals were scared to venture out at night for fear of kidnappings and robberies. Kumar is a methodical man who managed to reduce corruption and restore order to the violent streets of Patna after he first won control of Bihar in 2005. Poverty, however, has proved a tougher challenge. It is not just that Bihar is landlocked, in an era when manufacturing industry has tended to flourish in coastal regions connected by sea to trading partners abroad. For all the renowned agricultural fertility and natural wealth of the Gangetic plain, Bihar today is simply overpopulated.[2]

In the decade to 2011, the population of Bihar increased by more than a quarter to nearly 104 million. That increase of 21 million people roughly equates to the population of Australia, and Bihar now has more than twice as many inhabitants as Spain. By 2016, the population had reached about 117 million. With an average of 3.7 children over a woman's lifetime, Bihar is the state with the highest fertility rate in India, according to official statistics. Its population grew 2.2 per cent annually over the past decade, compared with 1.6 per cent for India as a whole.

Kumar thinks he has the solution: education for girls, because educated women have fewer children and start having them later. 'The big problem is the increasing numbers of the population,' Mr Kumar told me in an interview in Patna in 2013. 'So we have to stabilize it... And women's education is a must for stabilizing population.' Kumar said the fertility rate typically fell to about two when girls had completed two years of secondary education. 'And we came to this conclusion that unless we provide education to all our girl children this population cannot be controlled', he said. 'Nowadays we require more than 8,000 secondary schools. At this point in time we have 3,000 plus... So we are making our plans to open at least 1,000 schools every year.' Kumar, an engineer-turned-politician often seen as a potential future prime minister of India, made Bihar's economy the fastest-growing among India's twenty-nine states by tackling crime and promoting education from the start. In a very traditional, patriarchal north Indian society, he provided girls with free school uniforms and bicycles as an incentive for families to send their daughters to school. Bihar has also reserved half of its teaching posts and half of the seats in elected local government bodies for women.[3]

Yet even if Kumar succeeds, it will take many years for Bihar's population to stabilize, and the state's ability to provide basic services to its inhabitants remains constantly under threat from the rapid expansion of its population. Nor is Bihar even the largest state in the Indian union. The biggest is its western neighbour Uttar Pradesh, which with around 220 million people has more inhabitants than Brazil and would be the fifth-biggest nation on the planet if it were an independent country. It is true that in many southern Indian states such as Kerala and Tamil Nadu, fertility rates and population growth have declined sharply and the number of inhabitants is set to stabilize, partly as a result of urbanization and better education. It is also true that some places are doing worse than Bihar and India when it comes to managing their demography. Over the border in Pakistan, the mostly Muslim country that split from Hindu-majority India in the violent partition of 1947, each woman has an average of 3.8 children; the population has risen from 33 million at that time to 200 million today and is heading for more than 300 million by 2050. Karachi, the port at the mouth of the Indus River that gave India its name, was once known as the Venice of the East, but is now so grotesquely overcrowded that people live a dozen or more to an apartment, bus passengers are routinely packed onto the roof for lack of room inside, and fresh water is in short supply.[4]

Still it is India, because of the growth in the number of inhabitants in the Gangetic plain, that will overtake China to become the world's most populous nation in about 2025. India's population is set to rise from about 1.2 billion in 2010 to more than 1.7 billion in 2050 before—probably—levelling off in the second half of the century. In a few decades, in short, India is adding the equivalent of the entire population of Europe to the number of people it has to feed, house, educate—and provide with water. The strain on the country's natural resources (and on governments) is and will be immense.

The lands through which the Ganges flows have, by global standards, been densely populated by humans for millennia. Kameshwar Upadhyay, a Sanskrit scholar and astrologer in Varanasi, told me a curious demographic anecdote about Kapil Muni, the ancient sage whose fiery gaze is said to have burnt to ashes the 60,000 sons of King Sagar (and who thus helped bring the Ganges from the heavens to the earth when King Bhagirath persuaded the gods to release the holy river to purify his ancestors' remains). Kapil Muni, said Upadhyay, had declared that the maximum number of people who could live on earth was one times two times three and so on up to times 13. That gives a figure of 6,227,020,800 or 6.2 billion. The world's population today is already more than 1 billion above that, and rising fast. Most of the increase to date, globally and in India, has come since the start of the twentieth century, when the population of the territory that is now India was just 238 million—or one-sixth of the current total.

The threat of a life-extinguishing planetary 'population explosion' has been fearfully discussed for centuries, certainly from the time of the eighteenth-century economist Thomas Malthus if not from the Vedic era of Kapil Muni. Yet in recent years and among policymakers in much of the world, including India, there has been a reversal of

1. The valley where the Ganges has its source in a Himalayan glacier, with the ashrams of Bhujbas in the foreground.

2. Evening fire ceremony at the temple of Ganga the river goddess in Gangotri.

3. Swami Sundaranand—yogi, mountaineer, and photographer—pictured in Gangotri in 2013 lamenting the effects of climate change.

4. A woman trawls with mosquito netting for prawn seed in the Sunderbans.

5. Floods sweep over a statue of Shiva on the Ganges at Rishikesh, June 2013.

6. Crowds gather at the mouth of the Ganges for the annual festival at Sagar Island in the Bay of Bengal in January 2016.

7. Naga sadhus, the ascetic holy men of India, gather on the banks of the Ganges at the Kumbh Mela in Allahabad in 2013, arguably the largest gathering of humans in history.

8. Varanasi on the Ganges at dawn.

9. Boatmen row their craft along the foamy and polluted Yamuna River, a major tributary of the Ganges.

10. A gharial face to face with a grasshopper. Water-colour by Sita Ram, *c*.1820.

11. Indian security forces guard work crews repairing the vital Munak Canal that supplies Delhi after it was sabotaged by protesters in February 2016.

12. Villagers in Gusiyari in the drought-stricken Bundelkhand region carry water home at sunset from the village's only functioning sweet-water well, April 2016.

13. Film poster from the 1985 Bollywood hit *Ram Teri Ganga Maili* ('Ram, your Ganges has been sullied').

A BUDGEROW.

Drawn from Nature & on Stone by Captain J. Luard

Printed by Day & Son

14. Budgerows, the traditional boats of the Ganges. Lithograph by John Luard, *c.*1830.

The River Batar. Ganges in the fore ground and part of Lord Moira's Fleet

15. Lord Hastings's flotilla on the river, with many pinnace budgerows. By Sita Ram, *c.*1810–22.

16. Narendra Modi, Indian prime minister, promises to deal with lack of toilets and sanitation in his first Independence Day speech from the walls of the Red Fort in Delhi, 15 August 2014.

17. On the edge of India. A boy stands on one of the shifting islands of the Sunderbans at the mouth of the Ganges.

18. Three men sleep by the Hooghly River in Calcutta.

19. A woman tends her vegetable patch next to the Ganges under Chunar fort, where the river sweeps northwards to Varanasi.

20. A man prays at Devprayag, a holy river confluence where the Bhagirathi and Alaknanda meet to form the Ganges.

thought. Population growth, the thinking goes among many economists and investment analysts, is nothing to worry about. Rather, it is to be embraced because a rising population confers an economy with a 'demographic dividend' of a swelling workforce of young and creative inhabitants. Politicians, industrialists, and foreign economists and stock market analysts use this misleading phrase—a dangerous phrase, I argue—with wearisome regularity. I heard it spoken half a dozen times from the stage at a single event in Delhi to launch the 'Make in India' campaign, an initiative of Prime Minister Narendra Modi to boost manufacturing investment.[5] To understand how Indians became so complacent about the country's surging population, we have to go back a little in time and look at some demographic data.

In 1600, the population of India was already thought to be above 100 million,[6] and by the start of the twentieth century, 300 years later, the number of inhabitants within the present borders had more than doubled. At independence in 1947, it was above 300 million; the following year, S. H. Prater, who had been curator of the Bombay Natural History Society, lamented what he called 'the disastrous effect on the wild life of the country' of human encroachment in his preface to a field guide to Indian mammals.[7] It was in the 1960s, when the population rose above 500 million, that the neo-Malthusian Paul Ehrlich wrote *The Population Bomb*—and it was a taxi ride on a hot night in Delhi that provided him with the 'hellish' personal experience of the population crisis he believed he already understood intellectually. 'People eating, people washing, people sleeping. People visiting, arguing, and screaming. People thrusting their hands through the taxi window, begging. People defecating and urinating. People clinging to buses. People herding animals. People, people, people, people', he wrote in the prologue.

Today there are nearly three times as many Indians as there were then. At the beginning of the twenty-first century, India's population had reached 1 billion and in 2016 it was over 1.3 billion. It is obvious to anyone who travels in India that most of the land is occupied and much of it crowded. There is scarcely a spot along the length of the Ganges, except at the mountainous and swampy extremities near source and mouth, where you can be out of sight of people. Cities are becoming megalopolises, and towns are becoming cities as millions migrate from the overcrowded countryside to find work.

Back in 2007, Sheila Dikshit, then chief minister of the Indian capital territory of Delhi, complained that she was putting on weight because she was eating too much to overcome her anxiety about the half a million migrants arriving in the city each year. If her administration did not meet the needs of Delhi's inhabitants, she warned, one of the world's largest cities would slide downhill. 'Each one of them when they live in Delhi, they want more water, more power, they want more wages, more oil.'[8] They were prophetic words. With Delhi and its satellite cities and towns now home to some 25 million people, one of Dikshit's successes—the improvement of air quality by converting public buses and taxis from diesel to natural gas—has long since been cancelled by a surge in emissions of smoke and dust from trucks, power stations, and the burning of cow dung used as cooking fuel.[9]

The problem is not confined to Delhi. As I travelled around the country, I encountered many Indians—mystics, naturalists, ship captains, shopkeepers, farmers—who were concerned about excessive population growth. In Varanasi on the Ganges, a sweet-shop owner told the writer Piers Moore Ede: 'It was once the greatest city in the world, but now it is getting too crowded. Population is out of control.'[10] When the mountaineer Edmund Hillary travelled all the way up the Ganges from the mouth at Sagar Island to Haridwar on a jet-boat expedition in 1977, he wrote: 'I doubt whether we were ever completely out of sight of human beings; there was always somebody.'[11]

India after independence was the first country to implement a policy designed to slow population growth, for it was evident that increased numbers in what was already such a populous nation would strain any administration's ability to provide its citizens with health care, schooling, and roads, let alone food and water. However, despite the concerns of state chief ministers such as Dikshit in Delhi and Kumar in Bihar, India's national governments have in recent years been oddly reticent about addressing this most important of issues. The reasons for this reticence are many.

First, India suffers from a failing common in parliamentary democracies: neither bureaucrats nor politicians are good at assessing or addressing looming problems that will fully materialize only after the end of a national government's five-year term of office.

Second, family planning has become a 'toxic' political issue in India because of an earlier, crude attempt to limit the population. In the mid-1970s, after Indira Gandhi suspended democracy and imposed a state of emergency, India became notorious for its coercive sterilization 'camps'. In the 1976–7 year of the programme, 8.3 million Indian men and women were sterilized.[12] The abuses during that period under the leadership of Gandhi's son Sanjay, and the unpopularity of the emergency, prompted the suspension of family planning services for years and helps explain the delicacy with which the topic is approached by Indian officials to this day. (China's recent abandonment of its unpopular one-child policy—Beijing's own desperate if effective attempt to curb population growth—was seen in India as further evidence of the futility of a coercive approach to birth control.) In both China and India, furthermore, the combination of birth control and a preference for male heirs has created skewed populations characterized by a predominance of boys and a shortage of girls. Millions of girls have gone 'missing'—female infanticide and abortions targeting female foetuses are rife—and this tragedy of sex selection reinforces the view that it is folly to seek to control demography.[13]

A third reason for Indian national policymakers' lack of concern about their country's demographic profile is a failure to appreciate the long time lags between changed fertility rates and the resulting changes in population size. Around now, it is true, India's total fertility rate is predicted to have declined to around replacement levels. To be specific, an Indian woman in 1950 had an average of nearly six children in her lifetime, and that had halved to 2.34 by 2013. Replacement fertility in India is reckoned to be about 2.23 (the number is slightly higher than two children per couple because some children are killed by disease and some women die before they reach the end of their childbearing years). That replacement level might turn out to have been achieved in 2016, thanks in part to extensive use of contraception and voluntary sterilizations; in the southern states of Andhra Pradesh, Karnataka, and Tamil Nadu, the proportion of married women opting for sterilization has in some years exceeded 50 per cent, often with the aid of cash inducements.[14]

But 'population momentum' and an increase in the average age at which people die mean that it takes a generation for a replacement level of fertility to translate into a stable population. Even when the fertility rate of a fast-growing country (or the world) falls towards replacement levels, the population keeps increasing for decades because of the large cohorts of young women reaching child-bearing age. Then, in India, there is the north–south divide. The relatively well-educated women in the cities of southern India typically have few children, while those in the north have many. The greatest burden of

India's coming population growth will fall on the already crowded and resource-hungry states of the Ganges catchment area: Haryana, Delhi, Uttar Pradesh, and Bihar in particular.

The fourth reason for insouciance, or even boasting, about population growth is the belief that a greater number of people makes a country—or a region, or a religion, or a family—wealthier and more powerful. In India, right-wing Hindu leaders do not just want millions more Indians, they want more of them to be Hindus. Sakshi Maharaj, a maverick member of parliament for Modi's Bharatiya Janata Party, urged Hindu women to have at least four children each 'to save the religion'. Prominent Hindu nationalists such as Pravin Togadia joined the fray, calling for even more children to ensure the safety of Hinduism for 1,000 years. One holy man wanted eight babies per mother. Another recalled that Lord Krishna sired ten children by each of his 16,108 wives and was quoted as saying that 'the world will be ruled by those who have maximum population'. These appeals spring from an atavistic fear that Muslims are breeding so fast and converting vulnerable Hindu women at such a rate that they will soon overwhelm the Hindus who still account for four out of every five Indians. N. Chandrababu Naidu, chief minister of Andhra Pradesh, complained of a 'demographic crisis' in the Indian state and called for more Andhra babies.[15]

Misunderstandings proliferate. It is true that the Muslim share of the population in India, at about 15 per cent, has grown from about 10 per cent in the past sixty years—but that is not because Muslims were trying to outbreed their Hindu neighbours. Poorer, less-educated people tend to have larger families. Since partition in 1947, when many of the Muslim elite moved to Pakistan, Indian Muslims have been, on average, less well off than Indian Hindus. In the relatively prosperous state of Kerala, Hindus and Muslims have equally small families, and across India Muslim fertility rates are declining faster than those of Hindus, and converging with them.

Fortunately, narrow appeals to religious chauvinism are unlikely to make much impact on Indian women, at least not on a scale that would make an appreciable difference to birth statistics in a country of 1.3 billion people. 'Twenty per cent of the [existing] fertility is unwanted', says Poonam Muttreja, who heads the Population Foundation of India. 'Women barely want two children...Hindu women are not going to have more children because religious leaders are telling them to dilute the Muslim birth rate.'[16]

An equally insidious argument for more babies, the fifth and final part of the pro-growth argument and one with broader appeal for policymakers, is economic. Governments are inclined to relax their efforts to promote contraception and sterilization as a way of reducing family size because they are bewitched by the idea of national power and the so-called 'demographic dividend'. Government ministers in India have taken to gloating about the dynamism that will come from a huge, young population. They gleefully repeat economists' warnings about China, which has successfully curbed its population growth with the help of the draconian 'one child' policy. China, say the Indians, 'will grow old before it grows rich' because it will suffer the Japanese 'disease' of too many pensioners and not enough workers long before the Chinese are prosperous or the economy fully developed. Some even talk of a 'double dividend' of demography and democracy. Kamal Nath, an ebullient Congress Party politician and former minister of commerce and industry, called India an 'island of stability' in a region of turbulence and authoritarianism, 'a large country with a large popu- lation functioning as a democracy, a country with a young workforce that is raring to go'.[17]

Such statements smack of complacency given the dysfunctional nature of Indian politics and governance; the voting mechanics of the country's democracy have so far survived and prospered, but many of the other attributes of a successful free society—law and order, an effi- cient justice system, and competent government—are sadly wanting. As for demography, it is unlikely that India will be able to cash in the putative dividend of its vast young population any time soon. The 'tiger' economies of South-east Asia were able to do so from the 1970s, and China followed in the 1980s and 1990s, when manufacturing was transferred en masse from developed nations such as the UK, Germany, the United States, and Japan to Asian factories employing young, low- cost workers.

India, unfortunately, has largely missed that industrial boat. Two photographs starkly illustrate the point. In one, John Kerry, then US secretary of state, is shown visiting a new Ford car factory in Gujarat, home of Narendra Modi. Kerry was spreading US–India goodwill ahead of a trip to India by President Barack Obama, and is pictured benevolently surveying the work of an important US investor. The most striking feature of the picture, however, was not Mr Kerry but the shortage of other people: he was looking mainly at Kawasaki manufacturing robots. The second photograph, which I used to show to Indian government officials when asking about Modi's record on job creation, is of another car factory, this time for the Japanese company Honda in Rajasthan. It was used in an advertising campaign for the state's role in 'Make in India'. Not a single human is visible in the picture, which shows robots welding the pieces of the cars together in a shower of sparks. Mr Modi's 'Make in India' no doubt contributes to economic revival, but the automated factories of the twenty-first century make barely make a dent in the demand for 12 million new jobs a year from the country's poorly skilled and fast-growing workforce.

That leaves the service sector, long hailed as the potential saviour of the Indian economy. Unfortunately, employers in information technology and business process outsourcing face intense international competition and regularly complain about India's generally poor standards of education. There are simply not enough jobs for India's low-skilled workers, and not enough high-skilled Indians for the few million new jobs that might be available in high-end services. This is not a new conundrum (Rajat Nag, then managing director general of the Asian Development Bank, once warned that 'the demographic dividend can easily become a demographic curse' and foment social unrest if people were not properly provided with skills)[18] but Indian policymakers have been slow to grasp its significance.

Nor are service-sector jobs immune from the risks posed by automation and the adoption of new forms of information technology. The economist Ira Sohn recently wrote that it was in services, not the relatively small manufacturing sector, that developed countries should fear the impact of automation on jobs. In the United States, for example, more than 80 per cent of the workforce were employed in services, and so 'rapidly eliminating only 5 per cent of these jobs with the introduction of robots and artificial intelligence algorithms would be equivalent to idling about 50 per cent of current manufacturing employment, about 6 million jobs', Sohn wrote. 'The issue we should be discussing is not whether, but how quickly, the routine service jobs will disappear.'[19] India is not yet a developed economy and has a smaller proportion of its workforce in services, but the share is still over 50 per cent and will grow as tens of millions of farmers abandon their unprofitable lives on small plots of land in the countryside and move to towns and cities; manufacturing currently accounts for about 17 per cent of the Indian economy. Only about 10 million Indians are currently employed in private-sector companies with ten or more work-ers—an extraordinarily low number for a population of more than 1.3 billion.

Indian policymakers urgently need to acknowledge the reality of the country's fast-rising population and build the physical and social infrastructure—from sewage treatment plants and houses to schools and pension systems—to accommodate the additional hundreds of millions. The challenge is not unique to India. In just one century from 1950, the population of the arid African state of Niger, one of the world's poorest countries, is forecast to expand nineteenfold to an insupportable 50 million by the year 2050. In 1950, there were 221 mil-lion people living on the African continent; by 2030—that is, a couple of decades from now—there are likely to be around 1.5 billion Africans. But India is also densely populated and is unique because of the abso-lute size of its population—more than the whole of Africa—and its imminent overtaking of China as the most populous nation of all.

In today's high-population, low-mortality world—a world of increasing automation where the wearisome assembly line jobs of the past are performed by tireless robots—the despair sometimes expressed by the Japanese over their shrinking population and the insouciant delight of Indian politicians about the growth of theirs are both gro-tesquely misplaced. It is not hard to see why people think this way. Biology and human history favour population growth. 'In the multi-tude of people is the king's honour: but in the want of people is the destruction of the prince', is the biblical version in Proverbs 14:28. 'Virtually every rising power in history has also been a demographically expanding power', wrote two researchers in the United States a few months after the country's population rose above 300 million in 2006. 'In rising powers, higher fertility rates go hand in hand with greater faith in collective destiny.'[20]

This bias in favour of population growth is reflected in the choice of words used to describe demographic trends. Populations that are stable or shrinking are said to be 'stagnant', 'committing national sui-cide', or suffering from a self-inflicted disaster equivalent to the Black Death. Growing populations, by contrast, are 'young and energetic' and reaping the economic benefits of their 'demographic dividend'. A shrinking population, or declining population growth, is almost always defined in speeches and investment bank research papers as 'unfavourable', while a fast-growing population is inevitably 'positive'.

The 'losers' in this fantasy world are Japan, Russia, and Europe. The 'winners' are Bangladesh, Pakistan, Egypt, Mexico, Nigeria—and India. Yet no one who knows Pakistan or Nigeria, say, would conclude that these are inevitably future winners in anything other than a strictly demographic sense, or that they need more people of working age to boost their economies.

The main argument of the population boosters is that the slow-down or reversal of population growth will reduce the size of a nation's economy and impose a heavy financial burden on dwindling numbers of young workers who are obliged to support growing numbers of pensioners. Furthermore, innovation, which is vital for modern econ-omies, will wither because old people are not as inventive as the young. Whether in Japan or Italy, we are threatened with spectral images of moribund economies in which angry youths rebel against their elders and refuse to pay the taxes required to support the old and infirm. It is certainly true that many wealthy societies are ageing and that 'grey power' has become a political force in countries such as the United States. Indeed, one reason why we have underestimated population growth is that we did not expect longevity to increase as fast as it has. 'It's not that people suddenly started breeding like rabbits; it's just that they stopped dying like flies', was the way one UN consultant put it. 'The problem of ageing', the demographer Frank Notestein said half a century ago, 'is no problem at all. It is only the pessimistic way of look-ing at a great triumph of civilisation.'[21]

Fears about ageing are not unreasonable, particularly when a coun-try undergoes an abrupt transition from population growth to decline. But economists and the strategists of big international banks—who tend to see absolute economic growth as an essential sign of success—are wrong to conclude that the only remedy is to keep having more babies. The fundamental absurdity of this argument is that it envisages perpetual growth in the number of inhabitants in particular countries and on the planet as a whole. A better alternative is to aim for a gradual slow-down in population growth, followed by stabilization and per-haps a gentle decline.

There are also obvious weaknesses in the economic case for further population growth in India or anywhere else. First, increased longevity and better health care means that people can stay in the labour force (and often they want to) for many more years than previously thought. Second, several recent studies show high levels of innovation and productivity among the aged. Third, many societies, such as Japan and India, could do much more to bring women into the workforce and so alleviate the fiscal burden on other workers. Fourth, countries with labour shortages can import workers from 'young' countries with labour surpluses through immigration. Fifth, greater mechanization can reduce the need for younger workers and is already doing so. Sixth, the focus on the sheer size of an economy or its overall growth misses the point about the political and social purpose of economic expansion, which is to enhance people's welfare. Many African countries have growing economies purely by virtue of the fact that they have fast-growing populations, but it does not make people wealthier or happier. Per capita economic growth and per capita wealth are better measures of welfare, and they are not necessarily affected by declining numbers of people.

The vast population of young people hailed by countries such as India as a 'demographic dividend' may turn out to be a demographic disaster. The young will be expensive to house and educate and they may not find work in a high-technology world, and there is evidence that countries with large numbers of unemployed young men are more likely to succumb to war or violence. In short, the risks of elderly populations and the benefits of young ones are both overstated by the population-boosters.

Population decline, in any case, is limited to a small number of countries, and Europe is the only continent expected to see a fall in numbers between now and 2050. Globally, we are still in the midst of a population explosion. In mid 2016, 251 people were being born each minute and 108 were dying. We cannot even be sure that the world population will level off as forecast. Predictions of an eventual stabilization of human numbers depend crucially on population growth falling in places—in Africa, for example—where that has not yet happened.

After a period of concern half a century ago about the population explosion in India and on the planet as a whole, there are now some worrying signs of backsliding. At the end of the last century the United Nations predicted that the world population would rise to 8.9 billion in 2050, but in early 2007 it revised that upwards to 9.2 billion. In 2015, the UN made another upward revision. The world population, it said, would rise to 9.7 billion in 2050—and 11.2 billion in 2100. The increase from 2015 to 2050 is about the same as the entire global population as recently as 1950. And in its latest forecast the UN warned about the uncertainty of declining fertility in poorer countries:

Slower-than-projected fertility declines would result in much higher population totals in all subsequent time periods. For example, a scenario in which all countries had a fertility rate that was consistently half a child higher than in the medium variant would produce a population of 16.6 billion in 2100, more than 5 billion higher than the medium-variant projection.[22]

For all the carefully worded prose, these are terrifying numbers, as is the certainty (for it is in the past) that the world added about 1 billion to its human population in the 12 years to 2015.

As for India, many of the problems it faces—water shortages, the spread of infectious diseases, unemployment, heavy dependence on imported oil, and the effects of climate change—originate, at least in part, in the alarming growth of the national population. The bulge of young people today will in time become a bulge of pensioners in a country where only 11 per cent of the working-age population have formal pension arrangements. India will thus face the same problems of ageing and high dependency ratios as Japan and Europe today, only on a larger scale. Long before then, India's huge workforce of about 800 million could become more of a threat than an opportunity. Who will create employment for the 12 million or so new entrants to the job market each year, of whom only a fraction will find regular work? Who will feed them and supply them with water and fuel? India has 18 per cent of the world's population but only 4 per cent of its fresh water and just over 2 per cent of its land area.

Instead of bragging about the uncertain (and short-term) economic benefits of India's purported 'demographic dividend', Indian politicians and bureaucrats should be working out how to grow the food, provide the water, build and staff the schools, and construct the roads and power stations that the country's existing inhabitants, as well as its future ones, so desperately need. Water, the subject of the next chapter, will be among the biggest challenges.

11

Water and Wells

Why the Taps Run Dry

It's a crisis now and if we don't arrest it, then 10 years down the line we'll have water wars. Punjab and Haryana will be in flames in no time.

—Shashi Shekhar, water secretary, on inter-state battles over scarce water supplies[1]

Beti Aleem Khan is a domineering presence in the evening crowd around the old village well in Gusiyari. The 50-year-old Muslim woman has no hesitation in charging up to us to demand that we help provide the water that India's bureaucrats and politicians—from Prime Minister Narendra Modi down—have failed to supply. I have come with a colleague to this drought-stricken community on the southern side of the Gangetic plain, in the dry, pre-monsoon month of April 2016, to try to understand how a country with such abundant rainfall and such large rivers can be so short of water.

The village is in a region called Bundelkhand—it is near the Panna tiger reserve where I encountered the vultures—that straddles the border between Uttar Pradesh and Madhya Pradesh in the heart of India. Droughts are not new to this area, although the water shortage in 2016 was particularly severe, and many of those born here escape rural hardship to find work as migrant labourers in Saudi Arabia, Kuwait, or Dubai, or on the outskirts of Delhi. The large, brick-lined well where we find Khan and the other villagers on a hot afternoon is the only one that produces fresh water for Gusiyari's 3,500 inhabitants. They say it was built 300 years ago, and the bricks along its rim are furrowed by the ropes used to raise the water from 50 feet below in metal pots.

The village's government-installed wells, the long-handled metal hand-pumps seen all across rural India, produce water so salty that it is used mostly for washing utensils. I try the water from a pump about 100 metres from the brick well, and it is undrinkably saline. The villagers tell us that the problem is not just a lack of water for crops and farm animals. There is not even enough for them to wash themselves regularly, and the need to carry water long distances makes Gusiyari's men into unattractive marriage partners for potential brides. Next to the well, Khan shows us a filthy waterhole of green, viscous water in an otherwise dry riverbed and explains the situation in colourful Hindi:

The water crisis is acute here. It's a huge problem. A thousand rupees were spent to dig this hole here for water. All the women from the village bathe in this and wash their clothes. Every couple of weeks the water gets so dirty and smelly and is full of bacteria. Then everyone contributes half a litre of kerosene oil [diesel] and a pumping machine is bought to remove this water and then it takes a couple of days for the groundwater to resurface and the hole fills up with water again. Women have to take turns to come and bathe here since there is not enough room for too many people. So two or three women come to bathe here at a time. I am nearly 50 years old, and since my childhood we have been facing this problem of water here. Sweaty people smell awful but you can't bathe here every day. Some people don't wash for four days. And nobody wants their daughter to get married to someone from here because they think their daughters will die carrying water on their heads all their lives. Hindus of the village have an even bigger problem getting married. At least Muslims can marry girls from within the village. Hindus cannot get married to any girl from the same village. So all those people who come to this village looking for prospective grooms for their daughters, come and feast here on fried bread, vegetable curry, and sweets. But they return home merely to call on the phone and say, 'Hello, the village is really far and we don't want our daughters to go.' Our poor villagers lose whatever little money they have in trying to arrange for a bride for their sons.[2]

Rajesh Kumar Tiwari, a 48-year-old farmer who grows wheat and chickpeas, says there must be at least 'eighteen to twenty guys' in his neighbourhood who cannot get married due to the water crisis:

Since the time I was a child, I have seen this problem in our village. There is no provision for irrigation here, no tube-wells or canals. You can see the shortage of drinking water. You have just seen that hole that has been dug to provide for bathing water—animals, humans are all bathing in that dirty water. About three years ago Mr Rahul Gandhi [the Congress party politician and great grandson of Jawaharlal Nehru, the first prime minister] came here.

He spent a lot of time studying the problem. I had told him the same thing then—that if you really want to solve our problem, we should have tube-wells or canals. So many state and central governments have come and gone. They have done nothing to resolve our problem. There are three or four other villages in this Hamirpur district facing acute water crisis like us. The main problem here with the groundwater is that at about 160–70 feet, the ground is rocky and we do not have equipment to dig deeper. Even if we get water at that level, it's so salty that it cannot be used... Farmers in this area are on the verge of starvation, forced to commit suicide.

The Indian water crisis in early 2016 was particularly severe, with ten of India's twenty-nine states declaring an emergency, and was partly the result of relatively poor monsoon rains for the two preceding years. But India is facing a chronic crisis as well. Almost every farmer on unirrigated land (like Tiwari) demands an irrigation project or a tube-well. But as it is—even before new dams and pumps are deployed to extract water for farmers—the country's rivers, including the Ganges, sometimes cease to flow in the dry season for part of their length, and groundwater is already heavily over-exploited. On the upper reaches of the Ganges and on its tributaries, each barrage typically diverts most of the water for irrigation and leaves only a fraction to flow freely to the next diversion.

Even downstream in West Bengal, after the Ganges has been fed by tributaries from north and south, a big coal-fired power station at Farakka that relies on cooling water from the river had to suspend operations in March 2016, before the monsoon, because there was not enough water in the canal that supplies it. This deepening water crisis is caused by some of the international and Indian failings described in earlier chapters: climate change, excessive population growth, and bad management of resources. Its evolution will therefore depend on how those enormous challenges are tackled, and will help decide the fate of the Ganges and of India itself over the coming century.

Bundelkhand is by no means the only vulnerable part of India when it comes to water. Six weeks before I met Beti Khan at the village, I went to Sonipat just north of Delhi to report on an extraordinary act of sabotage that had cut most of the water supply to India's largest conurbation. At the time, few residents of the capital knew that Delhi depended for so much of its drinking water on sources so far away. Whole sections of the city ran dry when rioters in neighbouring Haryana state seized control of a canal and breached its banks. Troops were sent in to recapture the waterway and two people were killed. The riots, as it happens, were not about water: the protesters, who also burnt trucks and school classrooms and shut down factories, are members of the landed but often poorly educated Jat caste who were demanding the same access as lower castes to privileged placements in government jobs and universities. But the canal closure exposed the extreme water vulnerability of the Indian capital and prompted an immediate military response.

'It was the worst crisis Delhi has ever seen. Seven [of nine] water treatment plants were totally shut down', said Kapil Mishra, the Delhi state water minister. 'Right now the canal is damaged very badly. I've not seen anything like this . . . But there was no panic.' Supply was partially restored through another canal, but it took two weeks to repair the damage. Almost all of the 4 billion litres a day of water consumed in Delhi has its origins in the foothills of the Himalayas. It is extracted from the relatively clean upper reaches of the Yamuna, Ganges, and Sutlej rivers and sent southwards by various canals that pass through Haryana or Uttar Pradesh. It was the modern 'Carrier Lined Channel'—a 100-kilometre, leakproof aqueduct lined with cement and known as the Munak Canal—that was damaged by the Jat protesters. Delhi's water board sometimes cannot replace that supply with water direct from the Yamuna River that runs through the city because it is contaminated with ammonia from industries in Haryana.

'It's sabotage', said S. S. Chhikara, chief engineer of the Haryana irrigation department, as he watched the repair work. 'Delhi's drinking water depends on it [Munak], and Delhi's the capital of India. We cannot afford more problems.' Himanshu Thakkar, coordinator of a pressure group called the South Asia Network on Dams, Rivers and People, said the crisis showed how Delhi and other Indian cities need to manage their water resources better—by recycling waste water and by reviving local lakes, ponds, and traditional water reservoirs known as tanks during the monsoon season. 'Delhi is like a pampered child. Whenever it wants, it gets water from these far-off sources', he said. 'We should try and reduce this dependence as much as possible.'[3]

Water—its availability, its cost, its quality, and possible toxicity—is a common topic of conversation for urban Indians as well as for farmers. I lived in one of the more expensive parts of Delhi, but the house still received water for only a few hours a day. The pressure is not high enough to reach the taps, so most residents have the mains supply flow into a large plastic tank at ground level, to be pumped into the roof tank as required. For drinking, the water has to be filtered. Homes and offices typically have sophisticated purification devices to extract dirt and kill bacteria.

Shortly before I left Delhi, a friend suggested I read an eccentric graphic novel by Sarnath Banerjee about the politics of water in India. *All Quiet in Vikaspuri* is a *manga*-style, dystopian adventure set against the backdrop of 'the fictitious yet ever-so-real Water Wars of Delhi'. City districts such as Jangpura and Jor Bagh (the site of my office) fight for control of the precious resource. In the suburbs, the heedless residents of Gurgaon's luxury tower blocks consume vast quantities of water pumped from the ground (no fiction, this) yet 'speak of their buildings as if they are self-contained ecosystems in the Amazon'. In reality, Delhi-ites are not yet resorting to all-out war to secure their water, but the idea is not as far-fetched as it sounds.[4]

Two summers before the Munak Canal breach I went to Dwarka, a wealthy suburban part of the capital, to investigate a local water crisis there caused by the failure to connect the district to the same canal. (In India, local does not necessarily mean small; Dwarka is a fast-growing, satellite city of 500,000 people, many of them living in tower blocks.) There I found residents such as Lakhvinder Singh, a retired civil servant from India's Telecommunications Department, struggling to secure water for their homes. As the temperatures rose above 45 degrees centigrade, Singh and the other middle-class inhabitants of Dwarka found themselves haggling with local authorities and gangsters from the neighbouring state of Haryana to buy tanker-loads of water. 'We are getting one tanker per day from the DDA [the Delhi Development Authority], which is 10,000 litres, but I want 60,000 litres per day', said Singh, secretary of one of the 349 housing cooperatives that have built apartment blocks here since the DDA launched the project on farmland twenty-six years ago. 'When they planned this township they never bothered about the water problem. There was no management of the water system', he said. The housing cooperative of 120 apartments drilled its own borehole, but that stopped producing any drinkable water ten years earlier.

'Groundwater is the problem everywhere, especially in northern India', said Balvinder Kumar, DDA vice-chairman. 'Day by day, things will deteriorate, especially in terms of water availability . . . The water table is going down. That's a matter of great concern for the government of India as well as for planners.' Dwarka, Kumar insisted, was not the worst affected part of the Delhi megacity, but he admitted that the DDA was able to supply only half of Dwarka's demand of 40 million litres a day, some of it from seventy of its own tube-wells. Dwarka's population, furthermore, was eventually expected to more than double to 1.3 million as vacant lots were filled.

Sudha Sinha, general secretary of Dwarka's Federation of Cooperative Group Housing Societies, and her husband Mukesh, a property developer, said that in some places shortages had been so severe that residents had taken to using water reserves set aside for emergency firefighting. An anti-corruption campaign targeting the water mafia who brought tankers of water illegally from Haryana did not stop the trade; it simply doubled the cost of the water for those who needed to buy it. The couple live in a modern apartment in Sector 22. 'It's beautiful actually, it's a well-planned city', said Sudha Sinha. 'But surprisingly, when they built it, they never thought of the water supply.' The airport and the commercial zones of south Delhi are close and there are about 100 schools. 'Basically we have all the facilities. But we don't have water.'[5]

A year later, in 2015, Dwarka's immediate problem was solved when the canal was finally connected. And a year after that, attention turned again to the vast residential, industrial, and commercial city of Gurgaon (recently renamed Gurugram), which is on the southern fringe of Delhi but falls within the state of Haryana. The water table in this city of more than 2 million people is falling rapidly year by year, and there are frequent predictions that Gurgaon's aquifers will eventually run out of usable water altogether.

Once the monsoon arrived in July, however, drought was quickly replaced by flooding, cars were half-submerged on the roads, and Gurgaon was likened to a rather disgusting version of Venice. On the Ganges, the monsoon floods in 2016 broke records, just as the drought had done before the monsoon. In Patna, the height of the river was recorded at 50.52 metres on 26 August, slightly exceeding the previous record set in 1994, but some analysts said the real problem was not the arrival of the floodwaters but the fact that silt deposited in vast quantities over the years had raised the level of the riverbed.[6] Silt is both a blessing and a curse for the farmers who live in the river basin: it provides fertility, but on the plain it also changes the river's character and position from one year to the next, leading to unexpected floods and changes of course. On his progress up the river in the early nineteenth century, Lord Hastings remarked on the frequency of floods and on the richness of a land that produced three crops a year. 'If a tumbler-full of water be now taken from the Ganges, the earth which speedily subsides from it will occupy nearly a fourth part of the glass', he wrote in his diary.[7]

These common themes—droughts in the dry season and floods during the monsoon, large populations dependent on water imported from elsewhere, poor conservation practices, and rivalries between different groups of water-users—are repeated across India in and beyond the Ganges river system. And they are repeated decade after decade, with the situation usually deteriorating with each successive disaster.

In the south, Tamil Nadu and Karnataka have long been locked in a bitter dispute over the waters of the Cauvery River. I first went to Chennai, the Tamil Nadu capital, in 2006 to write about megacities and urbanization. I found a city stumbling into an ever deeper crisis over fresh water. Chennai is a typical Asian boomtown, a favoured destination for car manufacturers and investors in outsourced information technology services, but it suffers from the same pollution problems and shortages as other Indian towns. The city water company and hundreds of private water-sellers were transporting water from rivers and boreholes up to 100 kilometres from Chennai to supply the thirsty metropolis. Many houses in the city have their own boreholes, but overuse has depleted underground fresh water reserves and allowed salty water to seep in from the coast. The distant farmers who have sold the water under their land have suffered too, discovering too late that aquifers are exhausted. Bangalore, in the state of Karnataka, roves far to the east in the search for water, just as Chennai hunts to the west.

Chennai has since built a series of costly desalination plants—the fourth is on the way—to extract fresh water from the sea and solve its immediate shortages, but it has failed to address the other type of disaster caused by poor management of water: flooding. At the peak of the heavy 2005 monsoon, much of Chennai was under water for weeks because builders had constructed housing estates on old lake-beds and 'tanks', the traditional water storage ponds that were once found all over the subcontinent. 'When the rains came, all the old familiar routes [for flowing water] came back, and the entire city was pretty much flooded', said Bharath Jairaj of the Citizen Consumer and Civic Action Group. 'There are two big things about Chennai. One is the complete lack of planning. The second is the complete failure to look at the issue of water.' A decade later, in December 2015, Chennai was again submerged by heavy rains. Aircraft were marooned at the city's flooded international airport and companies such as Ford and Renault had to stop production at their factories. Modi, the prime minister, blamed climate change for the disaster—188 people were killed in flooding across eastern India—but bad urban planning was again at fault.[8]

Mismanagement of water is as bad in the north as it is in the south, and each village, town, and region inevitably fights for its own interests. Punjabi landowners, abetted by the state government, have used bulldozers to fill in an unfinished canal that would take water from the Sutlej River south to Haryana. 'It's a crisis now and if we don't arrest it, then ten years down the line we'll have water wars', said Shashi Shekhar, the secretary—the senior bureaucrat—at the Indian Water Ministry. 'Punjab and Haryana will be in flames in no time.' Brahma Chellaney, author of books on the international conflicts over water, said: 'We are having water wars in India already.'

In the drought-hit state of Maharashtra in the west, the authorities had to supply drinking water to the parched Marathwada area by truck and even by train in the first half of 2016. In the driest places they banned gatherings of more than five people around water supply points to prevent fights. And in the state capital Mumbai, judges demanded to know more about the 'criminal wastage' of water for cricket pitches after hearing a plea from environmental activists for the Indian Premier League tournament to be moved from Maharashtra.

The disaster was a repeat of the one that had afflicted the Marathwada area and many of its 20 million inhabitants (more than the population of Romania) three years earlier. When I went there in April 2013, I found that the government was keeping people and cattle alive with water tankers and fodder stations. Crops of grain and cotton had failed, leaving farmers without home-grown food, animal fodder, or cash. In orchard after orchard, the bright green leaves of the sweet-limes, a type of citrus tree, had turned brown and died in the absence of water for irrigation. The owners were hacking down the desiccated trees for firewood. Rivers, canals, and dams were dry. Big construction projects had stopped for lack of water.

Nyandu Maske told me he was not sure when he was born—he reckoned he was about 70 years old—but he remembered the year 1972: that was the last time there had been a drought as bad as this in Maharashtra.

'Then there was no food', said the unkempt, white-bearded farmer, sitting in the shade with his cattle in an emergency fodder camp south of Beed. 'Now there's no water either.' Environmentalists and government officials have blamed the recent droughts not only the erratic monsoons, but also on corruption in irrigation projects, the diversion of water to growing cities such as Aurangabad, illegal water pumping from rivers and aquifers by rich farmers, rapid population growth (the number of Maharashtra's inhabitants has more than doubled since the 1972 drought to more than 120 million today), and above all the promotion of sugar cane as a cash crop since the 1970s.[9]

Confronted with stories about both droughts and floods in India, often in the same place and the same year, we can be forgiven for becoming confused. Is India short of water or not? Is the Ganges doomed to suffer the fate of the Indus in Pakistan, where so much fresh water is extracted upstream for irrigation that the delta and its mangrove-fringed creeks are drying out and the salty Arabian Sea is spreading inland?[10]

The answer is that India, overall, is not dry in absolute terms. With over 1,000 mm of rain a year, it falls in the middle of the world rainfall rankings. Northern rivers such as the Ganges are also supplied with melted snow and ice from outside the country's borders in the Himalayas. But the rain is unevenly distributed in time and place—most of it comes in monsoon torrents from July until October, while the east is much wetter than the west—and the country's population is very large. According to Arunabha Ghosh, chief executive of the Council on Energy, Environment & Water, a research group, the average Indian had access to 5,200 cubic metres a year of water in 1951, shortly after independence when the population was 350 million. By 2010, that had fallen to 1,600 cu m, a level regarded as 'water-stressed' by international organizations. Today it is at about 1,400 cu m and analysts say it is likely to fall below the 1,000 cu m 'water scarcity' limit in the next two to three decades. On a per capita basis, then, India is neither over-endowed with water nor—so far—desperately short. It has less than its neighbours Myanmar and Nepal but more than Bangladesh and Pakistan. 'While population growth will have an impact, there's no inevitability of water scarcity', says Ghosh. 'I don't want to give this a Malthusian tilt.'

Apart from population growth, the causes of India's seasonal dearth of water are the inefficient way it transports and uses the stored surface water in some 5,000 large dams; the planting of water-intensive crops such as rice and sugar cane in dry areas by politically powerful landowners such as those in Maharashtra; and a failure to control demand for water because of free electricity and subsidized diesel provided to hundreds of millions of farmers for their pumps. 'We've always looked at the problem from the supply side, not from the demand side', says Shekhar at the Water Ministry. 'Neither the political class nor the intelligentsia have understood that a water crisis is literally staring us in the face. This sector has always been in the hands of technocrats, particularly structural engineers. They only know how to construct... The general feeling is, "We have plenty of water, it's available free of cost, it's the government's duty to provide me water."'

It is not just that canals leak and farmers waste the water sent to them by the state (that water ends up back in the groundwater anyway, and super-efficient water-exploitation tends to deprive downstream users of the resource). A bigger problem is that landowners can pump as much as they want from the ground. A recent European Commission study on Indian water legislation noted that the number of boreholes or tube-wells had risen from a few tens of thousands in the 1960s to more than 20 million today. In some parts of Punjab, that has led to a decline in the water table of up to three feet a year. India, the report said, pumps 230 billion cubic metres of groundwater, more than any other country.[11]

More than 60 per cent of India's irrigated agriculture, and 85 per cent of its drinking water, depend on this groundwater. (It is easy to make the mistake of assuming that privileged city-dwellers and industries steal water from India's rural poor, but figures from the UN's Food and Agriculture Organisation show that 91 per cent of India's water is withdrawn for irrigation and livestock, with 7 per cent going to municipalities and just 2 per cent to industry.) The FAO's Shyam Khadka reckons groundwater in the Punjab is now typically 400ft below the surface, four or five times as deep as it used to be and requiring much more energy to extract. 'The situation looks a little bit scary now from a groundwater perspective across India', he says. 'The situation is basically known to policymakers, but the political will to regulate groundwater usage is very low.'

Government data, already more than five years out of date, show that 839 of India's 5,723 administrative blocks were suffering from over-exploited groundwater in 2011. An added complication is that much of the groundwater in the whole river basin—60 per cent according to one report—is contaminated by salt and arsenic and unusable for drinking or irrigation, a danger that can be worsened by over-extraction and inadequate natural recharge of the groundwater. Contamination of groundwater by nitrates from fertilizer is another problem.[12]

Ghosh adds climate change to the list of water woes. Not only is north India expected to become a few degrees warmer, which increases water use, but the rains are also expected to become less predictable. Behind the scenes, there is broad agreement, even between the rival camps of the environmentalists and the development-minded national government, on most of the steps that need to be taken to avert a future water catastrophe—although many officials still tend to favour costly 'river-linking' projects regarded by green activists as damaging.

Some analysts say demand for water should be controlled by setting a price on it while restoring ancient and forgotten 'tanks' and local storage systems in towns and villages. Alongside those measures officials would also need to reduce leakage from poorly maintained canal systems, stop the growing of thirsty crops such as sugar cane in dry places, and manage water on the basis of entire river basins rather than state boundaries. Recycling of urban wastewater on a much bigger scale will also be needed. The alternative is to have India sink into a deeper water crisis with each successive drought, and to see entire blocks of land abandoned by their populations for lack of supply—something that already happens in the dry-season months when millions of rural Indians become temporary water refugees seeking work in the towns.

Few water experts are confident of swift action. 'The government has done some symbolic things', says Thakkar, 'but in terms of programmes, policy, and practices, there's absolutely no change.' For the FAO's Khadka, the good news is that India's low agricultural productivity means it has the chance to increase farm output while using its water more wisely, though he says water will soon be a 'huge issue' and fears the country is 'sleepwalking' into serious problems.

12

Dams and Droughts

Engineering the Ganges

*Whenever I see these great engineering works, I feel excited and exhilarated . . .
They are visible symbols of building up the new India and of providing life
and sustenance to our people.*

— Jawaharlal Nehru, India's first prime minister, on the dams he called
'the temples of modern India'[1]

If there's no water, then what can engineering do to improve things?
— Ramesh Chandra, water regulator at the Narora barrage on the Ganges[2]

How much water flows into the reservoir of a dam on the Ganges
in the dry season, and how much is allowed to continue downstream in the riverbed? The answers are 'Not very much' and 'Even
less'. Perhaps it should be obvious to someone who has learned about
irrigation and heard Indians along the length of the river complain
about the lack of water, but it is still shocking to see how much of the
holy river is extracted at each successive dam for the use of farmers.

I went to the Narora barrage, midway between Haridwar and
Kanpur, to find out for myself how it is that most of the water from
the upper Ganges, for most of the year, ends up in somebody's field
rather than flowing on down the river. The British built a weir here in
the late nineteenth century, and near a stone tower they constructed at
the western end of it is are two plaques facing each other, one in
English and one in Urdu: 'Lower Ganges Canal—Narora Water Sluices—
V.I. [Victoria Imperatrix, for Queen Victoria was also Empress of
India] Anno Domini 1877.' A new barrage, with its sixty-one sluice
gates, was built in the early 1960s. Twenty years later a second, huge

canal—the Parallel Lower Ganga Canal—was built next to the original to divert yet more water from the Ganges. There are two smaller offtakes to supply water to the Narora Atomic Power Station, whose cooling towers are visible downstream.[3]

The day is so hot that the big fruit bats hanging from the trees next to the reservoir are flapping their wings to keep cool, instead of resting, and taking turns to swoop down and drink from the surface in the middle of the day. On the sloping berm protecting the buildings of the Irrigation Department from the river is a large, painted concrete map showing the Ganges and Yamuna rivers and their various dams, barrages, and canals.

So how much water comes in and how much goes out? The numbers, measured in cusecs, or cubic feet per second of flow, tell the story. It is the driest time of the year (in May 2016) and Ramesh Chandra, the 'signaller' or water regulator, tells me the situation. The barrage upstream at Haridwar is normally supplied with water from melting snow in the mountains and should be receiving 12,000 cusecs, but is getting only half the amount because of the drought. Of that, only one-tenth, or 600 cusecs, is released for the Ganges (with the remainder diverted to the vital Upper Ganga Canal; the barrage normally sends water to the Eastern Ganga Canal too, but that is closed for lack of water).

By the time the river reaches Narora, it has been replenished, albeit artificially, by means of a canal that takes water from a dam on the Ramganga, the tributary whose natural outlet into the main river is much further downstream. So 2,700 cusecs is coming to the Narora barrage. Of this, Narora is obliged to release a minimum of 357 cusecs— just 10 cumecs or cubic metres per second—into the actual river. 'It's negligible', admits Chandra. On the day I visit, however, Narora is releasing a relatively generous 1,300 cusecs of the water down the river because the industrial city of Kanpur downstream is so desperately short of water. The remainder of the inflow to Narora—1,400 cusecs— is allocated to the Lower Ganga Canal. Consider that the capacity of the Lower Ganga Canal and its parallel twin are 8,500 and 8,900 cusecs respectively and you can begin to understand what a large share of the river's water is normally diverted for the benefit of north India's farmers (at least 60 per cent for large-scale irrigation, according to one estimate, and that was from data collected more than a decade ago).[4]

Sometimes, of course, there is too much water, not too little. Chandra and his colleagues draw a neat little map for me and annotate it with numbers: after the devastating floods on the Himalayan sources of the Ganges in June 2013 the flow passing Narora reached a record 610,859 cusecs, hundreds of times the minimum and more than the barrage's design capacity of 500,000 cusecs. Six lakhs (600,000), they tell me, is 'tricky'. But repeated dry season shortages such as those of 2016 demonstrate how tightly the river and its irrigation schemes have to be managed outside the monsoon season. Officials have to implement a priority system for the canals and limit their allocations. First comes the Upper Ganga Canal, then the pair of Lower Ganga Canals, then the Eastern Ganga Canal, and then the Central Ganga Canal from the Bijnor barrage. In the Irrigation Department's guesthouse is a picture of the new, cement-lined canal under portraits of Akhilesh Yadav, at the time the Uttar Pradesh chief minister, and his uncle Shivpal, then state minister of irrigation. But the lack of water to fulfil the official allocations in early 2016 suggests that the scope for grand new irrigation schemes favoured since the days of the British may be limited. 'We can do something only if there is water', says Chandra, who has worked for the irrigation department for thirty-six years and as signaller here for the past twenty. 'If there's no water, then what can engineering do to improve things?'

On the barrage itself, which doubles as a road bridge, Ram Krishna, an assistant engineer, shows me one of the unique features of Indian dams on the Ganges: a gap that is never closed which he calls the *Ram dhara*, or the god Ram's 'constant flow'. Next to a fish ladder, it is a metre-wide gap without a sluice-gate through which water always flows at the rate of 140 cusecs to comfort Hindus and assure them that the Ganges has not been stopped. 'In Hindu religion, you can never stop the Ganga flowing completely, so we always keep it.' Just below the barrage is the atomic power station ('ISO 14001—certified eco-friendly' it says at the gate), and another set of riverside steps called Ramghat. The much-diminished stream of the Ganges here, divided by sandbanks, is so shallow that a group of mourners are able to wade across to an island carrying a corpse wrapped in yellow cloth. A tractor and trailer follow with brushwood for the cremation.

Some Hindu devotees of the Ganges have always objected to attempts to control the flow of the Ganges, whether the perpetrators are Muslim princes, British engineers, or post-independence Indian governments. Nowadays, however, most worshippers seem undeterred. At the bathing *ghat* in the park on the reservoir's edge, near a marble

statue of the goddess Ganga, I come across Sanjay Parmar, a potato and
millet farmer from Agra. He has driven here with an extended family
of about thirty relatives in several carloads to prepare some idols for
installation in a new temple in his home village. He is immersing them
here in the holy water of the Ganges. 'So we are bathing our deities—
Lord Krishna, Lord Shiva, Lord Rama', he explains before launching
into a complaint about the destruction of his crops this year by drought.
I ask why he does not irrigate, and he replies that he does but the
pump cannot function most of the time because of power cuts. I ask
him how much land he has and he suddenly becomes defensive, perhaps thinking that I am asking too many questions and we might have
something to do with the tax authorities.

Upstream from Narora is a small town on the Ganges called
Anupshahr or 'Little Kashi'. The town's perceived holiness—it was
among the places visited by a Vedic sage called Bhrigu—connects it to
Varanasi or Kashi, the 'City of Light' down-river. A large poster on the
main street shows Manju Sharma—the chairwoman of the local council, pictured against the backdrop of the clear waters of the upper
Ganges—and a list of instructions: no broken idols, soap, or shampoo
in the river; no urinating or defecating (except in the toilets); and the
use of polythene is totally prohibited.

At the *ghat*, some hairy pigs are cooling themselves in the water
upstream and men in underpants are standing in the water up to their
knees. At the top of the steps, a lively conversation about the state of
the river quickly develops among the crowd that our arrival has
prompted (such crowds materialize instantly in India when strangers
arrive and ask questions). 'This kind of water is not available anywhere
in the world', says an old man to grunts of approval. 'The Ganges has
been considered holy for thousands of years', adds 62-year-old Tej
Singh, who is visiting from Mathura on the Yamuna.

Ashok Kumar, a 40-year-old ex-army man with short hair and jeans
and a yellow sailing shirt, jokes that there is too much plastic everywhere for India to become polythene-free. 'It's our mindset', he says.
'India itself is going to become plastic!' Kumar is the nephew of the
local BJP member of parliament and describes himself as a property
dealer in Mumbai. He praises Uma Bharti, the oft-criticized BJP minister responsible for water and the Ganges, and says she has been
achieving more than people realize. As for the river, 'for us, no matter
how dirty or impure it is, it is holy and pure', by which he means that

its spiritual purity cannot be affected by physical pollution. 'If you throw stones at God, he won't cease to exist', he says. 'I can see it's polluted but it's the most famous river in the country and it will never die.'

Since ancient times, India's villagers and city administrators have tried to ensure continuous supplies of drinking water for people and animals through the dry season, by digging or maintaining local ponds or 'tanks', as well as the wells and step-wells (you can walk down into them) that can be found across the subcontinent. Environmentalists, often hostile to large dams and irrigation projects, are rightly critical of governments in modern times for ignoring these local structures and water storage systems and for building over them in places such as Delhi and Chennai with predictable results: water shortages in dry periods and flooding in the monsoon.

Even in previous eras, however, Indian rulers were not averse to large-scale water diversion and irrigation schemes using the abundant waters of the country's big rivers. There is evidence of irrigated agriculture nearly 5,000 years ago in the Indus valley, and traces of irrigation projects dating back 3,700 years have been found in Maharashtra. Farmers in the Mauryan era, some 2,500 years ago, are reported to have paid taxes for irrigation water from rivers. The Grand Anicut (Kallanai) dam across the Cauvery River in Tamil Nadu was built by a Chola king about 1,800 years ago and the site is still in use today.[5]

In north India, the Yamuna was exploited from at least the fourteenth century. Firuz Shah Tughlaq, Sultan of Delhi, is credited with constructing what is now the Western Yamuna Canal in the 1330s to irrigate farms and supply water from the hills to his fort as Hissar, west of Delhi, though he may have been re-excavating and restoring channels built by earlier Rajput kings. Akbar, the Mughal emperor, ordered its restoration in the sixteenth century after it silted up, and in the seventeenth century Shah Jahan shifted the end-point of the canal from Hissar to Delhi to supply water to his fort there in the capital; the work was carried out by Ali Mardan Khan, a Safavid nobleman and former governor of Kandahar who took service with the Mughals.

The British were quick to see the social, political, and financial advantages of restoring the canal again in the nineteenth century. Francis Rawdon, the Marquess of Hastings and then known as Lord Moira, came across the vestiges of the canal as governor-general of India when he travelled up the Ganges from Calcutta on his grand tour of the territory in 1814–15:

This noble work of art formerly rendered the country through which it passed an absolute garden; and the sums paid by the several villages, in proportion to their respective population, for the privilege of drawing water from the canal, furnished a considerable revenue to the Government. The effects of the canal on the cultivation of the country were so striking, that it obtained the name of the Sea of Plenty.

Surface water in the area was brackish, said Hastings, and neglect of the canal had left villages in ruins and the country with 'an air of desolation'. A watercolour by Sita Ram, the Indian artist who accompanied him, shows the dry bed of the canal at Karnal, with soldiers marching down it and the encampment of the Raja of Patiala on either side. The canal was soon repaired with Hastings's approval.[6]

The restored Western Yamuna Canal is still in use today, as is the Eastern Yamuna Canal (another restoration from Mughal times) that is provided with water from the same point on the river. David Haberman, who wrote a book about the much-abused Yamuna, marvelled as I did at the extent of water abstraction for irrigation from India's rivers when he visited the Tajewala barrage (since replaced with a new diversion dam slightly upstream) from which these canals are supplied. Only a tenth of the volume of the Yamuna's water leaving the mountains reaches Delhi, he wrote, and during the dry months 'no water at all flowing from Yamunotri reaches the capital city. Clearly, dams have an enormous effect on the life of the river.'[7]

But the best-known and most important canal of north India—the Upper Ganga Canal, originally just the Ganges Canal—draws water from the Ganges itself at the holy city of Haridwar and helps to irrigate much of the fertile region known as the Doab ('two rivers') between the Ganges and Yamuna. It was the life's dream of Proby Cautley, the son of a rector from a Suffolk village, who became an engineer for the East India Company, helped construct the Eastern Yamuna Canal, and was appalled by the famine he witnessed in north India in 1838.

It was an ambitious task to persuade the East India Company's directors, distracted by the disastrous war in Afghanistan, to make the investment and then to tame the Ganges in such difficult terrain, but Cautley succeeded. When it was opened on 8 April 1854–thirteen years after the project was approved—its main channel was 560 kilometres long and its branches and sub-branches extended to more than 5,000 kilometres. It included a large aqueduct near Roorkee, visible today from the Delhi–Haridwar road, to carry the canal over the Solani River. The original canal brought irrigation to more than 3,000 square kilometres of land and 5,000 villages. The name of Cautley— who also hunted for fossils in the Shivalik hills and encountered the remains of a prehistoric giraffe, 'giant ostriches and cranes, the skulls of primitive cattle, the skeletal parts of lumbering mastodons, members of the rhinoceros family, and ancestors of the modern camel, all dating from the lower Pliocene period'—is still much mentioned today by Indians and Britons familiar with the history of the Ganges. At the time of its completion, it was said to be the world's largest irrigation canal in terms of the amount of water provided.[8]

In his final dispatch as governor-general of India, James Broun-Ramsay, known as the Earl of Dalhousie, boasted that the canal exceeded in length 'all the irrigation lines of Lombardy and Egypt'. It was also used as a freight highway, and during the Indian Mutiny of 1857 (Indians call the uprising the First War of Independence), the canal transported troops loyal to the British south from Roorkee to combat the rebel sepoys, 'the men rowing with the current, the white peaks of the Himalayas behind them and the sappers chanting "Gunga Jee Ka Jai" (victory to holy Ganges) for good luck every time they passed under a bridge'.[9]

Irrigation, however, was and remains the canal's main purpose, and the Ganges project and other canal works across British India were seen as triumphs of empire-building. 'A new Viceroy coming out to India learns many interesting lessons and sees many surprising things', Lord Curzon said in a speech in 1899 at Lyallpur, now Faisalabad in Pakistan. 'Among the most novel and gratifying of these is the operation of that great system of Irrigation which in England we dimly know has filled up immense blanks upon the map of India, has made the wilderness to blossom like a rose, and has provided sustenance and live-lihood to millions of human workers.' By the time the British left in 1947, public works had created '74,656 miles of main canals and distributaries which served some 32.8 million acres, approximately one-quarter of India's total cropped area'.[10]

Cautley's plans to dam and divert the holy waters of the Ganges did not go unopposed by the Hindu priests at Haridwar, although the British later placated them by ensuring there was a gap—like the one I saw at Narora—to allow at least some of the river to flow eternally and unchecked from the mountains to the sea. They also inaugurated the dam with a ceremony worshipping Lord Ganesh, god of new beginnings, and rebuilt the bathing *ghats*. When I first saw Haridwar, my immediate—and somewhat shocked—impression was that the holy *ghats* were not situated on the banks of the holy Ganges itself (as they are at Varanasi) but were actually on the man-made canal. In a way, that is the case, because the British engineers remodelled the relevant part of the river and converted it into the entrance point for the new canal.[11] The Ganges, as it so often is along its meandering course, has always been a rather complicated river here. In the nineteenth century, writes Kelly Alley in her study of the interplay between the river's physical pollution and spiritual purity:

the Ganga flowed through several channels that lay a mile across an open gorge. One channel, departing from the main stream 2¼ miles above Haridwar, flowed past Haridwar and the pilgrimage spaces of Mayapur and Kankhal before rejoining the parent river. On this branch of the Ganga, the government of India harnessed the river's flow and created the Upper Ganga Canal.[12]

Religious agitation against the canal works—led by Madan Mohan Malaviya, an Indian nationalist who founded the Banaras Hindu University, and the Maharajah of Jaipur—erupted again in the early twentieth century when the British decided to reorganize and enlarge the headworks of the canal. A compromise was negotiated, leading to an unusual resolution in 1916—still in force in modern times as a standing order for the Irrigation Department and referred to by Ganges activists eager to ensure the river's continuous flow. The agreement gives precise details of how much water should be allowed to go where, including a provision for a minimum flow of 1,000 cusecs past the *ghats* (except during maintenance) and a permanent gap in the weir to permit a permanent flow of at least 400 cusecs direct to the river in the dry season. Malaviya is renowned in India as a religious champion of the Ganges and its need to flow, just as Cautley is admired for his engineering prowess in exploiting the river to meet the needs of farmers.

Haridwar is in many respects a typical north Indian town, and its distinguishing features are the famous bathing *ghats* and the prohibition on alcohol and meat in deference to the city's sanctity for teetotal, vegetarian Hindus. It lies just 200 kilometres from the capital, but it takes hours to reach by road or rail and even the new sections of road leading to it from Delhi seem unreasonably bad, with car drivers and passengers flung up and down and from side to side in their seats as the

vehicle lurches from valley to crest on the uneven surface. The outskirts are littered with rotting garbage and irreducible plastic waste, but
the town centre and its cluster of hotels are cheerful and crowded with
pilgrims from across India.

Crippled beggars, perched on ankle-high makeshift trolleys equipped
with castors, propel themselves towards potential alms-givers by pushing on the ground with their hands. A man wielding a clutch of large,
circular magnets attached to a red rope hurls his device into the water
from time to time to trawl for lost jewellery and other metal objects.
Traders do brisk business selling plastic churns and bottles for the carriage home of the sacred *Ganga jal*. Even in the dry season, the current
in the canal/river rushing past the *ghats* is so fast that all but the most
proficient swimmers hang on the chains attached to the steps to avoid
being swept away. No one seems worried about the possibility that this
narrow waterway might be not the natural bed of the Ganges but a
man-made canal. Several kilometres down the road to Roorkee and
Delhi, I walk across to the canal and encounter a man on some steps
who insists that this waterway is the Ganges itself. I assure him he is
wrong—this canal is a straight as a ruler and the chaotic streams of
the real river stretch for hundreds of metres behind us on the other
side of the road—but I do not get the impression that he believes his
inconvenient foreign interlocutor.

From Nehru to Modi, the governments of independent India have
wholeheartedly adopted the colonial belief in the benefits of river
management and, when it comes to irrigation dams, the hitherto pre-
dominantly agricultural people of India have on the whole done the
same. 'In the economic modernization of India, large dams occupied a
rather special place', wrote the historian Ramachandra Guha. 'They
would, on the one hand, emancipate agriculture from the tyranny of
the monsoon and, on the other, provide the electric power to run the
new industries mandated by the five-year plans.' They could also be
used to control flooding. Nehru was so enchanted by dams that he
called them 'the temples of modern India', while the intellectuals of
newly independent India admired the hydrological achievements of the
Soviet Union and of the Tennessee Valley Authority in the United
States. 'Whenever I see these great engineering works, I feel excited and
exhilarated', Nehru wrote. 'They are visible symbols of building up the
new India and of providing life and sustenance to our people.'[13] Millions
of Indians shared his fascination, as did foreign admirers of India.

Not all dams have escaped criticism, of course, for most dams create victims of the villagers forced to move to make way for construction. Indian hydropower dams large and small have been fiercely opposed by locals and by vocal environmental activists. (Some dams perform both functions—generating electricity and diverting water for irrigation—but Indian dams designed primarily for power production tend to be sited upriver in steep gorges, while long, low irrigation barrages are generally down-river on the plains.)

Indian environmentalists have a particular loathing for the Tehri Dam, the country's tallest, which generates electricity from the Bhagirathi, the name given to the highest reach of the Ganges in the Himalayan foothills. They say the reservoir is destabilizing a fragile ecosystem already prone to severe earthquakes and landslides. The Mussourie-based writer Stephen Alter was stopped in his tracks by his first glimpse of the Tehri construction site on one of his walking pilgrimages to the sources of the Ganges. 'The opposite side of the valley, which had been hidden by the spur, was completely stripped of vegetation', he wrote. 'It was a scene of total devastation, a man-made disaster zone.' His reaction reminded me of Alice Albinia's shock when she walked to the source of the Indus and found the river completely stopped by a new dam in Chinese-controlled Tibet, or that of Edward Gargan, another writer who journeyed down the Mekong and found the river missing at the Dachoashan Dam, again in Tibet:

The Mekong was gone. Below the dam, dozens of immense concrete mixers and red-cabbed dump trucks, buses, cars and cranes were parked on the flattened and bone-dry river bottom. For geologic eras the Mekong had flowed here, gouging its passage through these hills, shaping the landscape even as the crush of the Indian and southeast Asian landmass crumpled the Earth's crust around it. Now it was gone.[14]

By Chinese standards, India has proceeded slowly in developing its hydro-electric potential, largely because it is a noisy and argumentative democracy in which infrastructure projects are repeatedly proposed and opposed or launched and cancelled. It took nearly three decades from the start of construction in 1978 for the Tehri Dam's first phase of 1,000 megawatts to open in 2006. Only about 16 per cent of India's hydropower potential (much of which lies in the remote eastern Himalayan state of Arunachal Pradesh) has been exploited, and hydropower's share of the country's rising electricity generating capacity has fallen over the years because of heavy investment in coal-fired power stations and now wind farms and solar power as well.

Brahma Chellaney, an expert on the politics of water, contrasts China's rapid implementation of projects with India's tendency to leave them on paper. The 1,450 MW Sardar Sarovar Dam across the Narmada River and its associated hydro-electric and irrigation projects in the dry western state of Gujarat were conceived in the 1950s and are still not entirely finished. 'By Chinese standards, it's not even a large dam', says Chellaney. He criticizes India for failing to harvest rainwater and develop fresh-water storage capacity (something that can be done without large dams anyway), and observes that India's per capita storage is about the same as Ethiopia's and a tiny fraction of China's. In its first two years in power the Modi government, he says, focused on cleaning the Ganges. 'That's the only thing. They still haven't formulated a national water strategy, as they are not treating water as a strategic resource.'[15]

India may not have as much hydropower as China or as much fresh water storage capacity per capita as Morocco, but it still has plenty of dams, and many of them are on the Ganges or its many tributaries. According to the Central Water Commission, the country has built 4,877 'large dams' (defined as those with a height of more than 15 metres from top to foundation), more than half of them completed in the dam-building heyday between 1970 and 1990. A further 313 are under construction. Merely on the tributaries of the upper Ganges in the Garhwal Himalayas, more than sixty hydropower projects have been mooted, many of them so-called 'run-of-the river' schemes where the river is diverted down a steep tunnel and through a turbine rather than stored in a large reservoir behind a dam; of those sixty, at least ten (including Tehri) have been built and a further fifteen are under construction or awaiting clearance.[16]

The main stream of the Ganges is blocked repeatedly, including twice at Haridwar (once for a hydropower project and again for the irrigation canals). Whether upstream or downstream, such dams are not without problems. Siltation is a double concern, because it reduces the effectiveness of hydropower dams by diminishing the size of the reservoir, while depriving downstream farmers of the life-giving silt that nourishes their crops. The Farraka barrage on the border with Bangladesh, designed to flush out the Hooghly and increase the nav-igability of the river on either side of Calcutta, has been particularly controversial since its commissioning in 1975, and not only among

Bangladeshis resentful of the diversion. (Under a 1996 bilateral treaty, Bangladesh is guaranteed half the water when the flow of the Ganges diminishes in the dry season.)

Like the Brahmaputra, the Ganges in spate on its lower reaches is already erratic and highly mobile from year to year, demolishing villages and fields on one bank and leaving space for new ones on the other. Farraka, its critics say, has made things worse: floods have been destroying communities with renewed frenzy because a build-up of sand behind the barrage has raised the riverbed by 7 metres and destabilized the natural water flow in the valley.[17] The state of Maharashtra, as green activist Himanshu Thakkar points out, has built more dams than any other state but still suffers from drastic water shortages because it has failed to address the fundamental reasons for its crisis, including over-extraction of groundwater for thirsty cash crops; the official data show that of the 5,190 large dams built or under construction in India, no less than 1,845 are in Maharashtra.[18]

Narendra Modi and his government have not been deterred by such criticisms, nor even by opposition among their Hindu fundamentalist supporters to the notion of restricting the flow of the holy Ganges. On the contrary, the building of infrastructure—especially water infrastructure such as dams and canals—is at the heart of Modi's plan to modernize India, create jobs, and help the country rival China as an Asian economic power. Modi's record as a sound economic manager of the state of Gujarat (a dry state, much of it semi-desert) during his thirteen-year tenure as chief minister was enhanced by the opening of the irrigation canal from the Narmada in 2008.

Since he became prime minister in 2014, his national government has eased and accelerated the previously laborious process of environmental clearances for big projects. As well as trying to clean the Ganges and revive river navigation routes, Modi has relaunched an old and immensely ambitious plan to transfer water from the wet regions of the north and east to the dry states of the centre, the west, and the south. This National River Linking Project, with its 15,000 km of canals, would in theory expand usable agricultural land by a third, add 34 gigawatts (34,000 MW) of hydro-electric capacity, control flooding, take twenty-five years to complete, and cost $168 billion. One commentator said Modi wanted 'to be remembered for building canals' and noted that the plan had been criticized as 'unbridled hydrological hubris on a par with China's superdams'.[19]

Uma Bharti, a devout Hindu and Modi's water minister, has tussled with other ministers about the fate of the holy waters of the Ganges (at one point she quoted the 1916 agreement on ensuring the flow of the river at Haridwar and said no more dams would be built on the three upper tributaries). But she had no hesitation in announcing less than six months after the government took office that all thirty river-linking projects could be completed within seven to ten years, 'provided states agree'. She said the river links would be a milestone in the nation's growth and would prove that development and environmental protection could go hand in hand. 'Inter-linking of rivers is the dream project of NDA government', she said, referring to the BJP-dominated coalition known as the National Democratic Alliance.[20]

Arun Jaitley, the finance minister, used his 2016 budget to outline what he called a 'transformative agenda' to double the income of India's hundreds of millions of farmers by 2022. It included spending the equivalent of $2.5 billion over the fiscal year to accelerate dozens of delayed irrigation projects.[21] Such moves prompted water activists to complain that an interministerial group on the Ganges was promoting more dams instead of ensuring a sustainable 'environmental flow' or 'e-flow' in the river. 'During discussions within the group, it had been noted that a minimum environmental flow of 75 per cent in winters and 50 per cent in summers should be ensured', one of them, Rajendra Singh, wrote in a dissenting note. 'However, the final report reduces these to 30 per cent and 20 per cent, respectively.' Projected new dams would 'destroy the Ganga as we know it today', he said.[22]

Even if the building of some dams and irrigation schemes does move quicker now than it has in the past, it is doubtful that the overarching scheme to connect entire river basins will proceed on Bharti's ambitious schedule. The idea was mooted and costed more than 130 years ago by Sir Arthur Cotton, the man who designed irrigation schemes on the Godavari and Krishna rivers in southern India and incidentally engaged in a vicious dispute with Proby Cautley over what he saw as the failings of Cautley's Ganges Canal.[23] The need for approval from India's individual states for schemes affecting their territory, an issue referred to in passing by Bharti, is likely to block or at best delay major canal schemes even if the villagers in the way allow them to proceed. As it is, new dams succeed in irrigating only fifty to seventy per cent of the areas they are supposed to, either because there is insufficient water or because farmers are growing the wrong crops, according to Shashi Shekhar, the national water secretary.

India's water crisis is grave and worsening, and the Ganges and its tributaries lie at the heart of the stricken area south of the Himalayas. Climate change is raising temperatures and melting the Himalayan glaciers that used to supply meltwater in the driest months of May and June before the monsoon. Deforestation and erosion have ravaged the landscape. (In 1938, 58 per cent of Bundelkhand was under forest, and the official minimum permitted now is 33 per cent, but the actual level is 1.21 per cent, according to a local anti-corruption campaigner. Over the past decade, the equivalent of $30 million has been spent on reforestation and every monsoon from July to October there is a drive to plant trees, but they are not maintained when the rains stop and usually die.)[24]

Soil quality is deteriorating because of incorrect use of subsidized fertilizers.[25] Dams and barrages do provide much-needed irrigation water to the farmers of north India, but each dam deprives the zone downstream of the water flow that would replenish the groundwater and supply the next dam in the chain. A continuing rise in the number of human inhabitants in what is already the most densely populated part of the planet, and their unchecked pumping of water from rivers and ever-deeper tube-wells, has put India on an unsustainable path.

This does not mean that catastrophe is unavoidable. Recent floods and droughts in India have reanimated discussions about the need to conserve, repair, and uncover the local water reservoirs, ponds, and tanks that existed for millennia as a way of absorbing water in the wet season and releasing it again in times of shortages. In Calcutta, the environmentalist Mohit Ray has documented the 5,000 or so small water bodies of the city and explained their importance. In western India, the journalist Meera Subramanian has analysed how Tarun Bharat Sangh, the so-called Rainman of Rajasthan, has helped create more than 12,000 water bodies to harvest rainwater and recharge groundwater in thirteen districts in the state. (She also points out that the pool at Hauz Khas in what is now a busy commercial area of bars and restaurants in New Delhi was constructed in 1295 as a source of irrigation water and to cool the royal pavilions.) In Delhi, Diwan Singh, an environmental activist and a resident of the new town of Dwarka, showed me a drying pond in the town's Sector 23 that he said should be desilted and deepened to become a 'model water body' that would help recharge the area's depleted groundwater.[26]

Above all, however, Indian governments need to end wastage and restrain agricultural demand for water. Demand today is effectively unlimited because the product (when it is available) is either free or so cheap to pump that it makes no difference. Demand management will mean either rationing water or making users pay for it, a change of policy that would require an extraordinary effort of political will in a country that has traditionally pandered unquestioningly to the demands of farmers and rural voters. Until that happens, groundwater levels will continue to fall ever deeper below the surface, rivers will run dry before each monsoon, and migrants will flee parched rural areas for the relative security of towns and cities in ever greater numbers. Some blocks of land, agriculture experts say, will simply become uninhabitable without water brought in from outside. 'The government has done some symbolic things but in terms of programmes, policy, and practices, there's absolutely no change', says Thakkar, the green lobbyist.

In Gusiyari village, the residents clustered around the village's only usable well are worried that their homes are already close to uninhabitable. Early 2016 was one of the driest times most of them could remember. One man says 60 per cent of the locals have already taken jobs in Ghaziabad, Delhi, Saudi Arabia, Dubai, or Kuwait, where they work as labourers or security guards. (Inevitably, because it has so many Muslim residents, some local Hindus call the village 'mini-Pakistan'.)

A boy with a bicycle pushes it away with four full blue plastic containers that he will sell for a total of 30 rupees. An angry Beti Khan has a parting shot at the politicians she blames for failing to help the village: 'Who do we ask? Akhilesh Yadav? Narendra Modi?' she roars. 'Our cattle are dying. We are tired of begging and pleading with people . . . We'll not vote for any political party.' A retired wrestler with a magnificent moustache and blue eye make-up lightens the mood by boasting of his past triumphs and making everyone laugh. 'I'm 80 but I'm hale and hearty', he declares, banging his chest with his fist. But the last word goes to another village elder who tells me the drought and heat sometimes get so bad in May and June that people 'wake up at 3 a.m. to get some nice cold water from the well'. And what if this well too dries up? 'Gusiyari village will cease to exist the day that happens', he replies.

13

A Bollywood Star

Ganga on Film

Listen to the words of Ganga:
All those who came to my banks,
They used to live by the rule
That once a promise is made, it must be fulfilled even at the cost of one's life.
Our river Ganga,
Our Ganga weeps as she cries out,
Oh Ram, your Ganga has been sullied
Washing away the sins of the sinners.
Oh Ram, your Ganga has been sullied
Washing away the sins of the sinners.
We are the citizens of the country where the Ganga flows.
The one who lived with the holy men is now surrounded by the wicked,
They have neither truth on their lips nor a clean heart,
They have spoiled the Ganga and now ask her for redemption.
What shall the pitiful one do?
Oh, what shall the pitiful one do?
She is being sunk to such depths of despair by her own!
Oh Ram, your Ganga has been sullied
Washing away the sins of the sinners!
…
The land and the River Ganga are the same, but her people have changed.
Their hands are stained with blood, their faces are glowing but their hearts are dark.
They forget their vows and make false promises
Their morals are low, but they walk with their heads held high.
These sinners,
Now these sinners cannot be purified even by the Ganga's holy water.
Oh Ram, your Ganga has been sullied
Washing away the sins of the sinners.

Title song of the Bollywood movie *Ram Teri Ganga Maili* (Ram, your Ganga has been sullied), music and lyrics by Ravindra Jain[1]

Anyone who wants to interfere with the Ganges, whether it be the canal-builder Proby Cautley in the nineteenth century or a prime minister such as Narendra Modi in the twenty-first, must reckon with the passions the river can arouse even among Indians who have never seen it. One of the many surprises for foreigners living in India is to find that the goddess Ganga is no less a living presence in contemporary Bollywood films than she was in the *Ramayana* more than two millennia ago. Egyptians and Britons worshipped the Nile and the Thames in ancient times, but scarcely give their rivers a religious thought today.

The Ganges is different: she is still a goddess and is still revered—actively revered—by hundreds of millions of Indians. For mundane engineers and politicians, the river's cultural centrality can be a help or a hindrance. Few Indians need persuading of the importance of the Ganges and the need to keep it clean and flowing; but equally (as Cautley found and post-independence Indian prime ministers have learned to their cost) Hindus may baulk at projects to divert the holy waters for the benefit of secular enterprises such as farms and factories.

Inevitably, the way the Ganges is portrayed has changed over the centuries. In the *Ramayana*, she is a numinous, mystical presence. After hearing the legend of Ganga's descent to earth from the sage Viswamitra, the prince-god Ram lies awake on the bank beside his sleeping brother, and listens to the sound of the river. 'She spoke to him secretly of strange and marvellous ages, and he was amazed that he could understand what she said. Like lucid dreams, primordial legends played themselves out before his mind's eye and the river was his guru under the moon.'[2] In the 1985 Bollywood hit *Ram Teri Ganga Maili* ('Ram, your Ganga has been sullied'), Ganga is a busty village girl who dances under a waterfall in see-through wet sari, is nearly sold into prostitution when she travels into the badlands downriver to find her loved one, escapes a rape attack by a *pandit* (a priest), is forced to become a dancer in Varanasi, and is sold as the mistress of a powerful businessman in Calcutta. Yet the underlying message remains the same in India's ancient epics and its contemporary films: Ganga is a source of purity and redemption in a wicked world of rape, thievery, and injustice.

Bollywood directors like to throw the name Ganga (also those of her fellow river-goddesses Yamuna and Saraswati) into their film titles, whether the film is in the Hindi language prevalent in north India, or in the Bhojpuri dialect, or in Bengali, Tamil, Telugu, or Malayalam.

Several productions are simply entitled *Ganga*; others include *Gangotri* (the holy town near the source), *Gangasangam* (the confluence where the Yamuna joins the Ganges), or *Gangaajal* (Ganges water). The technique gives film-makers an opportunity to make religious and moral allusions that are understood by all Hindus (and almost all non-Hindu Indians) and add a veneer of sophistication to otherwise simplistic plots; to delight urban audiences by prefacing the film with footage of the river's source at Gaumukh and the wild, Himalayan country around it; and to commission popular songs about love filmed in romantic, riverbank locations inaccessible to the slum-dwellers of Delhi, Calcutta, or Mumbai.

Ram Teri Ganga Maili, the last film directed by the famous Bollywood actor and film-maker Raj Kapoor, goes one step further, explicitly equating the heroine Ganga (played by Mandakini) with the river itself and including a parallel plot in which the Calcutta-based bad guys who try to sully her womanhood also attempt to pollute the river with an illegal factory. The story is loosely based on a Sanskrit drama by the classical writer Kalidasa 1,500 years ago, and he in turn was dramatizing a story from the *Mahabharata* epic. Yet the environmental references are contemporary—the film's release coincided with the preparation of the first Ganga Action Plan by Rajiv Gandhi, then the prime minister.

Narendra Sahai, the male hero of the film, is appalled about the plan for the factory (instigated by his cynical tycoon father) and goes off on a student trip to the upper Ganges, promising to bring back pure *Ganga jal*—the holy water—for his grandmother and donning an Alpine hat that would look more appropriate on a yodelling Austrian. It is there that he meets the beautiful Ganga when he hears alluring laughter coming from the direction of the river and admires the singing woman under the waterfall. They fall in love and she has a son (it is almost always a son in Bollywood) but the two are separated by the machinations of the wicked and are only reunited in the final scene after all of Ganga's adventures on the long journey from Gangotri to Calcutta to find her man.

Too much time spent watching Bollywood movies could make even the most starry-eyed innocent into a cynic about the societies through which the Ganges flows. Until the Bollywood star Amitabh Bachchan gallops into town on a white horse—his character does this a lot in the 1978 film *Ganga ki Saugand*, (Oath of the Ganges)—kind-hearted, low-caste peasants are at the mercy of cruel landlords, venal businessmen, and money-grabbing priests, usually in league with corrupt police officers. Rape and attempted rape are routine events in the villages. Unfortunately little of this is fantasy in the Gangetic states of Bihar, Uttar Pradesh, or Haryana. The fantasy lies in the scenes of vengeance and redemption, for Bollywood is a kind of escape valve for the anger of the downtrodden poor, an unreal world in which corrupt policemen are fired, wrongs are righted, and criminals go to jail instead of becoming members of parliament.[3]

Ganga ki Saukand has all of these regular filmic clichés, with the added bonus of moralizing scenes about the importance of tolerance between Hindus and Muslims and about the malign tendency in rural India (still strong in 2016) to exploit Hindu cow-worship for political or personal ends. After some rather faded footage of the upper Ganges and the mountains, and a *sadhu* pictured on a rock, the song *Maano to main Ganga Maa* lays out the message: 'If you have faith, I am mother Ganges. Without faith I am simply flowing water', the Hindi song says.

> *A gift from heaven to earth, I am a symbol of love.*
> *For centuries I've been flowing under the blue sky.*
> *For centuries my waters irrigated the soil of love...*
> *The immortal history of this nation is written on my waves.*
> *Some pray with my waters. Others bathe idols.*
> *Somewhere the* [low-caste] *cobbler washes leather,*
> *While in another place a* [high-caste] *priest quenches his thirst.*
> *Fights of religion and caste are foolishness on man's part.*

The film opens with the villainous 'young master' of the village, Thakur Jaswant Singh, raping a woman and having her corpse hurled into the Ganges from a bridge. Jeeva, the hero played by Bachchan, is in love with Dhaniya (played by Rekha), the daughter of the cobbler, and swears by the goddess Ganga to avenge his mother's death after she is expelled from the Thakur mansion; she has been secretly working as a maid there to support her son following the death of her soldier husband, the destruction of her fields by a Ganges flood, and her decision to pawn the family wedding jewellery. Jeeva attacks the moneylender, the wicked Thakur tries to rape Dhaniya, and Jeeva is framed by Thakur and the odious priest, who accuse him of allowing a holy cow to starve and persuade the village to punish him.

At this point Jeeva sees no choice but to become a *dacoit*—a bandit—but his actions are not so much those of a gangster as of a cross between Robin Hood and Mahatma Gandhi: he has even established a multi-denominational orphanage (it is decorated with the symbol Om, the word Allah written in Arabic, and a Christian cross). A dramatic final chase ends with Thakur escaping in a small yellow aircraft but crashing into the Ganges and meeting his timely end in the same place where the corpse of the woman he raped was flung at the start of the film. Jeeva shouts *'Jai Ganga Maya!'* ('Victory to Mother Ganges!'), and the film ends.

The river itself does not feature prominently in every film which includes the name Ganga in the title. *Jish Desh men Ganga Behti hai* ('The country through which Ganga flows'), a 1960 hit by Radhu Karmakar, stars Raj Kapoor as an orphan who joins a *dacoit* gang and has to decide whether his loyalty lies with violent gangsters or unscrupulous policemen.

The three-hour, 1961 Nitin Bose film *Ganga Jumna* features two brothers with the names of the two rivers. (Jumna is another spelling of Yamuna.) One of them, Ganga, has a fiery temperament but a good heart and supports the education of his brother Jumna in town, but when he saves his girl from a rape attempt by the *zamindar* he is sent to jail on a false charge of stealing grain and is unable to send money to Jumna. Jumna falls into destitution but refuses to countenance crime, is helped by a friendly policeman and joins the police himself, while an angry Ganga becomes a *dacoit*. That sets the scene for a holy confluence, a grand reunion of the two brothers/rivers ('Today Ganga and Jumna shall meet', goes the happy song), before the tragic finale in which Jumna does his duty by the law and shoots his *dacoit* brother.

In *Gangaajal* (Ganges water, 2003), by Prakash Jha, one of Bollywood's more political film-makers, the cruel joke in the crime drama set in Bihar is that *Gangaajal* is what the police call the acid they throw in the eyes of suspected criminals; they claim to be cleansing Indian society of evil. Jha released a sequel called *Jai Gangaajal* (Victory to Ganges water) in 2016, starring Priyanka Chopra as an honest police superintendent who fights to restore law and order in a society crippled by corruption, rape, and land-grabbing perpetrated by colluding politicians, businessmen, and police officers.

Not all films set in north India are so bleak or melodramatic. In Govind Moonis's charming 1982 village romance *Nadiya ke paar* (Across the river), the plot revolves around the film's most violent incident—a woman falling down the stairs by accident and dying. The songs amid the fields of sugar cane and rice have innocent lines such

as 'In which direction are you taking me, O cart driver?', the dancers
have sweaty armpits in the heat of rural Uttar Pradesh, and the men
spend a lot of time sitting on *charpoys* (the ubiquitous Indian bed of
wood and string) and talking to each other while the women work.
The death of the woman Roopa triggers the start of an arranged marriage between her widower Omkar and her sister Gunja so that Gunja
can care for the child, but Gunja has long been in love with Omkar's
loving brother Chandan; fortunately Gunja faints before the wedding
is complete, all is revealed, and Omkar blesses the union between his
brother and his sister-in-law.

The unnamed river is only a backdrop in *Nadiya ke paar*, but the
Ganges plays a more important role in the 1996 Hindi-French production *Jaya Ganga*. Directed by Vijay Singh and based on his own novel
Jaya Ganga: In Search of the River Goddess, the rather slow-moving film
is steeped in French romanticism and lacks the rollicking music and
songs of its Bollywood counterparts, but at times it paints an authentic
picture of the beauty and human folly to be found along the banks of
the Ganges.

Nishant, a young Indian writer living in Paris, is haunted by the
memory of Jaya, a fantasy woman who seems to symbolize romantic
love and whom he recalls disappearing around a corner up some steps
in Montmartre. He decides to journey down the Ganges to find himself
('If only I could flow like Ganga into the bosom of infinite seas') and
encounters various river characters: the servant of the absent holy man
who is supposed to be in Gangotri but finds it too cold and is away
visiting the prime minister; the boatmen who reject his complaint that
the river is polluted and insist it is nectar that 'can make a dead man
stand up'; the pestering *pandit* in Varanasi offering every kind of religious and secular service; an old friend who used to play Macbeth and
Hamlet but has now become a glorified *babu*, a bureaucrat who serves
as a district magistrate; and above all Zehra, a dancing girl, a real-life
counterpoint to the mystical Jaya and perhaps even the spirit of the
river itself. Nishant buys her out of the brothel for $2,000, they eat fish
on the banks of the Ganges, and sail down the river in a boat.

It all ends tragically when Nishant is summoned by telegram to
meet Jaya at Dasaswamedha Ghat in Varanasi (even though she para-
doxically keeps leaving a black glove and red paper heart inscribed in
French with the words 'Don't look for me. No one has ever found me.
I'm leaving...'). Nishant explains to an unsympathetic Zehra—'she's

a lunatic', she says of Jaya—that Jaya is in fact a tortured soul living a double existence of incarnation and reincarnation, switching between past and present lives because of a magic ring given to her by a *yogi* near Gangotri. While he glimpses Jaya at the *ghat* but fails to find her in the flesh, Zehra enters the river to bathe and disappears. Her drowned corpse is eventually found, leaving Nishant to mourn over her and cremate the body in the final scenes. A narrator explains that Zehra always wanted to be borne away as petals of ash on the Ganges. 'From the seas she had come and to the seas she now returned, summoned by the orders of an unpredictable destiny.'

Nearing the end of a marathon viewing binge of Indian films relating to the Ganges, I decided it would be unwise to end on such a cloying, sentimental note. There was no better antidote than *Gangaa Jamunaa Saraswathi*, a box office flop directed by Manmohan Desai and starring a slightly overweight Amitabh Bachchan that came out in 1988. It presses all the right buttons: ludicrous melodrama; singers with improbable costumes; stereotypical villains; slapstick comedy; and crude symbolism about the moral significance of India's rivers.

Ganga (played by Bachchan), Jamuna, and Saraswati are a man and two women locked into a kind of benign, cooperative love triangle who come into conflict with Thakur Hansraj. He is a local thug (and uncle of Ganga) whose villainy is underlined by his dark glasses; his bullwhip; his crocodile pond; and his urge to rape women, murder his relatives, steal from their widows, and terrorize the district so that property prices will fall and he can buy the land. 'Ganga Jamuna Saraswati are the message of love', runs the opening refrain. 'Where three hearts unite it's called confluence. The righteous path is very difficult and it's very easy to commit sins.' Jamuna sings on a train and Saraswati dances in the back of a Tata truck (He: 'Ganga will carry away Saraswati in his arms.' She: 'We'll be united for all eternity, let me be cremated by you.')

There is a corrupt police inspector (of course), jail sentences for the heroes, a famous male *qawali* singer unsubtly named Kawwal, and a cobra befriended by Ganga which blinds Thakur's unpleasant son and rescues Ganga from the crocodile pit by standing in as a rope. Jamuna at one point falls through a hole in the ice and Ganga has to save her by warming her naked body with his. They eventually have a child. Later, he saves her from Kawwal's burning house (where the policeman has tried to rape her) and then saves the house as well by hurling a well–aimed machete at the water tank. The ever-sacrificing Saraswati saves Ganga from his bullet wounds by standing in as his wife for a day and joining the women in praying for their husbands' lives to be long. ('I don't want a god greater than my husband', they sing.)

The intricate plot of the 187-minute movie is kept going by the clumsy device of Jamuna's amnesia after she and Ganga are ambushed on a bridge and end up in the fast-flowing Ganges below, where she hits her head on a rock. Incredibly, the amnesia ends after another blow to the head, when yet another bridge ambush deposits her in the river a second time. The climax is a mighty fist-fight between Thakur and Ganga, after a vengeful Ganga has entered the arena with a huge (and obviously stuffed) crocodile trussed up on his shoulders. Thakur, of course, dies in the jaws of the lifeless crocodile, the actor heroically throwing his head around inside to make it look as the though the beast is eating him. But still the drama is not over, for Saraswati has placed herself in the way of a bullet meant for Ganga's son, and is dying. 'I need to blend into the darkness', she says. 'Jamuna, I am leaving Ganga to you.' The film ends with her ashes being scattered in the Ganges.

14

Exotic River

Foreigners on the Ganges

The water is dark blue in colour with great waves rising in it. Although there are many strange monsters, they do people no harm. The water is sweet, and fine grains of sand come down with the current. According to the local popular records, this river is known as the Water of Blessedness.

—Xuanzang, Chinese Buddhist of the Tang dynasty, who visited India from 630 AD[1]

Here is great store of fish of sundry sorts, & of wild foule, as of swannes, geese, cranes, and many other things. The countrey is very fruitfull and populous . . . In this riuer of Ganges are many Ilands. His water is very sweete and pleasant, and the countrey adioyning very fruitfull.

—Ralph Fitch, English sixteenth-century merchant[2]

The capitaine of all the riever[s] of the world.

—English traveller Thomas Coryat praising the Ganges in a speech to Emperor Jehangir in 1616[3]

Without coming to India, the geographers and historians of the ancient world could not have guessed how the Ganges had been infused into Indian culture and religion since the beginning of history. But foreigners did at least know of the existence of the river and have an inkling of its importance—more than two millennia before the first Bollywood film bearing the name Ganga hit the screens. The Ganges, according to Megasthenes, a Greek ambassador thought to be the first Westerner to visit and describe the heart of India in about 302 BC, was 'the greatest river in India, worshipped by all Indians' and was sometimes so wide that it was impossible to see the far shore. The civilization along its banks was no less wondrous. On seeing the sixty-four gates and 570 towers of Pataliputra (now Patna), the capital of the emperor Chandragupta Maurya, Megasthenes is reported to have written: 'I have seen the great cities of the east. I have seen the Persian palaces of Susa and Ecbatana, but this is the greatest city in the world.'[4]

None of this would have been remarkable to those who lived along the Ganges. Indians by then had been worshipping the river, and using it as a trade route, for hundreds of years. To outsiders, however, both the Ganges itself and the unfamiliar habits of the people who lived on its banks must have been virtually unknown except in the form of rumours and fantastical tales transmitted down the precursors to the Silk Road. Megasthenes went to the court of Chandragupta as the ambassador of Seleucus, who ruled Western Asia after the death of Alexander the Great but had failed to extend Hellenistic power east-ward beyond the Indus. (As a young man, Chandragupta is said to have met Alexander and been inspired by his martial charisma; he married a Greek princess as part of a peace agreement with Seleucus.)

Megasthenes's original account of his journey by land via the Khyber Pass and the Punjab and by boat down the Yamuna and the Ganges does not survive, but he was extensively quoted by classical authors such as Strabo, the Roman geographer; Pliny, the Roman nat-uralist and author; and Arrian, the Greek historian of the Roman era. Megasthenes was the first Westerner known to have recorded that Indians worshipped the Ganges—as well as Zeus (or Indra), god of thunder and rain, and various local deities. He also wrote in detail about the caste system and mentioned that Chandragupta was pro-tected by a bodyguard of female warriors.

The Ganges was to become a byword in Western literature for a mighty river, with the added attraction of Eastern exoticism. Megas-thenes evidently saw the river in flood, for both Strabo and Arrian insisted that the Ganges was the world's largest river, greater even than the Nile or the Danube. (We now know that they were wrong in terms of length, but right in terms of water flow at its mouth, if one excludes the then undiscovered Amazon and Congo rivers.) Pliny[5] said that by some accounts the Ganges burst from its source with a thundering roar (true), tumbled down a steep and rocky channel (true), collected in a lake on the plain (false, though the story may derive from the Indian tradition that the holy lake of Manasarovar in Tibet is the source of India's holy rivers), and then went on its way with a width never less than 8 miles and averaging 11 miles and a depth never less than 20 fathoms (all false).

In the ninth book of the Aeneid, the Roman poet Virgil evokes the quiet power of the Ganges in a rather laboured river simile used to describe an advancing army 'like deep Ganges, swelling in silence with his seven placid streams'.[6] Juvenal mentions the Ganges in the second line of his tenth satire (known as The Vanity of Human Wishes) to illustrate the distance between east and west, just as the English writer Andrew Marvell did in his poem 'To His Coy Mistress' fifteen centuries later. The poet Ovid mentions the Ganges, too, when referring to Alexander. Ptolemy, the second-century astronomer and geographer based in Alexandria, collated different sources to create a map showing India and the Himalayas with the Ganges flowing south–south-east from the mountains to the delta in the Bay of Bengal. His division of India into *India intra Gangem* (the near side for Westerners, to the west of the river) and *India extra Gangem* (the eastern side), was followed for more than a millennium by subsequent map-makers and seems to have pushed them into inaccurately drawing the Ganges as a north–south river rather than the largely west–east one it really is.[7] Even when it was possible, geographical accuracy was not always the main concern of map-makers. Twelfth-century maps of Palestine based on the writings of Saint Jerome, one of the fathers of the early Christian Church, have Jerusalem at the centre, with the Nile to the right and the Ganges, the Indus, the Tigris, and the Euphrates above the city flowing down from the Caucasus and Armenia.[8]

Confusion in the West deepened in the Middle Ages in the absence of reliable new information. The Christian fathers had equated the Ganges with Phison, a river in the biblical Garden of Eden, which seemed an attractive idea because paradise was supposed to lie in the East and be abundantly fruitful. The author of the highly imaginative fourteenth-century text *The Travels of Sir John Mandeville* described paradise as the highest place on earth and said at its peak was a well from which issued all the world's sweet waters in the form of the four great rivers—the Phison or Ganges (containing many precious stones and 'much gravel of gold'), the Nile, the Tigris, and the Euphrates. 'The first river is clept [called] Pison, that is to say in their language, Assembly; for many other rivers meet them there, and go into that river. And some men clepe it Ganges, for a king that was in Ind, that hight [who was named] Gangeres, and that it ran throughout his land. And that water [is] in some place clear, and in some place troubled, in some place hot, and in some place cold.' The last sentence, at least, is demonstrably true of the Ganges.[9]

Some maps portrayed paradise as an island at the mouth of the Ganges. At the same time there was a belief dating back to Ptolemy that Africa and India were connected by a land bridge in the south, and that somewhere in one or the other lived the powerful Christian king Prester John surrounded by heathens. The Indus and the Ganges were also frequently conflated, leading to tall tales about the Gangetic exploits of Alexander the Great when he had in fact not reached the river. The linguistics and literature professor Steven Darian, to whom I am indebted for some of the historical references in the preceding sentences, recounts the legend of Eirek the Norwegian and his vow to find Eden:

After securing directions from the emperor of Byzantium, he set out for *Paradisus extra Gangem* [Paradise beyond the Ganges]. Encountering deep forests and endless plains, at last he came upon a lovely park encircled by a river, which he recognised from his instructions as paradise and the river Phison. The only access lay across a small stone bridge blocked by an enormous dragon. Whereupon Eirek drew his sword and marched into the dragon's mouth. At once the monster disappeared and Eirek passed over into paradise.[10]

Religious hope and geographical error were such that Christopher Columbus, relying heavily on Ptolemy, mistook America for Asia and the mouth of the powerful Orinoco River for one of the rivers of paradise. On his fourth voyage, he left Cuba bound westward for India, which he did not realize was more than half a world away on the other side of what we now know as the Americas and across the Pacific. He thought Honduras was China and on reaching the coast of Panama was convinced that India and the Ganges lay less than three weeks journey ahead of him. This he dutifully reported to the king of Spain in 1503, though lack of provisions obliged him to abandon the journey. He never reached India—though two legacies of his search for the westbound route to Asia and his belief that he had found it was the appellation of 'Indians' for native Americans and the naming of a group of Caribbean islands as the West Indies.

Most of the confusion and wild speculation in medieval Europe about the Ganges and India could have been avoided had scholars had access to Chinese texts. Chinese Buddhist scholar Fa Xian visited India in the early fifth century and wrote an account of his journey into India from central Asia, through the country and out from Tamralipti, then the principal port at the mouth of the Ganges, to Sri Lanka, and on to South-east Asia and back to China. He admires the 'beautiful and fruitful' land between the Ganges and the Yamuna, he says the people are 'numerous and happy' (and vegetarian), and he notes with satisfaction that Buddhists, Hindus, and Jains happily share each other's religious festivals in the great cities of the Gupta Empire centred on Patna. At Kannauj on the Ganges he describes a place on the river bank where the Buddha preached law to his disciples. 'It has been handed down that his subjects of discourse were such as "The bitterness and vanity (of life) as impermanent and uncertain", and that "The body is as a bubble or foam on the water." '[11]

But it is Xuanzang, a learned Buddhist of the early Tang dynasty, who is the most renowned of the Chinese pilgrims who came to India between the fifth and seventh centuries AD to visit Buddhist monasteries and collect manuscripts and images to take back to China. Known as Master of Law or Teacher of Dharma, his name is often transliterated in Indian and other texts as Hiuen Tsang or some other variant of Xuanzang. Not only did he travel and stay in India and criss-cross the Ganges between 630 and 645, he wrote a detailed account of his journey at the request of the emperor a year after his return, known as 'The Great Tang Dynasty Record of the Western Regions'.

Xuanzang travelled from China through central Asia and spent two years in Kashmir before setting eyes on the Ganges for the first time at the age of about 30, recording his impressions of the river and the manner in which it was worshipped by Hindus. 'The water is dark blue in colour with great waves rising in it', he wrote:

Although there are many strange monsters, they do people no harm. The water is sweet, and fine grains of sand come down with the current. According to the local popular records, this river is known as the Water of Blessedness. One's accumulated sins can be expiated by taking a bath in it. Those who drown themselves in the river will be reborn in heaven to enjoy happiness, and one whose corpse is thrown into the river will not fall into the evil states of existence in his next birth.[12]

Xuanzang, who survived capture by bandits who wanted to sacrifice him to the goddess Durga,[13] is best known in India for his description of what may be an early version of the Kumbh Mela at Prayag (now

Allahabad) in the company of the emperor Harsha. Like Fa Xian, he also witnessed Indian religious pluralism in practice, attending a philosophical discussion between adherents of the Hinayana and Mahayana Buddhist schools and various Hindu sects, arranged by Harsha in his capital at Kannauj.[14]

Next—albeit centuries later—it was the turn of the Muslims to investigate the mysteries of India. The scholar and astronomer Abu Rihan Al-Biruni, born in what is now Uzbekistan, travelled to India in 1017, more than 400 years after the departure of Xuanzang, and wrote about science, literature, and religion in his history of India. Like Xuanzang, he saw the austerities practised on the Ganges at Prayag, where the locals 'torment themselves with various kinds of tortures'. He noted that Hindus threw the cremated remains of their dead into the Ganges. He even recounted the myth of the river's descent to earth to liberate the souls of King Bhagirath's ancestors, and Shiva's intervention to catch the divine river and slow its violent arrival, although he thought the Ganges was male not female. An irritated Al-Biruni, in a complaint that echoes down the ages, also commented on the chauvinism of the self-satisfied Indians he met and the 'peculiarities of their national character'.[15]

Three hundred years later, by which time Muslim conquerors from the north had established themselves in Delhi, the Moroccan-born traveller Ibn Battuta reached India and stayed for fourteen years. For the first half of his stay he was in the service of Mohammed bin Tughluq, the Sultan of Delhi, and finally—after extensive travels in South and Central Asia, China, the Arab world, and Africa—he dictated a travel book now called simply as 'The Journey'. It was not known in the West until the early nineteenth century, but contains accounts of the Ganges and its importance for Hindu death rituals. He also reported that 'thousands upon thousands of people perished of want' in the seven-year famine in north India that began in 1335, mentioning that Indians were reduced to eating animal skins, rotten meat, and even human flesh.[16]

Nearly two millennia after Megasthenes had wondered at the glories of Pataliputra (Patna), the first envoys, traders, and travellers began to arrive in India from North-west Europe. Ralph Fitch, an English merchant, led an embassy to the emperor Jalaluddin Mohammed Akbar (Akbar the Great) in 1585 from Queen Elizabeth I. Her letter from 'Elizabeth by the Grace of God Defender of the Faith to the most

invincible and most mighty prince Zelabdin Echebar King of Cambaya'
requested 'mutual and friendly traffic of merchandise on both sides'.
Akbar, however, was too busy to meet Fitch. As the historian Michael
Wood points out, Akbar governed over 100 million people and was
establishing India as a world power, whereas Elizabeth ruled just 3 million subjects—'the equivalent of a small principality in the Deccan'—
on the outermost fringes of the inhabited world.[17]

The merchant adventurer Fitch nevertheless travelled on and,
unlike some of his companions, lived to write about his dangerous
journey to the East in a rather engaging stream-of-consciousness
manner that juxtaposes commercial information and travelogue with
social and religious commentary. Having landed in Goa as a prisoner
of the Portuguese and escaped from there to north India (where his
fellow-traveller William Leades served Akbar as a jeweller and was
provided with a house, a horse, five slaves, and a salary by the
emperor), he travelled down the Yamuna and the Ganges to the Bay
of Bengal. It took him five months, although he said he could have
done the journey faster. The rivers were obviously a well-estab-
lished trade route:

I went from Agra to Satagam [Saptagram] in Bengala, in the companie of
one hundred and fourescore boates laden with Salt, Opium, Hinge [asa-
foetida, a plant resin used in cooking], Lead, Carpets and divers other commodities down the river Iemena [Yamuna]. The chief merchants are Moores
and Gentiles. In these countries they haue many strange ceremonies. The
Bramanes which are their priests, come to the water and haue a string
about their necks made with great ceremonies, and lade vp water with both
their hands, and turne the string first with both their hands within, and
then one arme after the other out. Though it be neuer so cold, they will
wash themselves in cold water or in warme. These Gentiles will eate no
flesh nor kill any thing. They liue with rice, butter, milke, and fruits…The
Bramanes marke themselues in the foreheads, eares and throates with a kind
of yellow geare which they grind, & every morning they do it. And they
haue some old men which go in the streetes with a boxe of yellow pouder,
and marke men on their heads & necks as they meet them. And their wiues
do come by 10, 20 & 30. together to the water side singing & there do wash
themselues, & then vse their ceremonies, & marke themselues in their fore-
heds and faces, and cary some with them, and so depart singing. Their
daughters be maried, at, or before the age of 10. yeres. Their men may haue
7. wives. They be a kind of craftie people, worse then the Jewes. When they
salute one another, they heaue vp their hands to their heads, and say Rame,
Rame.[18]

As well as recording the 'Ram! Ram!' greeting still in use today, Fitch reached the Yamuna–Ganges confluence of Prayag (Allahabad) and accurately described the course of the river both upstream and downstream of the city. He remarked on the number of tigers, partridges, turtle-doves, and naked beggars. He evidently did not think much of these dedicated ascetics or any other non-Christian holy men, remarking on a naked *sadhu* in Prayag who had two-inch fingernails, had taken a vow of silence, and whose private parts were hidden only by his long hair. In Varanasi, the Hindus are 'the greatest idolaters that euer I sawe' and they worship 'euill fauoured' images and idols. Further down the river in Patna, he comes across a 'dissembling prophet' supposedly sleeping on a horse in the market place, where devotees clustered round to touch his feet. 'They tooke him a great man, but sure he was lasie lubber', says Fitch bluntly. 'The people of these countries be much giuen to such prating and dissembling hypocrites.' Like foreign travellers before and after, Fitch was, however, impressed with the waters of the Ganges and the natural wealth of India, albeit not, apparently, with the locals' pudding-bowl haircuts:

Here is great store of fish of sundry sorts, & of wild foule, as of swannes, geese, cranes, and many other things. The countrey is very fruitfull and populous. The men for the most part haue their faces shauen, and their heads very long, except some which bee all shauen saue the crowne : and some of them are as though a man should set a dish on their heads, and shaue them round, all but the crowne. In this riuer of Ganges are many Ilands. His water is very sweete and pleasant, and the countrey adioyning very fruitfull.[19]

For all Fitch's suspicion of the unfamiliar rituals of Hinduism, he notes the pilgrims coming from afar to Varanasi and describes the modes of dress and the various prayer ceremonies on or around the river—the threefold sipping of Ganges water, the offerings of grain to the idols, the half-completed cremations, and the grabbing of the calf's tail as I witnessed at Sagar Island—in such detail that they are recognizably the same as the practices of today. Varanasi was a 'great towne' with 'many faire houses' at the waterside, and Patna 'a very long and a great towne' now under the sway of the 'great Mogor [Moghul]'. Both were important trading centres dealing in cotton and fabrics—and sugar and opium in the case of Patna. Again he accurately describes the progress of the Ganges in Uttar Pradesh and Bihar, where it is fed by tributaries from the Nepalese Himalayas, for 'many very great riuers doe enter into Ganges; and some of them as great as Ganges, which cause Ganges to bee of a great breadth, and so broad that in the time of raine you cannot see from one side to the other'.[20]

Fitch, whose trip to the Near East and Asia was financed by the Levant Company and alluded to in Shakespeare's Macbeth, became an advisor to the East India Company after his return to England in 1591. He was followed by an increasing number of Britons and Continental Europeans into the heartland of north India, including Thomas Coryat, a keen walker and explorer from Somerset who learned Persian and gave a speech to the 'Great Mogoll'—the emperor Jehangir—in Ajmer in 1616. He had come to India, he said, not only to gaze on 'the blessed face of your Majesty, whose wonderfull fame hath resounded over all Europe and Mahometan countries' but also to look at elephants and 'to see your famous river Ganges, which is the capitaine of all the riever[s] of the world'.[21]

Coryat seems to have planned to visit Haridwar, although his account if he succeeded has not been found, because he wrote with relish of a plan to go to a 'memorable meeting' of about 400,000 pilgrims he believed would not only bathe in the river but also hurl in coins and great lumps of gold and perform 'other strange ceremonies most worthy the observation'. Like Fitch, he felt obliged to express Christian disapproval, but was obviously excited by the prospect of an awesome spectacle attracting devotees from the far corners of India. 'This shew doe they make once every yeere, comming thither from places almost a thousand miles off, and honour their river as their God, Creator, and Saviour; superstition and impiety most abominable in the highest degree of these brutish ethnicks, that are aliens from Christ and the common-wealth of Israel.' Coryat also requested an early version of a 'selfie', determining to have a picture of himself astride an Indian elephant in his next book. The wish was fulfilled (even if the artist had to use his imagination rather than seeing the elephant-borne Coryat in the flesh) while Coryat was in India, where he died of dysentery in 1617.[22]

Jean-Baptiste Tavernier, a prosperous French gem merchant who made six journeys to the East, including four to India, in the seventeenth century, was less overawed than Fitch by the sight of the Ganges, at least in the dry season. In December 1665, he is on his way from Agra to Bengal in the company of François Bernier, doctor to the Mughal emperor Aurangzeb, and somebody called Rachepot. They are:

surprised to see that this river which everyone makes such a fuss about is no wider than the River Seine in front of the Louvre, perhaps imagining that it was at least as broad as the Danube above Belgrade. There is so little water, even, from March until June or July when the rains begin to come that boats cannot come up this far.

In Allahabad, he admires the stone fort and meets Claude Maille of Bourges, a surgeon who helps the Persian doctors in tending to the sickly governor of the city. Tavernier, who relishes a good anecdote about India's unusual social mores, tells the sanguinary tale of the governor's chief Persian doctor in Allahabad. This doctor, it was said, grew jealous one day and hurled his wife from the battlements of the fort. In the event, she suffered only some broken ribs, but when her family pleaded with the governor for justice he fired the errant doctor, who put his injured wife in a palanquin and went on his way with his family. They had barely been gone three days when the governor felt poorly and recalled his doctor, whereupon this man—for reasons that Tavernier does not explain—stabbed his wife, his four children and thirteen slaves and returned to Allahabad. The governor took the doctor back into his service and said nothing.

   Later in Tavernier's voyage—during his eight-day stay in Patna, 'one of the greatest cities of India'—there is an account of another murder that intrigues the French traveller and leads him to conclude that 'the crime of sodomy does not go unpunished among Muslims'. A military commander rapes a young boy in his service despite repeated pleas from the boy about the captain's sexual advances, complaints that have gone as high as the governor himself; the boy avenges himself by killing the rapist with a sword on a hunting expedition; the boy confesses to the murder; but the governor refuses the demands of the captain's family to execute him and frees him after only six months. The governor 'feared the people, who thought the boy had done the right thing'. Tavernier leaves Patna by river for Dhaka (he says he would have taken a boat earlier, from Allahabad or Varanasi, had there been enough water, so it must have been an exceptionally dry winter) and after shooting some crocodiles on the way eventually arrives at Hooghly in February 1666.[23]

   At the other end of the river, the source of the Ganges remained a mystery to explorers for centuries, until James Baillie Fraser, a Scottish landscape artist, became the first European to reach Gangotri in 1815 and Captain J. A. Hodgson, a military officer and surveyor, reached the source at Gaumukh two years later. Both had also been to Yamunotri (the nearby source of the Yamuna) and were thrilled by the thin air, the cold, the wild aspect of the mountains and the rivers, and by the deep-blue sky of high altitudes. 'Fir-trees of immense size, and large fragments of others, are seen half buried in sand and gravel; and huge masses of earth and rock lay in wild confusion at the mountain feet', wrote Fraser of the Bhagirathi (the upper Ganges). For him, the landscape along the upper Ganges was even more dramatic than that of the upper Yamuna, with the character of the mountains 'not only different from that of any yet seen, but marked by features unspeakably more lofty, rugged, and inaccessible. There is even less of beauty, and more of horror; more to inspire dread, less to captivate.'[24]

By the early nineteenth century, however, most foreigners who saw the Ganges were not exploring the Himalayas but travelling from Calcutta to upcountry stations such as Allahabad and Kanpur (Cawnpore) as soldiers, officials, or traders for the East India Company. They therefore witnessed life on the lower and middle reaches of the river on the slow journey upstream and the faster one downstream; and they were enchanted by what they saw.

Some of them painted, too. In our age of digital photography and online video, it is hard to overemphasize the importance of the eighteenth- and nineteenth-century artists who showed the world what India was like. According to the art historian Jagmohan Mahajan, the most important reason for artists' seeking their fortunes abroad in the last quarter of the eighteenth century was 'the poor financial prospects of landscape painters in England'. The cult of the 'picturesque', furthermore, was in fashion, and India was nothing if not picturesque. The landscape artist William Hodges, who had accompanied Captain James Cook on his second voyage to the Pacific, arrived in 1780, and was followed by many more, including Thomas Daniell and his nephew William in 1786; the pair stayed seven years in India, much of the time on the Ganges:

The views of Calcutta, Rajmahal, the rocks of Sakrigali, Colganj and the Janghirah rock, the forts of Monghyr and Chunar, Varanasi and Allahabad which Hodges and the Daniells drew on the journey up the Ganga blazed a new trail in landscape painting. They gave the outside world—in fact, even the Indians themselves—the first ever visual pictures of the Ganga and the countryside through which it ran.

They were followed by other artists, some amateur and some profes-
sional, including Fraser (who went to Gangotri), Lieutenant-Colonel
Charles Forrest and Colonel Robert Smith and in the 1870s by Edward
Lear.[25]

The world's impressions of India were profoundly influenced for
generations by such paintings. They showed ancient ruins; the collapsed temple in the river at Varanasi; the palaces of potentates; religious fairs; mahouts washing elephants; moustachioed pilgrims bathing
at the *ghats*; a woman with a water jar on her head watched by some
storks in the shallows; a holy man under a giant banyan tree; gharials
on the river bank; sailing ships on the Ganges; or half-naked men hauling a *budgerow*, a shallow-draft river boat, against the current. It is
tempting to accuse the artists of Orientalism, and certainly what was
everyday life for the Indians along the Ganges was exotic to the visitor.
But such scenes were real and—except for the sailing ships and the
budgerow—are still real today. If, with the benefit of hindsight, we can
accuse them of anything the crime would be one of omission—of failing, for example, to portray the horror of famine and cholera—rather
than of commission.

The nineteenth-century diarist Fanny Parkes, the wife of a mentally
unstable official in charge of making ice in Allahabad, describes in
words the kind of images that attracted foreigners in India at the time
when she decides to sail up the Yamuna from Allahabad to see the
Taj Mahal:

The river is very picturesque; high cliffs, well covered with wood, rising
abruptly from the water: here and there a Hindu temple, with a great peepal
tree spreading its fine green branches around it: a ruined native fort: clusters
of native huts: beautiful stone *ghāts* jutting into the river: the effect greatly
increased by the native women, in their picturesque drapery, carrying their
vessels for water up and down the cliffs, poised on their heads. Fishermen are
seen with their large nets; and droves of goats and small cows, buffaloes and
peacocks come to the riverside to feed. But the most picturesque of all are the
different sorts of native vessels; I am quite charmed with the boats. Oh that
I were a painter, who could do justice to the scenery![26]

Parkes, far from being a snobbish, reserved colonial wife, learns
Hindustani and seems fascinated by everything Indian. She is described
by the historian William Dalrymple, who oversaw a modern edition of
her diaries, as 'an enthusiast and an eccentric with a burning love of
India that imprints itself on almost every page of her book'. By the

rivers—which she often refers to as Ganga-ji and Jumna-ji, adding honorifics in the Indian manner—the only scenes that shock her are those of hunger, disease, and the occasional floating corpse. She is appalled by the habit of throwing cremated bodies half-burnt into the Ganges, where they are savaged by crows and dogs. Otherwise, she repeats, 'how picturesque are the banks of an Indian river!'[27]

The journals of the Eden sisters, Fanny and Emily (their brother was George, Lord Auckland, governor-general of India) are undeservedly better known than those of Parkes (whom Fanny calls 'abundantly fat and lively'), for they are flippant and incurious about India. Emily thinks India has 'the most picturesque population, with the ugliest scenery, that ever was put together'.[28] But even they were impressed by the Ganges and their surroundings. 'The villagers here are nice looking people', Fanny writes at Rajmahal in the wet season of 1837. 'The Ganges is one side of us, looking like a smooth blue sea. The Hoogly is a very inferior article and the poor dear Thames a miserable stream, not to be named with either. That last sentence is what I call real Indian patriotism.'[29] Later she again describes the Ganges as being like 'a small sea' and praises the 'fine, hardworking' boatmen. 'Their singing is more like singing and less like screaming, than anything I have heard in India.'

We have records in both words and pictures of a particularly large colonial procession up the Ganges from Calcutta to north India in the early nineteenth century. Francis Rawdon, then the Earl of Moira and later Lord Hastings, was governor-general of Bengal and commander-in-chief—effectively the British ruler of India—from 1813 to 1823, a man who 'pursued a vigorous forward policy, considerably extending the frontier of British India'. On 28 June 1814 he embarked from his residence at Barrackpore on the Hooghly north of Calcutta and set off up-river to inspect Britain's possessions, meet Indian rulers and notables, and keep an eye on the war in Nepal.

With him was a flotilla of some 220 boats carrying his wife, their small children, his secretaries, and aides-de-camp; 150 sepoys of his bodyguard; a battalion of the Bengal Army; and all their horses, food, and baggage. (Hastings later reckoned there were 10,000 people in his camp when he finally left the river to march overland.)[30] The diary that Hastings kept on the trip was published in 1858, and in 1995 the British Library acquired a previously unknown collection of art that included 229 watercolours in ten albums of the journey by Sita Ram, an Indian artist trained in the so-called 'Company style'.

Captain Thomas Skinner called the scene at the beginning of such expeditions (he went on one a decade later) 'the most extraordinary that can be conceived'. He recalled:

Every officer had a sort of Noah's ark attached to his *budgerow*, and the uproar to fill it with its various animals was terrible: unwilling horses, and obstinate cows, with goats and sheep, running in all quarters; men, women, and children, of all colours and costumes; carriages, gigs, palanquins, coops of poultry, ducks, geese, and turkeys, scattered about, cackling and hissing with all their might, were to be seen in every direction.[31]

Among those who accompanied Hastings in his 'spectacular affair on a scarcely credible scale' was John Talbot Shakespear, superintendent of police for Bengal, Bihar and Orissa, and his wife Emily, who described in her journal the green-and-gold barges for Hastings's family and the activities along the way. 'Every now and then they stopped for a tiger hunt or an audience with the local raja, or an excursion on elephants, during which the Moiras [Hastings and his family] scattered largesse to the crowd.'[32]

The Ganges has been arousing the artistic sensibilities and scientific curiosity of foreigners for hundreds of years—even among those who have never set eyes on the river—and continues to do so in the present day. Gian Lorenzo Bernini's 1651 design for the 'Fountain of the Four Rivers' in the Piazza Navona in Rome has a statue of the divine Ganges—albeit a male god with muscular thighs and a beard holding an oar and looking rather like Father Thames, and not in the least like the goddess Ganga—representing Asia. (The statue's other rivers for Europe, Africa, and the Americas are the Danube, the Nile, and the River Plate.)

The name of the Ganges turns up in more-remote locations in the West as well, including Ganges, Ohio (previously known as Trucksville, the town was on an important grain trade route); Ganges in the Hérault department of France, a place known for the manufacture of silk stockings; and the village of Stoke Row in Oxfordshire in England, where Ganges water has been ceremoniously poured into the well built in the nineteenth century on the orders of the Maharajah of Benares (Varanasi) to relieve the effects of a drought. In the small town of Kiruna in Lapland, northern Sweden, three seventeenth-century French travellers felt the need to leave an inscription in Latin explaining how they had reached the end of the world after seeing Africa and the whole of Europe and 'drunk the Ganges'.[33] The nineteenth-century Russian poet Alexander Pushkin was so in love with Maria Raevskaya that he turned to India's famous river to illustrate her intoxicating beauty. To Pushkin, Maria's massed curls shone brighter than sunlight and were darker than the night. With olive skin she was, he said, '*la fille du Ganges*'.[34] The film director Jean Renoir was captivated by India and shot *The River* (1951)—a romance based on a coming-of-age novel by Rumer Godden, the daughter of a shipping agent in Bengal—on location on the Hooghly River.

Romance aside, an unavoidable part of the Ganges experience for traders and travellers was the river voyage itself. Boats and their crews and passengers are therefore the subject of the next chapter.

15

Storms and Sandbanks

Boats on the Ganges

[We saw] a number of persons floating down the stream by means of an empty earthenware jar (well corked) under each arm...This mode of voyaging has little of trouble in it, for it requires no exertion; but there is great peril from the alligators.

—Lord Hastings describing river commuters (downstream only) in 1814[1]

Our boats are large, flat-bottomed, shallow and broad country boats, on each of which a great house is built of bamboo and mats, and the roof is thatched...Such unwieldy vessels are very likely to be upset in a storm.

—The diarist Fanny Parkes in 1832

Sita Ram, an Indian artist trained in the 'Company style', accompanied Hastings on his journey upriver in the nineteenth century, giving us a detailed if selective notion of the people, the landscape, the wildlife, and the architecture—ruined and functional—of the river and its shores all the way from Calcutta to Haridwar. Ram—portrayed by a fellow artist as a venerable painter in a white robe and turban with matching white eyebrows and moustache, sitting barefoot with his skinny legs under a table—expertly painted everything from lemons and pomegranates to the great palaces, tombs, and mosques of north India.[2] He also spent a lot of time looking at boats.

Although the Ganges is a large river, it is erratic in its course through the plains, and its depth and volume vary immensely according to the season. Navigating the Ganges and the Yamuna was essential for the transport of cargo before the arrival of the railway, but it was an extraordinarily complex, laborious, and sometimes perilous enterprise. Dangers included intense squalls of wind, the unpredictable shallows on which ships and boats repeatedly ran aground, the constantly collapsing river banks of friable silt, and strong currents against which progress upstream—by dint of a line of men towing the boats from the river bank—could be agonizingly slow; one of Sita Ram's paintings that illustrates this practice, known as 'tracking', shows six men laboriously hauling a boat up-river by a rope attached to its mast, while the helmsman keeps the vessel away from the bank with a steering oar.

Hastings, in between admiring the scenery, expressing irritation with various maharajas, and visiting Varanasi, repeatedly describes accidents in which boats run aground or are overturned by squalls. On 29 July 1814, the river is very rough and three boats sink, with the loss of two men. Two days later another boat for the sepoys is wrecked as they try to haul it past the fort through the narrows at Munger, a pass described by Hastings as 'a seriously embarrassing one' that can delay vessels for up to three weeks. On 17 August, Hastings frets about the poor seamanship of the Indian sailors when the wind blows fresh 'and a vessel with baggage was overset owing to the incorrigible habit of the boatmen to tie the sheets [that is, the attaching ropes] of their sails in such a manner as that they never can suddenly be let fly'. Two days later he is ashore at Buxar, and:

going to the edge of the cliff on which the fort stands, in order to look at the reach of the river, I saw a boat overset by a sudden gust. Her crew, eight men and a boy, clung to the rigging, but were carried down the stream, and whirled in the eddies with great rapidity. Not a boat, of the many sailing near them, attempted to give them any succour. My own boat did not push off from the beach till after repeated calls from me, and then proceeded with a languor quite disgusting. The insensibility of the natives towards each other is astonishing. All the poor fellows belonging to the wrecked boat were saved.

By September, the flotilla has passed Varanasi and reached Allahabad, but there is little improvement when it comes to the safety of the boats: three are wrecked trying to round the fort and enter the Ganges from their anchorage in the Yamuna. On 24 September, at the tail end of the monsoon, numerous boats run aground and Hastings says it has been officially reported to him that the river has fallen 39 feet from its maximum of that year.[3]

The ways in which people travelled up, down and across the river were, in those days at least, wonderfully varied. Hastings describes:

a number of persons floating down the stream by means of an empty earthen-ware jar (well corked) under each arm. Nearer to Baughlipore, some of them carried milk-pots on their heads for sale at that place. This mode of voyaging has little of trouble in it, for it requires no exertion; but there is great peril from the alligators. That danger is solved to each individual by his belief that if it be his fate to be devoured by an alligator, the creature would come and take him out of his bed.

He goes on to say that some of those floating down with the pots have 'small umbrellas over their heads' and thus present 'a singular appearance'.[4] Presumably they walked along the bank to return upstream to their point of departure.

Another makeshift way of travelling along the river is shown in a sketch accompanying the journal of Reginald Heber, the Bishop of Calcutta who travelled up the Ganges and toured north India in 1824–5: the picture, captioned 'Fishermen on the Ganges', shows three men in a small boat. One is steering and the other two are standing and acting as human masts—one in the bows and one amidships—holding up large white sheets or cloths to catch a following wind; the top corners of their cloths are held out in their raised hands and the bottom cor-ners are wedged under their feet on either side of the boat, creating effective square sails.[5] The cross-river ferries pictured by Sita Ram, shallow-draft wooden boats with cross-beams serving as benches and packed with passengers, look much as they do today, although small diesel engines, often converted water pumps, have in many cases replaced the traditional paddles.

For his own transport Hastings has the pinnace *Sonamuckhee* (Sonamukhi, or 'golden-mouthed', the name given to the barges and boats of the governor-general or the viceroy) which he says 'is remark-ably convenient and sails very well. The children have another vessel equally good.' A picture of the flotilla by Sita Ram shows these two vessels to be two-masted ships with rectangular sterns like miniature warships and long bowsprits and jibs as well as the usual square sails suspended from the yards on the masts. This arrangement, as well as their keels, would have made them more stable and enabled them to sail closer to the wind than the lumbering *budgerows*, the passenger boats that made up most of the fleet, although their greater draft would have also made them more likely to run aground on the many sand-banks in the Ganges.

Wealthy Indian rulers along the river had their own state vessels, often gilded, ornate, colourful, and adorned with colourful pennants. In one picture, Sita Ram shows the state boat of the Rajah of Benares (Varanasi) with a horse figurehead, in front of his palace; in another, fantasy, portrayal of a river scene, he shows various royal boats, paddled furiously by rows of turbaned servants, for which the figureheads include an elephant and a peacock.[6] In Lucknow on the Gumti (a tributary of the Ganges), Fanny Parkes one day sees a large pleasure-boat belonging to the King of Oudh, Ghaziuddin Hyder, which was 'made in the shape of a fish, and the golden scales glittered in the sun'.[7] The *budgerow*, nevertheless, was the basic form of river transport for passengers in the colonial era, and it came in many varieties. Before his fall from grace in Amitav Ghosh's novel *Sea of Poppies*, the wealthy *zamindar* or landlord Raja Neel Rattan Halder takes to his 'stately barge' or 'palatial houseboat' on the river at Calcutta with his son and mis-tress; the vessel, we are told, has six large staterooms on the main deck and is a 'brigantine-rigged pinnace-budgerow, an Anglicized version of the humbler Bengali *bajra*'.[8] *Budgerows*, according to Mahajan:

had from twelve to twenty oars, and varied greatly in their sizes. Some were about eighteen metres long with very high sterns, and many of them were about three and a half metres from the edge of the water with sharp bows. They were fairly commodious, having in the centre an open portico with a door opening into a well-appointed cabin with windows on each side. This cabin was used as a sitting-cum-dining room, and adjacent to it was a bed-room. A large paddle was used for the purpose of steering the boats, and in the centre there was a mast on which a large square sail was hoisted. Though quite slow, the budgerow was steady, and a traveller could write or paint comfortably in the course of the journey. Besides this boat, a traveller of means would quite often be attended by two other boats; one which served as a kitchen, and the other to take him to the river bank and back, since more often than not the budgerow could not come close to the bank. The more affluent travellers had in addition boats for their servants and horses as well as for baggage not required during the journey.[9]

There was a *manjee* who served as captain and from twelve to twenty *dandees* as crew. Regular-sized *budgerows*, of course, were by no means the only boats on the river. When her household moved from Kanpur to Allahabad in 1832, Fanny Parkes mentioned 'six great country boats' for the furniture and 'an immense 900 man *paitailā*' containing cows, sheep, goats, guinea-fowls and turkeys:

Our boats are large, flat-bottomed, shallow and broad country boats, on each of which a great house is built of bamboo and mats, and the roof is thatched. The interior is fitted up with coloured chintz, like that used for tents. Such unwieldy vessels are very likely to be upset in a storm. The great *paitailā*, which contains the cows, etc., has given us much trouble; she has been aground several times being, from her height and bulk, almost unmanageable in a strong wind.

The ever-observant and practical Parkes provides a fascinating insight in the laborious day-to-day business of sailing up an Indian river when she decides to head upstream on the Yamuna from Allahabad to see the Taj Mahal at Agra in a newly acquired pinnace called *Seagull*. The locals are impressed by the boat's sailing abilities and tell her that *Seagull* 'goes before the wind like an arrow from a bow'. Accompanied by a dinghy and a small *pateli* as cook-boat, the *Seagull*, Parkes writes

was built in Calcutta to go to Chittagong and has a deep keel, therefore unfit for river work unless during the rains: two-masted, copper-bottomed and brig-rigged. She requires water up to a man's waist; her crew consist of twenty-two men, one *sarang*, who commands her, four *khalāsis*, who hold the next rank, one *gal'haiya*, forecastle man (from *galahi*, a forecastle), fourteen *dāndis*, one cook and his mate, all Musulmāns; total twenty-two. The crew, particularly good men, came from Calcutta with the pinnace; they cook their own food and eat and sleep on board. My food and that of the servants is prepared in the cook-boat.[10]

Each day they unmoor from the riverbank at six o'clock in the morning and sail or 'track' up-river until 7 o'clock in the evening, passing salt boats and 'hundreds of enormous boats laden with cotton'. The dangers are many—squalls, broken tow-ropes, sandbanks, submerged rocks, crocodiles (both types were common, but it was the marsh crocodiles, not the fish-eating gharials, that were the man-eaters), bandits, wolves— and progress is painfully slow. Twice the pinnace springs a leak, and on the second occasion, they discover that a main beam has been gnawed and weakened by white ants (termites) and rats. It takes them from 9 December to 28 January—more than seven weeks—to get within sight of the Taj Mahal, and a final sandbank stops the pinnace from completing the journey to Agra, forcing Parkes to make the remaining distance on horseback. As the crow flies, the distance is less than 450 kilometres, but the winding stream of the Yamuna is anything but direct.

Three years later, Parkes witnesses a disaster when she is aboard *Seagull* sailing up the Ganges in Kanpur ahead of twelve magazine boats bringing military supplies. A squall that overtakes them 'struck us all into picturesque attitudes, and sunk one of the magazine boats, containing Rs16,000 worth of new matchlocks. When the squall struck the little fleet they were thrown one against another, the sails shivered and the centre boat sank like a stone.' The Ganges, she concludes, can be a dangerous river, unlike the 'placid stream' of Kali Nadi, which enters the Ganges at Kannauj and whose passage through the meadows 'put me in mind of the Thames near Richmond'. The *Seagull*, complete with furniture, books, china, and wine, was wrecked in an early monsoon storm in the same year—1836—when she broke from her moorings and was driven against the broken bastions of the old city of Prayag/Allahabad. 'Alas! my beautiful *Seagull*; she has folded her wings for ever and has sunk to rest!' lamented Parkes. The crew swam for their lives and survived, but twenty large salt boats were wrecked in the same storm.

Parkes remained intrigued by everything to do with boats and ships to the end, mentioning among others the *surri*, a kind of shallow-draft *pateli*; the tiny, one-oared fishing boats (she even described the floats they used for their nets, made out of a light, spongy wood called *sola*, the same material used for the pith helmet or sola topee worn by colonials to keep off the sun); the *mor-pankhi*, 'a kind of pleasure boat, with the long neck and head of a peacock, most richly gilt and painted'; fanciful 'snake boats' for festivals; and, down the Hooghly off Calcutta, 'the fine merchant-ships, the gay, well-trimmed American vessels, the grotesque forms of the Arab ships, the Chinese vessels with an eye on each side the bows to enable the vessel to see her way across the deep waters, the native vessels in all their fanciful and picturesque forms, the pleasure-boats of private gentlemen'.[11]

Parkes had an eye for the sailing vessels, but lived in India just long enough to witness the arrival of the first steamer in Allahabad on 1 October 1828, after a twenty-six-day journey up-river from Calcutta. The same trip by sail and tracking in a *budgerow* typically took three months, rather than just over three weeks under steam, a travel time that fell further to about ten days by the 1840s after the British had surveyed the river and stationed local pilots at tricky passages along its navigable lengths. The early steamers, which towed the passengers in a vessel known as a flat, therefore transformed the ease and speed of

travel to north India from Calcutta for those who could afford it, usually travelling the long way via the Sunderbans and Dacca (now Dhaka)
to avoid the shallow chokepoint where the Hooghly departs the main
stream at Farraka. The early steamers, such as the *Lord William Bentinck*,
were paddlewheelers of about 100 feet in length that could plod steadily upstream against the current. The steamers in turn were replaced by
the railway in a matter of decades, while sail began a long decline that
accelerated dramatically with the rise of road transport in the second
half of the twentieth century.

Today, you could spend days on the Ganges and the Yamuna without seeing a single vessel of any sort under sail, although documentary
films of the river and Bollywood movies from as recent a time as the
early 2000s captured in their footage the occasional square-rigged
budgerow with rust-red sails or boats like dhows with giant lateen sails
such as those seen on the Nile.

Basil Greenhill, a British wartime naval officer who became a maritime historian and spent time studying the boats of Bengal, recalls
seeing one morning on the Brahmaputra 'at least five hundred sail in
sight at dawn'. Greenhill celebrates the scale and majesty of the rivers
of south Asia and the variety of craft that sailed on them: river boats,
delta boats, some rigged like Arab dhows, some like Chinese junks,
even seafaring dugouts carved from a single tree-trunk 60 feet long.
He is sympathetic, too, to the boating families who live on the water
and suffer from cholera, typhoid, dysentery—and thieves; one boatman
tells him how he fended off an attack by a group of river pirates, making his boat-boy go naked to give credence to his lament that he had
nothing to give them because the boat had already been pillaged by a
rival group of pirates further down the river.[12]

One challenge for any would-be builder of wooden boats now is the
shortage of good timber. On the Hooghly, small-boat owners have got
around this problem with an ingenious, and very cheap, one-person
craft constructed out a single sheet of galvanized corrugated steel, the
sort used for the roofs of houses and shacks. The sheet is folded together
and sealed at the stern (where the paddler sits between the two sides of
the sheet below the waterline), while the flat end—the bows, so to
speak—is curved slightly around a piece of wood and barely gives any
freeboard but is kept out of the water by the weight of the person at the
other end. These little metal canoes look surprisingly stable, but they
would very vulnerable to swamping by even modest-sized waves.

The makers of traditional wooden boats on the Ganges are fast disappearing. Eager to meet some, I was invited by a friend to meet a team of Bengalis near Dhaka on the Bangladeshi side of the border. They were, I was assured, the only remaining traditional craftsmen making large wooden vessels on the Ganges, but it turned out that the last full-sized boats they had made were built a decade ago for a French nautical enthusiast named Yves Marre, who had sailed to Bangladesh with a river barge and set up an eye charity. 'It was a long time back that I build one commercially', I was told by Kartik Chandra Sutradhar, one of the boatbuilders at Marre's riverside godown. Instead, I was shown into a darkened shed, to find a mini-museum on the floor of beautiful scale models of the *sampans*, *panchis*, and other boats they used to make full-size for sailing on the Ganges, models that can sell for high prices in Europe. 'This', said my friend, 'is the end of a 2,000 year tradition.'[13]

Since the dawn of the age of steam, adventurers foreign and Indian have travelled up the river from mouth to source and down it in the other direction—on foot, by car, by boat, by kayak, or some combination of the above. Their motivations have been as varied as their means of transport, although religious devotion and environmental campaigning are common themes. In 1977, Edmund Hillary, the New Zealand mountaineer who first reached the summit of Mt Everest with Sherpa Tenzing Norgay in 1953, led an expedition by three jet-boats from Ganga Sagar at the mouth to a point 275 kilometres upstream of Haridwar. Most of the final stretch is impossible to navigate in normal boats because of rapids, except for the inflatable boats whisked downstream in white-water rafting adventures. In 2015, eight women from eight countries, led by polar adventurer Ann Bancroft of the United States and Liv Arnesen from Norway, travelled downstream, on foot and by boat, to raise awareness about the need to save the world's rivers.

All rivers have an allure, but the Ganges—so varied in mood and flow, its waters so thick with silt and history—has a special attraction. As a young soldier, the writer Eric Newby spent six months on its banks near Kanpur and remembered first seeing it in the hot month of March, when the river was just a couple of hundred yards wide and 'a disagreeable shade of green' on which floated imperfectly cremated corpses and the occasional crocodile.

Then the rains came, clearing the sky and swelling the Ganges, turning it the colour of milky coffee and eventually transforming it into an inland sea. 'Everything in this landscape was brilliant and distinct. It was like the springtime of the world.' Cheerful men and boys perched on glistening water buffaloes urged their herd across the powerful stream (as they still do today), and then left him alone by the river. 'There was something about it, the ability it had shown to change in the space of an hour, to expand and stretch away to distant horizons, to the existence of which I had not even given a thought, that made me long to follow it on and on until it reached the sea.'[14] Twenty two-years later, he returned with his wife Wanda to do just that and write *Slowly Down the Ganges*, his classic travel book about India seen from a flimsy boat drifting down the river. Even in their shallow-draft boat in 1962, they ran aground time after time and had to hunt in frustration for what passed for the river's main channel. Today, the work of the Ganges navigator is more difficult still.

16

Trade Artery No More

Calcutta and Bengal

Into the Ganges flow multitudes of great rivers from each side, which give a matchless inland navigation. It receives in its course through the plains eleven rivers, some of which are equal in size to the Rhine and none lesser than the Thames: it maintains thirty thousand boatmen, by their carriage of salt and food for ten millions of people in Bengal and its dependencies, which occasions a vast expenditure; add to this the exports and imports, the common interchange of divers articles within its limits, its fisheries, and its travellers, which do all together occasion an expenditure of two millions of money.

—Thomas Pennant, 1798[1]

Let us sleep, let us sleep, and pray that Calcutta may be better to-morrow. At present it is remarkably like sleeping with a corpse.

—Rudyard Kipling on the stench of Calcutta in the Victorian era[2]

I have done this before in a boat and it is usually not good, I thought as we lurched to a sudden stop. I already had my doubts about the Modi government's ambitious plans to turn the Ganges and other rivers into a thriving freight transport network for modern India, and those doubts were convincingly reinforced when our ship ran aground in the Hooghly river north of Calcutta. No grave danger here—this was simply a sandbank in a shallow patch of the river, not a rock or a reef to rip the bottom out of the vessel—but it turned out to be only the first of three groundings for the *Paramhamsa* in a five-day journey. It was, furthermore, mid February, before the worst of the hot, dry season ahead of the monsoon, and there should still have been enough water in the river for a flat-bottomed, shallow-draft tourist vessel such as ours to proceed unhindered. (The Vivada company's ship is named after Ramakrishna Paramhamsa, a famous nineteenth-century holy man from this part of Bengal.)[3]

Nor were we the only victims. Back in January, one of the Vivada ships stuck fast on a sandbank in the main stream of the Ganges near the Kosi river, and the tourists had to be taken on by road. At a choke-point called the Mayapur channel, near where we first ran aground in the Hooghly, we came across another company's ship, the *Ganges Voyager II*, so embedded in a sandbank that a tug had been hired and was trying to pull her off. Two laden coal barges were waiting at anchor while dredgers tried to clear the channel. I concluded that the Ganges— for at the delta the waterway named the Hooghly is the biggest distributary channel of the river still within Indian territory—was short of water. For any river, this is a sad state of affairs. For one that is supposed to be navigable, it smacks of failure.

If the Gangetic city of Kanpur is about industry and Varanasi about religion and the ceremonies of death, Calcutta is about trade—or at least it was. After his election victory in 2014, Narendra Modi not only spoke about cleaning the holy river but also launched an ambitious plan to revive the country's waterways, including the Ganges, for freight transport as part of his drive to revive the economy. Nitin Gadkari, the transport minister regarded as one of the more effective members of a lacklustre cabinet, boasted that India had 14,500 kilometres of waterways that needed to be developed for this purpose, including the 1,620-km 'National Waterway 1' first declared in 1986. This highway would link Haldia at the mouth of the Hooghly via the Ganges to Allahabad in the heart of north India.

Gadkari announced plans for 2,000 ports along India's rivers, including thirty on the Ganges and roll-on, roll-off ('Ro-Ro') facilities for vehicle ferries at Haldia, Sahibganj, Patna, and Varanasi. He claimed that cargo could thus be transported on these routes at one-fifteenth of the cost of road transport. 'Varanasi, Haldia and Sahibganj will be developed as multi-modal hubs with roadways, waterways and railways. For this, we have acquired land, our designs are ready, we have given work order for all three places, so before March [2016] we will begin work', Gadkari told a business conference about 'smart cities', another much-trumpeted Modi initiative. 'India has huge potential for water transport... Not only this—we will develop our 1,300 islands as major tourist attraction.'[4]

The idea is not new. There have been ports on the Ganges since ancient times, although their locations have shifted with the shifting streams of this most variable of rivers. Under the British, before the advent of the railways, ships routinely went as far upstream as Kanpur. Job Charnock—preceded by other European traders, notably the Portuguese—set up his outpost for Britain's East India Company on the banks of the Hooghly in 1690 precisely because the river was navigable and the place was a convenient centre for trading with a vast and prosperous hinterland. Calcutta became one of the world's great commercial metropolises and remained the capital of British India until 1911.

Today, however, inland waterway traffic (apart from ferries to cross the many rivers) has all but disappeared in India. It is limited to a few tourist boats, and barges taking coal to power stations on the lower reaches of the Ganges–Hooghly, as well as the transport of oversized items such as giant turbines that are more easily carried by river than by road. By one measure, only 0.4 per cent of India's cargo is carried along its waterways, compared with about 8 per cent in China and the United States and more than 40 per cent in the Netherlands. So it is reasonable for the government to want to exploit the economic potential of rivers and canals, even if environmentalists are worried about the potentially damaging impact of dredging and of pharaonic 'river-linking' schemes, which are designed not primarily to facilitate trade but to shift surplus water from the Brahmaputra and lower Ganges in the east to the parched waterways of central and southern India.[5]

In reality, only projects amounting to a fraction of the government's grandiose schemes are ever likely to be put into practice and none of them can work at all—even those using the existing rivers—without adequate water. 'It's gradually diminishing', says Lakshmi Chowdhury, the pilot of our vessel, when asked about the river. I have joined him and the skipper on the bridge to discuss the state of the Ganges, and investigate why the water flow has been reduced. The replies are revealing: siltation, climate change, and population growth. 'There's a collection of reasons', says Chowdhury. 'First of all, the silt is increasing. Secondly, the seasons—before, you would know that the rainy season would start from such-and-such a time. And it's getting warmer. Neither the winter nor the rainy season are as long as they were before. There's less water coming, and the population is increasing.'[6] The traditional wells from which people used to pump their drinking water were found to contain poisonous arsenic—naturally occurring and brought down from the Himalayas into the floodplain over many centuries—so nowadays the water is pumped from the river, purified, and provided to the inhabitants of West Bengal. Near Barrackpore, the site of the British viceroy's suburban residence north of Calcutta, I noticed a large sign at a pumping station on the river bank: 'Mangal Pandey Water Treatment Plant—Arsenic-free surface water supply scheme'.

Chowdhury is 39 years old and works for the Inland Waterways Authority of India. A burly, smiling man dressed in grey tracksuit trousers and a green check shirt, he comes from a farming family near Katwa on the Hooghly. Of his two brothers, one looks after the farm, and the other secured a prized government job with the Central Reserve Police Force because of his sporting skills as a shot-putter. Although not an official pilot, Chowdhury maintains the navigational poles and other marks to guide the vessels in the river and says he knows the 650-kilometre stretch upstream from Calcutta by heart. 'I've been on this river for eighteen, twenty years. I've seen the changes in the channels. It's a continuous affair.' As he speaks, constantly scanning the milky water under a hazy sky, a chunk of sandy river bank collapses into the river from an island on our starboard side. 'I've been plying these waters so many years. But even if you've done it every day, you have to know the movement of the water—bubbles, waves—and you can see if sand is accumulating. I've got a gift.' He gives credit to Vivada for helping to revive the river traffic—the company has invested in freight transport and tourist trips—and says that if dredging is done properly 'nothing is impossible'.

Still, we keep coming back to the problem of the reduced water flow in the river. Without enough water, dredging the channel is pointless. Tapan Kumar Ghosh, the ship's captain, is ten years older than Chowdhury and just as cheerful, but he too says he has noticed a gradual reduction in the water level over the years and a stronger bore—the tidal wave (like the one in the Bristol Channel between England and Wales) that on occasion surges up the Hooghly and reaches as far as the power station at Triveni. Ghosh, who started as a ship's cook before progressing through the ranks as a deckhand and quartermaster to reach his current job as first-class master, says this is the first time for five years that he has run aground at this time of year. 'The river's shallower,' he says. 'Normally at this time the water is okay.'

I am looking at the water and it is not okay at all, but for the moment it is the quality rather than the quantity that is bothersome. Extraordinary quantities of garbage are floating down the river and littering the fields on both sides. I used to find it hard to imagine that Hindu ceremonies and the immersion of statues of gods and goddesses could be a serious contributor to pollution or vie with the damage caused by sewage and industrial effluents, but what I see in the Hooghly makes me think again. It is springtime and the season of Saraswati *pujas*, acts of worship of the river goddess who preceded Ganga in holding the affections of Indians and who is much revered even today in Bengal.[7] I watch dozens of images of Saraswati, mostly made of clay and straw but ornamented with dresses of synthetic fabric, plastic flowers, and ornaments, floating down the Hooghly. There are garlands of marigolds too—sometimes free and sometimes, perversely, wrapped tightly in plastic bags. And white plastic plates, massed on the river like a fleet of flying saucers on their way to the Bay of Bengal or lying in their hundreds under mango trees on the banks, where they have presumably been used for picnics.

When we land at Chandernagar, the old French outpost, we find the discarded, broken Saraswati images piling up in the shallows. One, yet to be immersed, has painted nails, is riding a swan and carrying a real wheat-sheaf (apparently her only biodegradable ornament). We encounter a small procession heading down to the river with yet another life-size Saraswati in a pink ball gown being transported by cycle-rickshaw. It is a peaceful evening by the Hooghly, the incoming tide is pushing the waters of the Ganges back up the river into India, and the stalls are selling fish and prawns. The worshippers cheerfully lift the image from the rickshaw, rotate it several times and then immerse the pink-robed Saraswati in the water, where she soon joins the other images in the shallows. Opposite the town an array of pumps are sucking mud from the riverbed and dumping it ashore to create flood defences for the coming monsoon.

Roman Catholics like bright images, too, and Chandernagore's 1691 church hosts statues of Jesus and the saints in primary colours, including a Madonna with child clutching a sceptre with a red light bulb at the end. As the boat drives upstream from Calcutta we are passing the architectural traces of the world's religions and the great European trading nations of the past: the British, the French, the Portuguese, Danish, and Dutch. On the left, a seventeenth-century Buddhist monastery; on the right, a mosque, a temple to Kali, and the mansion of a Marwari tycoon. There are brick kilns on all sides, and abandoned cargo wharves with cranes of rusting steel. The most notable sight in Kalna, once a big textiles port, is an unusual circular complex of 108 mini-temples dedicated to the god Shiva, each with its lingam, alternating in black and white, and built in the early nineteenth century. As we land, a group of men and women are shouting praise for Shiva, walking into the river from the *ghat* and collecting holy river water in pairs of pots that hang from poles carried on their shoulders.

The buildings are low-rise until the shape of a huge temple under construction starts to dominate the horizon at Mayapur: this is the headquarters of the International Society for Krishna Consciousness—ISKCON, better known abroad as the Hare Krishnas from their song of praise for the god Krishna. He is said to have manifested himself here 530 years back in the form of one of his own worshippers, who went on to found the organization.[8]

The existing temple is large, and decorated with paintings of Krishna and his lover Radha and his *gopis*, the female cowherds who attend him. But it is dwarfed by the new construction, a huge domed edifice of concrete and brick that looks in its unfinished state like the containment building of a particularly large nuclear power station. 'This', says Soumik Sarkar, a 27-year-old Krishna devotee and software engineer, 'is the biggest temple in the world coming up, the Temple of Vedic Planetarium'. The structure, to be painted in white, gold, and pale blue, will in fact rise to 113 metres, slightly higher than the 111-metre St Paul's Cathedral in London and lower than St Peter's Basilica in Rome—but with a wider dome. The latest cost estimates rise to some $90 million, of which Alfred Ford, great-grandson of Henry Ford and an heir to the motor industry fortune, a man known here as Ambarish Das, has donated $25 million. It will be finished, we are told, in 2022.[9]

Temples, churches, and mosques have long been the most prominent landmarks along the river in rural Bengal. Bandel—the name derives from Bandar, meaning port in Persian, though locals believe the word is Portuguese—is a typical riverside town of fishermen, rubbish heaps and a filthy stream. The local industry is the making of disposable clay cups for *chai*. But an old cannon barrel half exposed in the foundations of a house and the large basilica of Nossa Senhora do Rosario dating originally from 1599 are evidence of the long Portuguese presence here on the banks of the Hooghly. An old ship's mast displayed outside the church is cited as proof of one of several miracles associated with the church, for it was donated by a captain who had been caught in a storm in the Bay of Bengal and had prayed successfully to the Virgin Mary for deliverance. The Portuguese were here for the same reason as the British who followed them up the river in 1657: to trade.[10]

The Hooghly was a navigable but difficult waterway, and the reach of the river in the place that later became Calcutta, 232 kilometres up the river from the sea, was a large and protected anchorage where scores of ships could shelter simultaneously or load and unload cargo. After years of fighting and negotiations, the Mughal emperor Aurangzeb granted the English a new trade licence in 1690. Job Charnock, the agent of the East India Company, paid 3,000 rupees for the right to tax-free trade and made his way by ship up the Hooghly in the tempests of the monsoon season. 'At length on Sunday August 24, 1690, at noon, the weather-beaten band anchored, for the third time, in the long pool of Calcutta', wrote Nilmani Mukherjee in his history of the Port of Calcutta. 'With a poor guard of 30 soldiers, they scrambled up the steep mud bank which was from then on to grow uninterruptedly into the British capital of India.'[11]

The Portuguese and the British were by no means the first peoples to trade at the mouth of the Ganges. At the time of the Buddha in the fifth century BC, sea-going vessels were loaded with merchandise brought from Varanasi, and later from Pataliputra (now Patna) and Champa (now Bhagalpur);[12] all three are cities on the Ganges. Tributaries such as the Gandak entering the Ganges from the north were navigable too. Buddhist literature is scattered with references to ship traffic and ship construction along the Ganges, as well as ocean trade and shipwrecks. A Jain text mentions a wealthy potter who distributes his wares throughout the Ganges valley with his own fleet, while the *Artha Shastra*, a manual of statecraft thought to be from the Mauryan era, talks of a superintendent of ships responsible for ports and navigation, and a superintendent of commerce in charge of trade taxes.[13] The Ganges, wrote the literature professor Steven Darian, was thus at the centre of Indian civilization. 'We see great port cities strung out along the river, serving as entrepôts for an ever-widening hinterland, quickening the commercial and cultural life with their exchange of goods and their reports of new lands and people beyond the ocean. These ranged from Hastinapura, north of Delhi, to Tamralipti on the Bay of Bengal.'[14]

The *Periplus of the Erythraean Sea*, a Greek merchant's guide to the India trade from the late first century AD, says the Tamils ran trade up the east coast of India with big, sea-going catamarans of split logs. The author mentions the mouth of the Ganges: 'On it is an important trading post with the same name as the river, Ganges town, through which are exported malabathron and spikenard [a spice and a perfume, each made from leaves] and pears, and the finest quality muslins called "Gangetic". Beyond this country there lies a very great inland place called China, from which raw silk and silk yarn and Chinese cloth are brought overland..."[15]

Tamralipti, later known as Tamluk, on the Ganges delta south of Calcutta was an important port and centre of scholarship under the Buddhist emperor Ashoka, linking Bengal and inland India to Sri Lanka and beyond, and remained so for centuries. It is mentioned in Sanskrit and Chinese texts and by Ptolemy. The port's oceanic trade routes led past Burma (Myanmar) and the Malay Peninsula to the east, as well as to the west via south India and across the Arabian Sea. A third, inland, route took traders through northern India and across the Himalayas to the Silk Road.[16] As its channel silted up and its long dominance as the region's main harbour declined, Tamralipti was succeeded by Saptagram or Satgaon. The port flourished from the fourteenth century until superseded by the ports on the Hooghly patronized by the Europeans, and its commerce, a Venetian merchant reported in 1575, included 'rice, cloth of Bombast [silk] of diverse sortes, lacca, great abundance of sugar, mirabolans [a type of plum] dried and preserved, long pepper, oyle of zerzeline [sesame] and many other sortes of merchandise'.[17]

Once settled, Calcutta was destined to become the capital and the great port of British India, serving not only its immediate hinterland—the fertile delta region of Bengal—but the whole of the northern area of the subcontinent through which the Ganges flows and where it deposits its life-giving silt on the alluvial plain. Much of north and north-east India, writes Mukherjee, can be described as 'the gift of the Ganges'. Until a few centuries ago, furthermore, the main stream of the river turned south towards the sea in what is now independent India, whereas now most of the natural flow crosses the border into Bangladesh—where it is called the Padma and where it is joined by the mighty Brahmaputra—to find the sea on the eastern side of the delta. Mukherjee writes:

So far as can be ascertained from early traditions, descriptions of foreign travellers and cartographers and Indian literary evidence, the existence of old beds, and historic towns on the banks of the river, the main Ganges stream, from the dawn of history in Bengal, flowed south down the course of the present Bhagirathi to the vicinity of Tribeni or the confluence of the three rivers. This was the most natural and direct course to the sea. At Tribeni, the Ganges divided into three streams. The Saraswati flowed south-westward past Satgaon and emerged into the present Hooghly at Sankrail. The Jamuna followed the south-east direction along the route of the decayed stream of that name. A middle branch, which was the Bhagirathi proper, flowed south along the present Hooghly channel to Calcutta and then through the Adi Ganga (Tolly's Nullah) to the sea.[18]

Mukherjee's description gives some idea of the complexity of the Ganges delta, a dynamic and unstable fan of rivers whose streams have shifted over time and continue to shift year by year and affect navigation, with some (notably the Hooghly) becoming silted up and others turning from streams into rivers. (The naming of the rivers adds an additional layer of confusion, since the names of the biggest distributaries—Bhagirathi, Jamuna/Yamuna, and Saraswati—are the same as those given to tributaries or ancient rivers hundreds of kilometres upstream.)

It was at Calcutta, in any case, that the English made their fateful choice to land. Calcutta became the harbour for exports of treasure, indigo, jute, tea, and opium and eventually for the import of manufactured goods from Birmingham and Manchester. At the headquarters of the Kolkata Port Trust on Strand Road, the old heart of the city, the organization's historically minded chairman gave me a self-deprecating explanation for the choice of this region of Bengal on the part of the English as their point of entry. Raj Pal Singh Kahlon referred to Winston Churchill's discussions with Joseph Stalin in 1942, during which Churchill drew a crocodile to explain why the allies were eager to attack the underbelly of the Third Reich from North Africa rather than confront its jaws in Northern Europe. The English, Kahlon said, had been resisted in other parts of India as they poked about into its harbours:

Calcutta was easier, for plenty of reasons, to attack and to consolidate and to conquer. I myself am a Bengali so I can take the liberty of saying in front of my colleagues, Bengalis are very laid back and very contented and happy with life. It's not a martial race. There's a reason for that, because they were not at the forefronts of foreign invasions. The foreign invasions came from the west, especially Punjab, that was the biggest, everything that happened to the present day Pakistan and Punjab for the last 3,000–4,000 years, all the invaders came through there. Bengal was much more insulated and the land is very fertile. All you had to do was to throw the seed and the crop would grow. Then they have a saying, there are 12 months and 13 seasons, so when you have so much of leisure, you focus on celebrating festivals, writing literature, dance, drama, things like that, and you don't need to defend yourself. To be fair to them, it's not their necessity to defend themselves.[19]

The English, Kahlon concluded 'were very clever. It's alluvial soil, it's the Ganges delta, very, very fertile land. It's a beautiful land as well and they loved it here.' The port thrived, with the first pilot service up the river being introduced as early as 1668—before Charnock's definitive landing. The United States's first elephant, which arrived in New York in April 1796, had been loaded at Calcutta on the ship *America*. 'This most surprizing animal', the Argus newspaper reported four days later, was worth $10,000 and was 'remarkable for its sagacity, its courage in war, and its attachment to its keeper'. This particular specimen also 'drinks all kind of wine and spirituous liquors and eats every sort of vegetable; it will also draw a cork from a bottle with its trunk.'[20]

British India, however, exported people as well as commodities and unusual animals. After the abolition of slavery in the first half of the nineteenth century, 1.5 million indentured labourers, among them impoverished Biharis from the Gangetic plain, were transported from Calcutta between 1843 and 1917 to toil on the sugar, rubber, coffee, cotton, and tobacco plantations of the British Empire. They included 453,063 people sent to the island of Mauritius in the Indian Ocean, 238,909 to British Guiana (now Guyana) on the Caribbean coast of South America, and about 250,000 to Malaya. Others were shipped to Fiji, East Africa, and Natal in South Africa, where Mahatma Gandhi was later to make his name as a lawyer and campaigner for Indian rights.[21]

The novelist Amitav Ghosh, at the start of his trilogy about those involved in this commerce and in the opium trade from India to China, tells of a Bihari woman called Deeti who lives on the banks of the Ganges 400 miles from the sea and one day has a vision of a 'tall-masted ship'. Until this point, she is an ordinary farmer's wife, albeit one struggling to deal with an opium-addicted husband and an exploitative drug trade that leaves the peasants always short of money and fills the fields not with food crops but with poppies. '[F]or mile after mile, from Benares onwards, the Ganga seemed to be flowing between twin glaciers, both its banks being blanketed by thick drifts of white-petalled flowers.' Her daily routine includes bathing in the Ganges after shouting an invocation to the mother river. A series of adventures leads her into the arms of a new husband and down the river to escape, and they join a shipment of labourers bound for Mauritius on the *Ibis*, the tall-masted vessel of her earlier vision.

At the mouth of the holy river, they prepare to cross the inauspicious 'black water'—the ocean—dreaded by traditional Hindus. '[T]he very name Ganga-Sagar, joining as it did, river and sea, clear and dark, known and hidden, served to remind the migrants of the yawning chasm ahead; it was as if they were sitting balanced on the edge of a precipice, and the island were an outstretched limb of sacred *Jambudvipa*, their homeland, reaching out to keep them from tumbling into the void.' One character in the trilogy who helps evoke the nautical bustle and rich colloquial speech of Calcutta and its complex intermingling of colonial and Bengali social *mores* at the time is Zachary Reid, the mixed-race American ship's carpenter on the *Ibis*; he soon becomes a captain, has a torrid affair with an English lady in Calcutta and is sucked into the moral cesspit of the opium trade. Another is Jodu, a boatman's son who longs to go sea and to join the ranks of the lascars, that is the sailors—Chinese, Malays, Bengalis, Goans, Tamils, Arakanese, Africans, and Arabs—who have little in common except the Indian Ocean.[22]

Rudyard Kipling was equally enthused by the bustling life of Calcutta and its port. At the Shipping Office, where the ship captains engage their crews, he describes the motley collection of mariners who have run out of money and are waiting to be hired:

There are the Seedee boys, Bombay serangs and Madras fishermen of the salt villages; Malays who insist upon marrying Calcutta women, grow jealous and run amok; Malay-Hindus, Hindu-Malay-whites, Burmese, Burma-whites, Burma-native-whites; Italians with gold ear-rings and a thirst for gambling; Yankees of all the States, with Mulattoes and pure buck-niggers; red and rough Danes, Cingalese, Cornish boys fresh taken from the plough-tail, 'corn-stalks' from colonial ships where they got four pound ten a month as seamen; tun-bellied Germans, Cockney mates keeping a little aloof from the crowd and talking in knots together; unmistakable 'Tommies' who have tumbled into seafaring life by some mistake; cockatoo-tufted Welshmen spitting and swearing like cats; brokendown loafers, grey-headed, penniless and pitiful, swaggering boys, and very quiet men with gashes and cuts on their faces. It is an ethnological museum where all the specimens are playing comedies and tragedies.[23]

He wrote this characteristically ebullient passage in one of a series of articles about the city in 1888 collectively called *City of Dreadful Night*.[24] Kipling may not have liked Calcutta—and his other Indian works, notably *The Jungle Book* and *Kim*, are better known—but he relished the city as a writer, delighting in the drunken sailors, opium-smoking Chinese gamblers, and prostitutes rich and poor, who were Bengali ('Dainty Iniquity' and 'Fat Vice' are his nicknames for two of them), English, and Eurasian, and whom he interviews by night with the help of friendly police officers. He mocks the Indian and British politicians who have failed to build drains or deal with what he reckons to be the city's most notable feature: the Big Calcutta Stink. 'Benares is fouler in point of concentrated, pent-up muck, and there are local stenches in Peshawar which are stronger than the B.C.S.; but, for dif-fused, soul-sickening expansiveness, the reek of Calcutta beats both Benares and Peshawar. Bombay cloaks her stenches with a veneer of assafoetida and tobacco; Calcutta is above pretence.' Going to bed in Calcutta, he concludes, 'is remarkably like sleeping with a corpse'.

Charles Dickens, Kipling notes, would have loved Calcutta too, with its 'thick, greasy nights' and 'mysterious, conspiring tenements'. Like London and its riverine port on the Thames, its wealth and commerce attracted a colourful cast of criminals and people on the make. At the beginning of the British occupation, in the first half of the eighteenth century, the balance of trade was very much in favour of Bengal. Gold bullion, accounting for nearly three-quarters of the value of imports, was shipped in to pay for Bengal's exports of cotton, silk, sugar, salt, jute, saltpetre, and opium. For most of the century, there were 'constant raids by pirates, freebooters and slave-dealers'.[25] After the battle of Plassey on the east bank of the Hooghly in 1757, in which Clive and the East India Company defeated Siraj-ud-Daulah, the Nawab of Bengal, and his French allies, the British consolidated their rule and Calcutta prospered so much that traders complained of congestion. From 1750, about half of India's sea-borne trade—boosted by the export of tea and jute in the early nineteenth century—passed through Calcutta and its hinterland, which extended across north India as far as Punjab in the west.

Passengers, too, took ship from Calcutta to Europe and the Far East. It was from Calcutta that Swami Vivekananda, a nineteenth-century religious leader and global ambassador of Hinduism—and hero of Narendra Modi—left for his second visit to America in 1899, observing that 'there is a certain unforgettable fascination in our Ganga of Calcutta, muddy and whitish—as if from contact with Shiva's body—and bearing a large number of ships on her bosom'.[26] A 1961 survey by the Calcutta port commissioners—fourteen years after independence from Britain and half a century after the city had been supplanted by New Delhi as the capital and had begun its long decline—found that the port provided work directly or indirectly to one-third of the population of 5.5 million. These 1.8 million or so included 400,000 directly employed but excluded those working in banks, commercial houses, shops, factories, coal mines, and jute mills.[27]

Today the port and its satellite facilities employ only 20,000 directly—still a very large number by international standards, albeit one that includes the harbour at Haldia, halfway between Calcutta and the sea, which was commissioned in 1977 to cater for larger, ocean-going vessels unable to penetrate as far as the city. And Calcutta remains the main port not only for Bengal but also India's north-eastern states and the independent Himalayan nations of Nepal and Bhutan. According to Kahlon of the Port Trust, cargo throughput peaked at 57 million tonnes in 2007 and is now running at about 50 million tonnes a year, split between fuel imports, dry bulk trade such as coal and fertilizer, and container traffic.[28]

In the twentieth century, Calcutta was a crucial port for the British and the allies in the two world wars. In the Great War of 1914–18, no fewer than 1 million Indians fought with the British, and 70,000 died. Mahatma Gandhi, despite his support for non-violence, tried to recruit Indians into the army in the belief that their loyalty would advance the cause of independence. In 1917, Britain did promise 'responsible government' (that is, self-government) to India, but it took the shock of the Second World War—in which the Japanese took Singapore and pierced British India's eastern flank through Burma (Myanmar)—to launch independence in 1947 and finally dismantle the British Empire. The 2.5 million Indians fighting on the side of the Allies made up the largest volunteer army in history, but some Indians sided with the Japanese. Subhas Chandra Bose, who wanted the overthrow of British rule and led the Indian National Army on the side of the Axis powers, is a Bengali hero to this day, and Calcutta's international airport is named after him.[29] The turmoil during the war, including a Bengal famine and the humiliating flight home of 600,000 Indians from Burma (which killed 80,000 of them as they fled the Japanese onslaught), helped propel India towards independence.[30]

Winston Churchill, indeed, is detested by many Bengalis to this day, not so much for opposing Indian independence and calling Mahatma

Gandhi a 'half-naked' fakir but rather for his role in causing the famine of 1943. He refused to divert Australian wheat on its way to Europe and insisted on the continued export of Indian rice. Up to 1.5 million Bengalis starved to death in 1943, 'the year of the corpse'.[31] In fact, as so often happens in famines, the crisis was really about distribution and logistics rather than the availability of food. Historian Janam Mukherjee blames the premature application in 1942 of a misguided British plan to deny any invading Japanese force access to boats used in the vast delta at the mouth of the Ganges. Calcutta's docks were linked to a river and canal system 'that connected the port to the rice- and jute-rich regions of eastern Bengal along 1,127 miles of navigable waterways'. So-called 'country boats' were essential for transporting people, food, and equipment—for example to take farmers to *chars* or temporary fields on exposed mudbanks in the river. But of the 66,563 watercraft registered, 46,146 were confiscated (they were sunk, burnt, or stored in the open, where they rotted) and only 6,800 were officially allowed. Some 20,000 were hidden by locals for secret use, and had they not been the famine would have been even worse.

For all the importance of Calcutta and the Ganges river system for trade since ancient times, it cannot be emphasized enough what a difficult port and waterway they are. Damaging cyclones—their intensity apparently now increased by global warming—regularly make landfall on the shores of the Bay of Bengal.[32] Accounts of Calcutta's rise to wealth and prominence are interspersed with tales of cyclones, squalls, waterspouts, and wrecks.

On 30 September 1734, the weather was so bad that Calcutta 'looked like a place that had been bombarded by the enemy'.[33] On 16 October 1838, 200 troops and passengers died when the *Protector* was wrecked at the Sandheads near the river mouth.[34] On 5 October 1864, only twenty-three of the 193 vessels in port escaped damage and thirty-six were totally wrecked; the steamer *Mauritius*, Captain Haddock in command, broke her moorings and was blown ashore.[35] All were at risk. In August 1865, 265 of the 497 indentured labourers aboard the *Eagle Speed* under Captain Brinsden, bound for Demerara (British Guiana) from Port Canning south of Calcutta perished even before leaving India. The ship sprang a leak and the tug that took it in tow broke down. 'As if to add to the horrors of the story, several of the poor wretches who escaped drowning, when they landed on the mud islets near, were carried off by tigers', reported the Calcutta correspondent of

The Times. 'A story is told of two children who floated to shore. One had left his companion for a moment and returned to see him in a tiger's jaws. He again threw himself into the sea and was picked up at the last extremity.'[36] In the cyclone of 25 May 1887, the steamer *Sir John Lawrence*, with 750 passengers aboard, sank south of Palmyras Point. Most of them were pilgrims on their way to the Jagannath (Juggernaut) temple at Puri down the coast—still a major pilgrimage site—but their corpses were washed onto Sagar Island and the sandbanks in the river mouth.[37]

M. M. Beatie, who worked as a young pilot on the Hooghly and admired the fast, teak-built Arab sailing vessels from Jeddah and Muscat in the port at the close of the south-west monsoon, describes what it is like to be caught in a tropical squall at the Sandheads at the river mouth. 'There was perfect stillness for a few minutes, and then a belt of churned-up water came rushing towards us, and with a prolonged scream the squall hit us.'[38]

Tapan Ghosh and John Gomes, our own skipper and manager from the *Paramhamsa*, recall being caught in such an unheralded storm in the Sunderbans at the river mouth back in 2007. The glass tables were smashed and the ship dragged its anchor, but survived. Satellite-based weather forecasting, better preparations, and stronger ships and buildings have helped to protect the region's growing population from the effect of storms, but not entirely. In May 2008, Cyclone Nargis— one of the strongest cyclones ever recorded—made landfall in Myanmar to the east and killed 138,000 people. Cyclone Phailin, India's worst tropical storm for fourteen years, lashed eastern India in October 2013 and half a million residents on the coast were evacuated from their homes.

Even when the weather is good, the Hooghly is a notoriously hard river. Captain J. J. Biswas, Calcutta's chief hydrographer, calls it 'the river of three Bs': bores, bends, and bars. The bores are the tidal waves that sweep periodically up the river; the bends are many and tortuous; and the bars are the sandbanks that accumulate in river mouths over which ships must navigate to enter the waterway. About 100 vessels lie wrecked in the river, says Biswas, and he has detailed records of about forty of those.[39] Captain R. E. Mistry writes of the loneliness of piloting a large ship to or from Calcutta before the days of VHF radio communication. 'A deep leaded ship took 36 hours or more piloting and anchoring to get down the river', he writes. 'Turning a 550 feet long ship in a channel 850 wide in a vicious bore coming up the river at night is still the biggest hazard for a pilot.'[40]

Concerns about the silting of the Hooghly—and the consequent threat to Calcutta as a port—date almost from the time of the first British settlement. Look at a map of South Asia and it is strikingly clear that the main stream of the Ganges reaches the sea today not in India but in neighbouring Bangladesh, where the river is joined by the Brahmaputra River from Tibet before debouching into the Bay of Bengal. (This border did not exist, however, until the creation of Pakistan in 1947, and it was not until 1971 that Bengali-speaking East Pakistan won its independence from the western half of the country to become Bangladesh.)

The British dredged a canal between the main stream of the Ganges and the Hooghly more than 200 years ago to ensure navigation between Calcutta and the rest of India. 'As soon as the water of the river was led into it, the force of the stream achieved what was far beyond expectation', wrote Francis Rawdon, Lord Hastings, the governor-general of Bengal and British commander-in-chief, in his private journal at the start of a journey up the Ganges from Calcutta in 1814. 'It has ploughed a channel of considerable depth, about one hundred and fifty yards in breadth; and the flow of water through it is such as gives every reason to believe that the junction is secure for every season.' After independence, India started in 1962 to build the Farraka Barrage across the Ganges at the junction to guarantee the continued flow of water into the Hooghly. It was completed in 1975 but has been only partially effective in flushing the silt out of the Hooghly. An agreement with independent Bangladesh in 1996, furthermore, guaranteed a minimum flow of water for the main stream of the Ganges crossing the border into Bangladesh, where the river is named the Padma. According to Kahlon and Captain Biswas at the Kolkata Port Trust, the Hooghly needs a flow of 40,000 cusecs (cubic feet per second) to flush out the upper part of the river in the dry season, but in some years has had as little as 10,000–15,000 cusecs and is now receiving 20,000–23,000.

These numbers—or, more importantly, the evident lack of water in the river and the frequency of ships running aground—cast doubt on the government's plans to develop the waterways of India for freight, although the port officials do talk of plans to increase the amount of coal going up the river—to as much as 10 million tonnes a year—to serve power stations in Bihar as well as the one at Farraka. On the Indian side of the frontier, river-users grumble that too much water is sent to Bangladesh and on the other side they complain that too much is kept in India.

Vivada's 'promoter'—that is, the founder and chief investor—is Vijaya Nath, who came to Calcutta as a branch manager for a long-established shipping company called Darapsha B. Cursetjee and Sons and left to launch his own operation fifty years ago. He supplies fuel to ships in Haldia and Calcutta, sells diesel to fishing boats, and runs ferries in the Sunderbans and across the Hooghly. He transports petroleum, fly-ash (the ash from coal-fired power stations, sometimes used in cement) and oversized cargo such as turbines that are hard to move by road. 'It's growing', he says. 'There are a lot of factories, power plants, cement plants, which need over-dimension cargo as their equipment.'[41]

As recently as the 1970s, says Nath, there were about 5,000 large craft plying the inland waterways. Now there are only 150, although they are much bigger. There are opportunities in tourism, too, and in addition to the existing excursions to the Sunderbans and up the Ganges, the company is looking to open routes between Calcutta and Dhaka, the Bangladeshi capital, as well as to Guwahati in Assam via the Brahmaputra, and to Tripura. Such projects are likely to require dredging and careful river management, according to R. Sushila, Nath's executive director. 'The river', she says, 'has been kind of neglected.' The Calcutta port officials agree. 'It will be a freight thing only if the infrastructure comes up on both sides, if the embankments are firmed up, and if industry is set up on the sides on the river', says Kahlon. 'Again there's a problem, you take it by river but where do you offload it, unless you have easy accessibility? Right now we are going for the thermal power projects.'[42]

Bengal has always been a network of navigable waterways. In the past, the rivers of Bangladesh, according to one naval historian, constituted perhaps the most complete system of inland navigation in the world. 'The early European navigators and seamen were completely bewildered by their complexity—it was two hundred years before their courses were mapped at all accurately—and delighted by the relatively easy road they gave to the interior of the country.'[43]

Like West Bengal in India with which it shares the Ganges delta, Bangladesh is affected by all the upstream river engineering schemes to block or divert the Ganges and its tributaries in India, Nepal, and

China. 'With the exception of Chittagong, the whole of Bangladesh is built by sand carried by the two rivers [the Ganges/Padma and the Brahmaputra]. The land building process is still going on', says Ainun Nishat.[44] Professor emeritus at BRAC University's Centre for Climate Change and Environmental Research, he is one of Bangladesh's foremost water experts. A map on the wall of his office showing the dense networks of the country's 400 rivers—all 25,000 kilometres of them—looked to me when I first met him like a chart of the blood flow to somebody's lungs. Bangladesh, with 160 million inhabitants, is the world's most densely populated large country but the delta is so fertile and rich in fish that domestic food output has expanded steadily to meet demand since the famine of 1974 that followed the country's violent separation from Pakistan.[45] There is no doubt that Indian dams on some of the fifty cross-border rivers they share have had an impact on Bangladesh downstream, just as China's colossal engineering schemes on the Tibetan plateau have begun to affect the flow of Asia's other great rivers, including the Indus and the Mekong. Dhaka is just 8 metres above mean sea level, and Nishat says the Indian scheme to save Calcutta port by diverting water into the Hooghly from the Ganges— that is the purpose of the Farraka Barrage—caused a damaging increase in salinity on the lower reaches of the Ganges where the river meets the sea.

Making a river more easily navigable can have ecological consequences both bad and good: bad if it deprives another river of water flow or replaces the natural river with a lifeless canal, but good if it increases natural flow because governments decide to limit the diversion of water for other purposes in order to ensure sufficient river depths for shipping. 'If you can solve navigation then your problem of ecology is not there because there's sufficient water', says Nishat. There was substantial India–Bangladesh river traffic until 1965, he says, but the deep channels that were once maintained in the Brahmaputra—a complex, 'braided' river that tends to wander in ever-changing strands over its floodplain—have been lost. Nishat says the Brahmaputra, once typically 5–6 kilometres wide, is 15–16 kilometres across, and although the Bangladesh government is keen to restore the channel and the World Bank has offered to help, it would need as much as $100 billion and take twenty-five years. The natural vagaries and huge seasonal variations of the Ganges and the Brahmaputra, as well as relentless exploitation of upstream waters for hydro-electricity and irrigation, mean that the dream of turning either river into a significant freight highway is a long way from being realized.

The river ports of Calcutta and Dhaka have in any case lost out to more accessible harbours such as Paradip and Chittagong that can handle today's large, ocean-going cargo ships. Calcutta, usurped as British India's capital by Delhi in 1911, remained an important industrial and commercial centre for decades but its economic influence steadily declined and the city today rarely merits a visit by the foreign and Indian corporate executives who flock to Mumbai, Bangalore, Chennai, or Delhi's new satellite cities of Gurgaon and Noida. A Maoist insurgency and a hard-line, Communist-led state government elected in the late 1970s ushered in three decades of industrial decline, urban decay, and official hostility to capitalism. 'That dealt a death blow to industrialization and the ports', says Kahlon of the Port Trust. Investors, many of them commercially minded Marwaris originally from western India, were plagued with death threats and strikes. The mood was so sour, according to West Bengal finance minister Amit Mitra, that 56,000 factories shut down. Abhirup Sarkar, an economics professor, says the state's share of all Indian manufacturing fell from 12 per cent to just 2 per cent.

Mamata Banerjee, West Bengal's populist chief minister, has tried, somewhat erratically, to attract investors. Less than a decade ago, while in opposition, she led a campaign against a Tata Motors factory when the company wanted to make its low-cost Nano car in West Bengal. Hounded by protests over the land acquired for the plant, Tata moved its project to the business-friendly Gujarat of Narendra Modi on the other side of the country. These days, Banerjee insists she wants investors and boasts of her economic successes. 'Come to Bengal—Ride the Growth' was the most prominent billboard slogan in early 2016. It is nevertheless an uphill battle to persuade wary entrepreneurs that West Bengal has changed. Several big investors in Kolkata complain that corruption persists, while the *goondas* or thugs who used to enforce the will of the Communists have simply switched sides and support Banerjee's party now that it is in power.[46]

Calcutta and Bengal, furthermore, are exceptionally resistant to modernization. Look in one direction on a Calcutta street and you could be anywhere in fast-growing India, with scenes reminiscent of the 'tiger' economies of South-east Asia in the 1990s: canals run black with poisonous waste, builders are erecting metro lines and high-rise blocks of luxury apartments ('Eco-Homes—let the Eco-life begin!'), and malls urge shoppers to clothe themselves in Armani and Gucci. Glance in another direction, though, and you could only be in Calcutta. Old men with open sores lie half-naked by the road. Rats the size of small dogs forage in rubbish on the river banks. Whole trees whose seeds have landed on rooftops silently tear apart the unmaintained colonial edifices on Strand Road. The Botanical Gardens are overgrown with weeds, and mosquitoes attack those few who venture into the library of The Asiatic Society, founded by the philologist Sir William Jones in 1784. The taxis are all yellow Ambassadors, the iconic 1950s-designed vehicle of Hindustan Motors that the company stopped making a few years ago. And, astonishingly for the twenty-first century, the favoured mode of transport on the quiet side streets is not a cycle rickshaw or a motorized three-wheeled 'auto' but the old-fashioned two-wheeled rickshaw pulled by an old man with bare feet.

The Indian Coffee House, its ceiling fans churning the humid air, seems to embody all that makes Bengalis and foreigners nostalgic about the once-great metropolis. 'We take mental refreshment here', Siddharth Basu, a 56-year-old painter and writer of Bengali short stories, tells me gravely. He frequents the cafe, run by the Indian Coffee Workers' Co-operative Society, on Wednesdays and Saturdays. There is fare for the stomach as well as the mind—boiled eggs for Rs8 ($0.12) apiece or a mutton sandwich for Rs37 when I visited—and the cafe's cavernous hall echoes with the animated conversations of students, artists, and intellectuals. At one end of the room, a portrait of the poet and polymath Rabindranath Tagore presides serenely over the hubbub. Many of the locals lament Calcutta's cultural decline and dream of a new 'Bengal renaissance', the late nineteenth-century flowering of literary endeavour and social reform—not through poetry this time, but maybe in cinema, theatre, and modern music on the fast-growing suburban fringes of the old city.

Calcutta became India's first modern 'cosmopolis' under colonial rule, says Jadavpur University English professor Swapan Chakravorty, after the arrival of printing presses meant the serendipitous publication of Shakespeare plays and ancient Indian texts at the same time. 'If you imagine the Renaissance and the Enlightenment telescoped into one, you will get Bengal.' Today's Kolkata is very different. Overcrowded and impoverished, it reeks of the economic and cultural decline that followed the death of Tagore in 1941. Tourists tend to find a perverse charm in Kolkata's physical decay, just as some of the city's residents take a perverse pride in the eccentricities of the anti-capitalist political heritage often blamed for that decay. The 1980s, however, did not just lead to economic decline. According to Amit Chaudhuri, the novelist, poet, and musician who wrote a typically hyper-intellectual book about his return to his home city, Calcutta may stubbornly call itself a 'capital of culture' but is no longer any kind of centre at all. Above all, the paradox of Calcutta's lyricism—the notion 'that life and the imagination would hover most palpably over decay and dereliction'— was now unviable. '[I]t's not that it suddenly began to fail, but that its long history and aura of failure, cherished and even metamorphosed into something vital by the Bengali imagination, ceased to be intellectually or artistically instructive or illuminating. Without the transformative effect of the imagination, decay is just decay, disrepair plain disrepair.' Very few people from the city return to Calcutta today, says Chaudhuri, 'except to be with parents'.[47]

This melancholy perception of decline is shared by patrons of the Indian Coffee House. Chandidas Kumar, a retired bank clerk who refers airily to Dostoevsky and Maupassant, complains of declining values, behaviour, culture, and education. And yet, he says, Calcutta two centuries ago 'was a city so nice, more beautiful than London also— not only for the outward beauty but also for the inner beauty'.

For an antidote to any optimism, or to the romanticization of decline among the city's elderly intellectuals, one has to turn to the gritty realism of a Bengali writer such as Kunal Basu. In just one brief scene at the end of his novel *Kalkatta* (another alternative spelling for the city), the protagonist Jamshed Alam and his transvestite friend have a view of Calcutta from a boat in the middle of the Hooghly when the city—including the Howrah railway station and the Victoria Memorial with its angel standing on tiptoes on the dome—looks 'as a pretty as a film set'. For the rest of the novel, Calcutta emerges as a reeking, smoky city of corrupt policemen, vote-rigging politicians, unsanitary hospitals, kidney traders, drunks, pickpockets, a leper festooned with tin cans (to warn of his presence), beggars, *hijras* (transgender men who have adopted a female identity), purveyors of fake jewellery, and butchers who apply red dye to their meat to make it look as though it is fresh and running with blood. The Ganges–Hooghly, the navigable river that is the very reason for the existence of this vast Bengali metropolis, barely makes an appearance until the end.

Howrah Bridge roars to life when the sun rises. You might find half of Kalkatta's fourteen million on it, and none—including the dead—are allowed to enter or leave the city without crossing the Ganga that flows underneath. Nobody has found a good way to avoid wrestling with the millions on the bridge; the trampling and cursing causing serious disturbance to those who are in no hurry, simply enjoying the sights. It's no time to be polite to foreigners taking pictures of the city on their way out to Benares or Delhi. Or give way to a lady just because she was with child, and the rush was making her dizzy. It didn't matter if the holiest of rivers flowed under one's feet, as long as the river of bodies carried you forward to your destination.[48]

Our ship, having reached as far north as Murshidabad near the main stream of the Ganges, has survived its three groundings and returned under the Howrah Bridge to its base in Calcutta. It has been the last trip of the season so far upstream, and it will be months before the monsoon has filled the Ganges and its tributaries and distributaries with enough water to allow such large vessels to ply the rivers with passengers or cargo. As I disembark, I watch the waters of the Ganges—now shared among the many branching streams of the delta—patiently absorbing all the discarded filth of India's third-largest city and winding its muddy way towards the sea.

17

Mission Impossible?

How to Clean the Ganges

That noble river has really become a Stygian pool reeking with ineffable and unbearable horror.

—Benjamin Disraeli on the Thames, 1858[1]

In Köhln, a town of monks and bones,
And pavements fang'd with murderous stones
And rags, and hags, and hideous wenches;
I counted two and seventy stenches,
All well defined, and several stinks!
Ye Nymphs that reign o'er sewers and sinks,
The river Rhine, it is well known,
Doth wash your city of Cologne;
But tell me, Nymphs, what power divine
Shall henceforth wash the river Rhine?

—Samuel Taylor Coleridge comments on the Rhine in his poem Cologne in 1828

I've lost hope and surrendered . . . Ganga is more polluted than ever before.

—Kanpur environmental campaigner Rakesh Jaiswal in late 2016[2]

When Narendra Modi, who was then newly installed as Indian prime minister, met President Barack Obama for an informal White House dinner in September 2014, the talk turned almost immediately to environmental matters, including climate change and the fate of the Ganges. It was an odd dinner, not least because Modi was in the midst of a strict Hindu religious fast and ate nothing, but US officials said the men in charge of the world's two largest democracies quickly struck up a friendly relationship. Obama told Modi that the river in his native Chicago, once so filthy it used to catch fire, was now a place where fish were caught and eaten. 'That's exactly what I want for the Ganga', said Modi.[3]

The discussion about the Ganges did not make it into the official joint communiqué after the meeting, but US officials said there was no doubting Modi's commitment to environmental issues such as climate change.[4] India under Modi maintains a robustly independent—some would say truculent—approach to international negotiations on matters such as world trade and global warming. True, New Delhi has reluctantly accepted that climate change is potentially so dangerous, not least for India itself, that even developing countries with relatively low carbon emissions per capita must make some contribution to a solution. Yet the suspicion lingers among Indian policymakers that industrialized powers such as the United States and Europe, which emitted the most carbon into the atmosphere in the past, are seeking to stifle the economic opportunities of poor countries such as India by demanding curbs on carbon emissions.[5] When it comes to cleaning the Ganges, on the other hand, neither Modi nor his predecessors from the Congress Party have any such inhibitions: the river rises in India and remains in Indian territory for most of its length, so this is national project with national benefits. Even Indian nationalists such as Modi, rather than condemning the machinations of interfering foreign environmentalists, can hail foreign countries as examples to follow. India, after all, is not the first country to find that the growth of its population and the development of its modern industry and agriculture have poisoned the nation's rivers.

The successful clean-ups of the Thames in England and the Rhine in Continental Europe are the projects most often mentioned by Indians concerned about the Ganges. In 1957, the Natural History Museum in London is said to have declared that the River Thames in the city was biologically dead (although the actual findings were more nuanced—scientists found there were essentially no *fish* other than eels in the tidal Thames in greater London).[6] As a child I recall being told that close contact with the toxic Thames was something to be avoided at all costs: if you fell in, you would have to go to hospital to have your 'stomach pumped', a procedure that for children conjured up the image of a doctor with a device like a bicycle pump extracting poisoned river water from down one's throat (which is more or less the way it works in reality).

Fifty years later, the Thames in London is so clean that numerous types of fish have returned to the river, sea-horses have been found in the estuary, and financial traders can see seals at Canary Wharf. A lost whale even swam past the Houses of Parliament. I have seen kingfishers and herons along the canals of central London and cormorants fishing in the Thames under Southwark Bridge.

The fate of the Thames is instructive—there are many parallels in the way people have used and abused the Thames and the Ganges—because it was in Britain that the industrial revolution first took hold in the eighteenth century, which meant that London's river was among the first to undergo the cycle of fluvial death and eventual rebirth. Just as the tanneries of Kanpur pour their filthy waste into the Ganges today, so potteries in Fulham, porcelain factories in Chelsea, glassmakers in Vauxhall, the sugar refiners of Whitechapel, and the tanneries of Bermondsey did the same to the Thames in the past. Water was extracted at the source of the Thames for a canal and construction on the banks in London narrowed the river to a third of its natural breadth.[7]

Even before the building of modern industrial factories, the river in London—like the river in Varanasi—was sullied with sewage and the carcasses of animals. The London historian Peter Ackroyd quotes a royal complaint from Edward III as early as 1357 about the accumulation of dung and other filth on the banks and the 'fumes and other abominable stenches arising therefrom'. Friars complained that many of their number had been killed by the 'putrid exhalations' of the river. Pollution controls came early too, and an Act of Parliament in 1535 prohibited the casting of excrement and other rubbish into the Thames. Regulation, however, seems to have had as little effect in England hundreds of years ago as it had in industrializing South-east Asia in the late twentieth century or has in India today. The eighteenth-century writer Tobias Smollett was appalled by the need to drink water from the Thames 'impregnated with all the filth of London and Westminster', including human excrement but also 'all the drugs, minerals and poisons, used in mechanics and manufacture, enriched with the putrefying carcases of beasts and men; and mixed with all the scourings of all the wash-tubs, kennels and common sewers, within the bills of mortality'. The nineteenth century added ammonia, cyanide, and carbolic acid. The river, said the statesman Benjamin Disraeli, had become 'a Stygian pool reeking with ineffable and unbearable horror'. There were repeated cholera outbreaks from the 1830s to the 1860s.[8]

Corpses, animal and human, would wash up again and again with the tides at the steps—the English version of the *ghat*—in Wapping known as Dead Men's Stairs. The novel *Sweet Thames* (1992) by Matthew Kneale recreates the horror of the 1849 epidemic. In Kneale's recreation of events, the water of Dock Head Creek—like drains and foetid streams today in Kanpur or Delhi—is stained scarlet by the dyes of the leather dressers and 'covered with scum resembling a giant cob-web, through which loomed the patterned carcasses of animals that had tumbled in, as so many ill-wrapped packages'. People would still haul the water in buckets straight from such creeks into their houses to drink, and 14,000 died of cholera in that epidemic in London alone.[9]

In 1858, the so-called 'Great Stink' almost brought London to a stand-still. One cause of the exceptional pollution crisis was that residents had started using the new 'water closets'—flushing toilets—which increased the flow of sewage into the river. In the absence of any accompanying attempt at sewage treatment, this merely increased the volume of filth entering the river (a useful warning for contemporary Indian governments that have vigorously promoted the installation of toilets without simultaneously ensuring that sewage treatment plants are operated and maintained). So appalling was the stench in central London in the heat of summer that members of the newly constructed Houses of Parliament on the river at Westminster were unable to use the library. They tried drenching the curtains with a mixture of chloride and lime to disinfect the building and hide the smell. They considered moving to another location, even though the finishing touches were still being put to their new parliamentary workplace, the Palace of Westminster. ('Big Ben', the great bell, was installed in the belfry of the clock-tower later that year.)

But the stink was so bad that the MPs, after years of ignoring the pleas of public health campaigners, quickly passed a law to restore the River Thames. This was the dull-sounding Metropolis Local Management Amendment Act, which instructed the Metropolitan Board to complete as soon as possible 'the necessary Sewers and Works for the Improvement of the Main Drainage of the Metropolis, and for preventing as far as may be practicable, the sewage of the Metropolis from passing into the River Thames within the Metropolis'. The scientist Michael Faraday, who became the vocal champion of a Thames clean-up, had asked five years earlier: '[W]here are ye, ye civil engineers? Ye can remove mountains, bridge seas and fill rivers...can ye not purify the Thames, and so render your own city habitable?' This was Parliament's answer, for it authorized the Victorian civil engineer Joseph Bazalgette to proceed with his costly but necessary twenty-year project to build London's sewers, as well as the Victoria, Albert, and Westminster embankments and the tunnels beneath used by the District and Circle lines of the London Underground. Cleaning London's river and saving its citizens from cholera became one of the biggest infrastructure projects of the nineteenth century. The last cholera epidemic was in 1866 in the East End, which had not yet been connected to the sewer system.[10]

Even the robust and long-lived engineering works of Bazalgette were not enough. When the *Princess Alice*, a pleasure steamer, sank after a collision with a collier in September 1878, several of the few survivors who tried to swim to safety were overcome by the toxic pollutants emerging from the outfalls of his newly built sewage pumping stations; in all, more than 600 people died. The Thames, then, did not fully recover after Bazalgette's efforts in the late nineteenth century and eventually died a second time in the 1950s. Relentless population growth—from about 2 million in 1850 to nearly 5 million in 1880, and a further doubling to nearly 9 million today—produced more human waste flowing into the river. Industry and the resulting chemical pollution, including ammonia, phosphates, and heavy metals, grew as well. German bombing of London in the Second World War damaged some of the Victorian sewers. It was not until the post-war economic recovery in the 1960s that the quality of water in the river started to improve, as new sewage plants were constructed and companies began to treat the poisonous effluents from their factories. Awareness of our natural environment and the damage we were inflicting on it burgeoned around the world—Rachel Carson's *Silent Spring* was published in 1962—and Western governments went on to implement new laws to control pollution from chemicals, pesticides, and fertilizers.[11]

The work of keeping a river clean never ends. Even today, sewage from parts of London flows straight into the river each time rain swells the volume of waste water beyond the capacity of the treatment plants that are supposed to manage it, and 39 million tonnes of untreated sewage have been pouring into the river every year. Thames Water has embarked on the construction of two tunnels to capture the extra waste and take it to treatment plants for processing. One, the Lee Tunnel, is finished. The second, the 25-kilometre Thames Tideway

Tunnel under the river, is a vast project costing more than £4 billion due to be completed in 2023. Plastic waste—from plastic bags to the tiny plastic microbeads found in face-scrubs and other cosmetics—is another concern because of the damage it does to wildlife.[12]

On the whole, though, the Thames today is a clean river. As with the Ganges or the Yamuna along much of their length, one should not be deceived by the murkiness of the water, the result of the mud and sand churned up by the river's flow. It has seen a spectacular return of the plants and animals that were exterminated from the tidal stretch of the waterway in London by the capital's filth, so that the Thames is now 'one of the cleanest urban river catchments in Europe' and 'one of the most successful large-scale river restorations in history'.[13]

According to the Tudor chronicler Raphael Holinshed, the Thames at Richmond in the sixteenth century had such a supply of shrimp and fish that there was 'no river in Europe able to exceed it'.[14] In his biography of the river, Peter Ackroyd relished the names of the fish found in the medieval Thames—barbel, flounder, roche, dace, pyke, tench, eel, gudgeon, mullet, salmon, smelt, cod, bass, plaice, sole, whiting, lamprey, sturgeon, turbot, mackerel—before noting that by the 1950s there were said to be no fish at all in the Thames in all the 48 miles from Gravesend to Kew. Many have now returned. A salmon was found beyond Teddington Weir in 1976, the first in the non-tidal Thames for 140 years, and the estuary has become the largest spawning ground for sole in England. 'It is now also a cleaner river than at any time in its history. It is claimed, in fact, that the Thames is the cleanest metropolitan river in the world. It is a miracle of rejuvenation.'[15]

The Ganges, and its tributary the Yamuna in Delhi, are very different rivers from the Thames in London. Above all, they are harder to manage than the fairly predictable rivers of Northern Europe. In the monsoon season, the Ganges can become a raging torrent in the hills and change its course abruptly across the north Indian plain. In the dry season, especially now that the main river and its tributaries are blocked by dams for irrigation and hydro-electricity, the Ganges can disappear completely for long stretches. Still, it is not unreasonable to apply the lessons learned in southern England to north India. The artist and writer Robert Gibbings, boating and walking down the Thames during the Second World War, made an explicit reference to the Indian river as he observed Strand-on-the-Green. 'The houses are charming, but the river is filthy. Talk about the sacred Ganges. It is nothing to the

Thames at Chiswick', he wrote. 'And there were children bathing, swimming in water the colour of beer, with a sediment on its surface thick enough to be the beginning of a new continent.'[16]

Modi discussed the example of the Thames clean-up with a British politician a month before he discussed the Chicago River with Obama in Washington. On a visit to New Delhi three months after Modi was elected, Nick Clegg of the Liberal Democrats, then the UK's deputy prime minister, was pleasantly surprised to find Modi so interested in environmental topics such as climate change and water quality. 'Prime Minister Modi became most animated when talking about the environment and climate change', Clegg said. 'We talked through everything from the clean-up of the Ganges and whether the clean-up of the Thames could provide any help for that, through to using small-scale solar installations in remote farming communities in India, through to the disposal of urban waste in growing Indian cities ... If he does half the things he talked to me about, cleaning up the Ganges, more sustainable waste disposal in cities, more efficient energy consumption by Indian households, rollout of small-scale renewable energy generation capacity in rural communities—if he does half of that he will have met India's global climate change obligations already.' Clegg continued: 'I just said it [the Thames] used to be filthy and it's a lot cleaner now ... Cleaning up the Ganges is of course a challenge on a much, much bigger scale.' Clegg's hopes that India would join the United States and the UK in pushing for an ambitious international commitment to curb global warming at the Paris climate summit the following year were not to be fulfilled, but at least India did not block an agreement altogether.[17]

The Rhine—at more than three times the length of the Thames and thirty-five times the water flow—is a closer match to the Ganges in size and importance, and has been much cited by Indian policymakers and environmentalists as an example to follow. There are certainly similarities between the two rivers. Both rise in the mountains and run for hundreds of kilometres to a delta on the sea; both are navigable for much of their length; and both have been afflicted with pollution from sewage and industrial effluent since the English poet Samuel Taylor Coleridge paid his visit with William Wordsworth in 1828 and wrote his rude poem about the odour of the Rhine at Cologne. There are differences, too. The Rhine, in marked contrast to the highly seasonal Ganges, has a fairly stable rate of flow throughout the year, which makes it easier to dilute pollution and manage the riverine environment from the Alps to the North Sea. The Rhine, on the other hand, is an international river, running through or along six countries in the heart of Western Europe, which might have made it harder to reach a consensus on how to clean it; only one part of the lower Ganges is the responsibility of a country other than India, namely Bangladesh.

In modern times, the Rhine's pollution crisis peaked a few years later than that of the Thames, that is to say in the 1960s and 1970s rather than the late 1950s. By the 1960s, Europe was in the throes of its post-war economic and industrial resurgence. Rising levels of organic and inorganic pollution—sewage from cities, salts from the potash mines of Alsace, phosphates and nitrates from detergents and fertilizers, and chemicals and heavy metals such as mercury and chromium from the industries on the Ruhr (a tributary of the Rhine)—wiped out fish species, made the river unpleasant for swimming, and threatened the production of drinking water. This is roughly where the Ganges is today. (Like the Thames at London in 1957, the Yamuna is dead downstream of Delhi, but the Ganges at Varanasi is still a living, albeit polluted, river.)

European governments took action to stem the tide of pollution. Switzerland, France, Luxembourg, Germany, and the Netherlands formed the International Commission for the Protection of the Rhine against Pollution (ICPR) in 1953 to monitor pollution and find ways of reducing it. Among the measures taken were conventions to curb chemical and chloride contamination that were put into effect in 1976. Ten years later, on 1 November 1986, a pollution disaster caused by a fire at a Sandoz pesticide warehouse near Basel drew the public's attention to the fragility of the river and further energized official efforts to clean the river. Water sprayed on the fire washed chemicals into the river that killed eels in their thousands all the way to Karlsruhe more than 200 kilometres down-river.

Pollution control regimes have not returned the Rhine to its pristine state—which was never going to be possible—but they have succeeded to a great degree. By 1995, the amount of toxic heavy metals in the Rhine had fallen by over 90 per cent since the 1970s, while sewage treatment had reduced the levels of organic waste that nearly killed the lower reaches of the river; in two decades, Germany alone spent the equivalent of about $55 billion on sewage treatment plants. Levels of dissolved oxygen in the water, which had fallen to life-threatening levels of below 2 milligrams per litre in the summer months in the lower reaches of the river, rose to healthy levels of 9 to 10 milligrams per litre. Swimming was pleasant again.[18]

Fish returned, and in 1992 mature salmon were caught in the Rhine for the first time in decades. In 2001, the BBC reported from Basel on the Rhine's triumphant recovery. 'When I was first rowing, the Rhine was a very dirty river, full of chemicals and dye from the factories', said Martin Hug, who had been rowing on the river for thirty years. 'We used to say, "Oh it must be Thursday, because the river stinks like this", but now it's much better.' With the hard work of basic pollution control mostly done, the authorities in Europe were turning their attention to making it easier for fish to migrate up the river by building fish ladders. 'We really had to get together and clean it up and keep it clean', said Manfred Beubler, head of water quality for the Basel region. 'We realized it could be the death of the Rhine otherwise.'[19]

One reason why the work of controlling pollution can never be finished is that new industrial processes produce new pollutants whose dangers are not always immediately recognized. The ICPR, for example, is now looking at so-called 'micro-pollutants'. They include the tiny plastic beads used in cosmetics that are also found in the Thames (and the world's oceans), as well as hormones, biocides, anti-corrosion agents, and specialized substances used for everything from perfumes to medical imaging. But 96 per cent of the people in the catchment area of the Rhine are now connected to a waste-water treatment plant, river water quality has improved and the number of fish and plant species has increased. 'At present, 63 fish species live in the Rhine', says the ICPR. It adds that since 2006 'salmon, sea trout and eel as well as other migratory fish may migrate from the North Sea as far upstream as Strasbourg'.[20]

The first person to make the Rhine–Ganges comparison for me was Dutchman Onno Ruhl, then the World Bank's director for India. I warmed to him immediately when I met him in 2013 because he was articulate and passionate about the Ganges and because his ponytail and weather-beaten features suggested he was not the stereotypical, suit-wearing international bureaucrat from Washington. He is also an India-lover. Like me, he had recently bathed in the Ganges at the great Hindu religious festival of the Kumbh Mela in Allahabad, where the Yamuna River joins the Ganges at its holy *sangam* or confluence. And, like me, he had done so in the full knowledge that the river—even after the emergency closure of the tanneries upstream in Kanpur—was a long way from meeting the water quality standards of Northern Europe. ('I wasn't planning to because I know the Ganga's dirty and I'm not a Hindu, so I didn't think it would be worth my while to take the risk', he told me. 'When I was there and they took me to the place, it seemed the most natural thing to do, just to participate and be part of it, and that's what I did. It was an incredible experience and I don't know what it meant but just being part of something so big really lifted me up and I'm still happy I did it even a few days later.')[21]

Among Ruhl's jobs in India was to oversee a billion-dollar World Bank project for restoring the Ganges—one of the development bank's largest projects—but like other donors concerned about the river he has been in the curious position of struggling for years to persuade India to take the earmarked money and use it for purposes that everyone agrees are beneficial to health, environmental protection, and economic development. 'I think everybody who partners with India is trying to work this because it's such an important problem', he said, explaining that there were many issues that needed to be tackled simultaneously to ensure the future of the Ganges:

Many people say sanitation is the worst problem so let's just solve sanitation. It won't work. You have to make sure that the river flow stays high enough, so you have to work the efficiency of irrigation so that not all the water is used in irrigation and the river has enough water to clean itself, because rivers clean themselves through the flow. You have to work sanitation, you have to work solid waste management, you have to work industrial pollution, you have to improve the waterfront. Only if you do these things together do you actually get a healthy river back. And just to give you an example, this was done on the River Rhine in Europe, which of course is a very important river there. It cost about 40 billion euros to get to a sustainable outcome. The Ganges is bigger, has more people, has more pollution, so you would not expect cleaning the Ganges to be cheaper than cleaning the Rhine was.

But, I asked him, was India itself really on board with this whole programme to save its sacred river? It was an undiplomatic question, but Ruhl had a diplomatic answer. 'It's a big issue. The government [then the Congress-led administration of Manmohan Singh, Modi's predecessor] has established a National Ganga River Basin Authority, at the highest political level, chaired by the prime minister. This is unusual. There's a lot of political will to solve this.' Ruhl hinted at the obstacles that would need to be overcome (lack of planning, inconsistency, a shortage of capacity to implement projects) and the emotions that would need to be harnessed (the religious devotion to the river among Hindus) to ensure success. 'And even then it will take two decades at best', he said, before waxing philosophical in the way that people do when they have worked in India:

My own belief is that things that have to happen, inevitably at some point happen. The question is not whether but when. We have the institutional structure, we have the partnership. If we start working it now, ten years from now you could see a major difference. Our billion dollars—it's one of the biggest projects the World Bank has anywhere—it might not be enough, but it might be enough to show that if you cluster these activities in an area together you see the kind of impact that gives people the conviction that it's worthwhile trying. Truthfully, the problem is so big that many people might say it's not possible to solve it so why would we even try. So the key is to show that it's possible.

Indian state governments crippled by corruption; venal industrialists; the terrifying inertia of India's bureaucracy: all these will make restoring the Ganges to health an extraordinarily challenging task. But that task is not impossible. Rivers have been sullied for millennia, and they have been turned black and pungent by manufacturing industries for centuries, in England, in Germany, in the United States, in Japan, in China, in South-east Asia, and in India. And they have—like the Thames, the Rhine, and the Chicago River—recovered.[22]

Some prominent Indians have taken up the cause of cleaning the Ganges. I did not think the Ganges had ever been so polluted as to catch fire like the Chicago or the Cuyahoga rivers had done in the United States, but I discovered that the Indian river had indeed suffered that fate at least once. In 1984, the Ganges near the holy city of Haridwar burst into flames, a disaster that goaded the lawyer M. C. Mehta into filing a petition in the Supreme Court against the polluters involved. 'The effluents from two factories were so toxic that in 1984 somebody put a lit match into the river by chance and a whole one-kilometre stretch caught fire', he said later:

The fire went 20 feet high and could not be extinguished for three hours. I learned that there were many people who had become sick from the water. I filed a petition in the Supreme Court of India in 1985 against these two polluting factories. The scope of the case has now been broadened to include all the industries and all the municipal towns in the river basin—from the beginning to the end of the Ganga.[23]

History suggests that governments take decisive action to reduce pollution only when they are driven to do so, either by an acute environmental disaster that triggers public outrage or by a steady rise of public complaints about dirt or disease as an economy develops, wealth increases, and the middle class expands. The Chicago River, the Thames, and the Rhine have been restored to life. The once filthy urban canals of England have been transformed into longitudinal oases for walkers, cyclists, and pleasure-boaters. When he was mayor of the Seoul Metropolitan Government, the former businessman Lee Myung-bak trebled the green space in one of the world's largest cities, organized the destruction of a city-centre elevated highway and replaced it with the Cheonggyecheon stream that had been buried under the concrete; the stream immediately became a much-used pedestrian attraction in the heart of Seoul and its restoration helped Lee to win election in 2007 as the president of South Korea.[24]

Other countries, then, have cleaned and restored their waterways with policies and projects that India can emulate. But it is also worth looking at how and why Indian politicians have responded to other forms of pollution, with air pollution being the leading example. When she was chief minister of Delhi, Sheila Dikshit was obliged by a 1998 Supreme Court order to convert the city's buses from diesel to relatively clean compressed natural gas, and earned plaudits for making Delhi one of the first cities in Asia to start cleaning its filthy air. (The court order was at the instigation of the environmental lawyer M. C. Mehta, the same man who had campaigned against industrial pollution of the Ganges.) Delhi's air pollution crisis, after a few years of relief from the re-engineered buses, nevertheless continued to worsen in parallel with its water pollution crisis as the population and the number of private vehicles expanded.

In Delhi, there was no defining moment akin to the London smog disaster of 1952—which killed thousands of Londoners from respiratory ailments and prompted the Clean Air Act four years later—but by the time I arrived to live in the country in 2012 the air quality in the capital Delhi and many other cities of north India was among the worst in the world, with the levels of carcinogenic particles of dust and smoke often higher than in notoriously polluted Beijing. Four years later, I noticed that the view from my office window suggested a nearby forest fire. On one day, trees less than 100 metres away were obscured by smog and dust, and I could stare straight at the copper disc of the sun through the brown smoke of burnt wood, cow dung, coal, and diesel, all of which are used as fuel for cooking, generating electricity, or driving. Each day in winter, the automated weather apps on our smartphones described conditions in the Indian capital as 'smoke'. But there was no burning forest. Delhi is one of the world's largest cities—the population in the metropolitan area is about 25 million—and is at the heart of a public health disaster. Government medical tests of a sample of Delhi residents found a third of them to have impaired lung function, and for the first time in my life I found myself wheezing like an asthmatic. Often it is impossible to convert local pollution readings into the US Environmental Protection Agency's air quality index (AQI), because they would exceed the AQI maximum of 500; AQI numbers of 300–500 are considered hazardous for people to breathe.

Foreigners and wealthy Indians responded to the air catastrophe in the same way they had responded to the disaster of the city's water supply: they bought filters. After a couple of years in Delhi, I bought three Japanese-made filters for the office and three for our home. They were less effective than the water filters—in fact the larger models sold in India had to be provided with a special, cleanable pre-filter because they became clogged so quickly with oily dirt—but as with the water filters they allowed us to feel we were doing something to protect our children, our employees, and ourselves. India's central and state governments, however, have been slow to react. Sheila Dikshit seemed complacent about pollution when I met her in late 2013—even though the Delhi secretariat is next to the vile waters of the Yamuna River and I pointed out to her that the white object by the wall in her office was one of Delhi's first air filters. She lost power in an election the following month, and the man who replaced her as chief minister—anti-corruption campaigner Arvind Kejriwal—did eventually experiment with an 'odd–even' scheme to clean the city's air by keeping cars off the road on alternate days. The Supreme Court, meanwhile, announced a surprise ban on all diesel taxis in Delhi in April 2016 and then backtracked in the face of drivers' protests and decreed a gradual phase-out.[25]

These were small steps. Indian cities need determined measures to clean their air just as Indian rivers need determined measures to clean their waters. London's air underwent a sharp improvement after the ban on smoky coal in the Clean Air Act in the 1950s. As a child in London I remember thinking that bricks were black or dark brown, because that was the colour of the city's soot-coated brick buildings;

today those same buildings seem shockingly red—brick red, indeed—as a result of having been cleaned. London was rescuing the Thames from death by pollution at around the same time, and the success of the project over the decades was noticed far away in India. Sheila Dikshit travelled to London in 2000 to investigate, and returned with the news that the Yamuna could and would be cleaned in the same manner. The Delhi government promised to repair drains, treat the city's sewage, build fifteen plants to process industrial effluents, and monitor factories so that it could close those that breached the regulations. It also launched a drive to clean up the garbage on the riverbanks, and Dikshit was photographed in the newspapers doing her bit for the Yamuna in 2001 just as Modi was pictured cleaning the Assi *ghat* on the Ganges in his Varanasi constituency thirteen years later.

For the Yamuna, the results have been negligible, as sceptical environmentalists predicted at the time when they pointed out that not a single sewage treatment plant in the city was functioning. The Centre for Science and Environment, the country's most prominent environmental NGO, published an article in its magazine headlined 'The Great Sham' and saying the clean-up was 'more to create drama than to serve any real purpose'.[26]

The pollution crisis of the Ganges and its tributaries is as grave as it has ever been, although scientists and environmentalists have been saying for years that governments need take only a few simple steps to start ameliorating the problem. The word 'clean-up' is something of a misnomer, because the citizens of Britain, Germany, and the Netherlands did not have to scrub the Thames or the Rhine with expensive machinery to make them clean. All they had to do was to stop pollutants from entering the rivers. The eternal flow of the rivers did the rest.

Necessary measures to restore a river—any river—can be separated into three broad categories: first, collecting data about water quality and quantity; second, preparing policies and projects to deal with the problems revealed by the analysis of that data; and, third, implementing those policies and projects.[27] When it comes to the Ganges and its tributaries, Indian governments have been slow to collect reliable data, although they have organized some monitoring of water quality and flow; they have been prolific formulators of policies and plans for more than three decades; and they have failed dismally on implementation. This pattern is not confined to rivers—students of modern India will notice the similarities with, say, the shockingly poor state of public education and health care—and it reflects the dysfunctional nature of government at the centre and in the states of north India and the Gangetic plain.

To understand the first failure—data collection—it helps to visit the gloomy offices of the Central Pollution Control Board in east Delhi, on the other side of the Yamuna from the rest of the city. The CPCB is the central government body for collating data on the Ganges, while states have their own State Pollution Control Boards (SPCBs), which vary widely in effectiveness. After months of trying and failing to obtain an appointment with the CPCB, I simply showed up unannounced at the offices with a colleague in an attempt to obtain better information on Ganges pollution than the outdated and incomplete information on their website. The anti-pollution bureaucrats were friendly but did not reveal much that was new. In an office in which five-year-old reports on the river's water quality and 'guidelines for idol immersion' lay on dusty shelves, an environmental engineer told us of the World Bank project and the 113 locations along the river that had been identified for real-time water monitoring.[28] He also confirmed that the CPCB had little data on heavy metals because 'we are not equipped for that'.

A second, more senior official told us that in its work on the Ganges the CPCB was trying to emulate the monitoring and clean-up of the Thames. Since 2014, the organization had moved away from its previously 'conventional' operations and had now brought in 'innovative changes in our working', dividing the Ganges into four sections for monitoring: Gangotri-Haridwar, Haridwar-Narora, Narora-Varanasi, and Varanasi to the sea. Each day, he said, 501 million litres of industrial waste and six billion litres of sewage were entering the river, while the natural water flow was reduced by take-off for irrigation. At the Narora barrage, for example, 90 per cent of the Ganges was diverted, leaving only a tenth of the river to continue downstream. 'We are dirty. Our minds are dirty', he said.

Surprisingly, however, this CPCB official disagreed with me when I suggested that cleaning the Ganges was a huge task. On the contrary, he said, 'it's easy'. All you had to do was deal with three problems: first, agricultural run-off—pesticides and fertilizers; second, industry, which meant forcing factories to cut pollution or close, by ensuring the installation of effluent monitoring systems about which company owners were reluctant but from which they had 'no escape'; and third, sewage. 'Ultimately, what is our objective? The Ganga has to be healthy', he said, emphasizing the need to set targets for the interception and treatment of sewage. His superiors had 'big, big plans', he concluded. 'They have their vision, their action plan, and every day they keep on interacting with the international institutions—they make presentations to the prime minister. They have a nineteen-point Ganga Rejuvenation programme and even I'm not updated on that. There's a huge work they are planning on the Ganga.'[29]

'Huge works' for the Ganges are not a new idea. They have been planned and much money has been spent on them since the days of Prime Minister Rajiv Gandhi in the 1980s. There was a Ganga Action Plan (GAP I) and a Ganga Action Plan II. There was a Yamuna Action Plan (YAP I), financed by Japan, and a Yamuna Action Plan II, with so little achieved that environmentalists said it was all 'Yap Yap Yap'.[30] The GAPs and the YAPs, we know now, achieved next to nothing. As one water official explained, GAP I and GAP II 'successfully created' sewage treatment capacity of 961 million litres per day 'but with limited visible change' (because the plants were neither sufficient nor properly maintained). There was still time to learn from the Rhine, the Danube, the Thames, and Australia's Murray–Darling because the Ganges remained a living river, he said. But he added: 'There's a lot to be done.'

The Congress administration of Manmohan Singh established the National Ganga River Basin Authority in 2009, and the National Mission for Clean Ganga two years later; the five Ganges basin states each have a State Ganga River Conservation Authority. Modi re-energized the institutional focus on saving the Ganges after he took office in 2014, putting the name of the river in the relevant ministry so that it became the Ministry of Water Resources, River Development and Ganga Rejuvenation. He launched 'Namami Gange' (Obeisance to the Ganges), a national campaign under which the central government took control of the river clean-up, quadrupled its budget, and promised to spend 200 billion rupees (about $3 billion) in the five financial years to 2019–20. The programme has been sensibly split into three parts, starting with 'quick wins' for immediate, visible impact, including the collection of plastic waste, rural sanitation to cut sewage flow, the construction of crematoria to reduce the number of unburnt or partly burnt corpses in the river and the beautification of river *ghats*.

Then, in the medium term (over five years), the government will build additional municipal sewage treatment plants with a capacity of 2.5 billion litres a day, enforce industrial effluent controls, protect wildlife, plant 30,000 hectares of forest in the watershed to reduce erosion and install the 113 water monitoring stations. In the long term, a ten-year period that would extend into the mandate of the next government, the government will ensure adequate water flow (environmental flow or 'e-flow') in the river and improve the efficiency of irrigation.[31]

On the face of it, this frenzy of mobilization under Modi is good news for the Ganges; the lack of precise data before embarking on a clean-up does not matter when it is obvious that treating sewage would not only make the river cleaner but also reduce deaths and disease from waterborne diseases for millions of Indians.

What should give optimists pause for thought is the record of previous clean-up projects. It is not just that the river evidently remains filthy after they were supposedly implemented. No one is even sure how much money was spent or where it went. George Black, a journalist who has written articles for the New Yorker on the Ganges, said it was this confusion about funding that most surprised him when he tried to establish how Modi's plans compared with those of his predecessors. 'I found a good NGO critique, respected NGO, of the history of the failure and they said the government had spent $300m over the last thirty years', he said:

I thought well, that is not a huge amount, I'll check it and see what other estimates. I know it's difficult to establish things in India so I found another one: 700 million. I found another one: 230 million. I found another one: 6 billion. I thought, well, this is ridiculous, I'll go to the official sources because those are going to be the most accurate. You know, these are NGOs, they're independent analysts, whatever. So I found two reports, both from 2012, couldn't find anything more recent. One was from the cabinet compiling supposedly data from all the ministries, cabinet report to the prime minister: 600 million dollars had been spent, since 1986 when this started. I found another report from the government's Central Pollution Control Board, a very respected agency: 3 billion dollars. So the government figures vary by 500 per cent, and I suddenly thought, 'There you have Modi's problem in a nutshell.' No one is collecting accurate figures, there's no transparency, the government ministries who are involved are not coordinating with each other. You don't know how much was actually spent versus how much was budgeted. You don't know how much of what was budgeted disappeared into people's pockets before it got to the sewage treatment plants or the factory cleanups.

He learned, as I did, that anywhere between 30 per cent and 100 per cent of project money is stolen. 'All the money disappears, and they check it off on the list: "Project completed". And there is no project.'[32]

Any claims that Modi or his ministers make must therefore be treated with caution. After Modi's election in mid-2014, the Ministry of Defence proposed deploying forty 'eco-battalions'—40,000 serving and retired soldiers in all—to help rejuvenate the Ganges, although enthusiasm for the idea has waned since then.[33] Three months later, the central government revealed plans to spend Rs527 billion—around $8 billion (another new number)—by 2022 on sewage treatment and sanitation in all 118 towns and 5,000 villages along the river.[34]

A further four months after that, in early 2015, the government was summoned by the Supreme Court to respond to another case about the Ganges filed by the lawyer M. C. Mehta. With refreshing frankness, the court complained about 'bureaucratic jargon' and 'jumble'. The court said: 'You may call it Ganga mission or rejuvenation or conservation or whatever you may like but we would only want to understand it in terms of verifiable projects. You tell us in simple terms what you are going to do. Tell us what do we get when we lift a sample of water from the river.' Ranjit Kumar, the solicitor general, responded by insisting that the government wanted to clean the river by 2018 and would do so, in such a manner that the Ganges would not be an issue in the general election due in 2019.[35] In March 2015, the government gave the 118 Ganges municipalities and 764 factories from Haridwar to Diamond Harbour fifteen days to provide detailed plans for sewage and effluent treatment, although the deadline was repeatedly extended in the months that followed.[36] Other regulations and plans promulgated or proposed during Modi's first two years included the installation of real-time effluent sensors at almost every major factory; litter-free zones for 500 metres on each side the river in all towns, maintained by unemployed youths; a ban on all construction along the Ganges and its tributaries; and the installation of a 100 closed-circuit television cameras to stop people dumping rubbish and building debris in the Yamuna in Delhi.[37]

Efforts to clean the Yamuna suffer from exactly the same flaws as those for its better known sister-river the Ganges: a proliferation of institutions and uncoordinated projects, including the Unified Centre for Rejuvenation of River Yamuna or UCRRY (for bureaucrats love acronyms) set up in 2014; corruption and the consequent confusion about past and present spending; a complete failure to restore the river to health; and wild claims about the future. Estimates of the money spent on the Yamuna over the two decades up to 2014 have been as meaningless as those for the Ganges: among the figures quoted are $220 million, $500 million, $660 million, $740 million, and $1 billion.[38]

For the future, the Delhi administration and the central government announced a $120 million YAP III, a third Yamuna Action Plan, on May 7, 2016. 'We intend to clean the river', said Kapil Mishra, the Delhi water minister. 'After two to two-and-a-half years, not a drop of dirty water will flow into it. And the way things are moving, we can see that happening.' Two weeks later, it emerged that this was only part of a much larger, $900 million 'Yamuna Turnaround Plan' to ensure water supplies for the capital and clean the river.[39] Before those plans were even unveiled, Mishra had already promised that the river would be clean enough to bathe in by 2018, while tourism minister Jitender Singh Tomar talked about plans for boating and other water sports on the Najafgarh drain, a disgusting canal that pours the untreated sewage of millions of Delhi's residents straight into the Yamuna. The India head of the Japan International Cooperation Agency even said it would possible to drink the Yamuna's water straight from the river by 2017.[40]

National ministers have been upbeat as well, albeit cautious about the length of a time a full clean-up will take. Prakash Javadekar, the environment minister, insisted the Modi government would do better by the Ganges than its predecessors because it had learned from their mistakes. 'There is a tremendous focus and therefore we are very confident we will achieve our targets', he said two years after Modi took office. 'We are not saying that the whole Ganga mission will be complete in five years, no. Five years will ensure there is a marked difference but this is a long project... The Rhine and the Thames were in the same dirty state 50 or 60 years ago and it took nearly 20 years to change the overall ecology of that, and we will also achieve it within 10 to 15 years' time.'[41] In July 2016, Uma Bharti, the minister responsible for water and the Ganges, said 300 of the 1,000 projects envisaged for Namami Gange—including some for the beautification of *ghats* and the afforestation of river banks—had already been launched and the first impacts would be visible within three months.[42]

Shashi Shekhar, the water secretary, said the Ganges was harder to clean than the Thames, the Rhine, or the Danube because it was sometimes so short of flowing water (though it was better off than the

Murray–Darling in Australia). Even so, he said, 'in a time frame of five years we can deal with pollution'.[43] Benedito Braga, president of the World Water Council, an international think-tank, was optimistic about the Ganges when he visited India in 2016, although it had taken 'a hundred years' to clean the River Seine in France. 'I think India will be successful in this clean-up because the highest political authority in the country has made a political commitment that this will be done. It may take time.'[44]

But has Modi been any different from previous prime ministers in his approach to the Ganges and has he really learned the lessons of the past? He certainly knows what the problem is. 'I had no idea that things are so bad', he said at a private meeting in Delhi a year after taking office:

Not just the state of the Ganga—that is already known—but that the administration is totally unaware of what cleaning the Ganga is all about. Even now, what is the first proposal I got? That we will do lighting and decoration in Varanasi! You'd be surprised. That's the proposal I got. They thought this is about Varanasi [his parliamentary constituency] so Modi-ji will like it. I said, 'Nothing doing. Junk it.' What can one think if the system thinks that lighting the lamps will clean the Ganges, that cleaning the Ganges is about decoration and lighting!

By 2019, it should be clear whether Modi's government has overcome these systemic obstacles to cleaning the Ganges or whether it has been bogged down in the same morass of corruption and incompetence as those that preceded it.[45]

Ministers, environmentalists, and Hindu holy men these days routinely express the hope that Indians will emulate those who have restored cleanliness to the Thames and the Rhine, and water flow to the Murray–Darling river system. But outside the government there are also fears that nothing will actually change: that data collection will remain sporadic, that the formulation of plans and projects will be as haphazard as in the past, and that implementation will continue to be shockingly poor. The Delhi government completely banned plastic bags in 2012 ('no leniency'), but the rule has had no effect whatsoever.[46] The central government's initial steps to restore the Ganges have been exactly the kind of cosmetic changes—the cleaning of *ghats*, for example—that so irritated Modi, rather than the construction of sewage plants. Little seems to have changed at the Central Pollution Control Board or the state boards since the Indian Supreme Court dismissed them as toothless and useless five months after Modi took power. 'This is an institutional failure and your story is a complete story of failure, frustration and disaster', the court said. 'You need to stand up against the polluting units. It will take another 50 years if the task is left to you.'[47] The courts, unfortunately, have proved equally powerless. They have sought to play the role of government by ordering the enforcement of anti-pollution policies, but have been unable to force anyone to implement their edicts on the ground. In the words of Veer Bhadra Mishra, the late environmentalist priest in Varanasi: 'The Supreme Court can even order the Yamuna to flow backwards, but they still can't make it do so.'[48]

Vinod Tare, an environmental engineer from Kanpur who leads an effort by the elite Indian Institutes of Technology to research and restore the Ganges, understands better than anyone why India has failed even to start cleaning the Ganges after decades of trying. A balding, soft-spoken professor, Tare blames the delays on bureaucracy, corruption, political interference with the pollution control boards, and the short terms in office of politicians and senior officials:

In 1974, the Water Act has been passed. We are 38 years down the line—why have we not been able to implement? Why have we not been able to stop industrial pollution? We have looked at what is the structure of our state pollution boards. They are autonomous, but they are actually not autonomous. It is a politically governed process. Corruption comes from that only. But the whole structure is like that. If the CPCB chairman has to report to the joint secretary, how can he be independent of the government? Even if they shut down some industry, they get a call from the Ministry, 'How did you shut it down? Open it again!' How can it work like that?

Tare complained that state governments would do nothing for years and then, hearing of central government funds for pollution control, would rush to create projects for fear of losing the budget. 'No one worries if the project is actually needed or not.' Construction prices of sewage treatment plants would be inflated and little money would be allocated or spent on operations or maintenance, and officials would be transferred elsewhere before being held accountable for the resulting failure.[49]

The Modi government is planning to tackle this last problem by introducing public–private partnership (PPP) contracts that will spread the income to contractors from the construction of sewage plants over, say, fifteen years. Nevertheless, Tare's analysis of the way Indian governments work—or rather, do not work—should fill with fore-boding those who want to rescue the Ganges. He speaks from bitter experience, and the failures he describes are not specific to the Ganges or the result of Indian policymakers giving a low priority to environmental matters. They are systemic failures of Indian governance and the way the central government and the twenty-nine states interact.

Two years after the Modi government took office, Javadekar, his environment minister, claimed that industrial pollution of the Ganges had been cut by a third. Of the 764 'grossly polluting industries' on the river, 544 had installed a so-called OCEM—an online continuous effluent monitoring system, and 150—including sixty-eight tanneries—had been ordered to close for failing to install one. 'We started monitoring each one of them', said Javadekar. A brochure from his ministry said that nationwide 2,400 such systems had been installed to monitor air and water pollution, and if pollution norms for any parameter were exceeded continuously for more than fifteen minutes, then a text message was generated and sent to all concerned, including regulators.[50] These official declarations were greeted with a mixture of despair and incredulity by scientists, environmentalists, and factory owners.

At the tanneries in Kanpur, for example, they pointed out that in almost all cases the effluent monitoring devices did no more than measure the quantity of liquid and made no measurement of chromium or any other pollutant. 'I've lost hope and surrendered', said Rakesh Jaiswal, the Kanpur environmental activist. Expressing his view that pollution by the tanneries had not been cut, he stated: 'There is no reduction in wastewater generation by the tanneries. Ganga is more polluted than ever before.' Jaiswal went on, describing his experiences in Kanpur: 'PM Modi has rekindled the hope. He's allocated 20,000 crore rupees ($3 billion) towards the Ganga cleaning and keeps talking about Ganga cleaning but nothing is visible on the ground.' According to Jaiswal, there has been no material change in the flow of sewage or industrial effluent and no efforts have been made to augment the flow of the river.[51]

Nor is it clear that public concern about the river or the strength of religious devotion towards it among Hindus will be sufficient to propel Modi's Ganges projects towards greater success than those of previous governments. 'Here we have failed. The technology is known to us. It's a people problem, not only the government', said Kalyan Rudra, the Calcutta water expert and chairman of the West Bengal Pollution

Control Board, when I asked him why people simultaneously wor-shipped and polluted the Ganges. 'This is a paradox of culture.'[52] Mohit Ray, an environmental consultant in Calcutta, blamed the fact that Hinduism was not communal but 'very individual' and inward-looking. 'So this has made the average Hindu not bother much about outside things', he said. 'It's a philosophical licence to make pollution.' 'If some-thing is floating, you remove it, you do your bathing, and everything is purified.'[53]

This is more, then, than just a lack of civic pride. The river's sanctity may itself be part of the problem. B. D. Tripathi, head of environmental science at Banaras Hindu University, has been concerned about the Ganges since 1972, when he bathed with his mother and encountered the floating corpse of a cow. When he spoke of pollution and started measuring it, his mother and others were appalled. 'Varanasi is a reli-gious place', says Professor Tripathi. 'They said: "You are not a Hindu. The water of Ganga is the most pure."'[54]

Indian governments have spent hundreds of millions of dollars on projects to clean the Ganges since the 1980s, but most of the money was diverted by corrupt officials or simply wasted.[55] Yet cleaning the Ganges is far more important to India—religiously, economically, and socially—than the restorations of the Rhine or the Thames were to Germany, the Netherlands, or England. For Sanskrit scholar Diana Eck, we are watching a cultural and theological crisis as well as an environmental one: there is arguably nowhere in the world that should have a higher standard of river quality than India, 'for there is no other culture in which rivers have such a central role in the daily ritual lives of countless millions'. Indians bathe in river water, drink it, and make offerings of it to the departed, yet the 'rivers that are said to have descended to earth as sources of salvation are now, in their earthly form, in need of salvation themselves'.[56]

Yet what happens to the river in the next decade will be of more than religious significance. It will be a measure of the success or fail-ure of Modi's project to modernize India. 'Why protect the Ganga?' asks Tripathi in Varanasi. 'It's a question of survival, the survival of 450 million people. It's not religious sentiment . . . Ganga is a life-support system. It provides water, it provides nutrients, it enhances fertility of soil in the basin.'[57] Cleaning the Ganges will take large amounts of money, untapped reserves of political will and a national effort to suc-ceed. 'We need to bring a transformation in our country', says Tare.

'The government is very serious—no doubt about it. But the problem is so huge, it's not going to change overnight. The Thames took twenty or thirty years and the Ganga is much bigger, so it's going to take time.'[58]

For my last bath in the Ganges before leaving India, I went to the Parmarth Niketan ashram on the riverbank at Rishikesh to meet Pujya Swami Chidanand Saraswati, a jovial, hirsute, and very popular holy man who has long championed the need to save the Ganges from pollution. I watched him lead the sunset *Ganga aarti*, a ceremony of burnt offerings and songs in praise of Krishna and the river goddess, and then attend to the supplicants who come to him where he sits cross-legged under a tree in the ashram. He has known Uma Bharti, the water minister, since she was 9 years old, and seemed confident that the results of the Modi government's Ganges projects would begin to show in a matter of months.

'The journey will be from filth to faith', he said. (Like Modi, he enjoys puns and wordplay.) 'The river has spoken for us for ages, for centuries. Now we must speak for her. We have taken baths in her for ages and it's time for us to give *her* a bath.' The *swami* is well travelled and practical; he promotes the planting of trees and even suggested to me that he should stop the *aarti* for a day and replace it with a pledge to do something about the cholera, hepatitis, and other waterborne diseases that kill 1,200–1,500 Indian children under 5 each day. 'To me, Ganga is not mere water. She is a mother. I've played in her lap since I was a child. I've seen her colours, her beauty . . . To me she is everything. If Ganga dies, India dies. If Ganga thrives, India thrives. The lives of 500 million people is not a small thing.'[59]

18

Beautiful Forest

Where Ganga Meets the Ocean

It looks as if this bit of world had been left unfinished when land and sea were originally parted.

—Emily Eden, *Up the Country*[1]

And so to the sea and the river's end. By the time the Ganges reaches the Bay of Bengal, the first runnels of melted ice from its sources in the Himalayas have been joined by multiple mountain streams, by the clean waters of the Chambal and the filth of the Yamuna, by the Ramganga, the Son, the Punpun, and the Kiul. From Nepal to the north have come the Sarda, the Gomti, the Ghagra, the Gandak, and the Kosi, the latter a temperamental river whose habit of sudden, destructive migrations across the landscape has earned it the name 'the Sorrow of Bihar'. In Bangladesh, the river has been swollen by the Meghna and by the Brahmaputra sweeping down from Tibet and Assam; because the Brahmaputra is longer and more voluminous than the Ganges, one could argue that it is the Ganges and not the Brahmaputra that is the tributary here. In the alluvial mud of the delta spanning the India–Bangladesh border the river breaks apart, the turbid waters seeking their path to the ocean down a filigree of ever-shifting distributaries and tidal channels.

The pure water melted from the glacier at Gaumukh has by this point been subjected to all the follies and wonders of India. It has helped generate electricity at the Tehri Dam and been diverted by barrages and canals to the rice paddies and vegetable fields of Haryana and Uttar Pradesh or the taps of Delhi and the tanneries of Kanpur. At dam after dam, and pump after diesel pump, billions of litres are extracted from the river for farms and factories. What remains after evaporation and consumption has seeped back into the river as groundwater from the fields or as sewage from the cities, tainted now by faecal bacteria, industrial chemicals, and pesticide residues.

At Gaumukh in the highlands and at Sagar Island in the Bay of Bengal—at Gangotri, Haridwar, Allahabad, Bateswar, Varanasi, Patna, Calcutta, and everywhere in between—the water has also been worshipped as the goddess Ganga or the goddess Yamuna or both, garlanded with flowers, blessed with coconuts, and decorated with floating candles. Pilgrims in their thousands, sometimes in their millions, have plunged themselves and their idols into the stream, raised the water in cupped hands towards the rising sun and let it fall on their ecstatic faces. Grieving sons have scattered the ashes of their cremated parents in the river, while the less fortunate, unable to purchase enough firewood, have discreetly rolled the half-burnt corpses of their loved ones into the forgiving waters.

The main stream of the Ganges still teems with life along most of its length. It was from the villages and towns on the banks of the Ganges and its tributaries that millions of Indians, Bengalis, and Nepalese migrated to the Caribbean, the Pacific, the Middle East, and Europe in the nineteenth and twentieth centuries. It was in boats and ships down its lower reaches that many sailed to fight for the British in the First and Second World Wars. Before spending its waters in the sea, the Ganges has served a tenth of humanity in an area of more than a million square kilometres, passing on its way the monuments of the great civilizations and empires—Hindu, Buddhist, Muslim, and Christian—that have thrived on its bounty for thousands of years.

Humans are not the only animals to depend on the river. Many of India's few remaining tigers drink from its tributaries and wallow in the shallows; the toothy, long-snouted Gangetic dolphins and gharials hunt fish in its waters; and hundreds of thousands of wading birds strut along its sandbanks in the unending search for food.

After Dhaka and Calcutta, the last great cities to pour their filth into the Ganges, the journey down India's sacred river draws to a close. In its parting gift to the land, the river spews millions of tonnes of fertile silt on to the rice fields of Bengal and the mangroves of the Sunderbans (meaning 'beautiful forest' in Bengali) that fringe the Ganges delta. At its mouth the Ganges–Brahmaputra–Meghna has been counted as the world's third-biggest river by discharge of fresh water, second only to the Amazon and the Congo, with an average flow of more than 1.3 million cusecs or 38,000 cubic metres a second. The monsoon peak outflow from the main outlet in Bangladesh can reach nearly 5 million cusecs, or over 138,000 cubic metres a second—more than 10,000 times the minimum flow through the Narora barrage guaranteed for religious reasons.[2]

It is the bizarre and beautiful landscape of the world's largest mangrove forest, however, that is the most remarkable aspect of the geographical feature described on old maps as 'the mouths of the Ganges'. The British were (mostly) enchanted. The eighteenth-century Welsh naturalist Thomas Pennant recorded that the flat, tree-covered islands of the Sunderbans made up a mangrove forest 'as large as the whole principality of Wales' and were infested with large and extremely aggressive tigers as well as numerous examples of the one-horned rhinoceros (now extirpated from the area), which resorted to swampy places 'out of love of rolling itself like a hog in the mire'. He described passing through the forest in euphoric terms:

These passages afford a most grand and curious spectacle, a navigation of above two hundred miles through a forest divided by numberless isles, by a continual labyrinth of channels, so various in point of width, that a vessel has at one time her masts almost entangled in trees, at another, sails uninterruptedly on a capacious river beautifully skirted with woods. How particularly rapturous must this be to the naturalist, presented by each of the elements with the most singular or beautiful productions of nature![3]

Captain Thomas Skinner, sailing in the area in 1826, said the Sunderbans were uninhabited but rich in magnificent trees. 'Although a dismal swamp in many respects, all is exceedingly beautiful', he wrote. 'Nothing', agreed Godfrey Mundy, 'can exceed the luxuriant richness of the Sunderbund vegetation ... Whilst the eye is feasted by the infinite variety of tints in the foliage of the groves and banks, the scent is regaled, almost to surfeiting, with the spicy breezes which float through the atmosphere, loaded with sweets from the surrounding forest.'[4] The contemporary writer Amitav Ghosh introduces the Sunderbans in his novel *The Hungry Tide* by having Kanai Dutt, one of the protagonists, read a Bengali script that captures the beauty and danger of the mangroves and the wandering rivers in their midst:

'The islands are the trailing threads of India's fabric, the ragged fringe of her sari, the *achol* that follows her, half-wetted by the sea,' he reads on the train on the way to Canning. 'They number in the thousands, these islands; some are immense and some no larger than sandbars; some have lasted through recorded history while others were washed into being just a year or two ago. These islands are the rivers' restitution, the offerings through which they return to the earth what they have taken from it…The rivers' channels are spread across the land like a fine-mesh net, creating a terrain where the boundaries between land and water are always mutating, always unpredictable.'[5]

For more than 2,000 years, starting with the port of Tamralipti, merchants have used harbours on the delta to bring goods in and out of Bengal and the rest of the Ganges basin; villagers practised shifting agriculture in parts of the Sunderbans from the eleventh century; the Mughals later leased out forests on the edge of the mangroves; and the British of the East India Company systematically demarcated the land into numbered blocks, licensing the harvest of timber, bamboo, and other products and overseeing the conversion of forest into farmland. Between 1880 and 1950, cultivated land in the area expanded by 45 per cent, while the human population more than doubled to 13 million. Small farmers, landless labourers, and refugees from drought and famine, including many tribal people, poured in from poverty-stricken rural areas to the west. There were surges of incoming refugees from the east as well, first in 1947 when India was partitioned by the creation of Muslim Pakistan, and again in the 1970s when Bangladesh was fighting its war of independence.[6] 'The silt of the Ganges and its tributaries has fertilized the delta for millennia, and as such it is one of the most productive agricultural regions in India', wrote the historian Janam Mukerjee. 'The Padma [Ganges], Jamuna and Meghna rivers, with rich cultural as well as economic significance, converge in a seemingly infinite and shifting series of tidal estuaries, bayous and backwaters that constitute the coastal belt of Bengal.'[7]

The southern parts of the once vast mangrove forests are now protected as a National Park in India and as wildlife sanctuaries and forest reserves in Bangladesh. The area covers about 10,000 square kilometres (down from nearly 17,000 sq km in 1911), but is hemmed in by some of the world's largest, densest, and poorest populations and remains under intense pressure from farmers, fishermen, and timber gatherers. In Bangladesh, researchers found that about 50,000 hectares of mangroves—equivalent to 5 per cent of the whole Sunderbans zone—had been deforested in the country, mostly in the Sunderbans, in the decade to 2010. It was no coincidence that aquaculture, mostly prawn farms, had increased in the area by exactly the same amount. Nazmul Hasan, the scientist who led the investigation that produced this data, said satellite monitoring showed that the Sunderbans mangroves were not too badly affected on their southern fringes by devastating storms such as Cyclone Sidr in 2007 and Cyclone Aila in 2009. The problem was not the weather in the south but the people in the north. 'Contrary to the popular belief, the Sundarbans has been deforested along its northern front. It must be human aggression like the felling of trees, salt pans and *ghers* [enclosed shrimp ponds].'[8]

All the human-induced ills that afflict the upper and middle stretches of the Ganges—pollution, overpopulation, the relentless overexploitation of natural resources—are threats as well to the Sunderbans downstream and the millions who live along its fringes. Piyali Roy, the heroine of *The Hungry Tide*, is a marine biologist studying the threatened Irrawaddy dolphin in the delta with the help of a local fisherman. In *Tiger! Tiger!*, a short story by Kunal Basu, researcher Rowena Hawthorne witnesses an adulterous Sunderbans romance against the backdrop of a forest officer's fight against tiger poachers. 'Despite his muscles, he seemed soft compared to the men she met in the Sunderbans—men who made it their business to survive droughts and flash floods, tigers, corrupt officers, diseases and simply the rotten luck that comes with living on the edge.' Captain Singh is eventually killed by a tigress in the forest as his lover, the wife of an old-fashioned hunter, tries to lead him to safety from a new and violent gang of heavily armed poachers.

It could, of course, be worse. The Indus delta in Pakistan, on the other side of the Indian subcontinent, is so deprived of fresh water by upstream irrigation projects that the salty water of the incoming sea has killed date palms and rice fields and left freshwater fish with nowhere to live but the dribbles of sewage released into the riverbed. The writer Alice Albinia, who followed the river up to its source, was able to wade across the Indus near its mouth, a feat unimaginable on the Hooghly or the Meghna. She heard villagers complain that the government and the cotton farmers of the Punjab and northern Sindh had stolen the river water, and noted that the delta had shrunk from 3,500 square kilometres to 250 after the construction of the Kotri barrage in 1958:

Imagine the disbelief, had you told the British officials, who coveted the Indus from the early seventeenth century, that one day this darkly swirling river would actually run out; had you prophesied then that the exhaustion of this river in the twenty-first century would be in part the legacy of their irrigation projects. For three hundred years after the British first saw it, the Indus was the 'mighty river', capricious, frustrating, desirable. Nobody would have guessed that one day, down here in the Delta, there might be no fresh water left.[9]

Matters have not yet reached such a pass at the Ganges delta, thanks in large part to the vast contribution of fresh water from the Brahmaputra. But there has been damage to crops from increased salinity on the Bangladeshi side of the frontier. 'The Sundarbans are dying', Ainun Nishat, the Bangladeshi water expert, declared in 2010, blaming higher salinity at the mouths of the Ganges over the previous thirty years mainly on the Farraka barrage—an Indian dam, it should be recalled, that was designed specifically to divert some of the main stream of the Ganges down the Hooghly to increase navigability of the river and improve access to Calcutta's ports.'The salinity problem is compounded by climate change, but I am still convinced the main problem is Farraka because sea level rise is not that great—maybe ten centimetres.'[10]

When I met him six years later in Dhaka, Nishat did not repeat that the Sundarbans were dying, but he was still concerned about the salt water encroachment of Bangladeshi farmland on the northern fringes of the mangroves. 'In the Ganges-dependent area in Bangladesh, the salinity has gone up tremendously', he told me. Indian dams on the rivers in the Ganges system, including tributaries of the Ganges and the Hooghly, contribute to inland salinity and the lack of riverine 'flushing power' to deepen the beds of the main waterways, but such disadvantages are not confined to Bangladesh: neither Dhaka nor Delhi benefits as much as envisaged from the sharing of water flows enshrined in the 1996 treaty because the total flow has fallen unexpectedly sharply in the dry season. Nor is salinity caused entirely by the lack of fresh water flows. One hydrologist I met in Dhaka told me that the relative sea level was rising by as much as 5–6 millimetres a year (a lot by geological standards); about a third of that was attributable to tectonic plate movements, with Bengal sinking, especially in the east; another third was from the settling of sediment that was not being replaced at the levels of the past, largely because of dams and barrages; and the final third was blamed on rising sea levels caused by global warming.[11]

Even before the arrival of humankind on the river's banks, the mouths of the Ganges were constantly shifting. That was ensured by the daily ebb and flow of the tides, the annual waxing and waning of the monsoon floods, the occasional catastrophe of a cyclone in the Bay of Bengal, and finally by the relentless and sometimes violent northward push of the Indian tectonic plate into the Eurasian landmass—the geological crunch that gives us the young and still rising mountain range of the Himalayas. The turbulent waters of the lower Ganges unceasingly destroy and recreate. In India, Lochachara Island was submerged in the 1980s, leaving thousands without home or farmland. Today the once substantial island of Ghoramara, north of Sagar Island at the mouth of the Hooghly, is being steadily eroded by the tides, while new land—known as *char*—is being created by silt deposition south of Sagar. By one calculation, the rivers have been carrying a billion tonnes of sediment into the sea each year to create Bengal and the Sunderbans, 8 per cent of all the silt transported into the oceans by the world's rivers.

Any visitor to this watery world at the mouths of the Ganges is struck by how peaceful the villages seem—but also by how hard it must be to live here. The villagers ambling or bicycling along the muddy dykes around their homes and fields make their living from land that is barely above the high-tide mark in normal times and threatened with inundation or erosion whenever a tropical storm heaps up the water at the northern end of the Bay of Bengal. The inhabitants of the Sunderbans, doctors say, are afflicted not only by the diseases common across rural South Asia but also by those peculiar to the swampy environment. Women spend long hours in the water fishing for the valuable but now much depleted wild 'prawn seed'—the larvae of the tiger prawn *Penaeus monodon*.

Common illnesses include malaria, diarrhoea, hookworms, threadworms, giardia, skin diseases, and respiratory tract infections. In places such as Bastibari, a village of about 2,000 people in Sandeshkali surrounded by ponds for breeding prawns, eye problems are common too. The light here in the Sunderbans is searingly bright—the sky looks white in the middle of the day and the flat islands separating sea from sky are razor-thin on the horizon—but the bigger problem is the difficulty of finding the right treatment from self-appointed rural doctors who have a bad habit of prescribing steroids for everything. An eye charity offers help, but some farmers do not see the point of having their mothers undergo cataract operations when the women can still see well enough to carry out basic household tasks. 'Families are not keen on surgery for the elderly women even if it's free', says Sameera Ahmed of Sightsavers.[12]

Those who survive illness might, even today, be swept away to their deaths and drowned by the unpredictable rivers. In *The Japanese Wife*, another short story by Kunal Basu set in the Sunderbans, both parents of the teacher Snemahoy Chakrabarti have been killed by the Matla (the 'mad river'), and he himself expires from a mosquito-borne fever. For Salman Rushdie, the Sunderbans are a magical-realist hell-cum-paradise, teeming with ghosts, transparent maidens, three-inch leeches, pale-pink scorpions, poisonous snakes, and fruits so large they overturn a boat when they fall in the water. As the jungle grows in the monsoon, 'the huge stilt-roots of vast ancient mangrove trees could be seen snaking about thirstily in the dust, sucking in the rain and becoming thicker than elephants' trunks, while the mangroves themselves were getting so tall that, as Shaheed Dar said afterwards, the birds at the top must have been able to sing to God'.[13]

Villagers do lose legs in crocodile attacks. Tigers make regular kills, and are a particular danger for those collecting timber or honey in the forests. The natural resources are indeed rich, but notoriously hard to extract. While the women squat half-immersed in currents of muddy water dredging for prawn seed with converted mosquito nets, the men, watched by herons and giant monitor lizards, stand in the shallows and fling their circular weighted nets into the creeks in the hunt for fish.

Special hazards require special gods and saints and the placating of demons whose perceived forms are tailored by the desires and fears of islanders particularly vulnerable to the cruelties of the natural world. The principal goddess of the forest, worshipped by both Hindus and Muslims, is Bonobibi, sometimes Bonodevi to Hindus and equated in some Muslim texts to Fatima, daughter of the Prophet Mohammed. Amid multiple strands of mythology and iconography chaotic even by the standards of India, a recognizably Sunderban-esque theme emerges of Bonobibi triumphing over Dakshin Rai, the tiger god or tiger demon, who nevertheless maintains his fatal sway over the deep forest. According to a field guide to wildlife I obtained on one trip to the Sunderbans, the goddess Manasa 'is worshipped to satisfy the venomous snakes', with Jagatgouri specializing in cobras, Manik Pir tending to the welfare of cows, Olabibi or Olaichandi preventing cholera, and Satyanarayan-Satyapeer ensuring the general welfare of the people. The Gunins and Ojhas are like village doctors who are credited with supernatural powers to heal snakebites and drive away tigers. Sailors take oaths in the name of Badar Pir and various other holy men before starting their journeys. 'All these reveal the unique religious harmony among Hindus and Muslims', the authors assert. 'The difficult natural terrain combined with the calamities and threat of wild animals, especially tigers, have forced a peaceful coexistence in the region.'[14]

Tiger attacks are only the most gruesome example of the contest for space and resources between a growing human population and the beleaguered remnants of other species. Such attacks are uncommon these days elsewhere in India, largely because there are so few tigers and those that do exist are mostly known, named, numbered, and guarded in reserves. In the almost impenetrable mangrove swamps of the Sunderbans, tigers are harder to monitor. They are also of a variety—known as the Royal Bengal Tiger—that is large and aggressive, and are presented with a regular supply of human victims scouring their territory for crabs, fish, honey, and timber. By some reckonings fifty villagers were killed in 2014 and 2015. Most of them were men who left behind 'tiger widows' to fend for themselves. 'Tigers do not get sufficient prey in the forests', said local politician Achin Kumar Pain with brutal directness. 'The terrain makes it difficult for them to catch agile deers hence they prey on humans who are relatively easy to capture.' The bodies are rarely found. For want of a corpse, relatives often cremate a figurine made of flour and laid on a leaf.[15]

At Godkhali, a port and a tidal river junction, I found bare-chested men unloading a boat piled with big white plastic tubs of honey collected in the mangroves, as well as heaps of the freshly cut bamboo that is still used across Asia as scaffolding and as a building material for houses and boats. Sometimes locals are raped or robbed by pirates, or kidnapped for ransom. Members of one water-borne honey-collecting expedition from Kalitala near the frontier with Bangladesh described how they were ambushed at dusk by a dozen armed pirates in two boats. The gangsters not only stole 50 kilos of honey but kidnapped five of the villagers. In telephone calls from Bangladeshi mobile telephone numbers they demanded—and received—200,000 Indian rupees in exchange for the men's release. 'Lots of people migrate to other cities', is the sombre postscript of my guide Arun Sarkar, speaking as I head south out of the inhabited zone and into the wildlife sanctuary.[16]

There is a small and specialized wildlife tourism industry here (on both sides of the border), but few international tourists or wealthy Indians deviate from the Mughal treasures of Delhi, Agra, and Rajasthan to fly more than 1,000 kilometres east and study water birds, salt-resistant plants, and—if they are lucky—a muddy-pawed Bengal tiger from the hot deck of a boat in the swamps. One of the few Bollywood films to celebrate the horror and the beauty of the mangrove forests—the 2014 movie *Roar: Tigers of the Sunderbans*—was neither a commercial nor a critical success. It features a villainous poacher; a white tigress which avenges the death of its cub in a trap by killing a photojournalist; two beautiful women; and a heroic commando officer (the victim's brother) who seeks vengeance in his turn by leading a hunt for the tigress.

For naturalists, the Sunderbans are important in their own right as a 'biodiversity hot spot' of extraordinary richness: 250 species of fish, 44 of crabs, 20 of prawns, and scores of birds, as well as dolphins, crocodiles, and rare marine turtles, not to mention the mangrove plant species capable of excreting salt through glands in their leaves and taking in air through snorkel-like breathing tubes from their roots known as pneumatophores. Yet this, the largest surviving contiguous stretch of mangrove forest on the planet, is not only a delightful haven for peculiar wildlife. It is an essential resource for tens of millions of people in the Bay of Bengal, for two reasons: fish and cyclones.

Mangrove forests are known to be nutrient-rich nurseries for all kinds of marine life, and the Sunderbans—described as 'one of the largest detritus-based ecosystems of the world'—are no exception. Many species of commercially important fish found in the Indian Ocean depend on the mangroves, which act as nursery for 90 per cent of the aquatic species on India's east coast and sustain the sea and estuarine fisheries of Bangladesh as well. Some 4 million Bangladeshis are said to depend directly for their livelihoods on fish, crustaceans, timber, and other products from the Sunderbans. As for cyclones, people have recognized for centuries that the dense and securely rooted mangroves provide a protective barrier against the lethal winds and waves driven onto the coast by tropical storms. With coastal populations continuing to rise, this protection will be more important than ever if climate scientists are correct in assuming that global warming will generate cyclones more frequent and severe than in the past. Between 1877 and 1995, Bangladesh was hit by 154 cyclones, 43 of them severe. Such storms regularly swirl up into the Bay of Bengal, bringing with them winds of terrifying speed and alarming storm surges that raise the sea far above normal high-tide levels, demolishing dykes and inundating fields and villages.

On the Indian side, the young boatman Tapan Das knows these dangers from bitter experience. I have hired him to take me past the villages, the rice fields, the palm trees, and the mangroves and down the muddy tidal estuary to where the Ganges meets the ocean—the ocean from which she will rise again as water vapour and one day, cloud-bound, be driven by the south-west monsoon across the sub-continent to the Himalayas. There she will fall again as snow, replenish her mountain sources and so complete the eternal cycle of the life-giving Ganges.

Das, aged 26, is not an educated man, but he understands the tides and the moods of the river. I marvel at his skill in handling the boat in the fast-flowing tidal waters. There is no neutral or reverse gear, and the boat is powered by a simple diesel engine designed as a water pump and fuelled by subsidized cooking kerosene. He was 9 years old when a boat capsized and his father drowned in a storm, leaving him, the eldest of five siblings, as the family breadwinner. The boat-owner who rescued the rest of the family gave his destitute mother a sari and hired him as a helper for 300 rupees a month; now Das earns 4,000 rupees a month—roughly $60—as the skipper. He vividly recalls the destruction wrought by Cyclone Aila in 2009, when he says the water rose 5 feet higher than normal, submerged more than 100 islands, and destroyed nine of them permanently. Food was scarce for three months.

More than 2,000 kilometres from the river's glacial source at Gaumukh in the Himalayan foothills, and with the air 35°C warmer, Das is as much in awe of the power of the muddy Ganges at sea level as hotel owner Amod Panwar was on its fast-flowing upper reaches. He points to a spot where he watched a tiger on a mudbank a month ago. 'Storms and cyclones are happening more often than before', he says as silt surges from the depths in thick brown eddies of warm water around the boat. 'The current is faster and stronger.' Ahead of him on the horizon, the turbulent waters of the holy Ganges finally meet the Bay of Bengal and the open sea.

Notes

CHAPTER 1

1. Interview with the author 30 May 2016.
2. Nehru Memorial Museum and Library, http://nehrumemorial.nic.in/en/ gift-gallery.html?id=196&tmpl=component (accessed 20 September 2016).
3. Ashutosh Bhardwaj, 'By the Ganga, Modi talks of "spiritual stream" in himself', *Indian Express*, 18 May 2014, http://indianexpress.com/article/politics/ by-the-ganga-modi-talks-of-spiritual-stream-in-himself/ (accessed 21 September 2016).
4. Eck (1993), 214.
5. Wood, 87.
6. 'If the Ganga dies, India dies—Vandana Shiva', Bharata Bharati, 14 December 2010, https://bharatabharati.wordpress.com/2010/12/14/if-the-ganga-dies- india-dies-vandana-shiva/ (accessed 20 September 2016). From *Deccan Chronicle*, 13 December 2010.
7. Rashmi Sanghi and Nitin Kaushal, 'Introduction to Our National River Ganga via cmaps', in Sanghi (ed.), 11; the Ganges does not feature in Encyclopaedia Britannica's list of the fifteen longest, while Wikipedia ranks the Ganges at number thirty-four by length. https://en.wikipedia.org/ wiki/List_of_rivers_by_length (accessed 20 September 2016).
8. Miller (2010), 160.
9. Vidya Venkat, *The Hindu*, 3 April 2016. The article cited data from the Farraka barrage on the India–Bangladesh border to show that the flow of water on 29 March 2016 was 50,710 cusecs (that is, cubic feet per second), only just over half what it was on the same day in 2014 and 2015. 'The Ganga that has nourished the Indian civilisation for centuries has recorded a historically low inflow in its lower reaches this year.' Information in India, the world's largest democracy, is much more easily obtainable than it is in Communist China, although the article notes tartly that the Indian water-flow data was found even though it was 'not in the public domain, because the river is an international resource, protected for strategic purposes'.

CHAPTER 2

1. Hodgson, 116–17.
2. Interview with the author, 8 October 2013.

3. Hodgson, 75, 85, 98–9, 103–4, 116.
4. Hodgson, 117–18. He also refers to the idea that the legend of Shiva breaking Ganga's violent fall from heaven to earth with his hanging locks of hair has its origins in the icicles at the cave's mouth. 'From the brow of this curious wall of snow, and immediately above the outlet of the stream, large and hoary icicles depend; they are formed by the freezing of the melted snow water of the top of the bed, for in the middle of the day, the sun is powerful, and the water produced by its action falls over this place in cascade but is frozen at night.—The *Gangotri Brahmin* who came with us, and who is only an illiterate mountaineer, observed, that he thought these icicles must be MAHÁDÉVA'S [Shiva's] hair from whence, as he understood, it is written in the Shástra, the *Ganges* flows.—I mention this, thinking it a good idea, but the man had never heard of such a place, as actually existing, nor had he, or any other person to his knowledge, ever been here.—In modern times they may not, but *Hindus* of Research may formerly have been here, and if so, I cannot think of any place to which they might more aptly give the name of a Cow's Mouth than to this extraordinary *Debouche*.' Debouche means an opening or passage, from the French word for mouth. Hodgson, further, takes measurements similar to those of today, although by most accounts the glacier has receded a few kilometres. 'Measured by a chain, the mean breadth was 27 feet—The greatest depth at that place being knee deep, or 18 inches, but more generally a foot deep, and rather less just at the edges, say 9 or 10 inches—however, call the mean depth 15 inches.'
5. Eck (2012), xx.
6. Xuanzang, 18. The identification of Xuanzang's Brahmapura with modern-day Uttarkashi comes from historians quoted by Alter (146). A *Bodhisattva* is a person on the path to enlightenment, usually one chooses to help others before attaining nirvana.
7. Baillie Fraser, 469–73.
8. Trojanow, 2.
9. J. M. Shea et al., 'Modelling glacier change in the Everest region, Nepal Himalaya', *The Cryosphere*, 9 (2012), 1105–128, http://www.the-cryosphere. net/9/1105/2015/tc-9-1105-2015.pdf (accessed 28 September 2016).
10. Victor Mallet, 'India could be burnt by global warming', *Financial Times*, 1 February 2013, https://www.ft.com/content/50042992-2820-11e2-afd2-00144feabdc0 (accessed 28 September 2016).
11. Trojanow, 2.
12. Victor Mallet, 'Climate change blamed as thousands die in Indian heat', *Financial Times*, 29 May 2015, https://www.ft.com/content/d66381fc-05dd-11e5-b676-00144feabdc0 (accessed 28 September 2016). 'India's killer heat wave linked to climate change', *The Third Pole*, 28 May 2015, https://www.thethirdpole.net/2015/05/28/indias-killer-heat-wave-linked-to-climate-change/ (accessed 28 September 2016).

13. Pilita Clark, 'UN climate talks: 2016 set to be hottest year since records began', *Financial Times*, 14 November 2016, https://www.ft.com/content/54c53b6c-aa74-11e6-9cb3-bb8207902122 (accessed 9 December 2016).

14. See n. 12. For India and its neighbours at least, climate change is likely to be bad for the economy as well. The ADB has concluded that growth will be squeezed within a few decades if action is not taken to reduce the greenhouse gas emissions responsible for global warming. It calculated in one report that the six countries studied—India, Bangladesh, Nepal, Sri Lanka, Bhutan, and the Maldives—would on average lose 1.8 per cent of their gross domestic product by 2050 and 8.8 per cent by the end of the century, under a 'business as usual' scenario for global carbon emissions. Economic damage would be 'higher still if losses due to extreme weather events are added'. The impact on already vulnerable economies near the Himalayas would include more storms and flooding in low-lying parts of Bangladesh, damage to property and infrastructure, 'devastation of agricultural crops', reduced electricity generation from hydro-electric dams, and more disease—most of which are already happening.

15. Francis Rawdon, later Lord Hastings, in Losty, 141.

16. Alter, 170.

17. Cribb, 143.

18. Bond (2012), 102.

19. Alter, 182, 328.

20. Eck (2012), 132.

21. The comments from the *sadhus* and the temple priests are from conversations with the author, 8–11 October 2013.

22. Eck's translation from Eck (2012), 133.

CHAPTER 3

1. Padma Purana V 60.39, quoted by A. L. Basham, in foreword to Darian, xiv.

2. Ramayana, 47.

3. Quoted in Mehrotra and Vera, 51.

4. Prayag Magh Mela Research Group, 'Understanding the pilgrim experience: Findings from a three year Indo-British Research Collaboration funded by the Economic and Social Research Council' (2013), https://docs.google.com/viewer?a=v&pid=sites&srcid=Y2Jjcy5hYy5pbnxmYWN3ZWJ8Z3g6MWFlYzg5NzJiNTE5NzI5 (accessed 5 September 2016).

5. http://www.pilgrimsbooks.com (accessed 28 September 2016).

6. Wood, 92.

7. Xuanzang, 158–9.

8. Mahajan, 134.

9. I did not know it at the time, but it was at the same 2013 *mela* that Sir James Mallinson, an Oxford scholar of yoga and Sanskrit better known as

Jim, took his old friend Dominic West, the actor, to make a television programme about the event and about Mallinson's ceremonial elevation there
to the status of a *mahant*, or religious commander. The yogi who arranged
this is Mallinson's guru, referred to simply by the honorofic Baba-ji,
whom Mallinson met at his first Kumbh Mela in 1992. He was drawn to
the pot-smoking Baba-ji ('It's not a drug', says the guru, 'it's a gift from
Lord Shiva') and his order of the Thirteen Renouncer Brothers by his
reputation for being a master of *vajroli*, a mysterious and power-enhancing
yogic practice of urethral suction of fluids into the body. The practice, says
Mallinson (renamed as the *mahant* Jagdish Das) is 'the ultimate technique
of yoga' but has now been expunged from prudish translations of ancient
Sanskrit. Among the other practices of the sect is the *dhuni tap* or fire pen-
ance, an eighteen-year course in which the renouncers surround themselves with smoky, burning cow-dung and end up with it in a bowl on
their heads. In the television documentary, as they all arrive by boat at the
sangam, the sacred confluence of the rivers, Baba-ji says: 'This is the king
of all holy places.' James Mallinson, 'The making of a mahant: A journey
through the Kumbh Mela festival', *Financial Times*, 9 March 2013, https://
www.ft.com/content/d1e949a0-86bd-11e2-b907-00144feabdc0 (accessed
5 September 2016). 'West meets East', BBC 4, 8 September 2015.

10. Owen Bennett-Jones, 'Invented tradition and the religion of the ancients',
    BBC, 21 April 2014, http://www.bbc.co.uk/news/magazine-27049295
    (accessed 5 September 2016).

11. K. Sandeep Kumar, 'On banks of the "pure river", devotees opt for bottled
    water', *Hindustan Times*, 17 January 2013.

12. Victor Mallet, 'Pop-up megacity is lesson for India', 1 March 2013, with
    embedded video, https://www.ft.com/content/58a2b464-80a5-11e2-9c5b-
    00144feabdc0 (accessed 5 September 2016).

13. Ackroyd, 43.

14. Albinia, xv, 104, 106, 219–21, 242.

15. Darian, 58.

16. Albinia, 271.

17. Jayanth Jacob, 'PM Modi takes stock of Indus Waters Treaty, discusses options
    on Pak', *Hindustan Times*, 26 September 2016, http://www.hindustantimes.
    com/india-news/pm-modi-takes-stock-of-indus-waters-treaty-with-paki-
    stan-discusses-options/story-MMS59wEbU24r8uxwCNkVKM.html
    (accessed 28 September 2016).

18. Arundhati Roy, 'My seditious heart', *Caravan magazine*, http://www.
    caravanmagazine.in/essay/seditious-heart-arundhati-roy (accessed 5
    September 2016). Albinia, xvi.

19. Eck (2012), 183, 131–2.

20. Darian, xv, 37.

21. Interview with the author, 12 January 2016.

22. Hollick, 46.

23. Alter, 167.
24. Darian, 28.
25. *Mahabharata,* Loc 202.
26. *Ramayana,* 46–7
27. Eck (1993), 216.
28. Ibid. 219.
29. She says she adopted her signature colour scheme after visiting the famous 'pink city' of Jaipur in Rajasthan. PTI, 'Kolkata: Mamata Banerjee defends idea to paint city blue and white', *Firstpost,* 4 March 2015, http://www.firstpost.com/politics/kolkata-mamata-banerjee-defends-idea-to-paint-city-blue-and-white-2135911.html (accessed 5 September 2016).
30. Trojanow, 18.
31. Quoted in Mahajan, 132–3.

CHAPTER 4

1. This chapter is based on interviews and observations at the Allahabad Kumbh Mela in February 2013, at Ganga Sagar at the river's mouth in January 2016, and on presentations by Harvard University professors about the Kumbh Mela given in Mumbai on 18 January 2016. See also the following: the Harvard book on the 2013 event, *Kumbh Mela: Mapping the Ephemeral Megacity*; Victor Mallet, 'Delhi notebook: How the wedding syndrome could fix India', *Financial Times,* 8 February 2016, https://www.ft.com/content/e192bbf8-cb60-11e5-beob-b7ece4e953a0 (accessed 5 September 2016); Victor Mallet, 'Pop-up megacity is lesson for India', *Financial Times,* 1 March 2013, https://www.ft.com/content/58a2b464-80a5-11e2-9c5b-00144feabdc0 (accessed 5 September 2016).
2. Interviewed by the author at the Kumbh Mela.
3. Mehrotra and Vera, 152.
4. More cheerfully, he recalled going to see a Naga *sadhu* called Baba Rampuri of the Juna *akhara*. This man, who was supplied with a fresh *chillum* (a marijuana pipe) every twenty minutes or half an hour by an attentive *sadhvi*, turned out to have come originally from Beverly Hills. (He was born William Gans.)

CHAPTER 5

1. Victory speech in Varanasi, posted on YouTube by Great Indian Politics, 19 May 2014, https://www.youtube.com/watch?v=urjt5U_RE7I (accessed 6 September 2016).
2. PTI, 'BJP govt is Congress plus a cow, never seen a weaker PMO: BJP leader Arun Shourie', *Indian Express,* 27 October 2015, http://indianexpress.com/article/india/india-news-india/bjp-govt-is-congress-plus-a-cow-never-seen-a-weaker-a-pmo-says-arun-shourie/ (accessed 6 September 2016).

3. Twain, 271.

4. Victor Mallet, 'Modi shows political muscle in Indian holy city', *Financial Times*, 24 April 2014, https://www.ft.com/content/5bf9f990-cb8d-11e3-a934-00144feabdc0 (accessed 6 September 2016).

5. See n. 1.

6. Twain, 269.

7. Kipling (2010), 198.

8. Eck (1993), 5.

9. Kelly D. Alley, 'Ganga and Gandagi: Interpretations of pollution and waste in Benaras', *Ethnology*, 33(2) (Spring, 1994), 127–45, http://www.jstor.org/stable/3773893 (accessed 6 September 2016).

10. Sharma interviewed in Hindi by Jyotsna Singh, 9 February 2015; Shah interviewed by author, 9 February 2015.

11. Pennant, vol. III, 210.

12. In 2012, a special investigation team appointed by the Supreme Court exonerated Modi and his government.

13. Victor Mallet, 'India elections: Modi woos reluctant sari-weavers', *Financial Times*, 29 April 2014.

14. S. N. M. Abdi, 'Saffron isn't green: When religion is the pollutant, can Modi clean up Ganga?', *FirstPost*, 13 May 2015, http://www.firstpost.com/india/saffron-isnt-green-religion-pollutant-can-modi-clean-ganga-2241984.html (accessed 11 June 2016).

15. Siddhartha Roy, 'Varanasi on edge as tradition—and politics—clash with mission to clean Ganga', *The Wire*, 9 October 2015, http://thewire.in/12758/violence-in-varanasi-after-tradition-clashes-with-governments-clean-ganges-mission/ (accessed 6 September 2016).

16. Moore Ede, 103–9. Omar Rashid, 'Warrior for a river—Veer Bhadra Mishra 1938–2013' [obituary], *The Hindu*, 16 March 2013.

17. Hollick, 128.

18. Interview with the author 24 April 2014; Victor Mallet, 'Unholy pollution in India's holy waters', *Financial Times*, 29 April 2014, http://www.ft.com/cms/s/2/49d83172-ceef-11e3-ac8d-00144feabdc0.html#ixzz4BHnCePjV (accessed 6 September 2016).

19. Omar Rashid, 'Modi's drive to clean Ganga cosmetic, says Mahant', *The Hindu*, 15 December 2015. Excluded, apparently by accident, from a VIP enclosure for a *Ganga aarti* (a ritual lamp offering) hosted by Modi for Japanese Prime Minister Shinzo Abe in Varanasi in December 2015, Mishra rounded on the Indian leader and accused him of making only cosmetic efforts to clean the river and restore Varanasi. 'If Modi was serious about a fair assessment of the situation and concerned about highlighting Varanasi's woes, he should have taken Abe through broken roads and shown him drains, not the *aarti*', he said. After this improbable suggestion, Mishra went on: 'The Ganga [government] ministry has come up. But nothing concrete has been done. The same obsolete techniques are at play, like

installation of pipes. Indiscriminate medication without diagnosis of the disease can be disastrous.'

20. Praghya Singh, 'Noida upon the Ganges?' and '"By the time they're done, Banaras will be dead"', *Outlook magazine*, 2 March 2015. S. N. M. Abdi, 'Saffron isn't green: When religion is the pollutant, can Modi clean up Ganga?', *FirstPost*, 13 May 2015, http://www.firstpost.com/india/saffron-isnt-green-religion-pollutant-can-modi-clean-ganga-2241984.html (accessed 11 June 2016). Manmohan Rai, 'Varanasi still waiting for its Achche Din', *Economic Times*, 19 September 2014.

21. Bishwanath Ghosh, 'Grime on the ghat', *The Hindu*, 11 October 2015. Avijit Ghosh, 'Kashi's better, but not fully fit', *Sunday Times of India*, 17 May 2015.

22. Shivam Vij, 'Why a Bajrang Dal activist in Varanasi is unhappy with Modi', *HuffPost*, 10 December 2015, http://www.huffingtonpost.in/2015/12/10/bajrang-dal-modi_n_8756432.html (accessed 29 September 2016).

23. Times News Network, 'Uma says Saraswati not a myth, starts hunt for river', *The Times of India*, 13 August 2014.

24. PTI, 'BJP govt is Congress plus a cow, never seen a weaker PMO: BJP leader Arun Shourie', *Indian Express*, 27 October 2015, http://indianexpress.com/article/india/india-news-india/bjp-govt-is-congress-plus-a-cow-never-seen-a-weaker-a-pmo-says-arun-shourie/ (accessed 6 September 2016). Victor Mallet, '"Truthiness" takes hold of South Asian history', *Financial Times*, 17 May 2016.

25. Victor Mallet, 'Rajasthan spearheads India's reform drive', *Financial Times*, 21 January 2015, http://www.ft.com/intl/cms/s/0/89271888-a15e-11e4-8d19-00144feab7de.html#axzz4BGlrAf6h (accessed 6 September 2016).

26. Victor Mallet, 'Two years on, Modi struggles to realise India's dreams', *Financial Times*, 15 May 2016, http://www.ft.com/intl/cms/s/0/eec847fe-18d9-11e6-bb7d-ee563a5a1cc1.html#axzz4BGlrAf6h (accessed 6 September 2016).

27. Rev. M. A. Sherring, *The Sacred City of the Hindus: An Account of Benares in Ancient and Modern Times* (London, 1868); quoted in Khilnani, 119.

28. Gandhi, 240–1.

29. Eck (1993), 45, 56–7.

30. Kipling (2010), 191.

31. Quoted in Moore Ede, 97, from Panditaraja Jagannatha, *Ganga Lahari: The Flow of the Ganges*, trans. Boris Marjanovic (Indica Books, 2007), Verse 24, p. 69. However, it seems that Moore Ede has wisely had the original re-translated because I have the same Sanskrit–Hindi–English version of the poem as he and the English translations of that and other verses are in comically clunky if faithfully accurate prose.

32. *Ganga Lahari*, 13.

33. Eck (1993), 86.

34. Ibid. 87.

35. Varanasi is a good setting for fiction and films, too. Jeff Altman, a dissolute art journalist who is the protagonist in Geoff Dyer's novel *Jeff in Venice, Death in Varanasi*, finds himself (or loses himself) in the city and the Ganges after arriving on what is supposed to be brief travel reporting trip. The descriptions of the city's religious and secular life are pithy and humorous. The images of the gods are 'bright and cheerful as garden gnomes' and Varanasi is 'probably the most colourful city on earth'. In the end, though, Altman falls ill ('How had the connection between disease and excrement not been made? How could a culture with a horror of pollution be so indifferent to the most offensive form of pollution?'), loses contact with his friends back home, loses interest in the material things that once dominated his life, and—well, I will not spoil the end or try to explain the kangaroo on the *ghats*; let us just say that he is absorbed by India and Mother Ganges (Dyer, 250, 185). Varanasi is also the setting, or one of the settings, for numerous Indian films. Probably the best-known recent movie was *Masaan* (Crematorium), an Indo-French production of 2015 directed by Neeraj Ghaywan. Two plots are intertwined in this unusually gritty tale of inter-caste love in modern India. The Ganges and the death rituals of Varanasi play a central role, and at the end of the film the surviving half of each tragic pair meet by chance in Allahabad, where they console each other and share a boat to the *sangam*, the holy confluence of the Ganges and the Yamuna.

36. Moore Ede, 2.

37. Ibid. 27.

38. Ibid. 8.

CHAPTER 6

1. This chapter and the interviews in it are based on a visit to Varanasi in May 2016.

2. Syed Intishab Ali, 'Rajasthan hospital to try out cow urine "disinfectant"', *Times of India*, 17 September 2015, http://timesofindia.indiatimes.com/city/jaipur/Rajasthan-hospital-to-try-out-cow-urine-disinfectant/articleshow/48993649.cms (accessed 9 December 2016).

3. 'Ganga is defined by atomic theory', he said mysteriously. 'Ganga is the same as Gita [Bhagavad Gita, the divine song] and Gita is the same as atomic theory.' Gita meant knowledge, and knowledge meant energy radiation, he went on. 'Your different components of body are energy radiators and receivers, absorbers. It's energy quantum that's either going in or coming out...Ganga is entirely different in terms of energy.' Two plaques outside his apartment advertised 'The School of Ganga-Geeta-Atomic Theory', inaugurated in 2015 by Manoj Sinha, then minister of state for railways; and 'Nucleus of Mahamana Malvia Institute of Technology for the Ganga Management', inaugurated three years earlier by various

dignitaries, including Swami Chidanand Saraswati Muni, a holy man I subsequently interviewed at his ashram in Rishikesh, and Murli Manohar Joshi, an MP and former BJP president.

4. Sanjay Austa, 'Dom Raja: Untold story of the untouchable keeper of Varanasi's sacred flame', *YourStory*, 11 April 2015, http://yourstory.com/2015/04/dom-raja-of-varanasi/ (accessed 4 July 2016).

5. Moore Ede, 145–59. Lydia Smith, 'City of widows: The 38,000 forgotten women of Varanasi', *International Business Times*, 23 June 2015, http://www.ibtimes.co.uk/city-widows-38000-forgotten-women-varanasi-1505560# (accessed 6 September 2016).

6. Nitin Sethi, 'Modi invokes 1916 pact to justify dams on the Ganga', *Business Standard/The Wire*, 22 January 2016, http://thewire.in/19939/modi-invokes-1916-pact-to-justify-dams-on-the-ganga/ (accessed 6 July 2016). Agreement quoted in Alley (2002), 115. 'Govt using 1916 pact to allay fear on Ganga hydel projs', *Economic Times*, 26 May 2015, via Bullfax.com, http://www.bullfax.com/?q=node-govt-using-1916-pact-allay-fear-ganga-hydel-projs-pe-we (accessed 6 July 2016). Ganga Mahasabha, http://gangamahasabha.org/ (accessed 6 July 2016).

CHAPTER 7

1. Parts of this chapter are based on the author's article on the Ganges for the *Financial Times* weekend magazine: 'The Ganges: Holy, deadly river', 13 February 2015, as well as on subsequent reporting in Kanpur, Patna and other cities on the river. References to documents quoted can be found in subsequent notes.

2. Interview with the author in Kanpur, 11 May 2016.

3. 'Recommendations to address the issue of informal sector involved in e-waste handling', Moradabad, Uttar Pradesh, Centre for Science and Environment (2015), http://www.cseindia.org/userfiles/moradabad-e-waste.pdf (accessed 7 September 2016).

4. Victor Mallet, 'Blue sky dreaming for Delhi, a city where the sun doesn't shine', *Financial Times*, 11 January 2016, https://www.ft.com/content/31aaeb04-b844-11e5-bf7e-8a339b6f2164 (accessed 9 December 2016).

5. 'A report on Toxicity Load of Yamuna River in Delhi', Toxics Link (2014) http://toxicslink.org/docs/Yamuna-Report-Toxics-Link_12-12-2014.pdf (accessed 7 September 2016). Interview with Prashant Rajankar, 15 December 2014.

6. Darshan Malik et al., 'Heavy metal pollution of the Yamuna River: An introspection', *International Journal of Current Microbiology and Applied Sciences*, 3(10) (2014), 856–63, http://www.ijcmas.com/vol-3-10/Darshan%20Malik,%20et%20al.pdf (accessed 7 September 2016).

7. Sapna Chourasiya et al., 'Health risk assessment of organochlorine pesticide exposure through dietary intake of vegetables grown in the periurban sites

of Delhi, India', *Environmental Science and Pollution Research*, 22(8) (2014), 5793–806, https://www.researchgate.net/publication/277643675_Health_risk_assessment_of_organochlorine_pesticide_exposure_through_dietary_intake_of_vegetables_grown_in_the_periurban_sites_of_Delhi_India (accessed 7 September 2016).

8. Pritha Chatterjee and Aniruddha Ghosal, 'Pesticide on your plate', *The Indian Express*, 5 January 2015, http://indianexpress.com/article/cities/delhi/pesticide-on-your-plate/99/#sthash.WP3D7pCd.dpuf (accessed 7 September 2016).

9. Anand V. Singha and Jitendra Pandey, 'Heavy metals in the midstream of the Ganges River: Spatio-temporal trends in a seasonally dry tropical region (India)', *Water International*, 39(4) (2014), 504–16, published online 2 June 2014, http://www.tandfonline.com/doi/abs/10.1080/02508060.2014.921851?journalCode=rwin20 (accessed 7 September 2016). J. Pandey, K. Shubhashish, and Richa Pandey, 'Metal contamination of Ganga River (India) as influenced by atmospheric deposition', *Bulletin of Environmental Contamination and Toxicology*, 83 (2009), 204–9, published online 12 May 2009, http://www.ncbi.nlm.nih.gov/pubmed/19434353 (accessed 7 September 2016). Interview and email exchanges with Pandey, 12 January 2015.

10. 'NGT panel recommends Rs 120-cr fine on Art of Living for damage to Yamuna', *The Indian Express*, 8 March 2016, http://indianexpress.com/article/cities/delhi/ngt-panel-recommends-rs-120-cr-fine-on-art-of-living-for-damage-to-yamuna/ (accessed 7 September 2016). Kedar Nagarajan, 'NGT clears World Culture Festival, but with a Rs 5 crore slap on the wrist', *The Indian Express*, 10 March 2016, http://indianexpress.com/article/india/india-news-india/ngt-art-of-living-world-culture-festival-sri-sri-ravi-shankar-yamuna/#sthash.TQVAXLRv.dpuf (accessed 7 September 2016). Baishali Adak, 'Art of Living fest: Team Modi throws weight behind Sri Sri Ravi Shankar', *India Today/Mail Today*, 14 March 2016, http://indiatoday.intoday.in/story/art-of-living-fest-team-modi-throws-weight-behind-sri-sri-ravi-shankar/1/619341.html (accessed 7 September 2016). Gaurav Vivek Bhatnagar, 'A month later, Art of Living still to pay NGT fine', *The Wire*, 10 April 2016, http://thewire.in/2016/04/10/a-month-later-art-of-living-still-to-pay-ngt-fine-28582/ (accessed 7 September 2016).

11. Deepak Chhabra et al., 'Chronic heavy metal exposure and gallbladder cancer risk in India, a comparative study with Japan', *Asian Pacific Journal of Cancer Prevention*, 13(1) (2012), 187–90, http://www.apocpcontrol.net/paper_file/issue_abs/Volume13_No1/187-90%2012.11%20Jagannath.pdf (accessed 7 September 2016). Chelsea Anne Young, 'Scientists solve puzzle of arsenic-poisoning crisis in Asia', *Stanford Report*, 24 March 2009, http://news.stanford.edu/news/2009/april1/fendorf-arsenic-water-poison-asia-040109.html (accessed 7 September 2016). Dipankar Chakraborti et al., 'Groundwater arsenic contamination in India: A review of its magnitude,

health, social, socio-economic effects and approaches for arsenic mitigation', *Journal of the Indian Society of Agricultural Statistics*, 67(2) (2013), 235–66, http://www.isas.org.in/jsp/volume/vol67/issue2/07%20-%20Depankar%20Chakraborti-Col.pdf (accessed 7 September 2016).

12. 'Kanpur groundwater pollution', Blacksmith Institute, http://www.blacksmithinstitute.org/projects/display/28 (accessed 19 May 2016).

13. For a recent BBC television programme on the Ganges, my colleague Justin Rowlatt took an inspector into a randomly chosen tannery in Kanpur where filthy water was all over the floor and the visitors squelched through it by stepping on wet hides of the blue colour characteristic of chromium treatment.

14. Interviews with the author in Kanpur 18 February 2013. 'Inspecting a tannery in Kanpur, India', BBC video, 11 May 2016, http://www.bbc.co.uk/news/magazine-36252005 (acccessed 7 September 2016).

15. Young, 220–1.

16. Interviews with the author in Kanpur, 11 May 2016.

17. Shashi Shekhar interviewed by the author, 29 March 2016.

18. PTI, 'Build toilets first and temples later, Narendra Modi says', *The Times of India*, 2 October 2013, http://timesofindia.indiatimes.com/india/Build-toilets-first-and-temples-later-Narendra-Modi-says/articleshow/23422631.cms (accessed 23 May 2016).

19. Victor Mallet, 'Modi prioritises factories and toilets in Independence Day speech', *Financial Times*, 15 August 2014, http://www.ft.com/intl/cms/s/0/16335128-2438-11e4-be8e-00144feabdc0.html#axzz49OKJQfR6 (accessed 23 May 2016).

20. Puskal Upadhyay of the National Mission for Clean Ganga, 23 November 2015.

21. Victor Mallet, 'Delhi notebook: How the wedding syndrome could fix India', 8 February 2016, http://www.ft.com/intl/cms/s/0/e192bbf8-cb60-11e5-beob-b7ece4e953a0.html#axzz49OKJQfR6 (accessed 23 May 2016).

22. Private communication with the author in Delhi.

23. Victor Mallet and Jyotsna Singh, 'Narendra Modi's Ganges clean-up runs into the sand', 9 November 2015, http://www.ft.com/intl/cms/s/0/ad69b670-7952-11e5-933d-efcdc3c11c89.html#axzz49OKJQfR6 (accessed 23 May 2016).

24. Victor Mallet, 'India toilet campaign lifts lid on graft', *Financial Times*, 9 October 2012, http://www.ft.com/cms/s/0/7f900a34-0e15-11e2-8d92-00144feabdc0.html#ixzz49OKOt1nZ (accessed 7 September 2016). Neil Munshi, 'India's latest scandal: Down the pan', *Financial Times*, 27 April 2012, http://blogs.ft.com/beyond-brics/2012/04/27/indias-latest-scandal-it-happens/#axzz28KRA2Nsq (accessed 7 September 2016). 'Converting dry latrines in the District of Budaun, Uttar Pradesh: A story of commitment, determination and dignity. An initiative of the district administration, Budaun, UP', Unicef, August 2011.

25. Prakash Javadekar, briefing in New Delhi, 23 May 2016. Brochure, 'Ministry of Environment, Forest and Climate Change: New Initiatives and Efforts 2014–2016', May 2016. PTI, 'Industrial waste flowing into Ganga down by 35 per cent: Javadekar', *Times of India*, 15 May 2016.

CHAPTER 8

1. Victor Mallet and Clive Cookson, 'Toxic Ganges adds to spread of drug-resistant bacteria', *Financial Times*, 13 February 2015, https://www.ft.com/content/15af211a-b2c6-11e4-a058-00144feab7de (accessed 29 September 2016).
2. Gardiner Harris, '"Superbugs" kill India's babies and pose an overseas threat', *New York Times*, 3 December 2014.
3. See n. 1.
4. Gawande, 260–2.
5. Graham was interviewed by the author on 24 September 2014 and 16 January 2015, and we exchanged emails and articles. I am grateful for his help in reviewing this chapter. For non-scientists, his explanation of how the process of antibiotic resistance works and how it is measured is helpful: 'NDM-1 is an enzyme (i.e. active protein) that is made from bla_{NDM-1}, which is the gene sequence that codes for the amino acid sequence that defines NDM-1 manufacture. Cells store the code for making each protein in their DNA as gene sequences. In this case, bla_{NDM-1} is the DNA sequence for making NDM-1. When the cell needs a specific protein, it reads the DNA code (which is stored as a long series base) and makes the protein (building a long string of amino acids) using that code as a template. It is more complicated than this, but when we quantify bla_{NDM-1} in an environmental sample, we are not actually measuring NDM-1 itself, we are measuring the genetic capacity to make NDM-1. It is important to note that having bla_{NDM-1} in a cell does not mean NDM-1 is being made all the time. NDM-1 is only made when the cell needs it. This is why the gene can sit latent in a cell and we do not know it is there. The only time when NDM-1 is made is when the cell is stressed in a way that its manufacture is triggered. As an example, when you take a related antibiotic, the manufacture of NDM-1 is triggered is cells that carry bla_{NDM-1}...[T]hese genes are unique and very specific, therefore if you find the gene, it means it must be in an organism in which the gene could be expressed...

We measure the gene first because it is very difficult and less accurate to measure the protein itself (for a variety of reasons), therefore 99% of the people that study these systems in the environment measure the gene as a surrogate. DNA is stable, whereas protein is not. Therefore, we are measuring the gun and smoke, not the bullet.'

6. Senior medical scientists in India told me that while they agree the problem is alarming, they think solutions—including new antibiotics—may be found to limit the number of deaths.

7. 'Antimicrobial resistance: Tackling a crisis for the health and wealth of nations', by The Review on Antimicrobial Resistance, chaired by Jim O'Neill, December 2014, https://amr-review.org/sites/default/files/AMR%20Review%20Paper%20-%20Tackling%20a%20crisis%20for%20the%20health%20and%20wealth%20of%20nations_1.pdf (accessed 8 September 2016).

8. Ramanan Laxminarayan et al., 'Antibiotic resistance—the need for global solutions', The Lancet Infectious Diseases Commission, December 2014, originally published 21 November 2013. Gardiner Harris, '"Superbugs" kill India's babies and pose an overseas threat', New York Times, 3 December 2014.

9. Lhendup G. Bhutia, 'The Antibiotic Nation', Open magazine, 23 October 2015, http://www.openthemagazine.com/article/living/the-antibiotic-nation (accessed 8 September 2016).

10. Newby, 33.

11. Z. S. Ahammad et al., 'Increased waterborne bla_{NDM-1} resistance gene abundances associated with seasonal human pilgrimages to the upper Ganges River', Environmental Science & Technology, 48 (2014), 3014–20.

12. See n. 5.

13. Interviews with the author, 13 January 2015.

14. Amy Kazmin and Andrew Jack, 'India attacks resistant superbug study', Financial Times, 15 August 2010, https://www.ft.com/content/225917ee-a890-11df-86dd-00144feabdc0 (accessed 8 September 2016).

15. Ibid. Victor Mallet and Clive Cookson, 'Toxic Ganges adds to spread of drug-resistant bacteria', Financial Times, 13 February 2015, https://www.ft.com/content/15af211a-b2c6-11e4-a058-00144feab7de (accessed 8 September 2016). Lhendup G. Bhutia (see n. 9).

16. Timothy R. Walsh et al., 'Dissemination of NDM-1 positive bacteria in the New Delhi environment and its implications for human health: An environmental point prevalence study', The Lancet Infectious Diseases, 11 (2011), 355–62.

17. Anjana Ahuja, 'Big Pharma must lose its resistance to antibiotic research', Financial Times, 17 May 2015, https://www.ft.com/content/805e4746-fb0c-11e4-9aed-00144feab7de (accessed 8 September 2016).

18. Interview with the author, 12 January 2015.

19. Sumanth Gandra et al., 'Trends in antibiotic resistance among major bacterial pathogens isolated from blood culture tested at a large private laboratory network in India, 2008–2014', International Journal of Infectious Diseases, 50 (2016), 75–82.

20. O'Neill was elevated to the peerage and appointed commercial secretary to the Treasury while preparing his latest anti-microbial report. But he resigned from the Tory government of Theresa May in September 2016.

21. Andrew Ward, 'Big pharma risks public backlash on antibiotics, says Jim O'Neill', *Financial Times*, 14 May 2015, https://www.ft.com/content/8a6f6cf6-f95e-11e4-ae65-00144feab7de (accessed 8 September 2016).

22. Ibid.

23. David Graham et al., 'Underappreciated role of regionally poor water quality on globally increasing antibiotic resistance', *Environmental Science & Technology*, 1 October 2014.

24. *Ain-i-Akbari*, quoted in Mahajan, 25.

25. Foster, 299, 226.

26. Tavernier, vol. III, 98.

27. Hollick, 131.

28. M. E. Hankin, 'L'Action bactéricide des eaux de la Jumna et du Gange sur le microbe du choléra', *Annales de l'Institut Pasteur* (Paris, 1896), vol. X, 511–23, https://archive.org/stream/annalesdelinstit10inst#page/510/mode/2up (accessed 20 September 2016).

29. Twain, 279.

30. http://www.amazon.in (accessed 20 September 2016). Kumar Vikram, 'Now you can get a splash of Gangajal by post', *Mail Today*, 31 May 2016.

31. http://www.ebay.co.uk (accessed 20 September 2016).

32. Alley (2002), 7.

33. Personal communication with author.

34. Ackroyd, 250–1.

35. Interview with the author, 15 September 2016.

36. StaphTAME, http://www.gangagen.com/staphtame.html (accessed 20 September 2016).

37. Kuchment, xiii.

38. L. M. Marcuk et al., 'Clinical studies of the use of bacteriophage in the treatment of cholera', *Bulletin of the World Health Organisation*, 45(1) (1971), 77–83, http://www.ncbi.nlm.nih.gov/pubmed/4946956 (accessed 20 September 2016).

39. Personal communication with the author.

40. Kuchment, 11.

CHAPTER 9

1. Translation from Romila Thapar, *Aśoka and the Decline of the Mauryas* (Oxford University Press, 1997), 224, http://www.learn.columbia.edu/indianart/pdf/asoka_thapar.pdf (accessed 9 September 2016). There are question marks about the red-headed ducks (a pink-headed duck once found on the river is now thought to be extinct), the *nandi-mukhas* (possibly birds found in rice fields), and the Ganges animal (which may be the Gangetic dolphin).

2. Mr Dolphin Sinha, video documentary by Reporters Express Paris, 2008, directed by Christian Gallissian.

3. I addressed the wildlife themes in this and the preceding paragraphs in numerous articles while living in Delhi, including: 'Not common or in the garden', *Financial Times*, 20 April 2015, https://www.ft.com/content/551169c2-e416-11e4-9039-00144feab7de (accessed 9 September 2016); 'Flora and fauna of an Asian megacity', *Financial Times*, 2 October 2012, https://www.ft.com/content/627680f6-0c7e-11e2-a776-00144feabdc0 (accessed 9 September 2016); 'India: Our hates and loves', *Financial Times*, 30 May 2016, https://www.ft.com/content/9dc3fc18-2400-11e6-aa98-db1e01fabc0c (accessed 9 September 2016).

4. See previous note.

5. However, there was a reported sighting of the Baiji in late 2016. Tom Phillips, 'China's "extinct" dolphin may have returned to Yangtze river, say conservationists', *The Guardian*, 11 October 2016, https://www.theguardian.com/world/2016/oct/11/china-extinct-dolphin-returned-yangtze-river-baiji (accessed 10 December 2016).

6. Brac's name derives from its earlier incarnations as the Bangladesh Rehabilitation Assistance Committee and the Bangladesh Rural Advancement Committee.

7. Author's observations and interviews, 18 March 2016.

8. Uma Bharti, the minister responsible for water and restoring the Ganges, once said in parliament that the dolphins were being blinded by pollution, though there is no scientific evidence for that and the animals can barely see in any case. PTI, 'Yes, minister! Dolphins got blind because of pollution, says ministry', NDTV website, 31 August 2016. Unfortunately the article suggesting she was ignorant was illustrated by a stock picture of marine dolphins that have nothing to do with the Ganges. http://www.ndtv.com/india-news/yes-minister-dolphins-got-blind-because-of-pollution-says-ministry-1452833 (accessed 9 September 2016).

9. Jonathan Swinton and Whitney Gomez, 'Platanista gangetica', Animal Diversity Web, University of Michigan, Museum of Zoology, http://animaldiversity.org/accounts/Platanista_gangetica/ (accessed 25 July 2016). R. K. Sinha et al., 'Population status and conservation of the Ganges river dolphin (Platanista gangetica gangetica) in the Indian subcontinent', in *Biology, Evolution and Conservation of River Dolphins* (Nova Science Publishers, 2010), 419–43. Sandeep Kumar Behera et al. of WWF of India, 'Indicator species (gharial and dolphin) of riverine ecosystem: An exploratory of River Ganga', in Sanghi (ed.), 121–40.

10. See previous note.

11. Sinha interviewed by the author, October 2015; Dilip Kedia, research associate, interviewed by the author, 7 March 2013.

12. See n. 2.

13. WWF, 'World's top 10 rivers at risk' (2007), http://d2ouvy59p0dg6k.cloudfront.net/downloads/worldstop10riversatriskfinalmarch13_1.pdf (accessed 9 September 2016).

14. R. K. Sinha and K. Prasad, 'Management of water quality and biodiversity of the River Ganga', in *Ecosystems and Integrated Water Resources Management in South Asia*, ed. E. R. N. Gunawardena, Brij Gopal, and Hemesiri Kotagama (Routledge, 2012), 104–32. Prakash Nautiyal, Jyoti Verma, and Asheesh Shivam Mishra, 'Distribution of major floral and faunal diversity in the mountain and upper Gangetic plains zone of the Ganga: Diatoms, macroinvertebrates and fish', in Sanghi (ed.), 75–118.

15. Victor Mallet. 'Life and death among India's endangered vultures', *Financial Times*, 18 April 2016, https://next.ft.com/content/cc4afe2a-0307-11e6-af1d-c47326021344 (accessed 26 July 2016).

16. Interview with the author, 9 May 2015.

17. Alastair Lawson, 'Bangladesh "tiger boy" to return', BBC, 24 November 2008, http://news.bbc.co.uk/2/hi/south_asia/7746748.stm (accessed 27 July 2016).

18. Interview with the author, 18 February 2016.

19. Interview with the author, 18 March 2016.

20. Jo Johnson, 'Scandal of Indian tigers that disappeared', *Financial Times*, 29 March 2005, https://next.ft.com/content/dcc40f7a-9fd2-11d9-b355-00000e2511c8 (accessed 27 July 2016). Jay Mazoomdar 'A mockery of both science and sensibility: What's wrong with the tiger numbers', *Indian Express*, 19 April 2016, http://indianexpress.com/article/explained/tiger-population-in-india-2759532/ (accessed 27 July 2016).

21. Interview with the author, 8 April 2016. Kishor Rithe, 'Linking rivers—delinking life', *Sanctuary Asia*, 34(6) (2014), http://www.sanctuaryasia.com/magazines/conservation/9862-linking-rivers-delinking-life.html (accessed 27 July 2016).

22. Joseph Allchin, 'Low-lying Bangladesh targets jump in coal use', *Financial Times*, 30 December 2015, https://next.ft.com/content/241059fa-9424-11e5-bd82-c1fb87bef7af (accessed 28 July 2016).

23. 'Ganges: How the majestic Ganges has shaped the landscape, wildlife and culture of India', BBC/Travel Channel, 2007.

24. Sher Singh Rana was sentenced in August 2014 to life imprisonment for murdering Phoolan Devi in 2001. 'Life sentence to Sher Singh Rana for killing Phoolan Devi', *Times of India*, 14 August 2014, http://timesofindia.indiatimes.com/india/Life-sentence-to-Sher-Singh-Rana-for-killing-Phoolan-Devi/articleshow/40249822.cms (accessed 13 February 2017). Ten other accused were acquitted in the case.

25. Interview with the author, 2 June 2016.

26. See n. 23.

27. Interviews with the author, 5 June 2016. Sandeep Kumar Behera et al. of WWF of India (see n. 10). Ministry of Environment and Forests, Government of India, 'The gharial: Our river guardian', Undated, http://

www.moef.nic.in/downloads/public-information/Gharial%20booklet_
MoEF.pdf (accessed 28 July 2016).

28. Jay Mazoomdaar, 'River in peril: Bleeding the Chambal dry', *Tehelka magazine*, 16 March 2013, http://www.tehelka.com/2013/03/bleeding-the-
chambal-dry/ (accessed 29 July 2016).

29. Victor Mallet, 'Asia's dancing frogs, walking fish and sneezing monkeys',
Financial Times, 19 October 2015, http://www.ft.com/cms/s/0/65ed875c-
7427-11e5-a129-3fcc4f641d98.html#axzz4FlPlFR00 (accessed 29 July 2016).

30. Ashoka's 5th pillar edict, various translations, and see n. 1.

31. Hari Kumar, 'Stranded Indian elephant dies of heart attack, ending a
wretched journey', *New York Times*, 16 August 2016, http://www.nytimes.
com/2016/08/17/world/asia/bangladesh-elephant-dies-india.html
(accessed 9 September 2016).

32. Alter, 114.

CHAPTER 10

1. Heber, quote in Mahajan, 70.

2. This chapter is based on research and *Financial Times* columns about the
population issue over more than a decade, and on a piece entitled
'Demographic Dividend—or Disaster?' (Mallet, 2013).

3. Victor Mallet, 'Bihar's schools offer population solution', *Financial Times*,
18 March 2013, http://www.ft.com/cms/s/0/4ae4f62e-8ae7-11e2-b1a4-
00144feabdc0.html#axzz4FwccFSrA (accessed 31 July 2016).

4. Victor Mallet, 'Population, not politics, threatens Pakistan', *Financial Times*,
10 September 2014, http://www.ft.com/cms/s/0/67778df6-38ec-11e4-
a53b-00144feabdc0.html#axzz4FwccFSrA (accessed 31 July 2016).

5. The complacency did not come with the Modi government. Some of
his predecessors were similarly blasé about population growth. See for
example Kamal Nath, former trade and industry minister, in Victor
Mallet, 'The utopian myth of India's double dividend', *Financial Times*,
6 December 2007, https://www.ft.com/content/03a12b84-a339-11dc-
b229-0000779fd2ac (accessed 10 December 2016).

6. Sanyal, 167.

7. Prater, xiii.

8. Victor Mallet, 'The utopian myth of India's double dividend', *Financial
Times*, 6 December 2007, https://www.ft.com/content/03a12b84-a339-
11dc-b229-0000779fd2ac (accessed 10 December 2016).

9. Pilita Clark, 'Air pollution hits "catastrophic" levels', *Financial Times*,
12 May 2016, http://www.ft.com/cms/s/0/41d0d542-17ae-11e6-bb7d-
ee563a5a1cc1.html#axzz4FwccFSrA (accessed 1 August 2016).

10. Moore Ede, 94.

11. Quoted in Mahajan, 158.

12. Deborah Chambers, *A Sociology of Family Life* (Polity Press, 2012), 142.

13. Patti Waldmeir, Amy Kazmin, and Girija Shivakumar, 'Asia: Heirs and spares', *Financial Times*, 11 July 2011, https://www.ft.com/content/54751678-ab1a-11e0-b4d8-00144feabdc0 (accessed 10 December 2016).

14. Carl Haub and O. P. Sharma, 'India approaches replacement fertility', *Population Bulletin*, 70(1) (Population Reference Bureau, August 2015), http://www.prb.org/pdf15/india-population-bulletin.pdf (accessed 1 August 2016).

15. Ravi Reddy, 'Naidu wants people to have more children', *The Hindu*, 20 January 2015, http://www.thehindu.com/news/national/andhra-pradesh/chandrababu-naidus-remarks-on-population-stir-up-a-hornets-nest/article6805595.ece (accessed 10 December 2016).

16. Victor Mallet, 'Rightwing Hindus stir up "battle of the babies" in India', *Financial Times*, 22 January 2015, https://www.ft.com/content/13d13c20-a0d8-11e4-b8b9-00144feab7de (accessed 10 September 2016).

17. See n. 7.

18. Lorna Aldrich, 'Development bank official says inequality, governance challenges could derail Asian growth', *The National Press Club*, 22 May 2012, http://www.press.org/news-multimedia/news/development-bank-official-says-inequality-governance-challenges-could-derail-as (accessed 10 December 2016).

19. 'The dangers of being "relaxed" about robots', letter published in the *Financial Times*, 1 August 2016, http://www.ft.com/cms/s/0/a0e7fbd2-54d0-11e6-9664-e0bdc13c3bef.html#axzz4GDyTl8UL (accessed 3 August 2016).

20. Neil Howe and Richard Jackson, 'Rising populations breed rising powers', *Financial Times*, 9 February 2007, http://www.ft.com/cms/s/0/04f3c006-b7e3-11db-bfb3-0000779e2340.html?ft_site=falcon&desktop=true#axzz4SPFQdyKy (accessed 10 December 2016).

21. Frank Notestein wrote this in 1954 and has been extensively quoted, including in Ronald Schoenmaeckers and Irena Kotowska 'Population ageing and its challenges to social policy', Population Studies No. 50, Council of Europe Publishing (2005), http://envejecimiento.csic.es/documentos/documentos/ce-populationageing-01.pdf (accessed 10 December 2016).

22. UN Department of Economic and Social Affairs, 'World Population Prospects', 2015 Revision, https://esa.un.org/unpd/wpp/Publications/Files/Key_Findings_WPP_2015.pdf (accessed 3 August 2016).

CHAPTER 11

1. This chapter is based largely on research and interviews in February, March, and April 2016 for reporting and analysis of a severe drought in India. One feature that emerged was Victor Mallet, 'India: Water wars', *Financial Times*, 13 April 2016, http://www.ft.com/cms/s/0/96687242-009b-11e6-ac98-3c15a1aa2e62.html#axzz4GKKTDOLQ (accessed 4 August 2016).

2. Interview with the author, 7 April 2016.
3. Victor Mallet, 'Water wars hit Delhi as saboteurs strike', *Financial Times*, 26 February 2016, http://www.ft.com/cms/s/0/1e23dc86-dc4c-11e5-a72f-1e7744c66818.html#axzz4GKKTDOLQ (accessed 4 August 2016).
4. Victor Mallet, 'India's water shortage is more than a tale of town versus country', *Financial Times*, 2 May 2016, http://www.ft.com/cms/s/0/4dc0543c-0d49-11e6-b41f-0beb7e589515.html#axzz4GKKTDOLQ (accessed 4 August 2016).
5. Victor Mallet, 'Mismanagement blamed for New Delhi's water crisis', *Financial Times*, 19 June 2014, https://www.ft.com/content/584661f4-f5cb-11e3-afd3-00144feabdc0 (accessed 30 September 2016).
6. Navin Singh Khadka, 'India Ganges floods "break previous records"', BBC, 30 August 2016, http://www.bbc.co.uk/news/world-asia-india-37217679 (accessed 12 September 2016).
7. Losty, 54.
8. Victor Mallet, 'Water: Paying the price for years of neglect', *Financial Times*, 24 April 2006 (accessed via Factiva, 5 August 2016). James Crabtree and Victor Mallet, 'COP21: Floods kill 188 in India', 2 December 2015, https://next.ft.com/content/772ff6fe-98e3-11e5-bdda-9f13f99fa654 (accessed 5 August 2016).
9. Victor Mallet, 'Sugar leaves sour taste in Indian drought', *Financial Times*, 23 April 2013, https://next.ft.com/content/e4676692-aa2c-11e2-9c7b-00144feabdc0#slideo (accessed 5 August 2016).
10. Maria Thomas, 'The slow and dangerous death of Pakistan's Indus river delta', *Quartz India*, 9 July 2015, http://qz.com/448049/the-slow-and-dangerous-death-of-pakistans-indus-river-delta/ (accessed 5 August 2016).
11. Review of draft Indian water legislation and comparison with the European Water Framework Directive, European Commission, November 2015, http://eeas.europa.eu/archives/delegations/india/documents/report_review_india-eu_water_legislation.pdf (accessed 10 December 2016).
12. AFP, '60% of key S. Asian water basin not usable: Study', Yahoo! News, 30 August 2016, https://www.yahoo.com/news/60-key-asian-water-basin-not-usable-study-191125386.html (accessed 12 September 2016). WWF, 'World's top 10 rivers at risk' (2007), http://d2ouvy59p0dg6k.cloudfront.net/downloads/worldstop10riversatriskfinalmarch13_1.pdf (accessed 9 September 2016).

CHAPTER 12

1. Guha, 225.
2. Interview with the author, 6 May 2016.
3. This and the following paragraphs are based on a visit to Narora on 6 May 2016.

4. WWF, 'World's top 10 rivers at risk' (2007), http://d2ouvy59p0dg6k. cloudfront.net/downloads/worldstop10riversatriskfinalmarch13_1.pdf (accessed 9 September 2016), 22.

5. Irrigation in Southern and Eastern Asia in figures—Aquastat Survey 2011, 8–9.

6. Diary entry for 5 January 1815, Losty, 150–1. The original sentence in Losty reads 'The effects of the canal of the cultivation of the country were so striking…' which is either a misprint or a mistake of the writer.

7. Haberman, 6–7.

8. Kaushal Kishore, 'The Ganges Canal', Posted on Civil Engineering Portal http://www.engineeringcivil.com/the-ganges-canal.html (accessed 8 August 2016). See also the fictionalized account of Proby Cautley's canal project, Hutchison (2012), Loc 1152–9.

9. Mount, 416, 480.

10. Curzon: Speech on 3 April 1899 at Lyallpur, headquarters of the Chenab Irrigation District. *Cambridge Economic History of India*, ed. Dharma Kumar (Cambridge University Press, 1983), vol. II, *c.* 1751–*c.* 1970, 677, via Google Books (accessed 8 August 2016).

11. Kishore (see n. 8).

12. Alley (2002), 108.

13. Guha, 212–15, 225.

14. Alter, 61. Albinia, 284. Gargan, 87.

15. Interview with the author, 5 April 2016.

16. National Register of Large Dams, http://www.cwc.nic.in/main/downloads/New%20NRLD.pdf (accessed 10 August 2016). Kelly D. Alley, 'The developments, policies and assessments of hydropower in the Ganga River basin', in Sanghi (ed.), 285–305.

17. Hollick, 180–94.

18. See n. 16.

19. Anjana Ahuja 'In Modi's India, waterways are a geopolitical issue', *Financial Times*, 20 July 2014.

20. Nitin Sethi, 'NDA revives a 1916 pact for dams on the Ganga', *Business Standard*, 21 January 2016. Vishwa Mohan, 'Interlinking of rivers within 7–10 years: Uma', *The Times of India*, 18 October 2014.

21. Victor Mallet, 'India budget receives lukewarm response', *Financial Times*, 29 February 2016, https://www.ft.com/content/4100396e-dec4-11e5-b072-006d8d362ba3 (accessed 10 August 2016).

22. Mahim Pratap Singh, 'IMG's proposals will destroy Ganga, warns water conservationist', *The Hindu*, 11 April 2013, http://www.thehindu.com/todays-paper/tp-national/imgs-proposals-will-destroy-ganga-warns-water-conservationist/article4604592.ece (accessed 11 August 2016).

23. 'Master plan of Cotton maharishi', Letter from Gautam Pingle in *Financial Times*, 21 July 2014.

24. Ashish Sagar, interview with the author, 7 April 2016.

25. See PTI, 'Fertiliser use on the rise in India, soil health deteriorating', *The Hindu*, 22 March 2011. Often the problem is not the quantity of fertilizer but the type, and a consequent failure to provide the correct inputs of phosphorus and nitrogen.

26. Mohit Ray, *Five Thousand Mirrors: The Water Bodies of Kolkata* (Jadavpur University Press, 2015). Meera Subramanian, *Elemental India: The Natural World at a Time of Crisis and Opportunity* (HarperCollins India, 2015). Victor Mallet, 'Mismanagement blamed for New Delhi's water crisis', *Financial Times*, 19 June 2014, http://www.ft.com/cms/s/0/584661f4-f5cb-11e3-afd3-00144feabdc0.html#axzz4GKKTDOLQ (accessed 4 August 2016).

CHAPTER 13

1. Translation from the Hindi by Jyotsna Singh.
2. *Ramayana*, 54.
3. The Supreme Court ruled in 2013 that new convicts would thenceforth be banned from parliament. See Victor Mallet, 'Criminal MPs banned from Indian parliament', *Financial Times*, 10 July 2013, https://www.ft.com/content/4ac6d8dc-e966-11e2-9f11-00144feabdc0 (accessed 11 December 2016). Several senior ministers and chief ministers have been convicted of serious crimes, although opinion surveys show that many voters are unconcerned.

CHAPTER 14

1. Xuanzang, 127.
2. Fitch, 102–3.
3. Foster, 265.
4. Megasthenes quoted in Wood, 88–9.
5. Pliny the Elder, *The Natural History*, trans. John Bostock and H. T. Riley (London, 1855), via Tufts, http://www.perseus.tufts.edu/hopper/text?doc=Perseus%3Atext%3A1999.02.0137%3Abook%3D6%3Achapter%3D22 (accessed 13 September 2016).
6. Aeneid IX, lines 30–1.
7. Mahajan, 14.
8. Brotton, 96.
9. *The Travels of Sir John Mandeville: The version of the Cotton Manuscript in modern spelling*, (Macmillan, London, 1915), http://warburg.sas.ac.uk/pdf/ndb110b2285270.pdf (accessed 13 September 2016).
10. Darian, 176–7.
11. Fa-Hein (Fa Xian), 54. Sanyal, 121–4. Wood, 188–90.
12. Xuanzang, 127.
13. Darian, 95.

14. Mahajan, 17–21.
15. Ibid. 23. Alberuni (2011), vol. I, 22–3; Alberuni said: 'We can only say, folly is an illness for which there is no medicine, and the Hindus believe that there is no country but theirs, no nation like theirs, no kings like theirs, no religion like theirs, no science like theirs. They are haughty, foolishly vain, self-conceited, and stolid. They are by nature niggardly in communicating that which they know, and they take the greatest possible care to withhold it from men of another caste among their own people, still much more, of course, from any foreigner. According to their belief, there is no other country on earth but theirs, no other race of man but theirs, and no created beings besides them have any knowledge or science whatsoever. Their haughtiness is such that, if you tell them of any science or scholar in Khurasan and Persis, they will think you to be both an ignoramus and a liar. If they travelled and mixed with other nations, they would soon change their mind, for their ancestors were not as narrow-minded as the present generation is.'
16. Dunn, 204; Mahajan, 24.
17. Wood, 247.
18. Fitch, 100–2.
19. Ibid. 102–3.
20. Ibid. 109.
21. Foster 265.
22. Mahajan, 25; Foster, 247, 264–5, 269.
23. Tavernier, vol. III, 98, 103–4.
24. Fraser, 455–6.
25. Mahajan, 41–2.
26. Parkes, 177.
27. Ibid. 275.
28. Emily Eden, vol. I, 16.
29. Fanny Eden, 21.
30. Losty, 7–23.
31. Quoted in Mahajan, 53.
32. Mount, 227–8.
33. Mahajan, 39.
34. Ziegler, 137–9.

CHAPTER 15

1. Losty, 53.
2. Ibid. 10.
3. Ibid. 53–4, 56, 67–8, 87, 93.
4. Ibid. 53.
5. The picture is shown in Mahajan, 71.
6. Losty, 83, 48.
7. Parkes, 106.

8. Ghosh (2015b), 39.
9. Mahajan, 44–5.
10. Parkes, 170.
11. Ibid. 165ff, 172, 177, 182, 264–6, 284, 291–4.
12. Greenhill, 28, 38–9. He dedicates the book, published in 1971, to his first wife Gillian 'who shared all the travels which gave rise to this book and then died of amoebic hepatitis picked up somewhere in East Pakistan'.
13. Yves Marre's wife Runa Khan talks about preserving Bangladesh's wooden boat-building heritage in Gary Strauss, 'Anchoring Bangladesh's ancient boatbuilding technology', *National Geographic*, 17 November 2016, http://news.nationalgeographic.com/2016/11/Runa-Khan-explorer-moments-develops-living-museum-to-preserve-national-craft/ (accessed 11 December 2016).
14. Newby, 22–4.

<h2 style="text-align:center">CHAPTER 16</h2>

1. Pennant, vol. II, 166–7.
2. Kipling (2014), chapter 1, 'A Real Live City'.
3. The first part of this chapter is based on a boat journey up and down the Hooghly from 15–20 February 2016.
4. PTI, 'Govt plans to set up 2,000 waterports; 30 on Ganga between Varanasi-Haldia: Nitin Gadkari', via DNA India, 10 February 2016, http://www.dnaindia.com/money/report-govt-plans-to-set-up-2000-waterports-ro-ro-services-nitin-gadkari-2176356 (accessed 9 July 2016).
5. Environmentalists say the use of 101 Indian rivers for an integrated 'Inland Water Transport' system could threaten wildlife, introduce pollution in hitherto clean rivers, and have unpredictable results in the form of siltation, floods, the changing of river courses, and even the triggering of earthquakes. 'A fully integrated water transport with the inter-modal transport system requires addressing complex technical as well as infrastructural challenges in order to improve the inland waterway system and to integrate it with land based transportation', says Rajendra Singh, a conservationist who has been dubbed India's Water Man. 'Are we prepared for this?' Geologist Shashank Shekhar suggests the government should try some modest pilot projects rather than plunging unprepared into over-ambitious plans to restructure its waterways. 'This big bang development approach is fraught with risks', he says. See Neeta Lal, 'India plans to overhaul rivers for shipping', thethirdpole.net, 24 July 2015, https://www.thethirdpole.net/2015/07/24/india-plans-to-overhaul-rivers-for-shipping/ (accessed 9 July 2016).
6. See Chapter 2 for a discussion on how climate change is already affecting South Asia, especially the north Indian plains through which the Ganges flows.

7. The principal Saraswati River of western India disappeared thousands of years ago, and is now said to join the Ganges and the Yamuna invisibly at Allahabad, but there was also another by that name that was a distributary at the mouth of the Ganges in Bengal until after the medieval era.

8. Chaitanya Mahaprabhu, the founder of ISKCON.

9. Temple of the Vedic Planetarium website, https://tovp.org/ (accessed 13 July 2016).

10. Wood, 265.

11. Mukherjee (1968), 21.

12. Ibid. 13.

13. Darian, 91–2.

14. Ibid. 92.

15. Quoted in Wood, 134–5.

16. Ibid. 135–6.

17. Mukherjee (1968), 16.

18. Ibid. 3.

19. Interview with the author, 12 January 2016.

20. Kolkata Port Trust (2009), 77. 'April 13, 1796: First elephant arrives in America', *The Daily Dose*, http://www.awb.com/dailydose/?p=1097 (accessed 16 July 2016).

21. Kolkata Port Trust (2010), 73–8.

22. Ghosh (2015b), 3, 396.

23. Kipling (2014), chapter 4, 'On the Banks of the Hughli'.

24. The name came from a poem by James Thomson about London and had confusingly also been used by Kipling as the title of a vignette about Lahore.

25. Mukherjee (1968), 25, 27.

26. Kolkata Port Trust (2009), 51.

27. Mukherjee (1968), 208.

28. Kahlon was arrested at a Calcutta hotel by a police task force two months after I interviewed him, accused of receiving a 2 million rupee bribe from a company that handles containers at Kolkata Dock System. A director of Bharat Calcutta Containers Terminal Ltd was also arrested. Kahlon, who said he was being victimised for evicting people who had encroached on a plot of land, was replaced as the Port Trust chairman and released on bail after a month in detention. In arguing for bail, his lawyers said that the money was not recovered from his possession and that he had an unblemished civil service record. Jayanta Gupta, 'Kahlon loses his job as KoPT chairman', *Times of India*, 24 March 2016, http://timesofindia.indiatimes.com/city/kolkata/Kahlon-loses-his-job-as-KoPT-chairman/articleshow/51542907.cms (accessed 17 July 2016). Pooja Mehta, 'Kolkata Port Trust chairman arrested by Special Task Force for taking bribe', 10 March 2016, http://www.dnaindia.com/india/report-kolkata-port-trust-chairman-interrogated-by-cbi-after-lakhs-of-rupees-found-in-his-possession-2187476 (accessed 17 July 2016).

29. Bose died in an aircraft crash in 1945.
30. Victor Mallet, 'Tea, sex and one last cavalry charge', *Financial Times*, 25 March 2014, https://next.ft.com/content/33293afa-b358-11e3-b09d-00144feabdc0 (accessed 17 July 2016).Victor Mallet,'Tributes to the empire's forgotten warriors of second world war', *Financial Times*, 27 July 2015, https://next.ft.com/content/604a2956-343d-11e5-b05b-b01debd57852 (accessed 17 July 2016).
31. Mukherjee (2015), 158.
32. See Chapter 2 for a discussion of the effects of global warming on India.
33. Kolkata Port Trust (2009), 27.
34. Emily Eden, vol. I, 260, and *Calcutta Christian Observer*, vol. 8, 17–23, via Google Books.
35. Kolkata Port Trust (2009), 27.
36. *The Times*, 12 October 1865, quoted in Kolkata Port Trust (2010), 89.
37. Kolkata Port Trust (2010), 153.
38. Ibid. 120.
39. Interview with the author, 12 January 2016.
40. Kolkata Port Trust (2010), 131.
41. Interview with the author, 15 January 2016.
42. Interview with the author, 12 January 2016.
43. Greenhill, 19.
44. Interview with the author, 17 March 2016.
45. Food crop output, according to Nishat, has increased from 6.5 million tonnes at the time of Indian independence in 1947 to nearly 11 million tonnes at Bangladeshi independence in 1971, 25 million tonnes in 2005, and about 35 million tonnes today.
46. Victor Mallet,'Hollowed-out Bengal economy struggles to regain its vigour', *Financial Times*, 31 January 2016. Locals say the so-called 'Goonda Raj' of the Left remains under the government that supplanted it. See for example Sandip Roy,'Bengal's "Syndicate Raj":A left legacy that TMC has inherited', *HuffPost India*, 15 July 2016, http://www.huffingtonpost.in/2016/04/19/bengals-syndicate-raj-a-left-legacy-that-tmc-has-inherited/ (accessed 11 December 2016).
47. Chaudhuri, 71–3, 80, 111, 246.
48. Basu (2015), 311.

CHAPTER 17

1. Quoted in Ackroyd, 273.
2. Communication with the author, 9 September 2016.
3. Senior US official, speaking to journalists in New Delhi, 20 November 2014.The Chicago was one of four US rivers feeding the Great Lakes that caught fire; the best-known of the fires was on the Cuyahoga in 1969. See

John Hartig, *Burning Rivers: Revival of Four Urban-Industrial Rivers that Caught on Fire* (World Monograph Series, 2010).

4. US officials were particularly pleased with Modi's abandonment of earlier Indian objections to reducing emissions of hydrofluorocarbons or HFCs. These gases, used in refrigeration, replaced chlorofluorocarbons and hydro-chlorofluorocarbons (CFCs and HCFCs) under the Montreal Protocol that saved the world's protective ozone layer, but are substantial contributors to another environmental crisis: global warming.

5. Victor Mallet, 'COP21 Paris climate talks: India looms as obstacle to deal', *Financial Times*, 30 November 2015. https://www.ft.com/content/bfb36a16-94e5-11e5-bd82-c1fb87bef7af (accessed 11 December 2016).

6. I am indebted to Oliver Crimmen and Sandra Knapp of the Natural History Museum for answering my query on the lazy phrase 'biologically dead'. See Wheeler, 88–91.

7. Ackroyd, 190–1, 208.

8. Ibid. 270–5.

9. Ibid. 375. Kneale, 108–9, 313.

10. Cholera and the Thames, City of Westminster Archives, http://www.choleraandthethames.co.uk/ (accessed 25 August 2016); http://joseph-bazalgette.weebly.com/metropolis-local-management-amendment-act.html (accessed 25 August 2016).

11. Sophie Hardach, 'How the River Thames was brought back from the dead', BBC, 12 November 2015, http://www.bbc.co.uk/earth/story/20151111-how-the-river-thames-was-brought-back-from-the-dead (accessed 25 August 2016). Richard Gray, 'The clean up of the River Thames', *The Daily Telegraph* (UK), 13 October 2010, http://www.telegraph.co.uk/news/earth/wildlife/8059970/The-clean-up-of-the-River-Thames.html (accessed 25 August 2016). Ackroyd, 388–9.

12. London Tideway Improvements, Thames Water, https://sustainability.thameswater.co.uk/sustainable-drainage/london-tideway-improvements (accessed 16 September 2016).

13. The London NERC Doctoral Training Partnership, 'A battle against the odds: Restoring the Thames in the face of increasing urbanisation', http://london-nerc-dtp.org/2016/04/25/a-battle-against-the-odds-restoring-the-thames-in-the-face-of-increasing-urbanisation/ (accessed 25 August 2016).

14. Hardyment, 167.

15. Ackroyd, 277–80.

16. Gibbings, 221.

17. Interview with the author, 25 August 2014. Victor Mallet, 'Thames clean-up inspires Modi's Ganges plans', *Financial Times*, 25 August 2014, https://www.ft.com/content/d03ec636-2c73-11e4-8eda-00144feabdc0 (accessed 25 August 2016).

18. Karl-Geert Malle, 'Cleaning up the River Rhine', *Scientific American*, January 1996. Note that in this chapter I use milligrams per litre for dissolved oxygen in water. Elsewhere in the book—notably in Chapter 7—I have used parts per million. The units reflect the source material, usually scientific papers. Happily, they are equivalent measures at standard pressure and temperature: 1 mg/l = 1 ppm. See http://www.milwaukee-instruments.com/pdf/mg%20per%20liter%20and%20ppm.pdf (accessed 18 may 2017).

19. Imogen Foulkes, 'Rhine on path to recovery', BBC, 5 June 2001, http://news.bbc.co.uk/2/hi/europe/1371142.stm (accessed 26 August 2016).

20. ICPR, http://www.iksr.org/en/index.html (accessed 26 August 2016).

21. Interview with the author, 16 February 2013.

22. When I was researching a book in the 1990s about the industrial revolution in South-east Asia, I was struck by the similarities between descriptions of polluted rivers in Victorian England and those in contemporary Asia. Indeed they were so close that you could switch the names of the rivers and towns and struggle to work out which was which. 'Through the heart of this sore afflicted town flows the Sungei Segget, a river by only the most extravagant leap of the imagination', said the Malaysian writer Rehman Rashid of the pollution in the southern industrial city of Johor Bahru next to Singapore. 'To say it "flows" is to do hideous injustice to the word; the Sungei Segget is a rank, black, stagnant, noisome ditch, filling the town centre of Johor Baru with the aroma of raw sewage and rotting carcases. At the first sight and smell of the Sungei Segget, it is no longer difficult to imagine the river that must flow through hell.' About 140 years earlier, the novelist Charles Dickens described a typical industrial city of England (he was probably thinking of Preston in Lancashire) in his novel *Hard Times*. 'It was a town of machinery and tall chimneys, out of which interminable serpents of smoke trailed themselves for ever and ever, and never got uncoiled. It had a black canal in it, and a river that ran purple with ill-smelling dye... Down upon the river that was black and thick with dye, some Coketown boys who were at large—a rare sight there—rowed a crazy boat, which made a spumous track upon the water as it jogged along, while every dip of an oar stirred up vile smells.' Both quoted in Mallet (2000), 168. The Sungei Segget in Johor Bahru is now being dredged and cleaned.

23. Haberman, 146. Rajiv Malik, 'World's Most Effective Environmental Attorney', interviews of M. C. Mehta, *Hinduism Today*, October 1997, http://www.hinduismtoday.com/modules/smartsection/item.php?itemid=4913 (accessed 26 August 2016). The case launched in 1985 ended up focusing on the tanneries in Kanpur. It was concluded in 1987 with the Supreme Court ordering the closure of twenty-nine of those tanneries until they installed primary effluent treatment plants.

24. Victor Mallet, 'Welcome to Megacity', *Financial Times*, 4 August 2006, https://www.ft.com/content/599d57a4-22b8-11db-91c7-0000779e2340 (accessed 27 August 2016). Chuah Bee Kim, 'First phase of Johor Baru river rejuvenation to complete by year-end', *New Straits Times*, 22 June 2016, http://www.nst.com.my/news/2016/06/153704/first-phase-johor-baru-river-rejuvenation-complete-year-end (accessed 27 August 2016).

25. Victor Mallet, 'Blue-sky dreaming for Delhi, a city where the sun doesn't shine', *Financial Times*, 11 January 2016, https://www.ft.com/content/31aaeb04-b844-11e5-bf7e-8a339b6f2164 (accessed 27 August 2016). Sakshi Dayal, 'Another Supreme Court order 18 years ago and Delhi's first brush with CNG', *The Indian Express*, 3 May 2016, http://indianexpress.com/article/cities/delhi/supreme-court-ban-on-diesel-taxis-2781490/ (accessed 27 August 2016).

26. Haberman, 167–8.

27. See, for example, Subhajyoti Das, 'Lessons Learnt from the Thames and the Danube, in Ganga—Our Endangered Heritage', in Sanghi (ed.), 66.

28. With the help of the World Bank, the CPCB launched a pilot project to collect more detailed pollution data than the basic information previously amassed on the sewage from bacteria. Ten parameters are being measured, including salts, nitrates, and ammonia. The World Bank told me in early 2015 that the CPCB was doing the analysis and 'is in the process of making this data accessible to the public. Time lines are not known yet.'

29. Meetings at CPCB with officials who requested to remain anonymous, January 2015.

30. Haberman, 169.

31. Namami Gange, Prime Minister's Office (India), http://www.pmindia.gov.in/en/government_tr_rec/namami-gange/ (accessed 29 August 2016).

32. 'Meet the Journalist: George Black', 17 July 2016, http://pulitzercenter.org/education/meet-journalist-george-black (accessed 29 August 2016).

33. Pranav Kulkarni, 'Army plans to raise 40 eco-battalions to rejuvenate Ganga', *The Indian Express*, 29 July 2014.

34. Vishwa Mohan, 'Villages along Ganga to be open-defecation free by "22"', *The Times of India*, 13 September 2014. Pushkal Upadhyay, NMCG, speaking in Delhi 23 November 2015.

35. Utkarsh Anand, 'Ganga will be totally clean by 2018, Centre tells SC', *The Indian Express*, 15 January 2015.

36. National Mission for Clean Ganga notice in *Hindustan Times*, 24 March 2015. Amitabh Sinha, 'Ganga cleaning: Centre breather for industries', *The Indian Express*, 6 April 2016.

37. Neha Sethi, 'Centre to use sensors to monitor effluents flowing into Ganga', *Mint*, 22 August 2014. Vishwa Mohan, '500m along Ganga to be litter-free', *Sunday Times of India*, 19 April 2015. Amitav Ranjan, 'Govt takes in-principle decision to ban construction on Ganga', *The Indian Express*, 8 December 2015. Shalini Narayan, 'DDA will install cameras

at 26 spots along Yamuna to stop debris dumping', *The Indian Express*, 14 April 2015.

38. Suhas Munshi, 'DDA forms new panel for Yamuna', *Sunday Times of India*, 14 December 2014. Dhananjay Mahapatra, 'SC forms panel to take stock of Yamuna clean-up', *The Times of India*, 31 October 2012. '"3,500 crore spent, yet Yamuna dirty, why?" asks BJP', *The Hindu*, 10 March 2013. Dhananjay Mahapatra, 'Rs4,439 spent on Yamuna in 18 yrs', *The Times of India*, 30 October 2012. Neha Lalchandani, 'Rs6,500cr and 19yrs later, Yamuna dirty as ever', *The Times of India*, 11 March 2013. Neha Lalchandani, 'Babus bear stench of Yamuna on boat ride', *The Times of India*, 17 September 2015.

39. 'AAP govt, Centre join hands for Rs 825-cr Yamuna action plan', *The Indian Express*, 8 May 2016. Ritam Halder, 'DJB prepares "comprehensive" plan to revive Yamuna, to cost Rs6k crore', *Hindustan Times*, 23 May 2016. Damini Nath, 'Is this the last Yamuna plan?', *The Hindu*, 21 May 2016.

40. 'Yamuna will become good enough for a dip in 3 yrs: Minister', *Hindustan Times*, 29 November 2015. Faizan Haidar, 'Go boating "on" Najafgarh drain if govt's water park plan succeeds', *Hindustan Times*, 11 March 2015. 'You can drink Yamuna water and also swim in the river by 2017: JICA representative', *The Hindu*, 30 October 2014.

41. Interview with BBC, quoted in Justin Rowlatt, 'The River Challenge', *The Indian Express*, 14 May 2016.

42. ANI, 'Namami Gange Project will show its first impact by October: Uma Bharti', *The Indian Express*, 11 July 2016, http://indianexpress.com/article/india/india-news-india/namami-gange-project-will-show-its-first-impact-by-october-uma-bharti-2905484/ (accessed 30 August 2016).

43. Interview with the author, 29 March 2016.

44. News conference, New Delhi, 14 March 2016.

45. Modi spoke about his first year in office at a private gathering in New Delhi on 21 May 2015.

46. Victor Mallet, 'Delhi to outlaw plastic bags', *Financial Times*, 12 September 2012, https://www.ft.com/content/2a43a75a-fc9c-11e1-9dd2-00144feabdc0 (accessed 30 August 2016).

47. 'PCBs a "failure", SC hands Ganga to green tribunal', *The Indian Express*, 30 October 2014.

48. Haberman, 165.

49. Chicu Lokgariwar, '"Tare Ganga Par"', *India Water Portal*, 7 January 2015, http://www.indiawaterportal.org/articles/tare-ganga-par, and full interview of 19 October 2015 in attachment, http://www.indiawaterportal.org/sites/indiawaterportal.org/files/tare_interview.pdf (both accessed 30 August 2016). In 2010, Tare and his colleagues presented the previous (Manmohan Singh) government with a series of reports recommending river management plans for cities along the Ganges, essentially a data collection exercise for 250 towns that he said could have been financed by

World Bank funds. Four years later, government officials had done nothing on mapping the towns or collecting the data but said they were now
in rush to build facilities to stop pollution 'because the efficiency of a
government official is judged by the amount spent. He is in the process for
only three to five years. He is given a budget and thinks that if I do not
spend it this year, I will not get any money next year. His efficiency is
evaluated based on how much money entered his ministry that year, and
how much was spent. So he is in a hurry to distribute money. As soon as
the state government comes to know that the central government has a
scheme, the state government tries to find out how much money will
come to the state, and they make a project based on that. No one worries
if the project is actually needed or not. After that, suppose they are making
a STP [sewage treatment plant]. Money comes in for construction of the
STP, but not for operating it. So they amended it to include the operation
and maintenance costs for 10 years. That also is not a good idea. What happens is that the builder increases the capital expenditure and leaves only a
small amount for operation and expenditure. So he gets the full money for
commissioning. Formally, he has taken the contract for 10 years. But his
major payment has already been made—what interest does he have in
maintenance? For the first two to four years he satisfies the official by
some means or the other. After that the officials have also left and no one
is accountable any more, no one is responsible.'

50. Prakash Javadekar, briefing in New Delhi, 23 May 2016. Brochure 'Ministry
of Environment, Forest and Climate change: New Initiatives and Efforts
2014–2016', May 2016, http://www.moef.gov.in. PTI, 'Industrial waste flowing into Ganga down by 35 per cent: Javadekar', *Times of India*, 15 May 2016.

51. Jaiswal, communication with the author, 9 September 2016.

52. Interview with the author, 15 February 2016.

53. Interview with the author, 15 January 2016.

54. Interview with the author, 23 April 2014. This artificial division in people's
minds between the spiritual and physical properties of Ganges water
infuriates the more thoughtful holy men who live on India's rivers. In his
book on the Yamuna, Haberman encounters a holy man near the river in
Vrindabhan and asks him whether the goddess can survive even if the
river itself is destroyed. '"They're foolish!" he exclaimed. "If you destroy
the river, Yamuna-ji is finished! The river is the real goddess, not some lady
sitting on a turtle. That is just a symbol. The river is the main thing, the
main form of Yamuna. Those people who say the physical river is not
important are foolish people. They are the ones shitting in the river. They
don't know what life is, what this world is. They are so busying trying to
get things for themselves that they don't have time to think about the
nature of the world."' (Haberman, 139).

55. See Vinod Tare's detailed explanation of how corruption works in n. 49.

56. Eck (2012), 187–8.

57. Interview with the author, 23 April 2014.
58. Interview with the author, 12 August 2014.
59. Interview with the author, 30 May 2016.

CHAPTER 18

1. Emily Eden, vol. I, 4.
2. http://www.waterencyclopedia.com/Re-St/Rivers-Major-World.html (accessed 19 September 2016). Ganges–Brahmaputra–Meghna Basin, FAO Regional Water Report 37, 2011, http://www.fao.org/nr/water/aquastat/basins/gbm/index.stm (accessed 19 September 2016).
3. Pennant, vol. II, 151–4.
4. Both quoted in Mahajan, 51.
5. Ghosh (2012), 6.
6. Malavika Chauhan and Brij Gopal, 'Sundarban Mangroves: Impact of Water Management in the Ganga River Basin', in Sanghi (ed.), 143–66.
7. Mukherjee (2015), 63.
8. 'Human encroachment devastates Sundarbans: SRDI Study', *The Financial Express* (Bangladesh), 27 July 2013.
9. Albinia, 30–1.
10. Interviewed in Colopy, 315, 353.
11. Personal communication with the author.
12. Interviews with doctors and Sightsavers staff by the author, 8 May 2015. The Indian side of the Sunderbans is home to nearly 5 million people living on fifty-seven inhabited islands (a further fifty or so are uninhabited). With its current project, financed by Standard Chartered bank, Sightsavers aims to reach more than 2 million of them, carry out 27,000 cataract surgeries, and provide 13,000 pairs of spectacles for free or for a nominal sum.
13. Rushdie, 504.
14. Chowdhury, 40–1.
15. Deepa Philip, 'To eat or be eaten', *Tehelka magazine*, 7 November 2015.
16. Sayandeb Bandyopadhyay, 'B'desh pirates terrorise Sunderbans', *Hindustan Times*, 21 May 2015. Conversation with the author, 9 May 2015.

Bibliography

Acciavatti, A. (2015). *Ganges Water Machine: Designing New India's Ancient River.* Applied Research and Design Publishing.

Ackroyd, P. (2007). *Thames: sacred river.* Chatto & Windus.

Akihiko, M. (2006). *Shrinking Population Economics: Lessons from Japan.* Trans. Brian Miller. I-House Press.

Alberuni. (1971). *Alberuni's India.* Trans. Edward C. Sachau. Ed. Ainslie T. Embree. W. W. Norton.

Alberuni. (2011 [1910]). *Alberuni's India: An Account of the Religion, Philosophy, Literature, Geography, Chronology, Astronomy, Customs, Laws and Astrology of India about A.D. 1030.* Ed. Edward C. Sachau. Low Price Publications.

Albinia, A. (2009 [2008]). *Empires of the Indus: The Story of a River.* John Murray.

Alley, K. D. (1994). 'Ganga and Gandagi: Interpretations of pollution and waste in Benaras'. http://www.jstor.org/stable/3773893. *Ethnology*, 33(2) (1994), 127–45.

Alley, K. D. (2002). *On the Banks of the Gaṅgā: When Wastewater Meets a Sacred River.* University of Michigan Press.

Alter, S. (2001). *Sacred Waters: A Pilgrimage to the Many Sources of the Ganga.* Penguin Books.

Anam, T. (2012 [2011]). *The Good Muslim.* Penguin India.

Baillie Fraser, J. (1820). *Journal of a Tour through part of the Snowy Range of the Himala Mountains and to the Sources of the rivers Jumna and Ganges.* Rodwell and Martin.

Banerjee, S. (2015). *All Quiet in Vikaspuri.* HarperCollins Publishers India.

Basu, K. (2009 [2008]). *The Japanese Wife.* HarperCollins India with The India Today Group.

Basu, K. (2015). *Kalkatta.* Picador India.

Battacharji, R. (2002). *Lands of Early Dawn: North East of India.* Rupa & Co.

Battutah, I. (2003 [2002]). *The Travels of Ibn Battutah.* Ed. Tim Mackintosh-Smith. Picador.

Berwick, D. (1987 [1986]). *A Walk Along the Ganges.* Javelin Books.

Bond, R. (2012 [1992]). *All Roads Lead to Ganga.* Rupa Publications India Pvt Ltd.

Bond, R. (2015). *A Book of Simple Living: Brief Notes from the Hills.* Speaking Tiger.

Bond, R. (2015). *A Gathering of Friends: My Favourite Stories.* Aleph Book Co.

Brotton, J. (2013 [2012]). *A History of the World in Twelve Maps*. Penguin.

Buckley, M. (2014). *Meltdown in Tibet: China's Reckless Destruction of Ecosystems from the Highlands of Tibet to the Deltas of Asia*. Palgrave Macmillan.

Chaudhuri, A. (2013). *Calcutta: Two Years in the City*. Hamish Hamilton.

Chellaney, B. (2014 [2013]). *Water, Peace, and War: Confronting the Global Water Crisis*. Oxford University Press.

Chowdhury, B. R. and Vyas, P. (2005). *The Sunderbans*. Rupa.

Colopy, C. (2012). *Dirty, Sacred Rivers: Confronting South Asia's Water Crisis*. Oxford University Press.

Connelly, M. (2008). *Fatal Misconception: The Struggle to Control World Population*. The Belknap Press of Harvard University Press.

Cribb, J. (2010). *The Coming Famine: The Global Food Crisis and What We Can Do to Avoid It*. University of California Press.

Dalrymple, W. (ed.). (2002). *Begums, Thugs and White Mughals: The Journals of Fanny Parkes* (first published by Pelham Richardson, London, in 1850, as *Wanderings of a Pilgrim in Search of the Picturesque, during four-and-twenty years in the East; with Revelations of Life in the Zenana*). Eland Publishing.

Dalrymple, W. (2010 [2009]). *Nine Lives: In Search of the Sacred in Modern India*. Bloomsbury.

Darian, S. G. (2010 [1978]). *The Ganges in Myth and History*. Motilal Banarsidass Publishers Ltd Delhi.

Dasgupta, R. (2014). *Capital: A Portrait of Twenty-first Century Delhi*. Canongate.

Doniger, W. (2009). *The Hindus: An Alternative History*. Penguin.

Dorling, D. (2013). *Population 10 Billion: The Coming Demographic Crisis and How to Survive It*. Constable.

Doron, A. (2013). *Life on the Ganga: Boatmen and the Ritual Economy of Banaras*. Cambridge University Press India.

Dunn, R. E. (2004). *The Adventures of Ibn Battuta: A Muslim Traveller of the Fourteenth Century*. University of California Press.

Dyer, G. (2015 [2009]). *Jeff in Venice, Death in Varanasi*. Canongate Books.

Eck, D. (1993). *Banaras: City of Light*. Penguin Books India.

Eck, D. (2012). *India: A Sacred Geography*. Harmony Books.

Economy, E. C. (2004). *The River Runs Black: The Environmental Challenge to China's Future*. Cornell University Press.

Eden, E. (1866. *'Up the Country': Letters written to her Sister from the Upper Provinces of India by the Hon. Emily Eden. In two volumes*. Richard Bentley (vol. I via Google; vol. II Leopold Classic Library Reprint).

Eden, F. (1988). *Tigers, Durbars and Kings: Fanny Eden's Indian Journals 1837–1838*. Transcribed and ed. Janet Dunbar. John Murray.

Ehrlich, P. (1974 [1968]). *The Population Bomb*. Ballantine Books.

Eirik G. Jansen et al. (1994 [1989]). *The Country Boats of Bangladesh: Social and Economic Decision-making in Inland Water Transport*. The University Press Ltd, Dhaka.

Emmott, S. (2013). *10 Billion*. Penguin Books.

Forrest, Lt. Col. (2015 [1824]). *A Picturesque Tour along the Rivers Ganges and Jumna, in India, consisting of twenty-four highly finished and coloured views, a map, and vignettes, from original drawings made on the spot, with illustrations, historical and descriptive.* Niyogi Books.

Foster, William (ed.). (1921). *Early Travels in India 1583–1619.* Humphrey Milford—Oxford University Press.

Gandhi, M. K. (1993 [1957]). *Gandhi. An Autobiography: The Story of My Experiments with Truth. Translated from Gujarati by Mahadev Desai.* Beacon Press.

Gargan, E. A. (2003 [2001]). *The River's Tale.* Vintage Departures.

Gawande, A. (2014). *Being Mortal: Medicine and What Matters in the End.* Hamish Hamilton/Penguin Books India.

Ghose, S. (1993). *Jawaharlal Nehru: A Biography.* Allied Publishers, India.

Ghosh, A. (2012 [2004]). *The Hungry Tide.* HarperCollins.

Ghosh, A. (2015a). *Flood of Fire.* Hamish Hamilton.

Ghosh, A. (2015b [2008]). *Sea of Poppies.* Penguin.

Gibbings, R. (1948 [1940]). *Sweet Thames Run Softly.* J. M. Dent & Sons.

Gordon, S. (2008). *When Asia Was the World.* Da Capo Press.

Greenhill, B. (1971). *Boats and Boatmen of Pakistan.* David & Charles.

Griffiths, P. (1979). *A History of the Joint Steamer Companies.* Inchcape & Co.

Guha, R. (2007). *India After Gandhi: The History of the World's Largest Democracy.* Macmillan.

Haberman, D. L. (2006). *River of Love in an Age of Pollution: The Yamuna River of Northern India.* University of California Press.

Hankin, N. (2008). *Hanklyn Janklin.* 5th edn. Tara Press.

Hardyment, C. (2016). *Writing the Thames.* Bodleian Library.

Heber, R. (1828). *Narrative of a Journey through the Upper Provinces of India, from Calcutta to Bombay, 1824–1825.* John Murray.

Hodgson, C. J. (1822). 'Journal of a Survey to the Heads of the Rivers, Ganges and Jumna'. *Asiatick Researches or Transactions of the Society Instituted in Bengal for Enquiring into the History and Antiquities, the Arts, Sciences, and Literature, of Asia,* Chapter II, vol. 14, 60–152.

Hollick, J. C. (2007). *Ganga.* Random House India.

Horton Ryley, J. (1899). *Ralph Fitch: England's Pioneer to India and Burma. His companions and contemporaries. With his remarkable narrative told in his own words.* T. Fisher Unwin.

Hutchison, R. (2010). *The Raja of Harsil: The Legend of Frederick 'Pahari' Wilson.* The Lotus Collection/Roli Books.

Hutchison, R. (2012). *Garden of Fools.* New Delhi: Palimpsest Publishing House.

James, P. (1992). *The Children of Men.* Faber & Faber.

Karnad, R. (2015). *Farthest Field: An Indian Story of the Second World War.* William Collins.

Keay, J. (2005). *Mad about the Mekong: Exploration and Empire in South-east Asia.* HarperCollins.

Khilnani, S. (2004 [1997]). *The Idea of India.* Penguin.

Kipling, R. (1888). *City of Dreadful Night.* First published as eight articles in 1888 in *The Pioneer, The Pioneer Mail,* and *The Week's News.* This edition published by eBooks@Adelaide, University of Adelaide, and last updated 17 December 2014. https://ebooks.adelaide.edu.au/k/kipling/rudyard/city/index.html.

Kipling, R. (1984 [1894]). *The Jungle Book.* New York: Open Road, Integrated Media.

Kipling, R. (2010 [1901]). *Kim.* Collins Classics.

Kneale, M. (2001 [1992]). *Sweet Thames.* Penguin Books.

Kolkata Port Trust. (2009). *Bollards of Time.* Kolkata Port Trust, Maritime Archives & Heritage Centre.

Kolkata Port Trust. (2010). *Calcutta Port: Ageless Annals—Reflections in Print and Memory. An Anthology of Old and New Writings on the Port of Kolkata.* Kolkata Port Trust.

Kuchment, A. (2012). *The Forgotten Cure: The Past and Future of Phage Therapy.* Copernicus/Springer Science.

Losty, J. (n.d.). *Sita Ram: Picturesque views of India.* Roli Books.

Mahajan, J. (2004 [1984]). *The Ganga Trail: Foreign Accounts and Sketches of the River Scene.* Indica Books.

Malik, A. (2016). 'Navigating Namami Gange: India's Flagship River Project'. Article in Observer Research Foundation, Raisina Files, pp. 60–7.

Mallet, V. (2000 [1999]). *The Trouble with Tigers: The Rise and Fall of South-East Asia.* HarperCollins.

Mallet, V. (2013). 'Demographic Dividend or Disaster?' In McKinsey & Co *Reimagining India: Unlocking the Potential of Asia's Next Superpower.* Simon & Schuster (pp. 99–104).

Malthus, T. R. (1998 [1798]). *An Essay on the Principle of Population.* Prometheus Books.

Mehrotra, Rahul and Felipe Vera (2015) (eds). *Kumbh Mela: Mapping the Ephemeral Megacity.* Harvard University South Asia Institute/Niyogi Books.

Menon, R. (2004). *The Mahabharata: A Modern Rendering.* Kindle.

Menon, R. (2008 [2003]). *The Ramayana: A Modern Translation.* HarperCollins.

Miller, S. (2010 [2009]). *Delhi: Adventures in a Megacity.* Vintage.

Miller, S. (2014). *A Strange Kind of Paradise: India through Foreign Eyes.* Hamish Hamilton.

Montgomery, D. R. (2007). *Dirt: The Erosion of Civilizations.* University of California Press.

Moore Ede, P. (2015). *Kaleidoscope City: A Year in Varanasi.* Bloomsbury.

Mount, F. (2015). *The Tears of the Rajas: Mutiny, Money and Marriage in India 1805–1905.* Simon & Schuster.

Mukherjee, J. (2015). *Hungry Bengal: War, Famine and the End of Empire.* Hurst & Co.

300

BIBLIOGRAPHY

Mukherjee, N. (1968). *The Port of Calcutta: A Short History.* The Commissioners of the Port of Calcutta.

Murphy, D. (1983 [1977]). *Where the Indus Is Young: A Winter in Baltistan.* John Murray.

Newby, E. (1983 [1966]). *Slowly Down the Ganges.* Picador/Pan Books.

Pavan, A. (2005). *The Ganges: Along Sacred Waters.* Thames & Hudson.

Pennant, T. (1798). *The View of Hindoostan.* London: https://archive.org/details/viewofhindoostan01penn.

Prater, S. (1971 [1948]). *The Book of Indian Animals.* Bombay Natural History Society and Oxford University Press, India.

Ray, M. (2010). *Old Mirrors: Traditional Ponds of Kolkata.* Kolkata Municipal Corporation.

Ray, M. (2015). *Five Thousand Mirrors: The Water Bodies of Kolkata.* Jadavpur University Press.

Roberts, A. (2017). *Superfast Primetime Ultimate Nation: The Relentless Invention of Modern India.* PublicAffairs (Kindle edition).

Rushdie, S. (2008 [1981]). *Midnight's Children.* Vintage Books.

Sainath, P. (1996). *Everybody Loves a Good Drought: Stories from India's Poorest Districts.* Penguin Books India.

Sale, Roddy (2006) (ed.). *Lord Curzon: Speeches in India—A Selection from his Speeches as Viceroy and Governor-General of India 1898–1905.* Roddy Sale.

Sanghi, Rashmi (2014) (ed.). *Our National River Ganga: Lifeline of Millions.* Springer.

Sanyal, S. (2013 [2012]). *Land of the Seven Rivers: A Brief History of India's Geography.* Viking/Penguin Books India.

Shankar, S. (2016). *Ganga: A Journey.* Speaking Tiger.

Shrivastava, A. and Ashish, K. (2014 [2012]). *Churning the Earth: The Making of Global India.* Penguin.

Singh, R. (2003) [1992]. *The Ganges.* Thames & Hudson.

Spencer-Harper, A. (1999). *Dipping into the Wells: The Story of the Two Chiltern Villages of Stoke Row and Highmoor Seen Through the Memories of their Inhabitants.* Robert Boyd Publications.

Subramanian, M. (2015). *Elemental India: The Natural World at a Time of Crisis and Opportunity.* HarperCollins Publishers India.

Sundarananda, S. (2001). *Himalaya, through the lens of a Sadhu.* Tapovan Kuti Prakashan.

Tavernier, J. B. (1712). *Les Six Voyages de Jean Baptiste Tavernier, Ecuyer, Baron d'Aubone, qu'il a fait en TURQUIE, en PERSE, et aux INDES pendant quarante ans.* Rouen: Eustache Hérault.

Travel collection (1684). *Collections of Travels through TURKY into PERSIA and the EAST-INDIES Giving an Account of the Present State of those Countries . . . being The Travels of Monsieur Tavernier Bernier, and other great Men.* Moses Pitt.

Trojanow, I. (2011 [2003]). *Along the Ganges.* Translated from the German by the Author with Ranjit Hoskote. First published in Germany as *An den inneren Ufern Indiens.* The Armchair Traveller at the Book Haus.

Twain, M. (2016 [1897]). *Following the Equator: A Journey Around the World.* Jungle Land Publishing.

Vaishnav, M. (2017). *When Crime Pays: Money and Muscle in Indian Politics.* Yale University Press.

Verne, J. (1902 [1880]). *La Maison à vapeur. Voyage à travers l'Inde septentrionale* [pub. in English as *Demon of Cawnpore*]. Hetzel.

Wheeler, A. (1979). *The Tidal Thames: The History of a River and its Fishes.* Routledge.

Williamson, L. D. (1983). *An Illustrated History of The Maharajah's Well.* The Maharajah's Well Trust.

Wood, M. (2008 [2007]). *The Story of India.* BBC Books.

Xian, F. (1991 [1886]). *A Record of Buddhistic Kingdoms: Being an Account by the Chinese Monk Fa-Hein of Travels in India and Ceylon (AD 399–414) in Search of the Buddhist Books of Discipline.* Trans. and Annotated with a Corean Recension of the Chinese Text by James Legge. Munshiram Manoharlal Publishers.

Xuanzang (1996). *The Great Tang Dynasty Record of the Western Regions.* Translated by the Tripitaka-Master Xuanzang under Imperial Order. Composed by Sramana Bianji of the Great Zongchi Monastery. Taisho, Volume 51, Number 2087. Trans. Li Rongxi. Numata Center for Buddhist Translation and Research.

Young, B.-G. H. (1937). *The East India Company's Arsenals & Manufactories.* The Naval and Military Press.

Ziegler, D. (2015). *Black Dragon River: A Journey Down the Amur River at the Borderlands of Empires.* Penguin Press.

Publisher's Acknowledgements

We are grateful for permission to include the following copyright material in this book:

Excerpt from *Slowly Down the Ganges* reprinted by permission of HarperCollins Publishers Ltd. © Eric Newby (1966).

Title song from *Ram Teri Ganga Maili*, reprinted by permission of R. K. Films & Studios Pvt. Ltd.

The publisher and author have made every effort to trace and contact all copyright holders before publication. If notified, the publisher will be pleased to rectify any errors or omissions at the earliest opportunity.

Picture Acknowledgements

1   Victor Mallet
2   Victor Mallet
3   Victor Mallet
4   Victor Mallet
5   AP/Press Association Images
6   Victor Mallet
7   Reuters/Adnan Abidi
8   Victor Mallet
9   Gurinder Osan/AP/Press Association Images
10 British Library, London, UK/Bridgeman Images
11 Victor Mallet
12 Victor Mallet
13 Courtesy R. K. Films & Studios Pvt. Ltd.
14 British Library, London, UK/Bridgeman Images
15 British Library, London, UK/Bridgeman Images
16 Saurabh Das/AP/Press Association Images
17 Swastik Pal
18 Swastik Pal
19 Victor Mallet
20 Mustafah Abdulaziz

Index

reverence for 26–9, 162, 166, 176, 254
    beliefs about water quality 100–1, 108–13, 163–4, 251
    route xvii, 5–6, 253–4
    source 1–2, 4, 9, 10, 253; *see also* Gaumukh
    spelling xi
    unreliability 5–6, 171, 198, 234
Gangetic dolphins 5, 73, 92, 114–15, 116–20, 125, 127, 279 nn. 8, 9
Gangnani 19
Gangotri 2, 4, 9, 10, 12, 13, 17, 18, 20, 60, 194
Gargan, Edward 169
Gaumukh 1–2, 4, 8–9, 12, 38, 71, 110, 177
Gawande, Atul 96
Ghoramara Island 259
gharials (crocodiles) 5, 20, 60, 118, 121, 125, 126, 129–30, 131, 134, 192, 260
Ghaziuddin Hyder 201
Ghosh, Amitav 201, 216, 255
Ghosh, Arunabha 157, 159
Ghosh, Tapan Kumar 210, 221
Gibbings, Robert 234–5
girls:
    education 137
    infanticide 141
global warming 14–16, 220, 230, 235, 262
Godavari River 172
Godden, Rumer 197
Godkhali 261
Gomes, John 123, 221
goods and services tax (GST) 57
Graham, David 97, 101–2, 104, 108
Greeks 3, 183–5, 213–14
Greenhill, Basil 204
groundwater 158–9, 174
Guha, Ramachandra 168
Gupta, Shekhar 91
Gurgaon 154
Gusiyari 149–50, 174

Haberman, David 165, 294 n. 54
habitat destruction 115, 121
Hankin, Ernest 110
Hare Krishnas 212
Haridwar 4, 6, 7, 17, 24, 34, 72, 99, 102, 111, 140, 161, 165, 166, 167–8, 170, 172, 191, 239
Harrer, Heinrich 18
Harris, Gardiner 98
Harsha 25, 188
Hasan, Nazmul 257
Hastinapur wildlife sanctuary 121, 130
Hastinapura 31, 213
Hastings, Francis Rawdon, Marquess of 155, 164–5, 195, 196, 198–200, 222
Hauz Khas 173
heat stress 16
heavy metals 77–80, 81, 82, 84, 85, 236
Heber, Reginald, Bishop of Calcutta 136, 200
Hillary, Sir Edmund 17, 140, 205
Himalayas xvii, 1, 9, 11, 17, 122, 170, 173, 209
Hindu nationalism 21, 28, 50, 51, 56, 71, 142
Hinduism 20–1
    funeral rites 69–71, 188
    holy men 17–19, 23, 24, 25, 26; see also *rishis; sadhus*
    invention of traditions 25
    inward-looking nature 251
    myths and epics 7, 10, 11–12, 24, 29–33, 126–7
    origins of the word 'Hindu' 28
    pilgrims 19, 20, 23, 26, 35, 36, 37, 41, 42, 43, 99, 100, 101, 121, 124, 133, 190
    reverence for Ganges 26–9, 162, 166, 176
    beliefs about water quality 100–1, 108–13, 163–4, 251
    scriptures 27
    Varanasi 48–9
Hindustan 28
Hissar 164